STUDY GUIDE

HARVEY B. KING ◆ AVI J. COHEN
University of Regina *York University*

MACROECONOMICS

CANADA IN THE GLOBAL ENVIRONMENT

FOURTH EDITION

MICHAEL PARKIN ◆ ROBIN BADE

Toronto

ISBN 0-201-61389-1

Acquisitions Editor: Dave Ward
Developmental Editor: Suzanne Schaan
Production Editor: Marisa D'Andrea
Production Coordinator: Deborah Starks

1 2 3 4 5 04 03 02 01 00

Printed and bound in Canada.

Contents

Acknowledgments

This fourth edition of the *Study Guide* has benefited from help and advice from many sources. Colleagues have helped raise the quality of our questions with suggestions and corrections—we would especially like to thank Robin Bade, Brian Coulter, David Gray, Rod Hill, Eric Kam, Keith MacKinnon, Michael Parkin, and Keer Wilmut. Various students have pointed out mistakes and ambiguities they found in using the *Study Guide.* Thanks to My Chung, Peter Ogonowski, Kulvinder Saini, Corey Snider, and Karen Wong for helping us in this area. Thanks also to Joan MacMillan for her work on this project, and Suzanne Schaan for excellent editorial guidance and support. This edition is dedicated to the memory of Linda Scott and her abiding cheerfulness in encouraging editorial excellence, and to the memory of Dave Beattie for inspiring better teaching.

Harvey King
Avi Cohen
January 2000

Introduction

Before You Begin . . .

Our experience has taught us that what first-year economics students want most from a study guide is help in mastering course material in order to do well on examinations. We have developed this *Study Guide* to respond specifically to that demand. Using this *Study Guide* alone, however, is not enough to guarantee that you will do well in your course. In order to help you overcome the problems and difficulties that most first-year students encounter, we have some general advice on how to study, as well as some specific advice on how to best use this *Study Guide.*

Some Friendly Advice

The study of economics requires a different style of thinking than what you may encounter in other courses. Economists make extensive use of assumptions to break down complex problems into simple, analytically manageable parts. This analytical style, while not ultimately more demanding than the styles of thinking in other disciplines, feels unfamiliar to most students and requires practice. As a result, it is not as easy to do well in economics simply on the basis of your raw intelligence and high-school knowledge as it is in many other first-year courses. Many students who come to our offices are frustrated and puzzled by the fact that they are getting A's and B's in their other courses but only a C or worse in economics. They have not recognized that the study of economics is different and requires practice. In order to avoid a frustrating visit to your instructor after your first test, we suggest you do the following.

Don't rely solely on your high-school economics. If you took high-school economics, you will have seen the material on supply and demand that your instructor will lecture on in the first few weeks. Don't be lulled into feeling that the course will be easy. Your high-school knowledge of economic concepts will be very useful, but it will not be enough to guarantee high marks on exams. Your college or university instructors will demand much more detailed knowledge of concepts and ask you to apply them in new circumstances.

Keep up with the course material on a weekly basis. Read the appropriate chapter in the textbook before your instructor lectures on it. In this initial reading, don't worry about details or arguments you can't quite follow—just try to get a general understanding of the basic concepts and issues. You may be amazed at how your instructor's ability to teach improves when you come to class prepared. As soon as your instructor has finished covering a chapter, complete the corresponding *Study Guide* chapter. Avoid cramming the day before or even just the week before an exam. Because economics requires practice, cramming is an almost certain recipe for failure.

Keep a good set of lecture notes. Good lecture notes are vital for focusing your studying. Your instructor will only lecture on a subset of topics from the textbook. The topics your instructor covers in a lecture should usually be given priority when studying. Also give priority to studying the figures and graphs covered in the lecture.

Instructors do differ in their emphasis on lecture notes or the textbook, so ask early on in the course which is more important in reviewing for exams—lecture notes or the textbook. If your instructor answers that both are important, then ask the following, typically economic question: at the margin, which will be more beneficial—spending an extra hour re-reading your lecture notes or an extra hour re-reading the textbook? This question assumes that you have read each textbook chapter twice (once before lecture for a general understanding, and then later for a thorough understanding); that you have prepared a good set of lecture notes; and that you have worked through all of the problems in the appropriate *Study Guide* chapters. By applying this style of analysis to the problem of efficiently allocating your study time, you are already beginning to think like an economist!

Use your instructor and/or teaching assistants for help. When you have questions or problems with course material, come to the office to ask questions. Remember, you are paying for your education and instructors are there to help you learn. We are often amazed at how few students come to see us during office hours. Don't be shy. The personal contact that comes from one-on-one tutoring is professionally gratifying for us as well as (hopefully) beneficial for you.

Form a study group. A very useful way to motivate your studying and to learn economics is to discuss the course material and problems with other students. Explaining the answer to a question out loud is a very effective way of discovering how well you understand the question. When you answer a question only in your head, you often skip steps in the chain of reasoning without realizing it. When you are forced to explain your reasoning aloud, gaps and mistakes quickly appear, and you (with your fellow group members) can quickly correct your reasoning. The True/False/Uncertain questions in the *Study Guide* and the Critical Thinking questions at the end of each textbook chapter are good study group material. You might also get together after having worked the *Study Guide* problems, but before looking at the answers, and help each other solve unsolved problems.

Work old exams. One of the most effective ways of studying is to work through exams your instructor has given in previous years. Old exams give you a feel for the style of question your instructor may ask, and give you the opportunity to get used to time pressure if you force yourself to do the exam in the allotted time. Studying from old exams is not cheating, as long as you have obtained a copy of the exam legally. Some institutions keep old exams in the library, others in the department or at the student union. Upper-year students who have previously taken the course are usually a good source as well. Remember, though, that old exams are a useful study aid only if you use them to understand the reasoning behind each question. If you simply memorize answers in the hopes that your instructor will repeat the identical question, you are likely to fail. From year to year, instructors routinely change the questions or change the numerical values for similar questions.

Use the other study aids. In addition to the *Study Guide*, there are two other study aids that we believe are worth using for the help they will provide in mastering course material and doing well on examinations. However, don't just take our word for it—ask students who have used these aids for their opinions.

The Parkin-Bade Web site provides online quizzes, study tips, office hours, links, electronic Reading Between the Lines, a Point–Counterpoint feature that encourages students to participate in contemporary policy debates, and much more. You can reach the site at http://www.econ100.com.

Economics in Action is a state-of-the-art interactive software that covers all the main topics in the textbook. You can work through tutorials, answering questions that give instant explanations, manipulating graphs, and testing yourself in preparation for tests and exams.

Using the *Study Guide*

You should only attempt to complete a chapter in the *Study Guide* after you have read the corresponding textbook chapter and listened to your instructor lecture on the material. Each *Study Guide* chapter contains the following sections.

Key Concepts This first section is a one- to two-page summary, in point form, of all key definitions, concepts, and material from the textbook chapter. The summary is organized using the same major section headings from the textbook chapter. Key terms from the textbook appear in bold. This section is designed to focus you quickly and precisely on the core material that you must master. It is an excellent study aid for the night before an exam. Think of it as crib notes that will serve as a final check of the key concepts you have studied.

Helpful Hints When you encounter difficulty in mastering concepts or techniques, you will not be alone. Many students find certain concepts difficult and often make the same kinds of mistakes. We have seen these common mistakes often enough to have learned how to help students avoid them. The hints point out these mistakes and offer tips to avoid them. The hints focus on the most important concepts, equations, and techniques for problem solving. They also review crucial graphs that appear on every instructor's exams. We hope that this section will be very useful, since instructors always ask exam questions designed to test these possible mistakes in your understanding.

This section sometimes includes extra material that your instructor may add to the course, but that is not in textbook chapters. An example of extra material is the discussions in Chapter 3 of absolute advantage in producing a single good. This extra material is marked with the symbol ⓔ for extra, and may be skipped if your instructor does not cover it. The symbol ⓔ is used throughout the *Study Guide* to identify questions and answers based on extra material.

Self-Test This will be one of the most useful sections of the *Study Guide.* The questions are designed to give you practice and to test skills and techniques you must master to do well on exams. There are plenty of the multiple-choice questions that you are most likely to encounter on course tests and exams (25 for each chapter). There are other types of questions, described below, each with a specific pedagogical purpose. Questions (and answers) based on extra material covered in the Helpful Hints are marked with ⓔ so that you can easily skip them if your instructor does not assign the extra material. Before we describe the three parts of the Self-Test section, here are some general tips that apply to all parts.

Use a pencil to write your answers in the *Study Guide.* This will allow you to erase your mistakes and have neat, completed pages from which to study. Draw graphs wherever they are applicable. Some questions will ask explicitly for graphs; many others will not but will require a chain of reasoning that involves shifts of curves on a graph. *Always draw the graph.* Don't try to work through the reasoning in your head—you are much more likely to make mistakes that way. Whenever you draw a graph, even in the margins of the *Study Guide*, label the axes. You may think that you can keep the labels in your head, but you will be confronting many different graphs with many different variables on the axes. Avoid confusion and label. As an added incentive, remember that on exams where graphs are required, instructors will deduct marks for unlabelled axes.

Do the Self-Test questions as if they were real exam questions, which means do them *without looking at the answers.* This is the single most important tip we can give you about effectively using the *Study Guide* to improve your test and exam performance. Struggling for the answers to questions that you find difficult is one of the most effective ways to learn. The athletic adage—no pain, no gain—applies equally well to studying. You will learn the most from right answers you had to struggle for and from your wrong answers and mistakes. Only after you have attempted all the questions should you look at the answers. When you finally do check the answers, be sure you understand where you went wrong and why the right answer is correct.

If you want to impose time pressure on yourself to simulate the conditions of a real exam, allow two minutes for each true/false/uncertain and multiple-choice question. The short answer problems vary considerably in their time requirements, so it is difficult to give time estimates for them. However, we believe that such time pressure is probably *not* a good idea for *Study Guide* questions. A state of mind of relaxed concentration is best for work in the *Study Guide.* Use old exams if you want practice with time pressure, or use the Part Overview Midterm Examinations (see description on page x).

There are many questions in each chapter, and it will take you somewhere between two and five hours to answer all of them. If you get tired (or bored), don't burn yourself out by trying to work through all of the questions in one sitting. Consider breaking up your Self-Test over two (or more) study sessions.

The three parts of the Self-Test section are:

True/False/Uncertain and Explain These questions test basic knowledge of chapter concepts and your ability to apply the concepts. Some of the questions challenge your understanding, to see if you can identify mistakes in statements using basic concepts. These questions will quickly identify gaps in your knowledge and are useful to answer out loud in a study group.

When answering, identify each statement as *true* or *false*, or indicate that you are *uncertain* because the statement may be true or false depending on circumstances or assumptions. Explain your answer in one sentence. The space underneath each question is sufficient for writing your answer.

Multiple-Choice These more difficult questions test your analytical abilities by asking you to apply concepts to new situations, manipulate information, and solve numerical and graphical problems.

This is the most frequently used type of test and exam question, and the Self-Test contains 25 of them organized using the same major section headings from the textbook. The Test Bank that your instructor will likely use to make up exams contains most of the *Study Guide* multiple-choice questions, numerous questions that closely "parallel" the *Study Guide* questions, plus many similar questions.

Read each question and all five choices carefully before you answer. Many of the choices will be plausible and will differ only slightly. You must choose the one *best* answer. A useful strategy in working these questions is first to eliminate any obviously wrong choices and then to focus on the remaining alternatives. Be aware that sometimes the correct answer will be "none of the above choices is correct." Don't get frustrated or think that you are dim if you can't immediately see the correct answer. These questions are designed to make you work to find the correct choice.

Short Answer Problems The best way to learn to do economics is to do problems. Problems are also the second-most popular type of test and exam question—practise them as much as possible! Each Self-Test concludes with ten short answer numerical or graphical problems, often based on economic policy issues. In many chapters, this is the most challenging part of the Self-Test. It is also likely to be the most helpful for deepening your understanding of the chapter material. We have, however, designed the questions to teach as much as to test. We have purposely arranged the parts of each multipart question to lead you through the problem-solving analysis in a gradual and sequential fashion, from easier to more difficult parts.

Problems that require critical thinking are marked with the symbol ⓒⓣ, to alert you to the need for extra time and effort. These ⓒⓣ symbols give you the same indication you would have on a test or exam from the number of marks or minutes allocated to a problem.

Answers The Self-Test is followed by answers to all questions. But do not look at an answer until you have attempted a question. When you do finally look, use the answers to understand where you went wrong and why the right answer is correct.

Each true/false/uncertain and multiple-choice answer includes a brief, point-form explanation to suggest where you might have gone wrong and the economic reasoning behind the answer. At the end of each answer are page numbers in the textbook where you can go to find a more complete explanation. Answers to critical thinking questions are marked with ⓒⓣ to indicate why you might have struggled with that question! (We purposely did not mark which true/false/uncertain and multiple-choice questions were critical thinking, to stay as close as possible to a real test or exam format. In an exam, all multiple-choice questions, for example, are worth the same number of marks, and you have no idea which questions are the more difficult ones requiring critical thinking.)

The detailed answers to the short answer problems should be especially useful in clarifying and illustrating typical chains of reasoning involved in economic analysis. Answers to critical thinking problems are marked with ⓒ. If the answers alone do not clear up your confusion, go back to the appropriate sections of the textbook. If that still does not suffice, go to your instructor's or teaching assistant's office, or to your study group members, to get help and clarification.

Part Overview Problem and Midterm Examination Every few chapters, at the end of each of the ten parts of the textbook, you will find a special problem (and answer). These multipart problems draw on material from all chapters in the part, and emphasize policy and real-world questions (for example, the impact of cigarette smuggling on tax revenues). These overview problems will help you integrate concepts from different chapters that may seem unconnected but that are actually related. We often design exam questions similar to these problems.

Each Part Overview also contains a Midterm Examination, consisting of four to five multiple-choice questions from each chapter in the textbook part. The Midterm is set up like a real examination or test, with a scrambled order and a time limit for working the questions. Like the other multiple-choice questions in the *Study Guide*, there are answers with point-form explanations as well as page numbers in the textbook where you can go to find more complete explanations.

If you effectively combine the use of the textbook, the *Study Guide*, the Parkin-Bade Web site, *Economics in Action*, and all other course resources, you will be well prepared for exams. Equally importantly, you will also have developed analytical skills and powers of reasoning that will benefit you throughout your life and in whatever career you choose.

Do You Have Any Friendly Advice For Us?

We have attempted to make this *Study Guide* as clear and as useful as possible, and to avoid errors. No doubt, we have not succeeded entirely, and you are the only judges who count in evaluating our attempt. If you discover errors, or if you have other suggestions for improving the *Study Guide*, please write to us. In future editions, we will try to acknowledge the names of all students whose suggestions help us improve the *Study Guide*. Send your correspondence or e-mail to either of us:

Professor Avi J. Cohen
Department of Economics
Vari Hall, York University
Toronto, Ontario M3J 1P3
avicohen@yorku.ca

Professor Harvey B. King
Department of Economics
University of Regina
Regina, Saskatchewan S4S 0A2
Harvey.King@uregina.ca

Should the Study of Economics Be Part of Your Future?

by Robert Whaples (Wake Forest University) and Harvey King (University of Regina)

Should You Take More Economic Courses?

Soon you will learn about supply and demand, utility and profit maximization, employment and unemployment. Before, however, let's take a moment to look to the future.

- Should you take more classes or maybe even major in economics?
- What about graduate school in economics?

Economists generally assume that people try to make rational choices to maximize their own well-being. The purpose of this chapter is help you make that rational maximizing choice by providing low-cost information. Let us assess the benefits and see whether they outweigh the costs of studying economics.

Benefits from Studying Economics

Knowledge, Enlightenment, and Liberation

As John Maynard Keynes, a famous British economist, said, "The ideas of economists ... both when they are right and when they are wrong, are more powerful than is commonly understood. Indeed the world is ruled by little else. Practical men, who believe themselves to be quite exempt from any intellectual influences, are usually the slaves of some defunct economist." Studying economics is a liberating and enlightening experience. You don't want to be the slave of a defunct economist, do you? Liberate yourself. It's better to bring your ideas out in the open, to confront and understand them, rather than to leave them buried.

Knowledge, Understanding, and Satisfaction

Many of the most important problems in the world are economic. Studying economics gives you a practical set of tools to understand and solve them. Every day, on television and in the newspapers, we hear and read about big issues such as economic growth, inflation, unemployment, health care reform, welfare reform, the environment, and the transition away from Communism. Your introduction to economics will let you watch the news or pick up a newspaper and better understand these issues. As an added bonus, economics helps you understand smaller, more immediate concerns, such as: How much Spam should I buy? Is skipping class today a good idea? Should I put my retirement funds in government bonds or in the stock market? After all, as George Bernard Shaw put it, "Economy is the art of making the most of life." Mick Jagger, who dropped out of the London School of Economics, complains that he "can't get no satisfaction." Maybe he should have studied more economics. The economic way of thinking will help you maximize your satisfaction.

Career Opportunities

All careers are not equal. While the wages in many occupations have not risen much lately, the wages of "symbolic analysts" who "solve, identify, and broker problems by manipulating symbols" are soaring.[1] These people "simplify reality into abstract images that can be rearranged, juggled, experimented with, communicated to other specialists, and then, eventually, transformed back into reality." Their wages have been rising as the globalization of the economy increases the demand for their insights and as technological developments (especially computers) have enhanced their productivity. Economists are the quintessential symbolic analysts as we manipulate ideas about abstractions such as supply and demand, cost and benefits, and equilibrium. You can think of your training in economics as an exercise regimen, a workout for your brain.

You will use many of the concepts you will learn in introductory economics during your career, but it is the practice in abstract thinking that will really pay off. In fact, most economics majors do not go on to become economists. They enter fields that use their analytical abilities, including business, management, insurance, finance, real estate, marketing, law, education, policy analysis, consulting, government, planning, and even medicine, journalism, and the arts.

A recent survey of 100 former economics majors at one university included all of these careers. If you want to verify that economics majors graduate to successful and rewarding careers, just ask your professors or watch what happens to economics majors from your school as they graduate.

Statistics from the 1996 Canadian census show that economics majors earn a healthy salary. Table 1 shows the average yearly earnings for selected occupations, with those occupations that generally require a reasonable understanding of economics highlighted in italics.

TABLE 1 AVERAGE YEARLY EARNINGS, FULL-YEAR, FULL-TIME WORKERS (BOTH SEXES), 1995 (TOP 15 OCCUPATIONS, PLUS SELECTED OTHERS)

Occupation	**Average Yearly Earnings**
Judges	$126,246
Specialist physicians	$123,976
General practitioners and family physicians	$107,620
Dentists	$102,433
Senior managers – Goods production, etc.	$99,360
Senior managers – Financial, etc.	*$99,117*
Lawyers and Quebec notaries	*$81,617*
Senior managers – Trade, etc.	$79,200
Primary production managers	$76,701
Securities agents, investment dealers, and traders	*$75,911*
Petroleum engineers	$72,543
Chiropractors	$68,808
Engineering and science managers	$68,235
*University professors**	*$68,195*
Senior managers – health, education, social services, etc.	*$68,187*
Financial managers in administrative services	*$61,779*
Managers in financial services	*$59,113*
Government managers in economic analysis, etc.	*$58,695*
Economists and economic policy researchers and analysts	*$58,578*
Economic development officers and marketing researchers	*$49,793*
Average income, all occupations	$37,556

*Clearly, not *all* professors require an understanding of economics! The point is that becoming a professor is a high-paying option for an economics major.

Source: Statistics Canada, "1996 Census: Sources of income, earnings and total income, and family income," *The Daily*, 12 May 1998.

We can also see that economics degrees do well by examining data on entry level wages from the 1992 Survey of Graduates (*Source: Job Futures, Part 2: Career Outlooks for Graduates,* Human Resources and Development Canada, accessed at http://www.hdrc-dhrc.gc.ca/). In 1992, the average starting salary for a B.A. in economics was $31,700, roughly equal to the average starting salary for a B.A. Although this is lower than degrees in engineering ($35,000) or computing science, it is higher than the starting salary for a B.A. in the humanities (English degrees earned $26,000, French degrees $29,000), or for a B.A. in the other social sciences (psychology degrees earned $28,300, sociology degrees $28,700), or for a BSc in many of the sciences (geology degrees earned $30,500, chemistry $26,700). It was virtually identical to what was earned with a Bachelor of Commerce degree—$31,500.

You might like to consider graduate school in economics—the entry level wage for an M.A. in economics was roughly $42,700 in the 1992 Survey of Graduates!

In addition, the employment rate of economics majors is higher than that of many other majors, such as those in the humanities and other social sciences. Finally, the supply of new economics majors has been falling lately (down about 5 percent since 1985). Since the demand has remained high, the future promises even brighter prospects for economics majors.

The Costs of Studying Economics

Since the "direct" costs of studying economics (tuition, books, supplies) aren't generally any higher or lower than the direct costs of other courses, indirect costs will be the most important of the costs to studying economics.

Forgone Knowledge

If you study economics, you can't study something else. This forgone knowledge could be very valuable.

Time and Energy

Economics is a fairly demanding major. Although economics courses do not generally take as much time as courses in English and history (in which you have to read a lot of long books) or anatomy and physiology (in which you have to spend hours in the lab and hours memorizing things), they do take a decent amount of time. In addition, some people find the material "tougher" than most subjects because memorizing is not the key. In economics (like physics), analyzing and solving are the keys.

Grades

As Table 2 shows, grades in introductory economics courses are generally lower than grades in some other majors, including other social sciences and the humanities. On the other hand, grades in economics are similar to grades in some sciences and math.

TABLE 2 AVERAGE GRADES AND GRADE DISTRIBUTION IN INTRODUCTORY COURSES AT SEVEN ONTARIO UNIVERSITIES

Department	Mean Grade*	% (A + B)	% (D + F)
Music	3.02	72.1	9.7
English	2.76	64.0	9.4
French	2.69	61.1	12.4
Philosophy	2.54	57.6	15.3
Biology	2.52	54.5	19.7
Sociology	2.51	52.8	14.2
Political Science	2.49	55.6	14.1
Psychology	2.40	48.4	20.6
Physics	2.38	46.1	28.4
Mathematics	2.19	44.4	33.9
Chemistry	2.18	42.9	30.9
Economics	2.18	41.6	30.7

*A = 4, B = 3, C = 2, D = 1, F = 0.

Source: Paul Anglin and Ronald Meng, "Evidence on Grades and Grade Inflation at Ontario's Universities," *University of Windsor Working Paper*, Nov. 1999. Used with permission.

Caveat Emptor (Buyer Beware): Interpreting Your Grades Is Not Straight Forward

High grades provide direct satisfaction to most students, but they also act as a signal about the student's ability to learn the subject material. Unfortunately, because the grade distribution is not uniform across departments, you may be confused and misled by your grades. You may think that you are exceptionally good at a subject because of a high grade, when in fact nearly everyone gets a high grade in that subject. The important point here is that you should be informed about your own school's grade distribution. Just because you got a B in economics and an A in history does not necessarily mean that your comparative advantage is in learning history rather than economics. Everyone—or virtually everyone—may receive an A in history. Earning a B or a C in economics could mean that it is the best major for you because high grades are much harder to earn in economics. It is fun to have a high GPA in college, but maximizing GPA should not be your goal. Maximizing your overall well-being is probably your goal, and this might be obtained by trading off a tenth or so of your GPA for a more rewarding major—perhaps economics.

Potential Side Effects from Studying Economics

Studying economics has some potential side effects. I'm not sure whether they are costs or benefits and will let you decide.

Changing Ideas About What Is Fair

A recently completed study compared students at the beginning and end of the semester in an introductory economics course.[2] It found that by the end of the semester, significantly more of the students thought that the functioning of the market is "fair." This was especially true for female students. The results were consistent across a range of professors who fell across the ideological spectrum.

For example, the proportion of students who regarded it as unfair to increase the price of flowers on a holiday fell almost in half. The proportion that favoured government control over flower prices, rather than market determination, fell by over 60 percent. The study argues that these responses do not reflect changes in deep values, but instead represent the discovery of previous inconsistencies and their modification in the light of new information learned during the semester.

Changing Behaviour

Many people believe that the study of economics changes students' values and behaviour. Some think that it changes them for the worse. Others disagree. In particular, it is argued that economics students become more self-interested and less likely to cooperate, perhaps because they spend so much time studying economic models, which often assume that people are self-interested. For example, one study reports experimental evidence that economics students are more likely than nonmajors to behave self-interestedly in prisoners' dilemma games and ultimatum bargaining games.[3]

This need not mean that studying economics will change you, however. Another study compares beginning freshmen and senior economics students and concludes that economics students "are already different when they begin their study of economics."[4] In other words, students signing up for economics courses are already different; studying economics doesn't change them. However, there are reasons to question both of these conclusions, because it is not clear whether these laboratory experiments using economic games reflect reality. One experiment asked students whether they would return money that had been lost. It found that economics students were more likely than others to say that they would keep the cash.

However, what people say and what they do are sometimes at odds. In a follow-up experiment, this theory was tested by dropping stamped, addressed envelopes containing $10 in cash in different campus classrooms. To return the cash, the students had only to seal the envelopes and mail them. The results were that 56 percent of the envelopes dropped in economics classes were returned, while only 31 percent of the envelopes dropped in history, psychology, and business classes were sent in.[5] Perhaps economics students are less selfish than others!

Obviously, no firm conclusions have been reached about whether or how studying economics changes students' behaviour.

Cost Versus Benefits

Suppose that you've weighed the costs and benefits of studying economics and you've decided that the benefits are greater than or equal to the costs. Obviously, then, you should continue to take economics courses. If you can't decide whether the benefits outweigh the costs, then you should probably collect more information—especially if it is good but inexpensive. In either case, read the rest of this section.

The Economics Major

The study of economics is like a tree. The introductory microeconomics and macroeconomics courses you begin with are the tree's roots. Most colleges and universities require that you master this material before you go on to any other courses. The way of thinking, the language, and the tools that you acquire in the introductory course are usually reinforced in intermediate microeconomics and macroeconomics courses before they are applied in more specialized courses that you take. The intermediate courses are the tree's trunk. Among the specialized courses that make up the branches of economics are econometrics (statistical economics), financial economics, labour economics, resource economics, international trade, industrial organization, public finance, public choice, economic history, the history of economic thought, mathematical economics, current economic issues, and urban economics. The branches of the tree vary from department to department, but these are common. It will pay to check your school calendar and discuss these courses with professors and other students.

Graduate School In Economics

Preparing for Graduate School in Economics

You can prepare for graduate school in economics by taking several math classes. This would probably include one year of calculus plus a couple of courses in probability and statistics and linear/matrix algebra. Ask your advisor about the particular courses to take at your university. In addition, the mathematical economics and econometrics courses in the economics department are essential. (*Helpful hint:* Even if you aren't going to graduate school, these mathematical courses can be valuable to you, just as more economics courses can be valuable for nonmajors.)

If your school offers graduate level economics courses, you might want to sit in on a few to get accustomed to the flavour of graduate school.

Most graduate programs require strong grades in economics, a good score on the Graduate Record Examination (GRE) for U.S. schools, and solid letters of recommendations. It is a good idea to get to know a few professors very well and to go above and beyond what is expected so that they can write glowing letters about you.

Financing Graduate School

Unlike some other graduate and professional degree programs, you probably won't need to pile up a massive amount of debt while pursuing an M.A. or Ph.D. in economics. Most graduate programs hire their economics graduate students as teaching or research assistants. Teaching assistants begin by grading papers and running review sessions and can advance to teaching classes on their own. Research assistants generally do data collection, statistical work, and library research for professors and often jointly write papers with them. Most assistantships will pay for tuition and provide you with enough money to live on.

Where Should You Apply?

The best graduate school for you depends on a lot of things, especially your ability level, geographical location, areas of research interests, and, of course, financing. You should talk with your professors about ability level and areas of research. In addition, for U.S. schools there are informative articles that give overall departmental rankings and rankings by subfield. See especially John Tschirhart, "Ranking Economics Department in Areas of Expertise," *Journal of Economic Education,* Spring 1989, and David Colander, "Research on the Economic Profession," *Journal of Economic Perspectives,* Vol. 3, no. 4, Fall 1989, pp. 137–148. There will probably be more up-to-date rankings by the time you apply. Ask a professor or reference librarian to help you track them down. For smaller specialties (e.g., economic history, urban economics) it is especially important to get up-to-date information on any particular program.

What You Will Do in Graduate School

Most students who go on to graduate school do only an M.A. These degrees typically take one year for the non-thesis route and about two years for the thesis route. Course work will include 2–4 courses in economic theory, plus 4–6 courses in specific subfields.

Most Ph.D. programs in economics begin with a year of theory courses in macroeconomics and microeconomics. After a year you will probably take a series of tests to show that you have mastered this core theory. If you pass these tests, in the second and third year of courses you will take more specialized subjects and perhaps take lengthy examinations in a couple of subfields. After this you will be required to write a dissertation—original research that will contribute new knowledge to one of the fields of economics. These stages are intertwined with work as a teaching and/or research assistant, and the dissertation stage can be quite drawn out. In the social sciences the median time that it takes for a student to complete the Ph.D. degree is about 7.5 years.[6] Be aware that a high percentage (roughly 50 percent) of students do not complete their doctoral degree.

What Is Graduate School Like?

Graduate school in economics comes as a surprise to many students. The material and approach are distinctly different from what you will learn as an undergraduate. The textbooks and journal articles you will read in graduate school are often very theoretical and abstract. A good source of information is sitting in on courses or reading the reflections of recent students. See especially *The Making of an Economist* by Arjo Klamer and David Colander (Boulder, Colo.: Westview Press, 1990).

The Committee on Graduate Education in Economics (COGEE) undertook an important review of graduate education in economics and reported its findings in the September 1991 issue of the *Journal of Economic Literature.* COGEE asked faculty members, graduate students, and recent Ph.D.s to rank the most important skills needed to be successful in the study of graduate economics. At the top of the list were analytical skills and mathematics, followed by critical judgment, the ability to apply theory, and computational skills. At the bottom of the list were creativity and the ability to communicate. If you are interested in economic issues but do not have the characteristics required by graduate economics departments, there are other economics-related fields to consider, such as graduate school in public policy. Many economics majors go to business schools to obtain an MBA and are often better prepared than students who have undergraduate degrees in business.

Economics Reading

If you decide to make studying economics part of your future, or if you're hungry for more economics, you should immediately begin reading the economic news and books by economists. Life is short. Why waste it watching TV?

The easiest way to get your daily recommended dose of economics is to keep up with current economic events. Here are a few sources to pick up at the newsstand, bookstore, or library over your summer or winter break.

The Globe and Mail *or the* National Post

Many undergraduates subscribe to the *Globe and Mail* or the *National Post* at low student rates. Join them! Not only are these well-written business newspapers, but they also have articles on domestic and international news, politics, the arts, travel, and sports, as well as lively editorial pages. Reading one of these papers is one of the best ways to tie the economics you are studying to the real world and to prepare for your career.

Magazines and Journals

The Economist, a weekly magazine published in England, is available at a student discount rate. Pick up a copy at your school library and you will be hooked by its informative, sharp writing. *Business Week* is also well worth the read.

Also recommended are *Challenge* magazine and *The Public Interest,* two quarterlies that discuss economic policy, as well as *Policy Options,* a bimonthly publication of the Institute for Research on Public Policy. Finally, there is the *Journal of Economics Perspectives,* which is published by the American Economic Association and written to be accessible to undergraduate economics students.

Books by Economists

Robert Whaples recently asked a group of economics professors (members of the Teach-Econ computer discussion list) the following question: "A bright, enthusiastic student who has just completed introductory economics comes up to you, the professor, and asks you to recommend an economics book for reading over the summer. What do you suggest?'

Here is what they suggested that you, the bright, enthusiastic student, should read:

Top Choices

Milton Friedman, *Capitalism and Freedom.*

Robert Heilbroner, *The Worldly Philosophers: The Lives, Times, and Ideas of the Great Economic Thinkers.*

Steve Landsburg, *The Armchair Economist: Economics and Everyday Life.*

Other Good Choices

Alan Blinder, *Hard Heads, Soft Hearts: Tough-Minded Economics for a Just Society.*

Victor Fuchs, *How We Live.*

Patrick Luciani, *Economics Myths: Making Sense of Canadian Policy Issues.*

Paul Krugman, *Peddling Prosperity: Economic Sense and Nonsense in the Age of Diminished Expectations.*

Donald McCloskey, *If You're So Smart: The Narrative of Economic Expertise.*

Russell Roberts, *The Choice: A Parable of Free Trade and Protectionism.*

In addition, Adam Smith's *The Wealth of Nations* is a must read for every student of economics. Written in 1776, it is the most influential work of economics ever. Its insights are still valuable today.

Endnotes

1. This term is used by Robert Reich in *The Work of Nations.* The quote is from p. 178.

2. Robert Whaples, "Changes in Attitudes about the Fairness of Free Markets among College Economics Students," *Journal of Economic Education,* Vol. 26, no. 4, Fall 1995.

3. Robert H. Frank, Thomas Gilovich, and Dennis T. Regan, "Does Studying Economics Inhibit Cooperation?' *Journal of Economic Perspectives,* Vol. 7, no. 2, Spring 1993, pp. 159-171.

4. John R. Carter and Michael D. Irons, "Are Economists Different, and If So, Why?" *Journal of Economic Perspectives,* Vol. 5, no. 2, Spring 1991, pp. 171-177.

5. "Economics Students Aren't Selfish, They're Just Not Entirely Honest," *Wall Street Journal,* January 18, 1995, B1.

6. See Ronald Ehrenberg, "The Flow of New Doctorates," *Journal of Economic Literature,* Vol. 30, June 1992, pp. 830–875. If breaks in school attendance are included, this climbs to 10.5 years. Of course, some students attend only part time, and most have some kind of employment while completing their degrees.

Chapter 1
What Is Economics?

KEY CONCEPTS

A Definition of Economics

The fundamental economic problem is **scarcity**.

- Because wants exceed the resources available to satisfy them, we cannot have everything we want and must make choices.
- **Economics** studies the choices people make to cope with scarcity.

Big Economic Questions

Five questions summarize all economic choices.

- *What* **goods and services** are produced and in *what* quantities?
- *How* are goods and services produced?
- *Who* consumes the goods and services produced?
- *Where* are goods and services produced?
- *When* are goods and services produced?

Big Ideas of Economics

Eight ideas summarize the economic way of thinking.

- A choice is a **tradeoff**—we give up something to get something else—and the **opportunity cost** of any action is the highest-valued alternative forgone. Opportunity cost is the single most important concept for making choices.
- We make choices in small steps, or at the **margin**, and choices are influenced by **incentives**.
  - Economic choices are made by comparing the *additional* benefit—**marginal benefit**—and *additional* cost—**marginal cost**—of a small increase in an activity. If marginal benefit exceeds marginal cost, we choose to increase the activity.
  - By choosing only activities that bring greater benefits than costs, we use our scarce resources in the way that makes us as well off as possible.
  - Given a change in incentives—inducements to take particular actions—we can predict how choices will change by looking for changes in marginal benefit and marginal cost.
- **Voluntary exchange** makes *both* buyers and sellers better off. **Markets** are an **efficient** way to organize exchange in allocating resources to where they are valued most. Less efficient **command systems** use top-down order-giving to organize the economy.
- Sometimes government actions are needed to overcome **market failure**—when the market does not use resources efficiently.
- For the economy as a whole, **expenditure** equals **income** equals the **value of production**.
- Living standards improve when **productivity**—production per person—increases.
- **Inflation**—the process of rising prices—occurs when the quantity of money increases faster than production.
- **Unemployment** can result from market failure, but some unemployment is productive.

What Economists Do

Economists study

- **microeconomics**—decisions of individual households and firms.

- **macroeconomics**—the national and global economy and how economic aggregates grow and fluctuate.

Economics, as a social science, distinguishes between

- *positive* statements—statements about what *is*, that can be tested by checking them against the facts.
- *normative* statements—statements about what *ought* to be, that depend on values and cannot be tested.

Economic science attempts to understand the economic world and is concerned with positive statements. Economists try to discover positive statements that are consistent with observed facts by

- observation and measurement.
- building **economic models**—abstract, simplified representations of the real world with two components:
  - *Assumptions* about what is essential versus inessential detail.
  - *Predictions* that can be tested by comparison with observed facts.
- testing economic models to develop **economic theories**—generalizations for understanding economic choices and economic performance.

Useful economic models and theories isolate important economic forces and disentangle cause and effect. This requires

- ***ceteris paribus*** assumptions to hold other things equal to isolate the effects of one force at a time.
- avoiding errors of reasoning including the
  - fallacy of composition—the false statement that what is true of the parts is true of the whole, or what is true of the whole is true of the parts.
  - *post hoc* fallacy—the false claim that event *a* caused event *b* just because event *a* occurred first.

Economists agree on a wide range of questions about how the economy works.

HELPFUL HINTS

1 The definition of economics (explaining the choices we make using limited resources to try to satisfy unlimited wants) leads us directly to two important economic concepts—choice and opportunity cost. If wants exceed resources, we cannot have everything we want and therefore must make *choices* among alternatives. In making a choice, we forgo other alternatives, and the *opportunity cost* of any choice is the highest-valued alternative forgone.

2 Marginal analysis is a fundamental tool economists use to predict people's choices. The key to understanding marginal analysis is to focus on *additional*, rather than total, benefits and costs. For example, to predict whether or not Taejong will eat a fourth Big Mac, the economist compares Taejong's *additional* benefit or satisfaction from the fourth Big Mac with its *additional* cost. The total benefits and costs of all four Big Macs are not relevant. Only if the marginal benefit exceeds the marginal cost will Taejong eat a fourth Big Mac.

3 In attempting to understand how and why something works (for example, an airplane, a falling object, an economy), we can try to use description or theory. A description is a list of facts about something. But it does not tell us which facts are essential for understanding how an airplane works (the shape of the wings) and which facts are less important (the colour of the paint).

Scientists use theory to abstract from the complex descriptive facts of the real world and focus only on those elements essential for understanding. Those essential elements are fashioned into models—highly simplified representations of the real world.

In physics and some other natural sciences, if we want to understand the essential force (gravity) that causes objects to fall, we use theory to construct a simple model, then test it by performing a controlled experiment. We create a vacuum to eliminate less important forces like air resistance.

Economic models are also attempts to focus on the essential forces (competition, self-interest) operating in the economy, while abstracting from less important forces (whims, advertising, altruism). Unlike physicists, economists cannot easily perform controlled experiments to test their models. As a result, it is difficult to conclusively prove or disprove a theory and its models.

4 Models are like maps, which are useful precisely because they abstract from real-world detail. A map that reproduced all of the details of the real world (street lamps, fireplugs, electric wires) would be useless. A useful map offers a simplified view, which is carefully selected according to the purpose of the map. Remember that economic models are not claims that the real world is as simple as the model. Models claim to capture the simplified effect of some real force operating in the economy. Before drawing conclusions about the real economy from a model, we must be careful to consider whether, when we reinsert all of the real-world complexities the model abstracted from, the conclusions will be the same as in the model.

5 The most important purpose of studying economics is not to learn what to think about economics but rather *how* to think about economics. The "what"—the facts and descriptions of the economy—can always be found in books. The value of an economics education is the ability to think critically about economic problems and *to understand how* an economy works. This understanding of the essential forces governing how an economy works comes through the mastery of economic theory and model-building.

SELF-TEST

True/False/Uncertain and Explain

1 Economics explains how we use unlimited resources to satisfy limited wants.

2 If Fred slept in instead of either going to lecture or jogging, the missed lecture is his opportunity cost of sleep.

3 When the opportunity cost of an activity increases, the incentive to choose that activity increases.

4 For the economy as a whole, expenditure, income, and the value of production are all equal.

5 Inflation occurs when there is a shortage of money.

6 A positive statement is about what is, while a normative statement is about what will be.

7 Economics is not a science since it deals with the study of wilful human beings and not inanimate objects in nature.

8 Testing an economic model requires comparing its predictions against real-world events.

9 *Ceteris paribus* means "after this, therefore because of this."

10 Observers are correct in noting that economists disagree on most questions.

Multiple-Choice

A Definition of Economics

1 The fact that human wants cannot be fully satisfied with available resources is called the problem of

- **a** opportunity cost.
- **b** scarcity.
- **c** normative economics.
- **d** what to produce.
- **e** who will consume.

2 The problem of scarcity exists

- **a** only in economies that rely on the market system.
- **b** only in economies that rely on the command system.
- **c** in all economies.
- **d** only when people have not optimized.
- **e** now, but will be eliminated with economic growth.

3 Scarcity can be eliminated through

- **a** voluntary exchange.
- **b** efficient markets.
- **c** productivity increases.
- **d** market failure.
- **e** none of the above.

4 Scarcity differs from poverty because
a resources exceed wants for the rich.
b wants exceed resources even for the rich.
c the rich do not have to make choices.
d the poor do not have any choices.
e the poor do not have any wants.

Big Economic Questions

5 The five big economic questions
a all arise from scarcity.
b describe the scope of economics.
c are about goods and services.
d describe choices we make.
e are all of the above.

6 The big economic questions about goods and services include all of the following *except*
a *what* to produce.
b *why* produce.
c *when* to produce.
d *where* to produce.
e *who* consumes what is produced.

Big Ideas of Economics

7 The most fundamental economic problem is
a market failure.
b budget deficits.
c inflation.
d unemployment.
e scarcity.

8 When the government chooses to use resources to build a dam, those resources are no longer available to build a highway. This illustrates the concept of
a a market system.
b macroeconomics.
c opportunity cost.
d voluntary exchange.
e the fallacy of composition.

9 Renata has the chance to either attend an economics lecture or play tennis. If she chooses to attend the lecture, the value of playing tennis is
a greater than the value of the lecture.
b not comparable to the value of the lecture.
c equal to the value of the lecture.
d the opportunity cost of attending the lecture.
e zero.

10 Which of the following sayings best describes opportunity cost?
a "Make hay while the sun shines."
b "Money is the root of all evil."
c "Boldly go where no one has gone before."
d "There's no such thing as a free lunch."
e "Baseball has been very good to me."

11 Marginal benefit is the
a total benefit of an activity.
b additional benefit of a decrease in an activity.
c additional benefit of an increase in an activity.
d opportunity cost of a decrease in an activity.
e opportunity cost of an increase in an activity.

12 Monika will choose to eat a seventh pizza slice if
a the marginal benefit of the seventh slice is greater than its marginal cost.
b the marginal benefit of the seventh slice is less than its marginal cost
c the total benefit of all seven slices is greater than their total cost.
d the total benefit of all seven slices is less than their total cost.
e she is training to be a Sumo wrestler.

13 Market failure can be caused when
a too many producers compete in a market.
b producers take into account pollution costs they impose on others.
c goods can be consumed by everyone without exclusion, creating a free-rider problem.
d prices rise so that fewer consumers can afford a good.
e prices fall so that producer profits suffer.

14 Government policies to overcome market failure include
a antitrust laws.
b environmental protection laws.
c taxes.
d subsidies.
e all of the above.

15 Living standards improve from an increase in
a prices.
b population.
c productivity.
d expenditure.
e all of the above.

16 Unemployment may
- **a** fluctuate over the business cycle.
- **b** be productive.
- **c** be normal and efficient.
- **d** result from market failure.
- **e** be all of the above.

What Economists Do

17 The branch of economics that studies the decisions of individual households and firms is called
- **a** macroeconomics.
- **b** microeconomics.
- **c** positive economics.
- **d** normative economics.
- **e** home economics.

18 Microeconomics studies all of the following *except* the
- **a** decisions of individual firms.
- **b** effects of government safety regulations on the price of cars.
- **c** global economy as a whole.
- **d** prices of individual goods and services.
- **e** effects of taxes on the price of beer.

19 Macroeconomic topics would *not* include the
- **a** reasons for a decline in the price of orange juice.
- **b** reasons for a decline in average prices.
- **c** effect of the quantity of money on inflation.
- **d** effect of the government budget deficit on employment.
- **e** determination of total income.

20 A positive statement is
- **a** about what ought to be.
- **b** about what is.
- **c** always true.
- **d** capable of evaluation as true or false by observation and measurement.
- **e** **b** and **d**.

21 Which of the following is a positive statement?
- **a** Low rents will restrict the supply of housing.
- **b** High interest rates are bad for the economy.
- **c** Housing costs too much.
- **d** Owners of apartment buildings ought to be free to charge whatever rent they want.
- **e** Government should control the rents that apartment owners charge.

22 "The rich face higher income tax rates than the poor" is an example of a
- **a** normative statement.
- **b** positive statement.
- **c** predictive statement.
- **d** theoretical statement.
- **e** *ceteris paribus* statement.

23 A normative statement is a statement regarding
- **a** what is usually the case.
- **b** the assumptions of an economic model.
- **c** what ought to be.
- **d** the predictions of an economic model.
- **e** what is.

24 Which of the following statements is/are normative?
- **a** Scientists should not make normative statements.
- **b** Warts are caused by handling toads.
- **c** As compact disc prices fall, people will buy more of them.
- **d** If income increases, sales of luxury goods will fall.
- **e** None of the above.

25 An economic model is tested by
- **a** examining the realism of its assumptions.
- **b** comparing its predictions with the facts.
- **c** comparing its descriptions with the facts.
- **d** the Testing Committee of the Canadian Economic Association.
- **e** all of the above.

Short Answer Problems

1 What is meant by scarcity, and why does the existence of scarcity mean that we must make choices?

2 If all people would only economize, the problem of scarcity would be solved. Agree or disagree and explain why.

3 Ashley, Doug, and Mei-Lin are planning to travel from Halifax to Sydney. The trip takes one hour by airplane and five hours by train. The air fare is $100 and train fare is $60. They all have to take time off from work while travelling. Ashley earns $5 per hour in her job, Doug $10 per hour, and Mei-Lin $12 per hour.

Calculate the opportunity cost of air and train travel for each person. Assuming they are all economizers, how should each of them travel to Sydney?

4 Suppose the government builds and staffs a hospital in order to provide "free" medical care.

a What is the opportunity cost of the free medical care? The foregone income from paid med. care

b Is it free from the perspective of society as a whole? No

5 Branko loves riding the bumper cars at the amusement park, but he loves the experience a little less with each successive ride. In estimating the benefit he receives from the rides, Branko would be willing to pay $10 for his first ride, $7 for his second ride, and $4 for his third ride. Rides actually cost $5 apiece for as many rides as Branko wants to take. This information is summarized in Table 1.1.

TABLE **1.1**

Ride	1st	2nd	3rd
Marginal benefit	10	7	4
Marginal cost	5	5	5

a If Branko chooses by comparing total benefit and total cost, how many rides will he take?

b If Branko chooses by comparing marginal benefit and marginal cost, how many rides will he take?

c Is Branko better off by choosing according to total or marginal benefit and cost? Explain why.

6 Assume Branko's benefits are the same as in Short Answer Problem 5. Starting fresh, if the price of a bumper car ride rises to $8, how many rides will Branko now take? Explain why.

7 Indicate whether each of the following statements is positive or normative. If it is normative (positive), rewrite it so that it becomes positive (normative).

N **a** The government ought to reduce the size of the deficit in order to lower interest rates.

b Government imposition of a tax on tobacco products will reduce their consumption. P

8 Consider the following paradox. If one farmer has a bumper crop, her income increases. On the basis of the experience of the individual farmer, you predict that, in general, bumper crops cause rising farm incomes. But when all farmers have bumper crops, the excess supply causes prices to fall drastically and farm income actually decreases. What error in reasoning ruined your prediction? Explain.

9 Suppose we examine a model of plant growth that predicts that, given the amount of water and sunlight, the application of fertilizer stimulates plant growth.

a How might you test the model?

b How is the test different from what an economist could do to test an economic model?

10 Suppose your friend, who is a history major, claims that economic theories are useless because the models on which they are based are so unrealistic. He claims that since the models leave out so many descriptive details about the real world, they can't possibly be useful for understanding how the economy works. How would you defend your decision to study economic theory?

ANSWERS

True/False/Uncertain and Explain

1 F Limited resources and unlimited wants. (2)
2 U Opportunity cost is highest-valued alternative forgone; don't know whether lecture or jogging more valuable to Fred. (6)
3 F Incentive decreases because activity is now more expensive. (7)
4 T Big idea 5 (10).
5 F Inflation occurs when there is "too much money chasing too few goods." (11)
6 F Normative statements are about what *ought* to be. (11–12)
7 F Science not defined by subject, but by method of observation, measurement, and testing of theoretical models. (12–14)
8 T Test predictions, not assumptions. (13–14)
9 F *Ceteris paribus* means "other things being equal." Other quote is *post hoc ergo propter hoc.* (14–15)
10 F There is agreement on a wide range of (mostly positive) questions. (16)

Multiple-Choice

1 b Definition. (2)
2 c With infinite wants and finite resources, scarcity will never be eliminated. (2)
3 e Scarcity is an inescapable fact of life. (2)
4 b Poverty is a low level of resources. But wants exceed resources for everyone, necessitating choice. (2)

5 e Economics explains choices about goods and services created by scarcity. (2–5)
6 **b** The other question is *how* to produce. (2–5)
7 e Scarcity and the need for choice underlies all economic problems. (6)
8 c Highway is forgone alternative. (6)
9 **d** Choosing lecture means its value > tennis. Tennis = (highest-valued) forgone alternative to lecture. (6)
10 **d** Every choice involves a cost. (6)
11 c Definition; **e** is marginal cost, **b** and **d** are nonsense. (7)
12 a Choices at made at the margin, when marginal benefit exceeds marginal cost. (7)
13 c **a** true if too *few* producers; **b** true if produces do *not* take cost into account; rising and falling prices part of market allocation process. (9).
14 e All can restore efficiency. (9)
15 c Others can increase the dollar value of production, but living standards depend on real production/person. (10)
16 e Some unemployment part of efficient functioning of markets while some results from wasteful fluctuations in expenditure over the business cycle. (11)
17 **b** Definition. (12)
18 c Macroeconomic topic. (12)
19 a Price of individual good is a microeconomic topic. (12)
20 e Definition. (12–13)
21 a While **a** may be evaluated as true or false, other statements are matters of opinion. (12–13)
22 **b** Positive statements describe facts about what *is.* (12–13)
23 c Key word for normative statements is *ought.* (12–13)
24 a Key word is *should.* Even statement **b** is positive. (12–13)
25 **b** Assumptions not realistic descriptions; are simplified representations of world. (13–14)

Short Answer Problems

1 Scarcity is the universal condition that human wants always exceed the resources available to satisfy them. The fact that goods and services are scarce means that individuals cannot have all of everything they want. It is therefore necessary to choose among alternatives.

2 Disagree. If everyone economized, then we would be making the best possible use of our resources and would be achieving the greatest benefits or satisfaction possible, given the limited quantity of resources. But this does not mean that we would be satisfying all of our limitless needs. The problem of scarcity can never be "solved" as long as people have infinite needs and finite resources for satisfying those needs.

3 The main point is that the total opportunity cost of travel includes the best alternative value of travel time as well as the train or air fare. The total costs of train and air travel for Ashley, Doug, and Mei-Lin are calculated in Table 1.2.

TABLE **1.2**

Traveller	Train	Plane
Ashley		
(a) Fare	$ 60	$100
(b) Opportunity cost of travel time at $5/hr	$ 25	$ 5
Total cost	**$ 85**	**$105**
Doug		
(a) Fare	$ 60	$100
(b) Opportunity cost of travel time at $10/hr	$ 50	$ 10
Total cost	**$110**	**$110**
Mei-Lin		
(a) Fare	$ 60	$100
(b) Opportunity cost of travel time at $12/hr	$ 60	$ 12
Total cost	**$120**	**$112**

On the basis of the cost calculation in Table 1.2, Ashley should take the train, Mei-Lin should take the plane, and Doug could take either.

4 **a** Even though medical care may be offered without charge ("free"), there are still opportunity costs. The opportunity cost of providing such health care is the highest-valued alternative use of the resources used in the construction of the hospital, and the highest-valued alternative use of the resources (including human resources) used in the operation of the hospital.

b These resources are no longer available for other activities and therefore represent a cost to society.

ⓒ **5 a** If Branko rides as long as total benefit is greater than total cost, he will take 3 rides.

Total benefit (cost) can be calculated by adding up the marginal benefit (cost) of all rides taken. Before taking any rides, his total benefit is zero and his total cost is zero. The first ride's marginal benefit is $10, which when added to 0 yields a total benefit of $10. The first ride's marginal cost is $5, which when added to zero yields a total cost of $5. Total cost is greater than total benefit, so Branko takes the first ride. For the first and second rides together, total benefit is $17, which is greater than total cost of $10. For all 3 rides together, total benefit is $21, which is greater than total cost of $15.

b If Branko compares the marginal benefit of each ride with its marginal cost, he will only take 2 rides. He will take the first ride because its marginal benefit ($10) is greater than its marginal cost ($5). After the first ride, he will still choose to take the second ride because its marginal benefit ($7) is greater than its marginal cost ($5). But he will quit after the second ride. The third ride would add a benefit of $4, but it costs $5, so Branko would be worse off by taking the third ride.

c The marginal rule for choosing will make Branko better off. It would be a mistake to pay $5 for the third ride when it is only worth $4 to Branko. He would be better off taking that final $5 and spending it on something (the roller coaster?) that gives him a benefit worth at least $5.

You will learn much more about applying marginal analysis to choices like Branko's in Chapters 3 and 6.

ⓒ **6** If the price of a bumper car rises to $8, Branko now takes only 1 ride. He will take the first ride because its marginal benefit ($10) is greater than its marginal cost ($8). After the first ride, he will quit. The marginal benefit of the second ride ($7) is now less than its marginal cost ($8).

7 a The given statement is normative. The following is positive: If the government reduces the size of the deficit, interest rates will fall.

b The given statement is positive. The following is normative: The government ought to impose a tax on tobacco products.

8 The paradox is an example of the fallacy of composition—the (false) statement that what is true of the parts is true of the whole. We cannot always generalize from the parts to the whole, and the prediction that bumper crops cause rising incomes for all farmers is a false generalization from the parts to the whole.

9 a The prediction of the model can be tested by conducting the following controlled experiment and carefully observing the outcome. Select a number of plots of ground of the same size that have similar characteristics and are subject to the same amount of water and sunlight. Plant equal quantities of seeds in all the plots. In some of the plots apply no fertilizer and in some of the plots apply (perhaps varying amounts of) fertilizer. When the plants have grown, measure the growth of the plants and compare the growth of the fertilized plots and the unfertilized plots. If plant growth is greater in fertilized plots, we provisionally accept the model and the theory on which it is based. If plant growth is not greater in fertilized plots, we discard the theory (model), or modify its assumptions. Perhaps the effective use of fertilizer requires more water.

Then construct a new model that predicts that, given more water (and the same amount of sunlight), fertilized plants will grow larger than equivalently watered unfertilized plants. Test that model and continue modifying assumptions until predictions are consistent with the facts.

b Economists cannot easily perform such controlled experiments and instead must change one assumption at a time in alternative models and compare the results. Then differences in outcomes can only be tested against variations in data that occur naturally in the economy. This is a more difficult and less precise model-building and testing procedure than exists for the controlled fertilizer experiment.

ⓒ **10** A brief answer to your friend's challenge appears in Helpful Hint 3. Models are like maps, which are useful precisely because they abstract from real-world detail. A useful map offers a simplified view, which is carefully selected according to the purpose of the map. No mapmaker would claim that the world is as simple as her map, and economists do not claim that the real economy is as simple as their models. What economists claim is that their models isolate the simplified effect of some real forces (like optimizing behaviour) operating in the economy, and yield predictions that can be tested against real-world data.

Another way to answer your friend would be to challenge him to identify what a more realistic model or theory would look like. You would do well to quote Milton Friedman (a Nobel Prize winner in economics) on this topic: "A theory or its 'assumptions' cannot possibly be thoroughly 'realistic' in the immediate descriptive sense. … A completely 'realistic' theory of the wheat market would have to include not only the conditions directly underlying the supply and demand for wheat but also the kind of coins or credit instruments used to make exchanges; the personal characteristics of wheat-traders such as the color of each trader's hair and eyes, … the number of members of his family, their characteristics, … the kind of soil on which the wheat was grown, … the weather prevailing during the growing season; … and so on indefinitely. Any attempt to move very far in achieving this kind of 'realism' is certain to render a theory utterly useless."

From Milton Friedman, "The Methodology of Positive Economics," in *Essays in Positive Economics* (Chicago: University of Chicago Press, 1953), p. 32.

Chapter 2

Making and Using Graphs

KEY CONCEPTS

Graphing Data

Graphs represent quantity as a distance. On a two-dimensional graph,

- horizontal line is *x-axis.*
- vertical line is *y-axis.*
- intersection (0) is the *origin.*

Main types of economic graphs:

- **Scatter diagram**—shows relationship between two variables, one measured on *x-axis,* the other measured on *y*-axis.
- **Time-series graph**—shows relationship between time (measured on *x*-axis) and other variable(s) (measured on *y*-axis). Reveals variable's level, direction of change, speed of change, and **trend** (general tendency to rise or fall).
- **Cross-section graph**—shows level of a variable across different groups at a point in time.

Misleading graphs often omit origin or stretch/squeeze measurement scale to exaggerate or understate variation. Always look closely at the values and labels on axes before interpreting a graph.

Graphs Used in Economic Models

Graphs showing relationships between variables fall into four categories:

- **Positive (direct) relationship**—variables move together in same direction: upward-sloping.
- **Negative (inverse) relationship**—variables move in opposite directions: downward-sloping.
- Relationships with a maximum/minimum:
  - Relationship slopes upward, reaches a maximum (zero slope), and then slopes downward.
  - Relationship slopes downward, reaches a minimum (zero slope), and then slopes upward.
- Unrelated (independent) variables—one variable changes while the other remains constant; graph is vertical or horizontal straight line.

The Slope of a Relationship

Slope of a relationship is change in value of variable on *y*-axis divided by change in value of variable on *x*-axis.

- Δ means "change in."
- Formula for slope is $\Delta y/\Delta x$ = rise/run.
- Straight line (**linear relationship**) has constant slope.
  - A positive, upward-sloping relationship has a positive slope.
  - A negative, downward-sloping relationship has a negative slope.
- Curved line has varying slope, which can be calculated
  - *at a point*—by drawing straight line tangent to the curve at that point and calculating slope of the line.
  - *across an arc*—by drawing straight line across two points on the curve and calculating slope of the line.

Graphing Relationships Among More Than Two Variables

Relationships among more than two variables can be graphed by holding constant the values of all variables except two. This is done by making a ***ceteris paribus*** assumption—"other things remaining the same."

HELPFUL HINTS

1 Throughout the text, relationships among economic variables will almost invariably be represented and analysed graphically. An early, complete understanding of graphs will greatly facilitate your mastery of the economic analysis of later chapters. Avoid the common mistake of assuming that a superficial understanding of graphs will be sufficient.

2 If your experience with graphical analysis is limited, this chapter is crucial to your ability to readily understand later economic analysis. You will likely find significant rewards in occasionally returning to this chapter for review. If you are experienced in constructing and using graphs, this chapter may be "old hat." Even so, you should skim the chapter and work through the Self-Test in this *Study Guide.*

3 Slope is a *linear* concept since it is a property of a straight line. For this reason, the slope is constant along a straight line but is different at different points on a curved (nonlinear) line. For the slope of a curved line, we actually calculate the slope of a straight line. The text presents two alternatives for calculating the slope of a curved line: (1) slope at a point and (2) slope across an arc. The first of these calculates the slope of the *straight line* that just touches (is tangent to) the curve at a point. The second calculates the slope of the *straight line* formed by the arc between two points on the curved line.

4 A straight line on a graph can also be described by a simple equation (see Text Mathematical Note, pages 32–33). The general form for the equation of a straight line is

$$y = a + bx$$

If you are given such an equation, you can graph the line by finding the y-intercept (where the line intersects the vertical y-axis), finding the x-intercept (where the line intersects the horizontal x-axis), and then connecting those two points with a straight line:

To find the y-intercept, set $x = 0$.

$$y = a + b(0)$$
$$y = a$$

To find the x-intercept, set $y = 0$.

$$0 = a + bx$$
$$x = -a/b$$

Connecting these two points ($x = 0$, $y = a$) and ($x = -a/b$, $y = 0$)) or $(0, a)$ and $(-a/b, 0)$ allows you to graph the straight line. For any straight line with the equation of the form $y = a + bx$, the slope of the line is b. Figure 2.1 illustrates a line where b is a *negative* number, so there is a *negative* relationship between the variables x and y.

FIGURE **2.1**

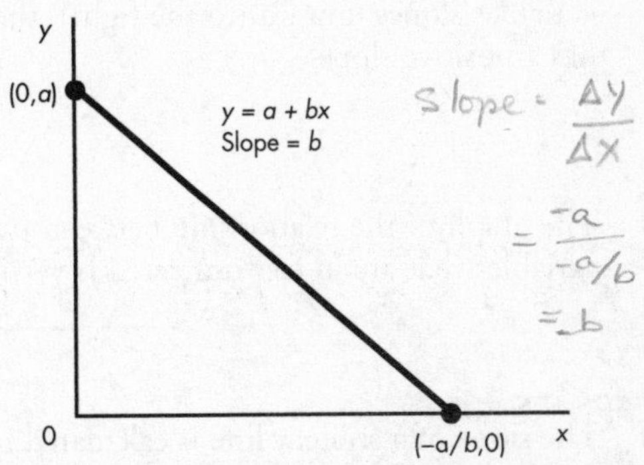

To see how to apply this general equation, consider this example:

$$y = 6 - 2x$$

To find the y-intercept, set $x = 0$.

$$y = 6 - 2(0)$$
$$y = 6$$

To find the x-intercept, set $y = 0$.

$$0 = 6 - 2x$$
$$x = 3$$

Connecting these two points, (0, 6) and (3, 0), yields the line in Fig. 2.2.

FIGURE **2.2**

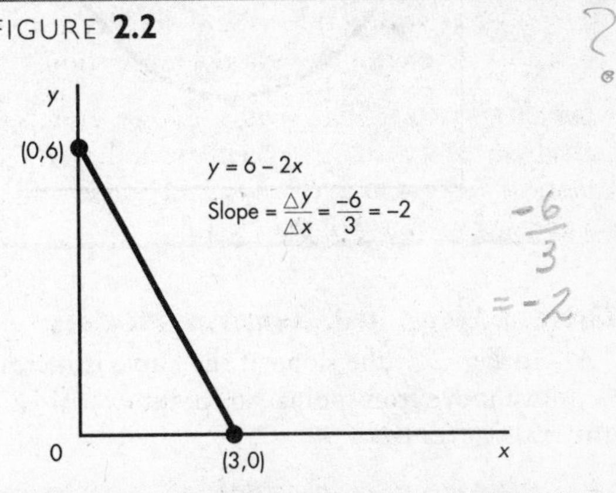

The slope of this line is –2. Since the slope is negative, there is a negative relationship between the variables x and y.

SELF-TEST

True/False/Uncertain and Explain

1 A graph that omits the origin is misleading.

2 If the graph of the relationship between two variables slopes upward (to the right), the graph has a positive slope.

3 The graph of the relationship between two variables that are in fact unrelated is vertical.

4 The slope of a straight line is calculated by dividing the change in the value of the variable measured on the horizontal axis by the change in the value of the variable measured on the vertical axis.

5 In Fig. 2.3, the relationship between *y* and *x* is first negative, reaches a minimum, and then becomes positive as *x* increases.

FIGURE **2.3**

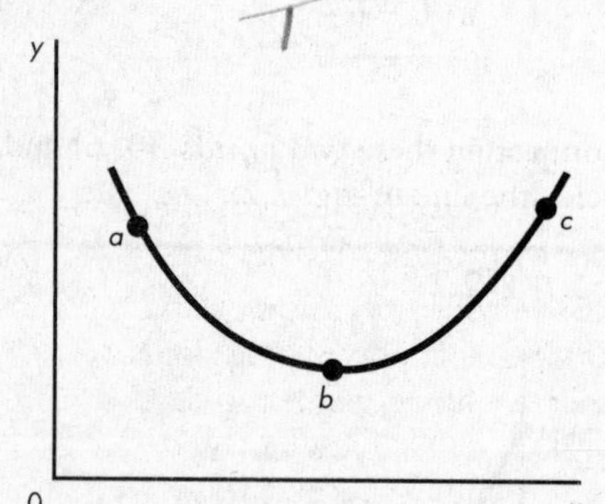

6 In Fig. 2.3, the slope of the curve is increasing as we move from point *b* to point *c*.

7 In Fig. 2.3, the slope of the curve is approaching zero as we move from point *a* to point *b*.

8 In Fig. 2.3, the value of *x* is a minimum at point *b*.

9 For a straight line, if a small change in *y* is associated with a large change in *x*, the slope is large.

10 For a straight line, if a large change in *y* is associated with a small change in *x*, the line is steep.

Multiple-Choice

Graphing Data

1 Fig. 2.4 is

a a one-variable time-series graph.
b a two-variable time-series graph.
c a cross-section graph.
d a scatter diagram.
e none of the above.

FIGURE **2.4**

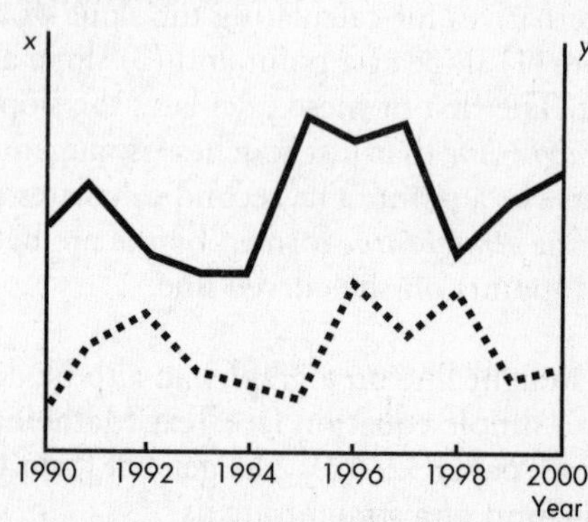

2 The dotted line in Fig. 2.4 represents variable *y*. Which of the following statements best describes the relationship between *x* and *y* in Fig. 2.4?

a *x* and *y* tend to move in opposite directions over time.
b *y* tends to move in the opposite direction from *x*, but one year later.
c *x* and *y* tend to move together over time.
d *x* tends to move in the same direction as *y*, but one year later.
e *y* tends to move in the same direction as *x*, but one year later.

3 The tendency for a variable to rise or fall over time is called its

- **a** slope.
- **b** trend.
- **c** *y*-coordinate.
- **d** level.
- **e** correlation.

Graphs Used in Economic Models

4 From the data in Table 2.1, it appears that

- **a** *x* and *y* have a negative relationship.
- **b** *x* and *y* have a positive relationship.
- **c** there is no relationship between *x* and *y*.
- **d** there is first a negative and then a positive relationship between *x* and *y*.
- **e** there is first a positive and then a negative relationship between *x* and *y*.

TABLE **2.1**

Year	x	y
1990	6.2	143
1991	5.7	156
1992	5.3	162

5 If variables *x* and *y* move up and down together, they are said to be

- **a** positively related.
- **b** negatively related.
- **c** conversely related.
- **d** unrelated.
- **e** trendy.

6 The relationship between two variables that move in opposite directions is shown graphically by a line that is

- **a** positively sloped.
- **b** relatively steep.
- **c** relatively flat.
- **d** negatively sloped.
- **e** curved.

The Slope of a Relationship

7 In Fig. 2.5 the relationship between *x* and *y* as *x* increases is

- **a** positive with slope decreasing.
- **b** negative with slope decreasing.
- **c** negative with slope increasing.
- **d** positive with slope increasing.
- **e** positive with slope first increasing then decreasing.

FIGURE **2.5**

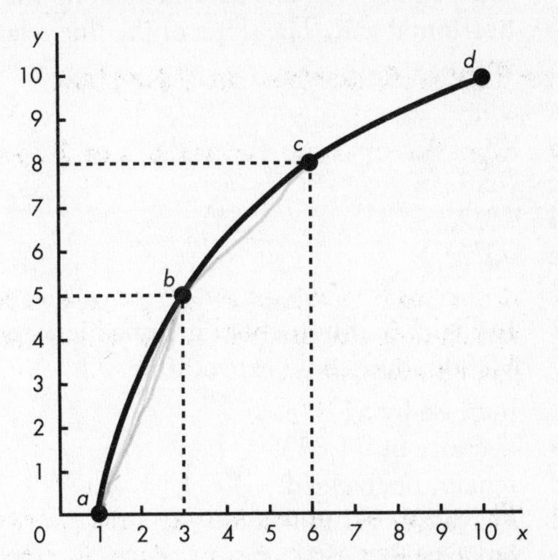

8 What is the slope across the arc between *b* and *c* in Fig. 2.5?

- **a** 1/2
- **b** 2/3
- **c** 1
- **d** 2
- **e** 3

9 In Fig. 2.5, consider the slopes of arc *ab* and arc *bc*. The slope at point *b* is difficult to determine exactly, but it must be

- **a** greater than 5/2.
- **b** about 5/2.
- **c** between 5/2 and 1.
- **d** about 1.
- **e** less than 1.

10 In Table 2.2, suppose that *w* is the independent variable measured along the horizontal axis. The slope of the line relating *w* and *u* is

- **a** positive with a decreasing slope.
- **b** negative with a decreasing slope.
- **c** positive with an increasing slope.
- **d** negative with a constant slope.
- **e** positive with a constant slope.

TABLE **2.2**

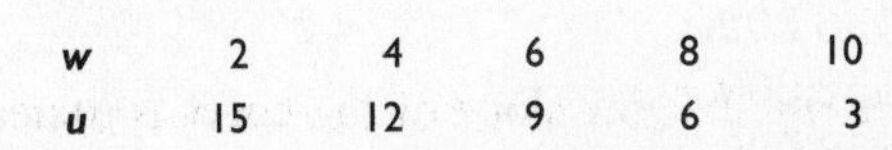

w	2	4	6	8	10
u	15	12	9	6	3

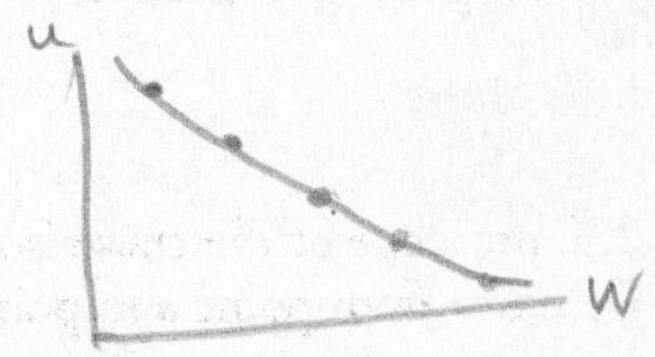

11 Refer to Table 2.2. Suppose that w is the independent variable measured along the horizontal axis. The slope of the line relating w and u is

- **a** +3.
- **b** –3.
- **c** –2/3.
- **d** +3/2.
- **e** –3/2.

12 In Fig. 2.6, if household income increases by \$1,000, household expenditure will

- **a** increase by \$1,333.
- **b** decrease by \$1,333.
- **c** remain unchanged.
- **d** increase by \$1,000.
- **e** increase by \$750.

FIGURE **2.6**

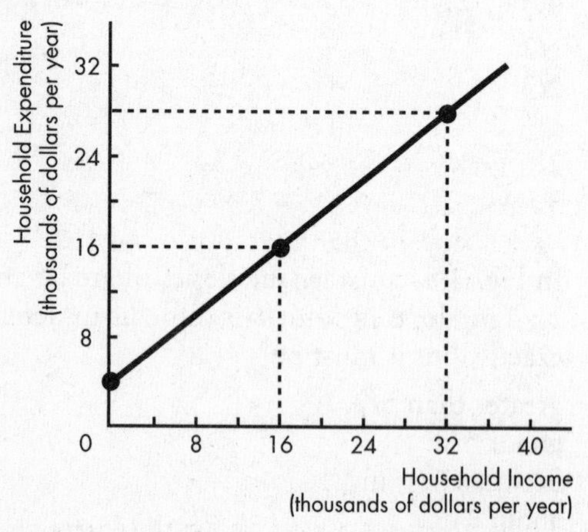

13 In Fig. 2.6, if household income is zero, household expenditure is

- **a** 0.
- **b** –\$4,000.
- **c** \$4,000.
- **d** \$8,000.
- **e** impossible to determine from the graph.

14 In Fig. 2.6, if household expenditure is \$28,000, household income is

- **a** \$36,000.
- **b** \$32,000.
- **c** \$28,000.
- **d** \$25,000.
- **e** none of the above.

15 At all points along a straight line, slope is

- **a** positive.
- **b** negative.
- **c** constant.
- **d** zero.
- **e** none of the above.

16 What is the slope of the line in Fig. 2.7?

- **a** 2
- **b** 1/2
- **c** 3
- **d** 1/3
- **e** –3

FIGURE **2.7**

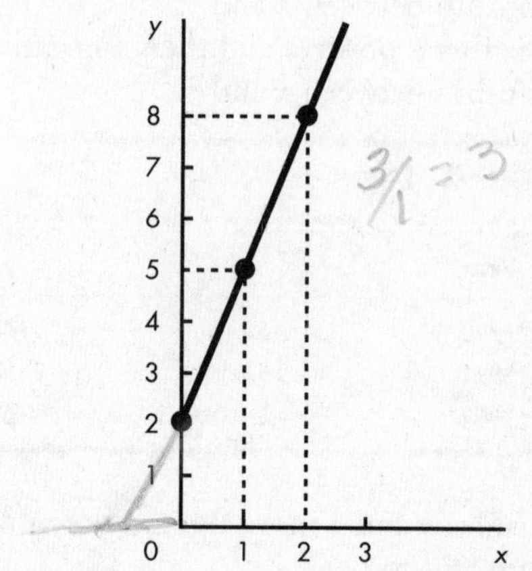

17 If the line in Fig. 2.7 were to continue down to the x-axis, what would the value of x be when y is zero?

- **a** 0
- **b** 2
- **c** 2/3
- **d** –2/3
- **e** –3/2

18 If the equation of a straight line is $y = 6 + 3x$, then the slope is

- **a** –3 and the y-intercept is 6.
- **b** –3 and the y-intercept is –2.
- **c** 3 and the y-intercept is 6.
- **d** 3 and the y-intercept is –2.
- **e** 3 and the y-intercept is –6.

19 If the equation of a straight line is $y = 8 - 2x$, then the slope is

- **a** –2 and the x-intercept is –4.
- **b** –2 and the x-intercept is 4.
- **c** –2 and the x-intercept is 8.
- **d** 2 and the x-intercept is –4.
- **e** 2 and the x-intercept is 4.

Graphing Relationships Among More Than Two Variables

20 To graph a relationship among more than two variables, what kind of assumption is necessary?

a normative
b positive
c linear
d independence of variables
e *ceteris paribus*

21 Given the data in Table 2.3, holding income constant, the graph relating the price of strawberries (vertical axis) to the purchases of strawberries (horizontal axis)

a is a vertical line.
b is a horizontal line.
c is a positively sloped line.
d is a negatively sloped line.
e reaches a minimum.

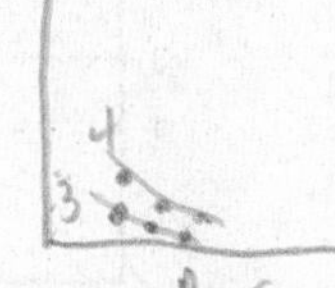

TABLE **2.3**

Weekly Family Income ($)	Price per Box of Strawberries ($)	Number of Boxes Purchased per Week
300	$1.00	5
300	$1.25	3
300	$1.50	2
400	$1.00	7
400	$1.25	5
400	$1.50	4

22 Given the data in Table 2.3, suppose family income decreases from $400 to $300 per week. Then the graph relating the price of strawberries (vertical axis) to the purchases of strawberries (horizontal axis) will

a become negatively sloped.
b become positively sloped.
c shift to the right.
d shift to the left.
e no longer exist.

23 Given the data in Table 2.3, holding price constant, the graph relating family income (vertical axis) to the purchases of strawberries (horizontal axis) is a

a vertical line.
b horizontal line.
c positively sloped line.
d negatively sloped line.
e positively or negatively sloped line, depending on the price that is held constant.

24 In Fig. 2.8, x is

a positively related to y and negatively related to z.
b positively related to both y and z.
c negatively related to y and positively related to z.
d negatively related to both y and z.
e greater than z.

FIGURE **2.8**

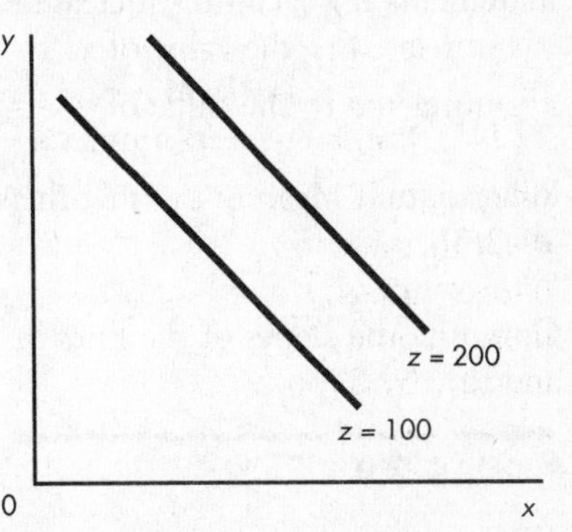

25 In Fig. 2.8, a decrease in the value of z will cause, *ceteris paribus*,

a a decrease in the value of x.
b an increase in the value of x.
c an increase in the value of y.
d no change in the value of y.
e no change in the value of x.

Short Answer Problems

1 Consider the data in Table 2.4.
a Draw a time-series graph for the interest rate.
b Draw a two-variable time-series graph for both the inflation rate and the interest rate.
c Draw a scatter diagram for the inflation rate (horizontal axis) and the interest rate (vertical axis).
d Would you describe the general relationship between the inflation rate and the interest rate as positive, negative, or unrelated?

TABLE **2.4**

Year	Inflation Rate (%)	Interest Rate (%)
1970	5.4	6.4
1971	3.2	4.3
1972	3.4	4.1
1973	8.3	7.0
1974	11.8	7.9
1975	6.7	5.8
1976	4.9	5.0
1977	6.5	5.3
1978	8.6	7.2
1979	12.3	10.0

2 Draw a graph of variables x and y that illustrates each of the following relationships:

a x and y move up and down together.
b x and y move in opposite directions.
c as x increases y reaches a maximum.
d as x increases y reaches a minimum.
e x and y move in opposite directions, but as x increases y decreases by larger and larger increments for each unit increase in x.
f y is unrelated to the value of x.
g x is unrelated to the value of y.

3 What does it mean to say that the slope of a line is –2/3?

4 Compute the slopes of the lines in Fig. 2.9(a) and (b).

FIGURE **2.9**

(a)

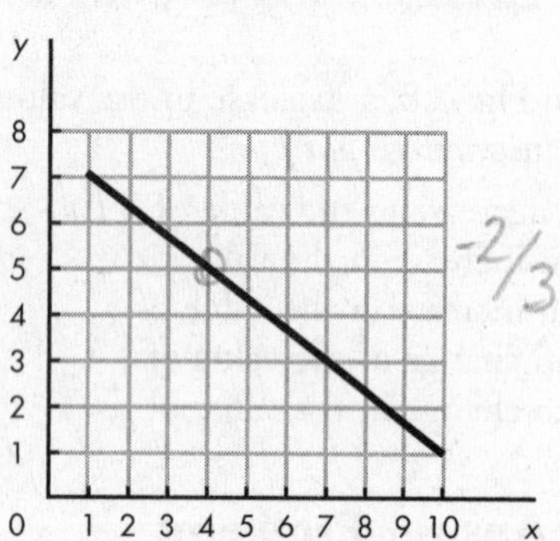

(b)

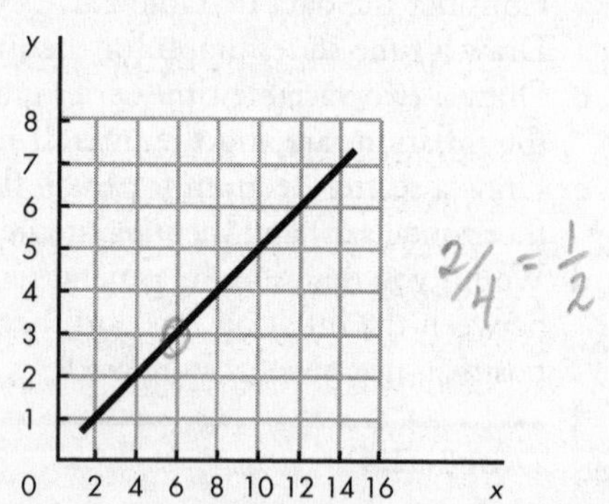

5 Draw each of the following:

a a straight line with slope –10 and passing through the point (2, 80)
b a straight line with slope 2 and passing through the point (6, 10)

6 The equation for a straight line is $y = 4 - 2x$.

a Calculate: the y-intercept; the x-intercept; the slope.
b Draw the graph of the line.

7 Explain two ways to measure the slope of a curved line.

8 Use the graph in Fig. 2.10 to compute the slope

a across the arc between points a and b.
b at point b.
c at point c, and explain your answer.

FIGURE **2.10**

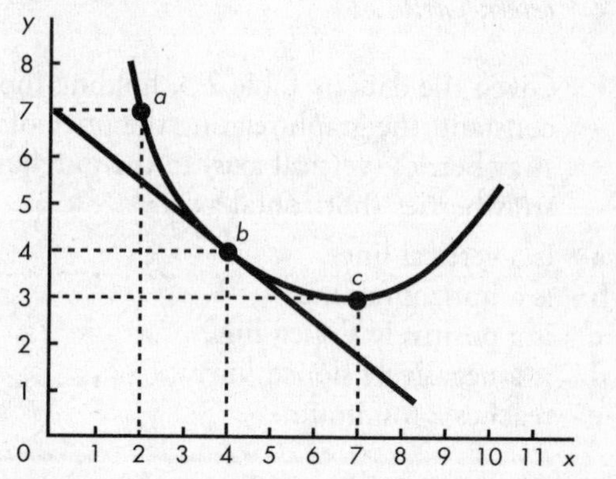

9 How do we graph a relationship among more than two variables using a two-dimensional graph?

10 In Table 2.5, x represents the number of umbrellas sold per month, y represents the price of an umbrella, and z represents the average number of rainy days per month.

a On the same diagram, graph the relationship between x (horizontal axis) and y (vertical axis) when $z = 4$, when $z = 5$, and when $z = 6$. On average, it rains six days per month. This implies a certain average relationship between monthly umbrella sales and umbrella price. Suppose that the "greenhouse effect" reduces the average monthly rainfall to four days per month. What happens to the graph of the relationship between umbrella sales and umbrella prices?
b On a diagram, graph the relationship between x (horizontal axis) and z (vertical axis) when $y = \$10$ and when $y = \$12$. Is the relationship between x and z positive or negative?
c On a diagram, graph the relationship between y (horizontal axis) and z (vertical axis) when $x = 120$ and when $x = 140$. Is the relationship between y and z positive or negative?

TABLE **2.5**

Umbrellas Sold per Month (x)	Price per Umbrella (y)	Average Number of Rainy Days per Month (z)
120	$10	4
140	$10	5
160	$10	6
100	$12	4
120	$12	5
140	$12	6
80	$14	4
100	$14	5
120	$14	6

ANSWERS

True/False/Uncertain and Explain

1 U Sometimes it's misleading, sometimes omitting origin enables graph to reveal its information. (22)
2 T Upward-sloping curves/lines have positive slopes. (28–29, 32–33)
3 U Graph of unrelated variables may be vertical or horizontal. (27)
4 F Slope = (Δ variable on vertical (*y*) axis)/(Δ variable on horizontal (*x*) axis). (28–29)
5 T Arc *ab* would have negative slope, arc *bc* positive slope. (24–27)
6 T Curve becomes steeper, meaning Δ*y* increasing faster than Δ*x*, so slope increasing. (28–30)
7 T At *b*, tangent has slope = 0, since Δ*y* = 0 along horizontal line through *b*. (28–30)
8 F Value of *y* is minimum at point *b*. (26–27)
9 F Large slope means large Δ*y* associated with small Δ*x*. (28–29)
10 T Steep line has large slope, meaning large Δ*y* associated with small Δ*x*. (28–29)

Multiple-Choice

1 b Two variables are *x* and *y*. Cross-section graphs and scatter diagrams don't have time on an axis. (22–23)
2 e For example, *x* begins falling in 1991, *y* begins falling in 1992. (24–26)
3 b Definition. (23)
4 a Higher values *x* (6.2) associated with lower values *y* (143). (24–26)
5 a Definition. (24–26)
6 d Graph may be steep, flat, or curved, but must have negative slope. (25–26)
7 a Slope of arc *ab* = +2.5. Slope of arc *bc* = +1. (28–30)
8 c Δ*y* = 3(8 – 5); Δ*x* = 3(6 – 3). (29–30)
9 c 5/2 is slope of *ab*, while 1 is slope of *bc*. (29–30)
10 d As *w* increases, *u* increases. Δ*u*/Δ*w* is constant. (28–30)
11 e Between any two points, Δ*u* = 3, Δ*w* = –2. (28–30)
12 e Slope (Δ*y*/Δ*x*) = 3/4. If Δ*x* (Δ household income) = $1,000, then Δ*y* (Δ household expenditure) = $750. (28–30)
13 c Where the line intersects the household expenditure (*y*) axis. (28–30)
14 b From $28,000 on vertical (expenditure) axis, move across to line, then down to $32,000 on horizontal (income) axis. (28–30)
15 c Along straight line, slope may or may not be **a**, **b**, or **d**. (28)
16 c Between any two points, Δ*y* = 3 and Δ*x* = 1. (28–29)
ⓒⓣ **17 d** Equation of line is *y* = 2 + 3*x*. Solve for *x*-intercept (set *y* = 0). (28–30, 32–33)
18 c Use formula *y* = *a* + *bx*. Slope = *b*, *y*-intercept = *a*. (28–30, 32–33)
19 b Use formula *y* = *a* + *bx*. Slope = *b*, *x*-intercept = –*a*/*b*. (28–30, 32–33)
20 e Must hold constant other variables to isolate relationship between two variables. (30–31)
21 d Look either at data in top 3 rows (income = 300) or data in bottom 3 rows (income = 400). Higher price associated with lower purchases. (30–31)
ⓒⓣ **22 d** At each price, fewer boxes will be purchased. (30–31)
ⓒⓣ **23 c** For *P* = 1, two points on line are (5 boxes, $300) and (7 boxes, $400). Same relationship for other prices. (30–31)
24 c Increased *y* causes decreased *x* holding *z* constant. Increased *z* causes increased *x* holding *y* constant. (30–31)
ⓒⓣ **25 a** Decreased *z* causes decreased *x* holding *y* constant. Decreased *z* causes decreased *y* holding *x* constant. (30–31)

Short Answer Problems

1 a A time-series graph for the interest rate is given in Fig. 2.11(a).
b Fig. 2.11(b) is a two-variable time-series graph for both the inflation rate and the interest rate. The inflation rate is the dotted line; the interest rate is the solid line.
c The scatter diagram for the inflation rate and the interest rate is given in Fig. 2.11(c).
d From the graphs in Fig. 2.11(b) and (c), we see that the relationship between the inflation rate and the interest rate is generally positive.

FIGURE **2.11**

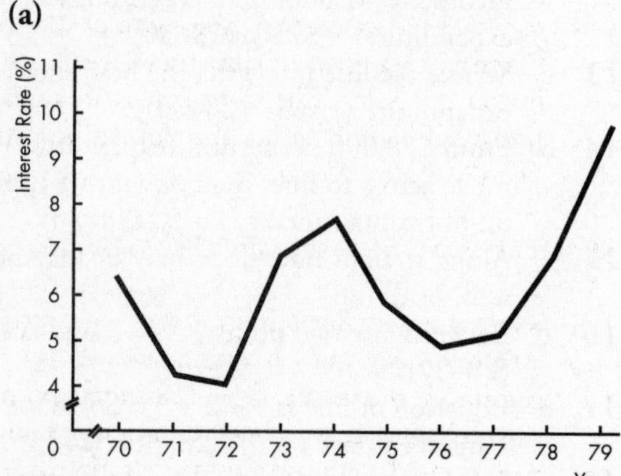

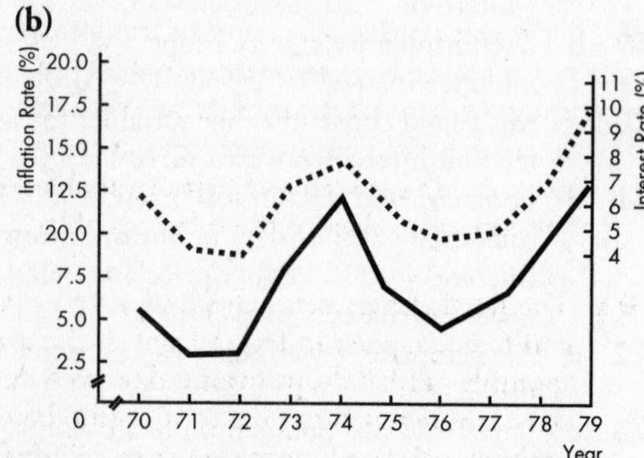

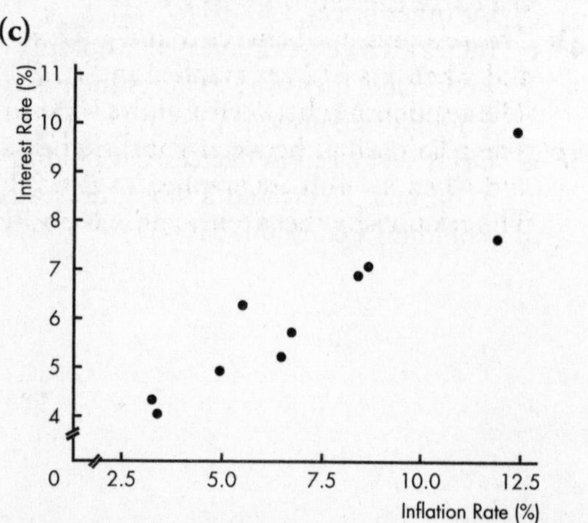

2 Fig. 2.12(a) through (g) illustrates the desired graphs.

FIGURE **2.12**

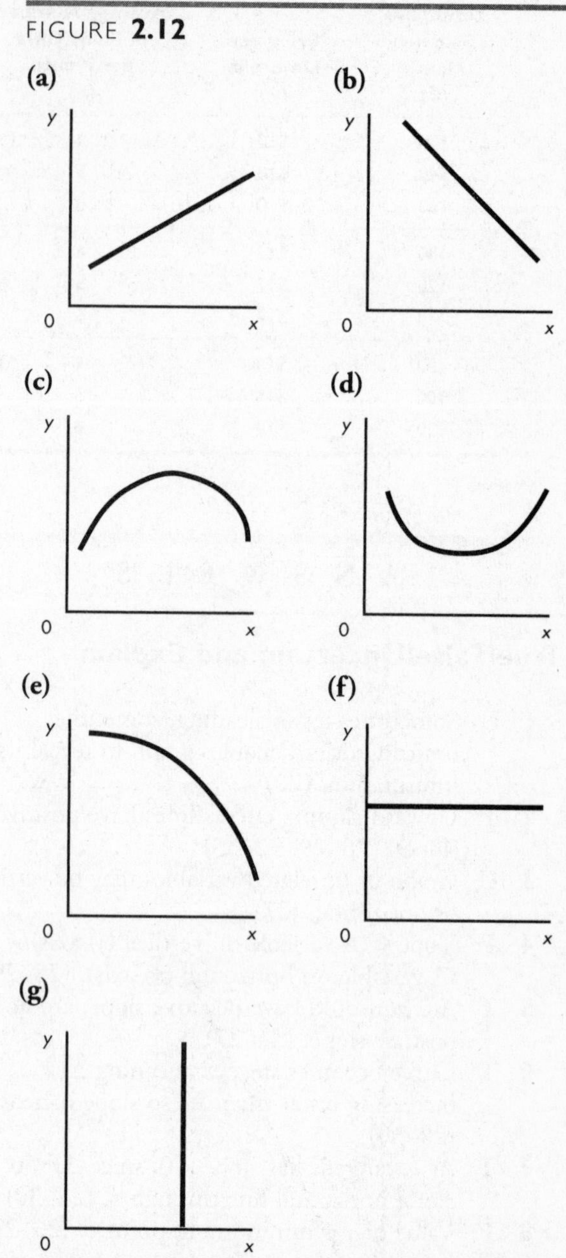

3 The negative sign in the slope of –2/3 means that there is a negative relationship between the two variables. The value of 2/3 means that when the variable measured on the vertical axis decreases by 2 units (the rise or Δy), the variable measured on the horizontal axis increases by 3 units (the run or Δx).

4 To find the slope, pick any two points on a line and compute $\Delta y/\Delta x$. The slope of the line in Fig. 2.9(a) is –2/3, and the slope of the line in Fig. 2.9(b) is 1/2.

5 a The requested straight line is graphed in Fig. 2.13(a). First plot the point (2, 80). Then pick a second point whose y-coordinate decreases by 10 for every 1 unit increase in the x-coordinate, for example, (5, 50). The slope between the two points is $-30/3 = -10$.

b The requested straight line is graphed in Fig. 2.13(b). First plot the point (6, 10). Then pick a second point whose y-coordinate decreases by 2 for every 1 unit decrease in the x-coordinate, for example, (5, 8). The slope between the two points is $-2/-1 = 2$.

FIGURE **2.13**

(a)

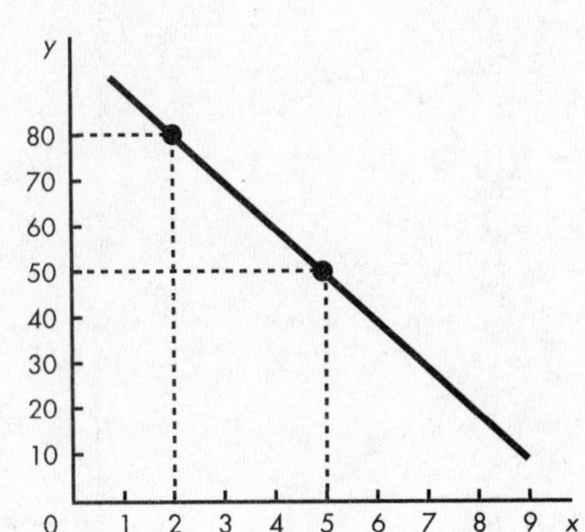

(b)

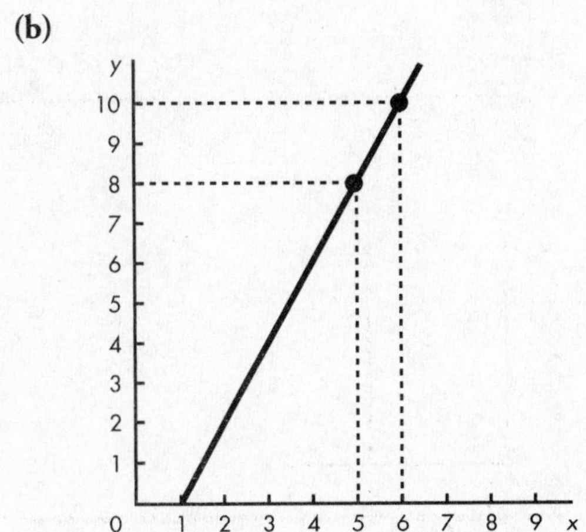

6 a To find the y-intercept, set $x = 0$.

$$y = 4 - 2(0)$$
$$y = 4$$

To find the x-intercept, set $y = 0$.

$$0 = 4 - 2x$$
$$x = 2$$

The slope of the line is -2, the value of the "b" coefficient on x.

b The graph of the line is shown in Fig. 2.14.

FIGURE **2.14**

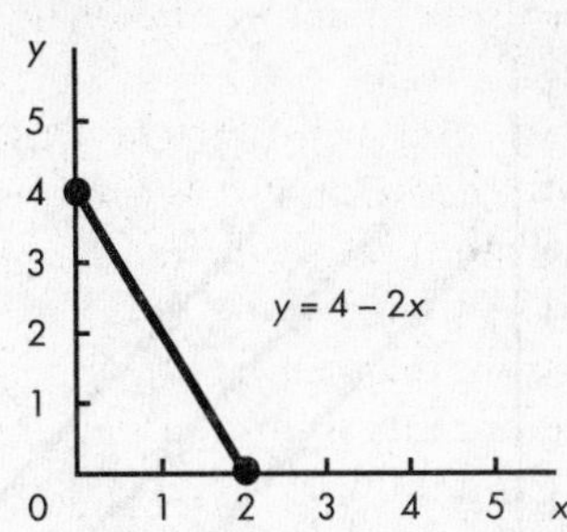

7 The slope of a straight line can be measured at a point or across an arc. The slope at a point is measured by calculating the slope of the straight line that is tangent to (just touches) the curved line at the point. The slope across an arc is measured by calculating the slope of the straight line that forms the arc.

8 a The slope across the arc between points a and b is $-3/2$.

b The slope at point b is $-3/4$.

c The slope at point c is zero because it is a minimum point. Nearby a minimum point the slope changes from negative to positive and must pass through zero, or no slope, to do so.

9 To graph a relationship among more than two variables, we hold all of the variables but two constant, and graph the relationship between the remaining two. Thus we can graph the relationship between any pair of variables, given the constant values of the other variables.

10 a The relationships between x and y for $z = 4$, 5, and 6 are graphed in Fig. 2.15(a). If the average monthly rainfall drops from 6 days to 4 days, the curve representing the relationship between umbrella sales and umbrella prices will shift from the curve labelled $z = 6$ to $z = 4$.

b The relationships between x and z when y is \$10 and when y is \$12 are graphed in Fig. 2.15(b). The relationship between x and z is positive.

c The relationships between y and z when $x = 120$ and when $x = 140$ are graphed in Fig. 2.15(c). The relationship between y and z is positive.

FIGURE **2.15**

(a)

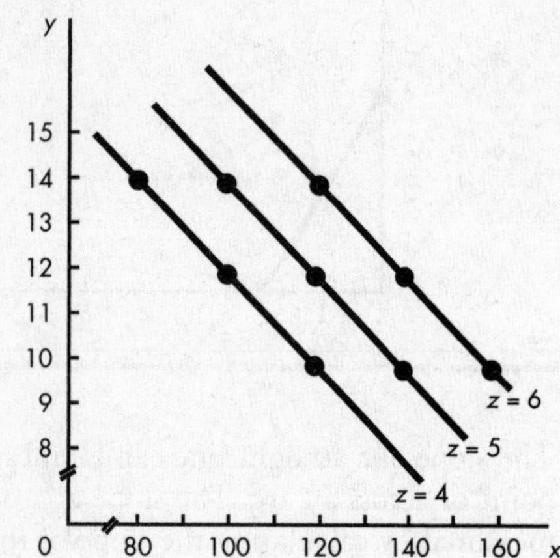

(b)

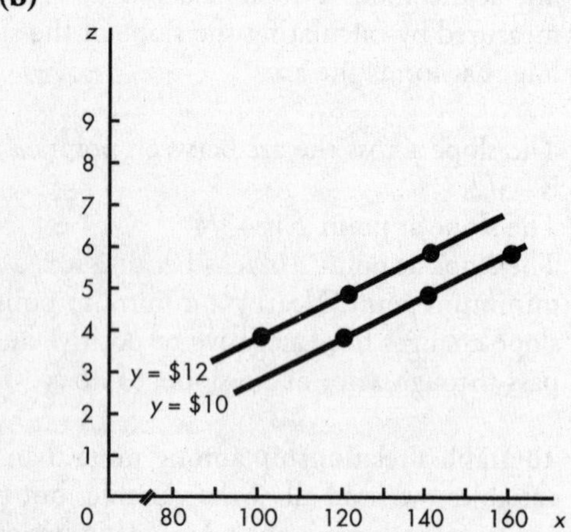

(c)

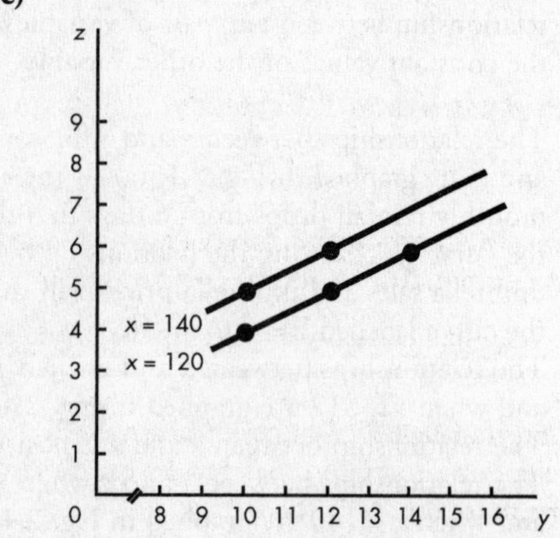

Chapter 3

The Economic Problem

KEY CONCEPTS

Resources and Wants

Scarcity arises because we have

- limited resources—**labour**, **land**, **capital** (including **human capital**—knowledge and skill obtained from education and training), **entrepreneurship**.
- unlimited wants.

The fundamental economic problem is to use limited resources to produce items we value most highly. **Economics** explains the *choices* people make to cope with scarcity.

Resources, Production Possibilities, and Opportunity Cost

The **production possibility frontier** (*PPF*)

- is the boundary between those combinations of goods and services that can be produced and those that cannot.
- shows maximum combinations of outputs (goods and services) that can be produced with given resources and technology.

PPF characteristics:

- Points on *PPF* represent **production efficiency**—more of one good cannot be produced without producing less of another good.
- Points inside *PPF* are inefficient—attainable, but not maximum combinations of outputs; they represent unused or misallocated resources.
- Points on *PPF* are preferred to points inside *PPF*.
- Points outside *PPF* are unattainable.
- Choosing among efficient points on *PPF* involves an **opportunity cost** and a **tradeoff**.

*PPF*s are generally bowed outward (concave), reflecting increasing opportunity costs as more of a good is produced.

- *PPF* is bowed outward because resources are nonhomogeneous—resources are not equally productive in all activities. Resources most suitable for a given activity are the first to be used.
- Bowed-out-shaped *PPF* represents increasing opportunity cost—opportunity cost of good increases as its quantity produced increases.
- In moving between two points on *PPF*, more good *X* can be obtained only by producing less good *Y*. Opportunity cost on *PPF* of additional *X* is amount of *Y* forgone.
- No opportunity cost in moving from point inside *PPF* to point on *PPF*.

Using Resources Efficiently

To choose among points on *PPF*, compare

- **marginal cost**—opportunity cost of producing one more unit of a good.
  - marginal cost curve slopes upwards because of *increasing opportunity cost.*
- **marginal benefit**—benefit (measured in willingness to forgo other goods) from consuming one more unit of a good.
  - marginal benefit curve slopes downwards because of *decreasing marginal benefit.*

We choose a point on *PPF* where resource use is **efficient**

- where we produce the goods and services valued most highly.
- where marginal benefit = marginal cost.

Economic Growth

Economic growth is the expansion of production possibilities—an outward shift of *PPF*.

- *PPF* shifts from changes in resources or technology.
- **Capital accumulation** and **technological change** shift *PPF* outward—economic growth.
- Opportunity cost of increased goods and services in future (economic growth through capital accumulation and technological progress) is decreased consumption today.

Gains from Trade

Production increases if people specialize in the activity in which they have a comparative advantage.

- Person has **comparative advantage** in producing a good if she can produce at lower opportunity cost than anyone else.
- When each person specializes in producing a good at which she has comparative advantage and exchanges for other goods, there are gains from trade.
- Specialization and exchange allow consumption (not production) at points outside *PPF*.
- Person has **absolute advantage** in producing all goods if, using the same quantity of inputs, she can produce more of all goods than anyone else.
  - Absolute advantage is irrelevant for specialization and gains from trade.
  - Even a person with an absolute advantage gains by specializing in activity in which she has a comparative advantage and trading.
- **Dynamic comparative advantage** results from specializing in an activity, **learning-by-doing**, and over time becoming the producer with the lowest opportunity cost.

The Market Economy

Trade is organized using the social arrangements of

- **property rights**—governing ownership, use, and disposal of resources, goods, and services.
- **markets**—coordinating buying and selling decisions through price adjustments.

HELPFUL HINTS

1 This chapter reviews the absolutely critical concept of opportunity cost—the best alternative forgone—that was introduced in Chapter 1. Opportunity cost is a *ratio*. A very helpful formula for opportunity cost, which works well in solving problems, especially problems that involve moving up or down a production possibility frontier (*PPF*), is:

$$\text{Opportunity Cost} = \frac{\text{Give Up}}{\text{Get}}$$

Opportunity cost equals the quantity of goods you must give up divided by the quantity of goods you will get. This formula applies to all *PPF*s, whether they are bowed out as in Text Fig. 3.1 or linear as in Text Fig. 3.7. To illustrate, look again at the bowed-out *PPF*.

FIGURE **3.1**

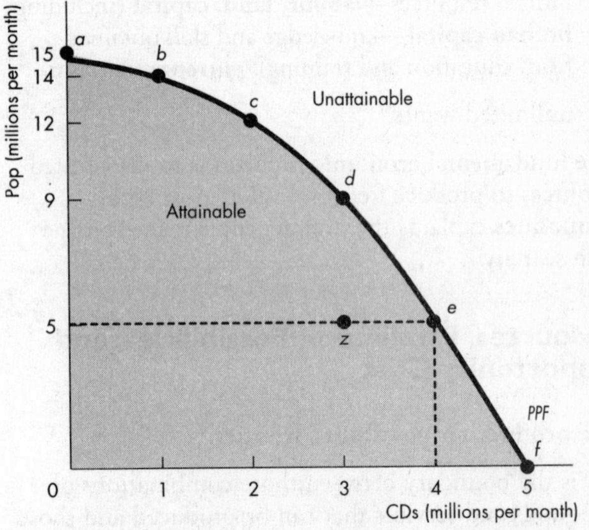

First, consider an example of moving down the *PPF*. In moving from *c* to *d*, what is the opportunity cost of an additional CD? This economy must give up 3 million bottles of pop (12 – 9) to get 1 million CDs (3 – 2). Substituting into the formula, the opportunity cost is:

$$\frac{\text{3 million pop}}{\text{1 million tapes}} = \text{3 pop per tape}$$

Next, consider an example of moving up the *PPF*. In moving from *d* to *c*, what is the opportunity cost of an additional pop? We must give up 1 million CDs (3 – 2) to get 3 million bottles of pop (12 – 9). Substituting into the formula, the opportunity cost is:

$$\frac{1 \text{ million tapes}}{3 \text{ million pop}} = \frac{1}{3} \text{ tape per pop}$$

Opportunity cost is always measured in the units of the forgone good.

ⓔ **2** Opportunity cost can also be related to the slope of the *PPF*. As we move down between any two points on the *PPF*, the opportunity cost of an additional unit of the good on the horizontal axis is:

$$|\text{slope of } PPF|$$

The slope of the *PPF* is negative, but economists like to describe opportunity cost in terms of a positive quantity of forgone goods. Therefore we must use the absolute value of the slope to calculate the desired positive number.

As we move up between any two points on the *PPF*, the opportunity cost of an additional unit of the good on the vertical axis is:

$$\left|\frac{1}{\text{slope of } PPF}\right|$$

This is the *inverse* relation we saw between possibilities *c* and *d*. The opportunity cost of an additional CD (on the horizontal axis) between *c* and *d* is 3 pop. The opportunity cost of an additional pop (on the vertical axis) between *d* and *c* is 1/3 CD.

3 All points on a *PPF* achieve productive efficiency in that they fully employ all resources. But how do we pick a point on the *PPF* and decide *what* combination of goods we want? The *PPF* provides information about resources and *costs*. But choosing what goods we want also requires information about *benefits*.

This choice, like all economic choices, is made at the margin. To decide what goods we want, compare the marginal cost (*MC*)and marginal benefit (*MB*) of different combinations. Marginal cost is the opportunity cost of producing one more unit. The marginal cost of producing more of any good increases as we move along the *PPF*. Marginal benefit is the benefit received from consuming one more unit. Marginal benefit decreases as we consume more of any good.

If the marginal cost of a good exceeds the marginal benefit, we decrease production of the good. If the marginal benefit exceeds the marginal cost, we increase production. When marginal cost equals marginal benefit for every good, we have chosen the goods that we value most highly. The decision rule of $MB = MC$ yields an *efficient* allocation of resources.

Text Fig. 3.4 is crucial for explaining all economic decisions. Make sure you spend time on it even though it may be hard to fully understand. You will understand Text Fig. 3.4 better after we spend time in future chapters elaborating the concepts of marginal cost and marginal benefit.

4 The CD/pop production possibility frontier assumes nonhomogeneous resources, that is, resources that are *not* equally useful in all activities. As a result of this assumption, opportunity cost increases as we increase the production of either good. In moving from possibility *c* to *d*, the opportunity cost per CD is 3 pop. But in increasing CD production from *d* to *e*, the opportunity cost per CD increases to 4 pop. In producing the first 1 million CDs, we use the resources best suited to CD production. As we increase CD production, however, we must use resources that are less well suited to CD production—hence increasing opportunity cost. A parallel argument accounts for the increasing opportunity cost of increasing pop.

It is also possible to construct an even simpler model of a *PPF* that assumes homogeneous resources, resources that are equally useful in all activities. As a result of this assumption, opportunity cost is constant as we increase production of either good. Constant opportunity cost means that the *PPF* will be a straight line (rather than bowed out). As you will see in some of the following exercises, such a simple model is useful for illustrating the principle of comparative advantage, without having to deal with the complications of increasing opportunity cost.

ⓔ **5** The text defines absolute advantage as a situation where one person has greater productivity than another in the production of all goods. We can also define *absolute advantage in the production of one good*. In comparing the productivity of two persons, this narrower concept of absolute advantage can be defined in terms of either greater output of the good per unit of inputs or fewer inputs per unit of output. It is useful to understand these definitions of absolute advantage only to demonstrate that absolute advantage has no role in explaining specialization and trade. The gains from trade depend only on differing comparative advantages. People have a comparative advantage in producing a good if they can produce it at lower opportunity cost than others.

6 This chapter gives us our first chance to develop and use economic models. It is useful to think about the nature of these models in the context of the general discussion of models in Chapter 1. For example, one model in this chapter is a representation of the production possibilities in the two-person and two-good world of Tom and Trish. The model abstracts greatly from the complexity of the real world in which there are billions of people and numerous different kinds of goods and services. The model allows us to explain a number of phenomena that we observe in the world such as specialization and exchange. The model also has some implications or predictions. For example, countries that devote a larger proportion of their resources to capital accumulation will have more rapidly expanding production possibilities. The model can be subjected to "test" by comparing these predictions to the facts we observe in the real world.

SELF-TEST

True/False/Uncertain and Explain

Refer to the production possibility frontier (*PPF*) in Fig. 3.2 for Questions **1** to **4**.

FIGURE **3.2**

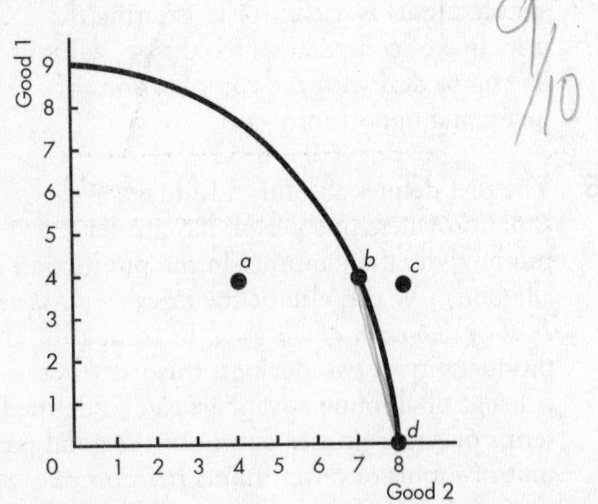

1 Point *a* is not attainable.

2 The opportunity cost of increasing the production of good 2 from 7 to 8 units is 4 units of good 1.

3 Point *c* is not attainable.

⊚ **4** In moving from point *b* to point *d*, the opportunity cost of increasing the production of good 2 equals the absolute value of the slope of the *PPF* between *b* and *d*.

5 The marginal benefit of good *X* is the maximum amount of good *Y* a person is willing to forgo to obtain more *X*.

6 Economic growth, by shifting out the *PPF*, eliminates the problem of scarcity.

7 In a model where capital resources can grow, points on the *PPF* that have more consumption goods yield faster growth.

8 With specialization and trade, a country can produce at a point outside its *PPF*.

9 Canada has no incentive to trade with a cheap-labour country like Mexico.

10 The incentives for specialization and exchange do not depend on property rights but only on differing opportunity costs.

Multiple-Choice

Resources and Wants

1 All of the following are resources *except*

a natural resources.
b tools.
c entrepreneurship.
d government.
e land.

2 The knowledge and skill obtained from education and training is

- **a** labour.
- **b** human capital.
- **c** physical capital.
- **d** entrepreneurship.
- **e** technological know-how.

Resources, Production Possibilities, and Opportunity Cost

3 If Harold can increase production of good *X* without decreasing the production of any other good, then Harold

- **a** is producing on his *PPF*.
- **b** is producing outside his *PPF*.
- **c** is producing inside his *PPF*.
- **d** must have a linear *PPF*.
- **e** must prefer good *X* to any other good.

4 The bowed-out (concave) shape of a *PPF*

- **a** is due to the equal usefulness of resources in all activities.
- **b** is due to capital accumulation.
- **c** is due to technological change.
- **d** reflects the existence of increasing opportunity cost.
- **e** reflects the existence of decreasing opportunity cost.

5 The economy is at point *b* on the *PPF* in Fig. 3.3. The opportunity cost of producing one more unit of *X* is

- **a** 1 unit of *Y*.
- **b** 20 units of *Y*.
- **c** 1 unit of *X*.
- **d** 8 units of *X*.
- **e** 20 units of *X*.

FIGURE **3.3**

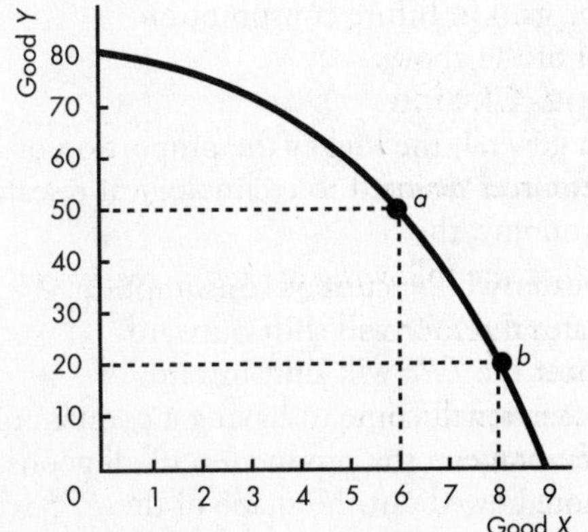

6 Refer to the *PPF* in Fig. 3.3. Which of the following statements is *false*?

- **a** Resources are nonhomogeneous.
- **b** Points inside the frontier represent unemployed resources.
- **c** Starting at point *a*, an increase in the production of good *Y* will shift the frontier out.
- **d** The opportunity cost of producing good *Y* increases as production of *Y* increases.
- **e** Shifts in preferences for good *X* or good *Y* will not shift the frontier.

7 Refer to Fig. 3.4, which shows the *PPF* for an economy without discrimination operating at maximum efficiency. If discrimination against women workers is currently occurring in this economy, the elimination of discrimination would result in a(n)

- **a** movement from *a* to *b*.
- **b** movement from *b* to *c*.
- **c** movement from *a* to *c*.
- **d** outward shift of the *PPF*.
- **e** inward shift of the *PPF*.

FIGURE **3.4**

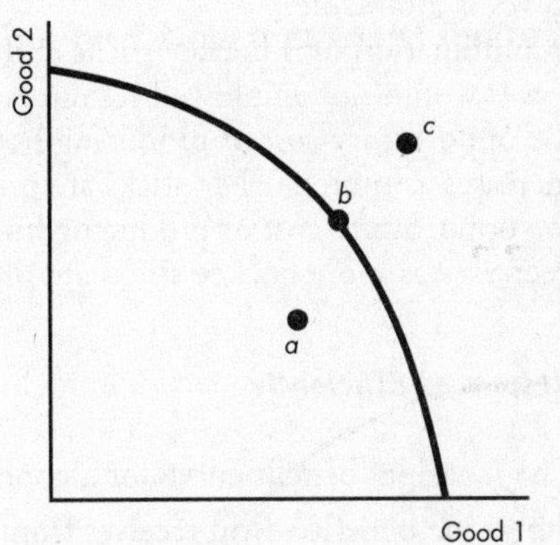

Suppose a society produces only two goods—hockey sticks and maple leaves. Three alternative combinations on its *PPF* are given in Table 3.1. Use the information in Table 3.1 to answer Questions **8** and **9**.

TABLE **3.1** PRODUCTION POSSIBILITIES

Possibility	Units of Hockey Sticks	Units of Maple Leaves
a	3	0
b	2	3
c	0	9

8 In moving from combination *c* to combination *b*, the opportunity cost of producing one additional hockey stick is

a 2 maple leaves.
b 1/2 maple leaves.
c 6 maple leaves.
d 1/6 maple leaves.
e 3 maple leaves.

9 According to this *PPF*

a resources are homogeneous.
b a combination of 3 hockey sticks and 9 maple leaves is attainable.
c a combination of 3 hockey sticks and 9 maple leaves would not employ all resources.
d the opportunity cost of producing hockey sticks increases as more hockey sticks are produced.
e the opportunity cost of producing hockey sticks decreases as more hockey sticks are produced.

Using Resources Efficiently

10 The marginal benefit curve for a good

a shows the benefit a firm receives from producing one more unit.
b shows the maximum amount a consumer is willing to pay for one more unit.
c is upward-sloping.
d is bowed out.
e is none of the above.

11 With increasing production of food, its marginal benefit

a increases and marginal cost increases.
b increases and marginal cost decreases.
c decreases and marginal cost increases.
d decreases and marginal cost decreases.
e decreases and marginal cost is constant.

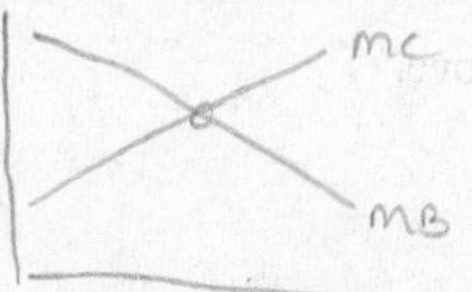

12 Suppose the *PPF* for skirts and pants is a straight line. As the production of skirts increases, the marginal benefit of skirts

a increases and marginal cost is constant.
b is constant and marginal cost increases
c decreases and marginal cost decreases.
d decreases and marginal cost increases.
e decreases and marginal cost is constant.

13 If resources are being used efficiently, then for each good produced, marginal

a benefit equals marginal cost.
b benefit is at its maximum.
c benefit exceeds marginal cost by as much as possible.
d cost exceeds marginal benefit by as much as possible.
e cost is at its minimum.

Economic Growth

14 The *PPF* for wine and wool will shift if there is a change in

a the price of resources.
b the unemployment rate.
c the quantity of resources.
d preferences for wine and wool.
e all of the above.

15 A movement *along* a given *PPF* will result from

a technological change.
b change in the stock of capital.
c change in the labour force.
d all of the above.
e none of the above.

16 The opportunity cost of pushing the *PPF* outward is

a capital accumulation.
b technological change.
c reduced current consumption.
d the gain in future consumption.
e all of the above.

17 In general, the higher the proportion of resources devoted to technological research in an economy, the

a greater will be current consumption.
b faster the *PPF* will shift outward.
c faster the *PPF* will shift inward.
d closer it will come to having a comparative advantage in the production of all goods.
e more bowed out the shape of the *PPF* will be.

18 Refer to the *PPF* in Fig. 3.5. A politician who argues that "if our children are to be better off, we must invest now for the future" is recommending a current point like

a *a.*
b *b.*
c *c.*
d *d.*
e *e.*

FIGURE **3.5**

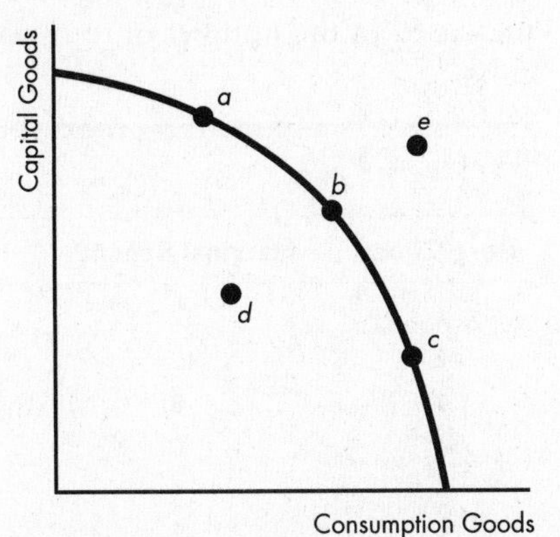

19 Refer to the *PPF* in Fig. 3.5. The statement that "unemployment is a terrible waste of human resources" refers to a point like

a *a.*
b *b.*
c *c.*
d *d.*
e *e.*

Gains from Trade

In an eight-hour day, Andy can produce either 24 loaves of bread or 8 kilograms of butter. In an eight-hour day, Rolfe can produce either 8 loaves of bread or 8 kilograms of butter. Use this information to answer Questions **20** and **21**.

⊜ **20** Which of the following statements is *true*?

a Andy has an absolute advantage in butter production.
b Rolfe has an absolute advantage in butter production.
c Andy has an absolute advantage in bread production.
d Andy has a comparative advantage in butter production.
e Rolfe has a comparative advantage in bread production.

21 Andy and Rolfe

a can gain from exchange if Andy specializes in butter production and Rolfe specializes in bread production.
b can gain from exchange if Andy specializes in bread production and Rolfe specializes in butter production.
c cannot gain from exchange.
d can exchange, but only Rolfe will gain.
e can exchange, but only Andy will gain.

22 Mexico and Canada produce both oil and apples using labour only. A barrel of oil can be produced with 4 hours of labour in Mexico and 8 hours of labour in Canada. A bushel of apples can be produced with 8 hours of labour in Mexico and 12 hours of labour in Canada. Canada has

a an absolute advantage in oil production.
b an absolute advantage in apple production.
c a comparative advantage in oil production.
d a comparative advantage in apple production.
e none of the above.

23 In Portugal, the opportunity cost of a bale of wool is 3 bottles of wine. In England, the opportunity cost of 1 bottle of wine is 3 bales of wool. Given this information,

a England has an absolute advantage in wine production.
b England has an absolute advantage in wool production.
c Portugal has a comparative advantage in wine production.
d Portugal has a comparative advantage in wool production.
e no trade will occur.

24 Learning-by-doing is the basis of

a absolute comparative advantage.
b dynamic comparative advantage.
c intellectual property rights.
d financial property rights.
e none of the above.

The Market Economy

25 Trade is organized using the social arrangements of

a real property rights.
b financial property rights.
c intellectual property rights.
d markets.
e all of the above.

Short Answer Problems

1 Why is a *PPF* negatively sloped? Why is it bowed out?

2 Suppose that an economy has the *PPF* shown in Table 3.2.

TABLE **3.2** PRODUCTION POSSIBILITIES

Possibility	Maximum Units of Butter per Week	Maximum Units of Guns per Week
a	200	0
b	180	60
c	160	100
d	100	160
e	40	200
f	0	220

a On graph paper, plot these possibilities, label the points, and draw the *PPF*. (Put guns on the *x*-axis.)
b If the economy moves from possibility *c* to possibility *d*, the opportunity cost *per unit of guns* will be how many units of butter?
c If the economy moves from possibility *d* to possibility *e*, the opportunity cost *per unit of guns* will be how many units of butter?
d In general terms, what happens to the opportunity cost of guns as the output of guns increases?
e In general terms, what happens to the opportunity cost of butter as the output of butter increases? What do the results in parts *d* and *e* imply about resources?
f If (instead of the possibilities given) the *PPF* were a straight line joining points *a* and *f*, what would that imply about opportunity costs and resources?
g Given the original *PPF* you have plotted, is a combination of 140 units of butter and 130 units of guns per week attainable? Would you regard this combination as an efficient one? Explain.
h Given the original *PPF*, is a combination of 70 units of butter and 170 units of guns per week attainable? Does this combination achieve productive efficiency? Explain.

3 If the following events occurred (each is a separate event, unaccompanied by any other event), what would happen to the *PPF* in Short Answer Problem 2?
a A new, easily exploited, energy source is discovered.
b A large number of skilled workers immigrate into the country.
c The output of butter increases.
d A new invention increases output per person in the butter industry but not in the guns industry.
e A new law is passed compelling workers, who could previously work as long as they wanted, to retire at age 60.

4 The Borg produce only two goods—cubes and transwarp coils—and want to decide where on their *PPF* to operate. Table 3.3 shows the marginal benefit and marginal cost of cubes, measured in the number of transwarp coils per cube.

TABLE **3.3**

Borg Cubes	Marginal Benefit	Marginal Cost
1	12	3
2	10	4
3	8	5
4	6	6
5	4	7
6	2	8

a If the Borg are efficient (and they are!), what quantity of cubes will they produce?
b If the Borg were to produce one more cube than your answer in **a**, why would that choice be inefficient?

5 Suppose the country of Quark has historically devoted 10 percent of its resources to the production of new capital goods. Use *PPF* diagrams like Text Fig. 3.6 on page 46 to compare the consequences (costs and benefits) of each of the following:
a Quark continues to devote 10 percent of its resources to the production of capital goods.
b Quark begins now to permanently devote 20 percent of its resources to the production of capital goods.

6 Lawyers earn $200 per hour while secretaries earn $15 per hour. Use the concepts of absolute and comparative advantage to explain why a lawyer who is a better typist than her secretary will still specialize in doing only legal work and will trade with the secretary for typing services.

7 France and Germany each produce both wine and beer, using a single, homogeneous input—labour. Their production possibilities are:

- France has 100 units of labour and can produce a maximum of 200 bottles of wine or 400 bottles of beer.
- Germany has 50 units of labour and can produce a maximum of 250 bottles of wine or 200 bottles of beer.

a Complete Table 3.4.

TABLE **3.4**

	Bottles Produced by 1 Unit of Labour		Opportunity Cost of 1 Additional Bottle	
	Wine	**Beer**	**Wine**	**Beer**
France				
Germany				

Use the information in part **a** to answer the following questions.

ⓔ **b** Which country has an absolute advantage in wine production?

ⓔ **c** Which country has an absolute advantage in beer production?

d Which country has a comparative advantage in wine production?

e Which country has a comparative advantage in beer production?

f If trade is allowed, describe what specialization, if any, will occur.

ⓒⓣ **8** Tova and Ron are the only two remaining inhabitants of the planet Melmac. They spend their 30-hour days producing widgets and woggles, the only two goods needed for happiness on Melmac. It takes Tova 1 hour to produce a widget and 2 hours to produce a woggle, while Ron takes 3 hours to produce a widget and 3 hours to produce a woggle.

a For a 30-hour day, draw an individual *PPF* for Tova, then for Ron.

b What does the shape of the *PPFs* tell us about opportunity costs? about resources?

c Assume initially that Tova and Ron are each self-sufficient. Define self-sufficiency. Explain what the individual consumption possibilities are for Tova, then for Ron.

d Who has an absolute advantage in the production of widgets? of woggles?

e Who has a comparative advantage in the production of widgets? of woggles?

f Suppose Tova and Ron each specialize in producing only the good in which she/he has a comparative advantage (one spends 30 hours producing widgets, the other spends 30 hours producing woggles). What will be the total production of widgets and woggles?

g Suppose Tova and Ron exchange 7 widgets for 5 woggles. On your *PPF* diagrams, plot the new point of Tova's consumption, then of Ron's consumption. Explain how these points illustrate the gains from trade.

9 The Netsilik and Oonark families live on the Arctic coast, west of Hudson Bay. They often go fishing and hunting for caribou together. During an average working day, the Netsiliks can, at most, either catch 6 kilograms of fish or kill 6 caribou. The Oonarks can either catch 4 kilograms of fish or kill 4 caribou.

a Assuming linear *PPFs*, draw each family's *PPF* on the same diagram. Put fish on the horizontal axis and caribou on the vertical axis.

b Complete Table 3.5.

TABLE **3.5**

	Opportunity Cost of 1 Additional	
	Fish (kg)	**Caribou**
Netsiliks		
Oonarks		

c Which family has a comparative advantage in catching fish? in hunting caribou?

d Can specialization and trade increase the total output of fish and caribou produced by the two families? Explain.

10 Explain the interdependence that exists between households and firms in Text Fig. 3.9 on page 51.

ANSWERS

True/False/Uncertain and Explain

1 F Attainable but not an optimal point. (39–40)

2 T Moving from *b* to *d*, production good 1 decreases by 4 units. (40–41)

3 T Outside *PPF*. (39)

ⓔ **4 T** See Helpful Hint 2. (40–41)
5 T Marginal benefit is also the maximum amount a person is willing to pay for one more unit, but payment in money ultimately represents an opportunity cost in goods forgone. (43)
6 F Cost of growth is forgone current consumption. (45)
7 F Points with capital goods yield faster growth. (45–46)
8 F Can *consume* at point outside *PPF.* (48–49)
9 F Mutually beneficial trade depends on comparative advantage, not absolute advantage. (49)
10 F Property rights prerequisite for specialization and exchange. (50)

Multiple-Choice

1 d Government is a social institution. (38)
2 b Definition. (38)
3 c For 0 opportunity cost, must be unemployed resources. (39–40)
4 d **a** would be true if *un*equal resources; **b** and **c** shift *PPF.* (41)
5 b To increase quantity *X* to 9, must decrease quantity *Y* from 20 to 0. (40–41)
ⓒⓣ **6 c** Increased production *Y* moves up *along PPF.* (39–41)
7 a Discrimination causes underemployment of resources. Women not allowed to produce up to full abilities. (39–41)
8 e Give up 6 maple leaves to get 2 hockey sticks: 6/2 = 3 maple leaves per hockey stick. (40–41)
ⓒⓣ **9 a** Constant opportunity cost means resources equally useful for producing all goods—see Helpful Hint 4. (39–41)
10 b Benefits apply to consumers; curve is downward-sloping. (43)
11 c Principles of diminishing marginal benefit and increasing marginal cost. (42–44)
ⓒⓣ **12 e** Diminishing marginal benefit, but linear *PPF* means constant opportunity and marginal costs. (42–44)
13 a Whenever $MB \neq MC$, efficiency improves by reallocating resources to produce more goods with high marginal benefits, causing a decrease in their marginal benefit and increase in marginal cost. (44)
14 c Only changes in resources or technology shift *PPF.* (45)
ⓒⓣ **15 e** **a**, **b**, and **c** all shift *PPF.* (45–46)
16 c **a** and **b** cause outward shift *PPF,* not opportunity cost; **d** effect of outward shift *PPF.* (45–46)
17 b Technological change shifts *PPF* outward at cost of current consumption. (45–46)
18 a Producing more capital goods now, shifts *PPF* outward in future. (45–46)
19 d Points inside *PPF* represent unemployed resources, whether labour, capital, or land. (39–40, 45–46)
ⓔ **20 c** Andy produces 3 loaves bread per hour; Rolfe produces 1 loaf per hour—see Helpful Hint 5. (47–49)
ⓒⓣ **21 b** Andy has comparative advantage (lower opportunity cost) bread, Rolfe has comparative advantage butter production. Both gain if they trade at a ratio in between their respective opportunity costs (e.g., if Andy trades 12 bread for 6 butter). See Chapter 35. (49)
ⓒⓣ **22 d** Opportunity cost oil in bushels of apples—Canada 2/3, Mexico 1/2. Opportunity cost apples in barrels of oil—Canada 3/2, Mexico 2. (47–49)
23 c Opportunity cost wine in bales of wool—Portugal 1/3, England 3. Opportunity cost wool in bottles of wine—Portugal 3, England 1/3. (47–49)
24 b Definition. (49)
25 e Property rights and markets keys to trade. (50)

Short Answer Problems

1 The negative slope of the *PPF* reflects opportunity cost: in order to have more of one good, some of the other must be forgone.

It is bowed out because the existence of nonhomogeneous resources creates increasing opportunity cost as we increase the production of either good.

2 a The graph of the *PPF* is given in Fig. 3.6.

FIGURE **3.6**

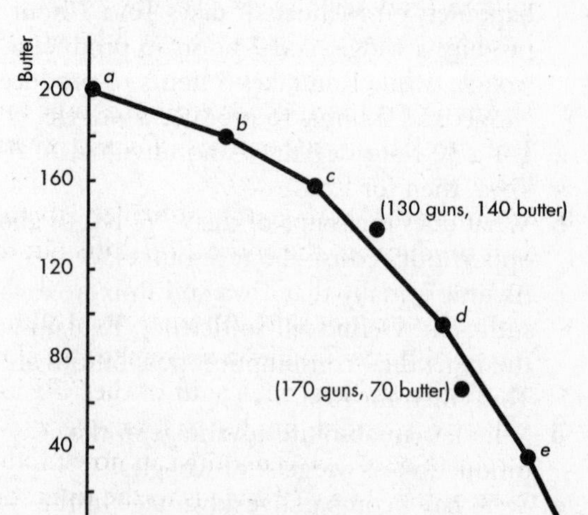

b In moving from *c* to *d*, in order to gain 60 units of guns, we must give up 160 – 100 = 60 units of butter. The opportunity cost per unit of guns is

$$\frac{60 \text{ units butter}}{60 \text{ units guns}} = 1 \text{ unit butter per unit of guns}$$

c In moving from *d* to *e*, in order to gain 40 units of guns, we must give up 100 – 40 = 60 units of butter. The opportunity cost per unit of guns is:

$$\frac{60 \text{ units butter}}{40 \text{ units guns}} = 1.5 \text{ unit butter per unit of guns}$$

d The opportunity cost of producing more guns increases as the output of guns increases.

e Likewise, the opportunity cost of producing more butter increases as the output of butter increases. Increasing opportunity costs imply that resources are nonhomogeneous; that is, they are not equally useful in gun and butter production.

f Opportunity costs would always be constant, regardless of the output of guns or butter. The opportunity cost per unit of guns would be

200/220 = 10/11 units of butter

The opportunity cost per unit of butter would be

220/200 = 1.1 units of guns

Constant opportunity costs imply that resources are homogeneous; that is, they are equally useful in gun and butter production.

g This combination is outside the *PPF* and therefore is not attainable. Since the economy cannot produce this combination, the question of efficiency is irrelevant.

h This combination is inside the *PPF* and is attainable. It is inefficient because the economy could produce more of either or both goods without producing less of anything else. Therefore some resources are not fully utilized.

3 a Assuming that both goods require energy for their production, the entire *PPF* shifts out to the northeast as in Fig. 3.7(a).

b Assuming that both goods use skilled labour in their production, the entire *PPF* shifts out to the northeast.

c The *PPF* does not shift. An increase in the output of butter implies a movement up along the *PPF* to the left, not a shift of the *PPF* itself.

d The new invention implies that for every level of output of guns, the economy can now produce more butter. The *PPF* swings to the right, but remains anchored at point *f* as in Fig. 3.7(b).

e The entire *PPF* shifts in towards the origin.

FIGURE **3.7**

(a)

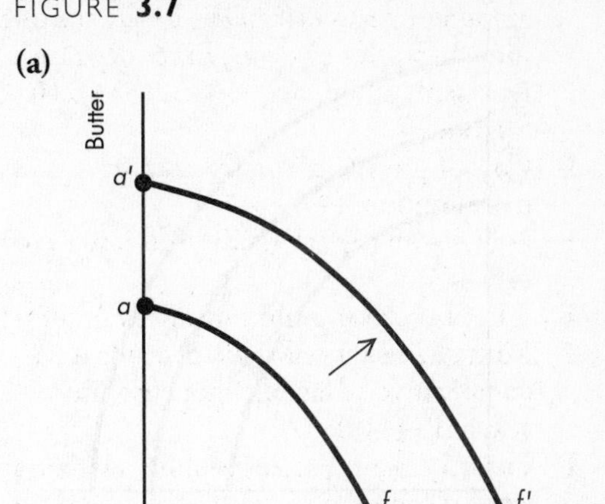

(b)

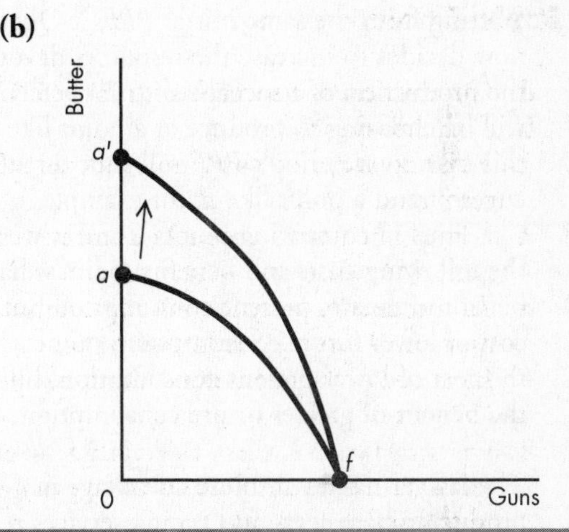

4 a At the efficient quantity of output, marginal benefit = marginal cost. The Borg will produce 4 cubes ($MB = MC$ = 4 transwarp coils/cube).

b At 5 cubes, marginal benefit = 4 and marginal cost = 7. Since $MC > MB$, the Borg could get better use from their resources by shifting production out of cubes and into transwarp coils.

5 a The situation for Quark is depicted by Fig. 3.8. Suppose Quark starts on *PPF* 1. If it continues to devote only 10 percent of its resources to the production of new capital goods, then it is choosing to produce at a point like *a*. This will shift the *PPF* out in the next period, but only to the curve labelled 2 (where, presumably, Quark will choose to produce at point *b*).

FIGURE **3.8**

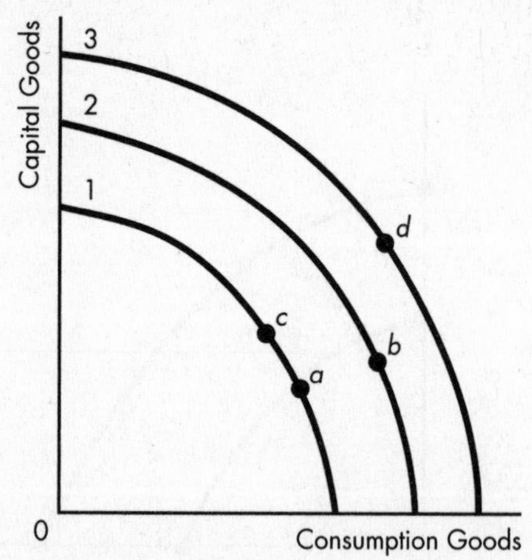

b Starting from the same initial *PPF*, if Quark now decides to increase the resources devoted to the production of new capital to 20 percent, it will be choosing to produce at a point like *c*. In this case, next period's *PPF* will shift further—to curve 3, and a point like *d*, for example.

Thus in comparing points *a* and *c*, we find the following costs and benefits: point *a* has the benefit of greater present consumption but at a cost of lower future consumption; point *c* has the cost of lower present consumption, but with the benefit of greater future consumption.

6 The lawyer has an absolute advantage in producing both legal and typing services relative to the secretary. Nevertheless, she has a comparative advantage in legal services, and the secretary has a comparative advantage in typing. To demonstrate these comparative advantages, we can construct Table 3.6 of opportunity costs.

TABLE **3.6**

	Opportunity Cost of I Additional Hour ($)	
	Legal Services	**Typing**
Lawyer	200	200
Secretary	>200	15

Consider first the lawyer's opportunity costs. The lawyer's best forgone alternative to providing 1 hour of legal services is the $200 she could earn by providing another hour of legal services. If she provides 1 hour of typing, she is also forgoing $200 (1 hour) of legal services. What would the secretary have to forgo to provide 1 hour of legal services? He would have to spend 3 years in law school, forgoing 3 years of income in addition to the tuition he must pay. His opportunity cost is a very large number, certainly greater than $200. If he provides 1 hour of typing, his best forgone alternative is the $15 he could have earned at another secretarial job.

Thus Table 3.6 shows that the lawyer has a lower opportunity cost (comparative advantage) of providing legal services, and the secretary has a lower opportunity cost (comparative advantage) of providing typing services. It is on the basis of comparative advantage (not absolute advantage) that trade will take place from which both parties gain.

7 a The completed table is shown here as Table 3.4 Solution.

TABLE **3.4** SOLUTION

	Bottles Produced by I Unit of Labour		Opportunity Cost of I Additional Bottle	
	Wine	**Beer**	**Wine**	**Beer**
France	2	4	2.0 beer	0.50 wine
Germany	5	4	0.8 beer	1.25 wine

ⓔ **b** Germany, which can produce more wine (5 bottles) per unit of input, has an absolute advantage in wine production.

ⓔ **c** Neither country has an absolute advantage in beer production, since beer output (4 bottles) per unit of input is the same for both countries.

d Germany, with the lower opportunity cost (0.8 beer), has a comparative advantage in wine production.

e France, with the lower opportunity cost (0.5 wine), has a comparative advantage in beer production.

f The incentive for trade depends only on differences in comparative advantage. Germany will specialize in wine production and France will specialize in beer production.

ⓒ **8 a** The individual *PPF*s for Tova and Ron are given by Fig. 3.9(a) and (b) respectively.

FIGURE **3.9**

(a)

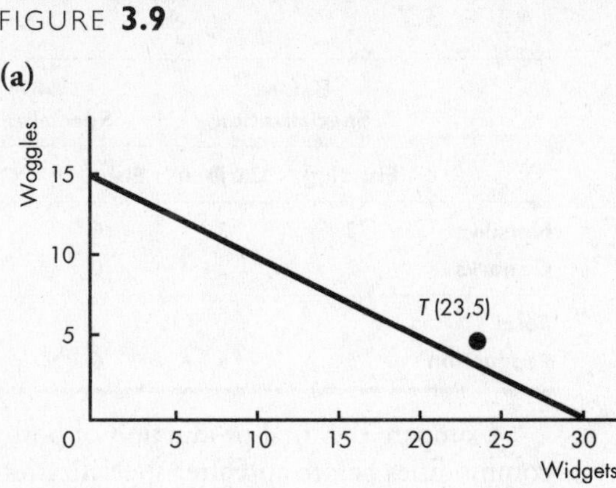

(b)

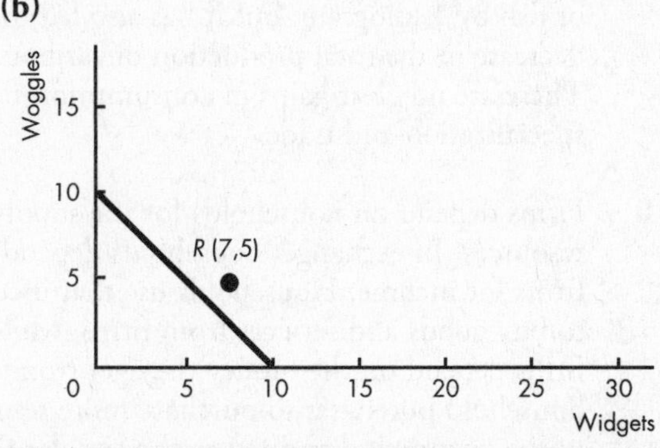

b The linear shape of the *PPF*s tells us that opportunity costs are constant along each frontier and that resources are homogeneous.

These linear *PPF*s with constant opportunity costs abstract from the complexity of the real world. The world generally has increasing opportunity costs, but that fact is not essential for understanding the gains from trade, which is the objective of this problem. Making the model more complex by including increasing opportunity costs would not change our results, but it would make it more difficult to see them.

c Individuals are self-sufficient if they consume only what they produce. This means there is no trade. Without trade, Tova's (maximum) consumption possibilities are exactly the same as her production possibilities—points along her *PPF*. Ron's (maximum) consumption possibilities are likewise the points along his *PPF*.

d Tova has an absolute advantage in the production of both widgets and woggles. Her absolute advantage can be defined either in terms of greater output per unit of inputs or fewer inputs per unit of output. A comparison of the *PPF*s in Fig. 3.9 shows that, for given inputs of 30 hours, Tova produces a greater output of widgets than Ron (30 versus 10) and a greater output of woggles than Ron (15 versus 10). The statement of the problem tells us equivalently that, per unit of output, Tova uses fewer inputs than Ron for both widgets (1 hour versus 3 hours) and woggles (2 hours versus 3 hours). Since Tova has greater productivity than Ron in the production of all goods (widgets and woggles), we say that overall she has an absolute advantage.

e Tova has a comparative advantage in the production of widgets, since she can produce them at lower opportunity cost than Ron (1/2 woggle versus 1 woggle). On the other hand, Ron has a comparative advantage in the production of woggles, since he can produce them at a lower opportunity cost than Tova (1 widget versus 2 widgets).

f Tova will produce widgets and Ron will produce woggles, yielding a total production between them of 30 widgets and 10 woggles.

g After the exchange, Tova will have 23 widgets and 5 woggles (point *T*). Ron will have 7 widgets and 5 woggles (point *R*). These new post-trade consumption possibility points lie outside Tova's and Ron's respective pre-trade consumption (and production) possibilities. Hence trade has yielded gains that allow the traders to improve their consumption possibilities beyond those available with self-sufficiency.

9 a The *PPF*s of the Netsiliks and Oonarks are shown in Fig. 3.10.

FIGURE **3.10**

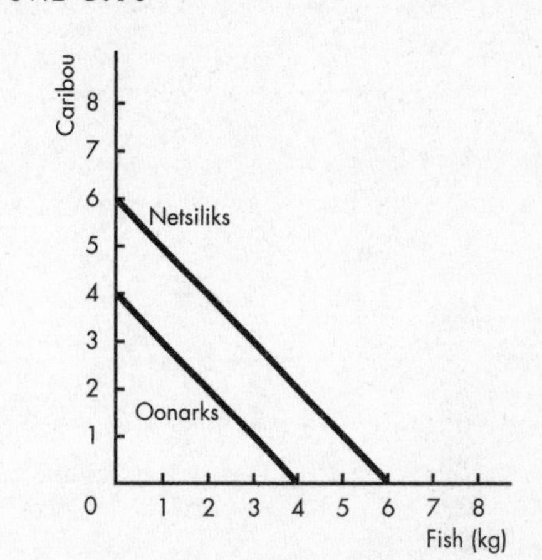

b The completed table is shown here as Table 3.5 Solution.

TABLE **3.5** SOLUTION

	Opportunity Cost of 1 Additional	
	Fish (kg)	Caribou
Netsiliks	1 caribou	1 kg fish
Oonarks	1 caribou	1 kg fish

c Neither family has a comparative advantage in catching fish since the opportunity cost of fish is the same (1 caribou) for each family. Similarly, neither family has a comparative advantage in hunting caribou since the opportunity cost of a caribou is the same (1 kg fish) for each family.

d Gains from specialization and trade are due to the existence of comparative advantage. In this case, no family has a comparative advantage in either fishing or hunting, so there are no gains from specialization and trade.

To illustrate the absence of gains, suppose that initially each family devoted half of its time to each activity. Then suppose that the Netsiliks specialized completely in catching fish and the Oonarks specialized completely in hunting caribou. Production before and after specialization is shown in Table 3.7.

TABLE **3.7**

	Before Specialization		After Specialization	
	Fish (kg)	Caribou	Fish (kg)	Caribou
Netsiliks	3	3	6	0
Oonarks	2	2	0	4
Total Production	5	5	6	4

Compare the total production of both commodities before and after specialization. Specialization has increased the total production of fish by 1 kilogram, but it has also led to a decrease in the total production of caribou by 1. There are no clear gains in consumption from specialization and trade.

10 Firms depend on households for the supply of resources. In exchange, households depend on firms for income. Households use that income to buy goods and services from firms, while firms depend on the money they get from household purchases to purchase more resources in the next period and renew the circular flow.

Chapters

1–3

Part I Overview

Understanding the Scope of Economics

PROBLEM

The economy is a mechanism that allocates scarce resources among competing uses. But how do those allocation decisions get made? In the Canadian economy, markets are the primary institutions that coordinate individual decisions through price adjustments.

Suppose, for simplicity, the Canadian economy produced only two outputs—child-care services and televisions. The production possibility frontier (*PPF*) for the economy appears in Fig. P1.1 below. The economy is operating at point *a*, producing Q^0_{cc} units of child-care services and Q^0_{tv} televisions.

FIGURE **P1.1**

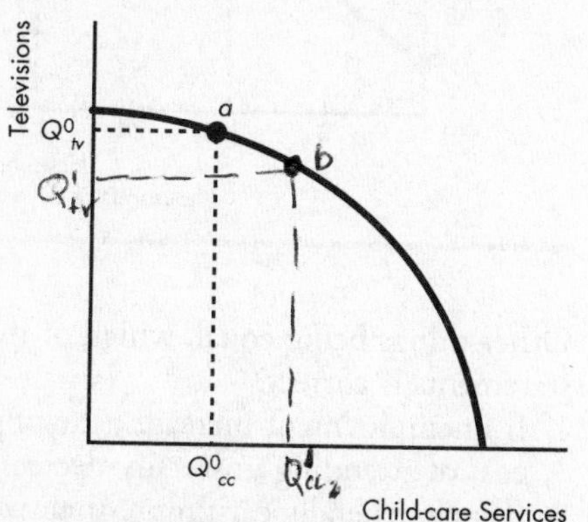

a What does the bowed-out (concave) shape of the *PPF* imply about resources? opportunity costs?

b As more women enter the labour force, there is increased demand for child-care services. As a result, the price and quantity of child-care services both increase. At the same time, the demand for televisions falls (perhaps to save money to pay for the additional child-care services). As a result, the price and quantity of televisions both decrease.

On the *PPF* in Fig. P1.1, label as point *b* a new combination of child-care services and televisions reflecting the changes in demand.

c Explain how the economy came to produce these new quantities in response to the changing demands of households.

d What determines the distance of the *PPF* from the origin? What determines the precise point on the *PPF* at which the economy operates? What is the true cost of moving from point *a* to point *b* on the *PPF*? The # of tv's given up.

MIDTERM EXAMINATION

You should allocate 30 minutes for this examination (15 questions, 2 minutes per question). For each question, choose the one *best* answer.

1 A *PPF* shows that

a there is a limit to the production of any one good.

b to produce more of one good, we must produce less of another good.

c there are limits to total production with given resources and technology.

d all of the above are true.

e none of the above is true.

2 The data in Table P1.1 could *not* be represented by

a two one-variable time-series graphs.
b one two-variable time-series graph.
c a three-variable time-series graph.
d a scatter diagram.
e any of the above.

TABLE **P1.1**

Year	x	y
1990	6.2	143
1991	5.7	156
1992	5.3	162

Suppose a society produces only two goods—guns and butter. Three alternative combinations on its *PPF* are given in Table P1.2. Use the information in Table P1.2 to answer Questions 3 and 4.

TABLE **P1.2** PRODUCTION POSSIBILITIES

Possibility	Units of Butter	Units of Guns
a	8	0
b	6	1
c	0	3

3 In moving from combination *b* to combination *c*, the opportunity cost of producing *one* additional unit of guns is

a 2 units of butter.
b 1/2 unit of butter.
c 6 units of butter.
d 1/6 unit of butter.
e 3 units of butter.

4 According to this *PPF*

a a combination of 6 butter and 1 gun would not employ all resources.
b a combination of 0 butter and 4 guns is attainable.
c resources are homogeneous.
d the opportunity cost of producing guns increases as more guns are produced.
e the opportunity cost of producing guns decreases as more guns are produced.

5 Which of the following is a normative statement?

a Pollution is an example of an external cost.
b Pollution makes people worse off.
c Firms that pollute should be forced to shut down.
d Pollution imposes opportunity costs on others.
e None of the above.

6 The graph of the relationship between two variables that are negatively related

a is horizontal.
b slopes upward to the right.
c is vertical.
d slopes downward to the right.
e is linear.

7 In Fig. P1.2, the slope of the line is

a 1.50.
b 1.25.
c 1.00.
d 0.75.
e 0.50.

FIGURE **P1.2**

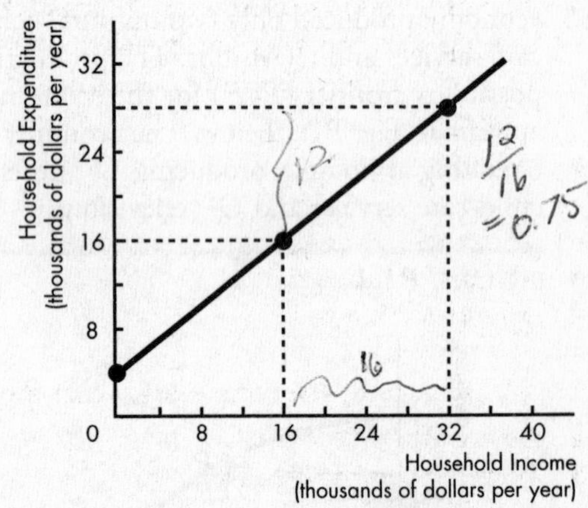

8 Other things being equal, which of the following statements is correct?

1 If unemployment increases, the opportunity cost of attending university decreases.
2 If men generally earn more than women in the labour market, the opportunity cost of attending university is higher for men than for women.

a 1 only
b 2 only
c 1 and 2
d neither 1 nor 2
e impossible to judge without additional information

9 The economy is at point *b* on the *PPF* in Fig. 1.3. The opportunity cost of increasing the production of *Y* to 50 units is

a 2 units of *X*.
b 6 units of *X*.
c 8 units of *X*.
d 20 units of *Y*.
e 30 units of *Y*.

FIGURE **P1.3**

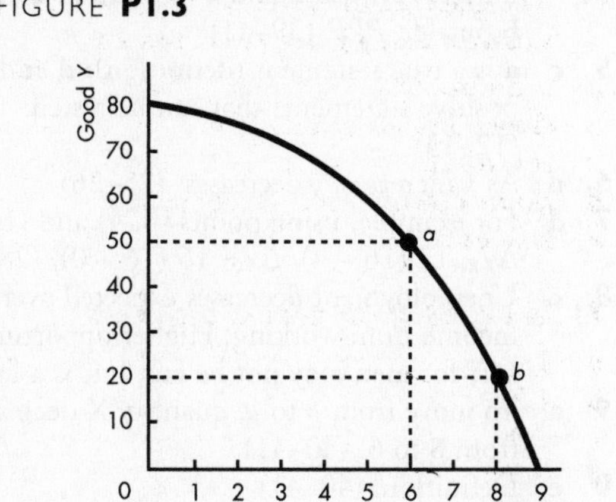

10 Because productive resources are scarce, we must give up some of one good in order to acquire more of another. This is the essence of the concept of

a specialization.
b monetary exchange.
c comparative advantage.
d absolute advantage.
e opportunity cost.

11 The scarcity of resources implies that the *PPF* is

a bowed inward (convex).
b bowed outward (concave).
c positively sloped.
d negatively sloped.
e linear.

12 If additional units of any good can be produced at a constant opportunity cost, the *PPF* is

a bowed inward (convex).
b bowed outward (concave).
c positively sloped.
d perfectly horizontal.
e linear.

13 Marginal cost is the

a total cost of an activity.
b additional benefit of a decrease in an activity.
c additional benefit of an increase in an activity.
d opportunity cost of a decrease in an activity.
e opportunity cost of an increase in an activity.

14 If variables *x* and *y* move in opposite directions, they are said to be

a positively related.
b negatively related.
c intimately related.
d unrelated.
e siblings.

9/15

15 *Ceteris paribus* is a Latin term meaning

a "After this, therefore because of this."
b "What is true of the parts is true of the whole."
c "What is true of the parts is *not* true of the whole."
d "Other things being equal."
e "Your place or mine."

ANSWERS

Problem

a The bowed-out shape of the *PPF* implies that resources are nonhomogeneous; they are not equally productive in all activities. With nonhomogeneous resources, there are increasing opportunity costs as production increases of either child-care services or televisions.

b See Fig. P1.1 Solution.

FIGURE **P1.1** SOLUTION

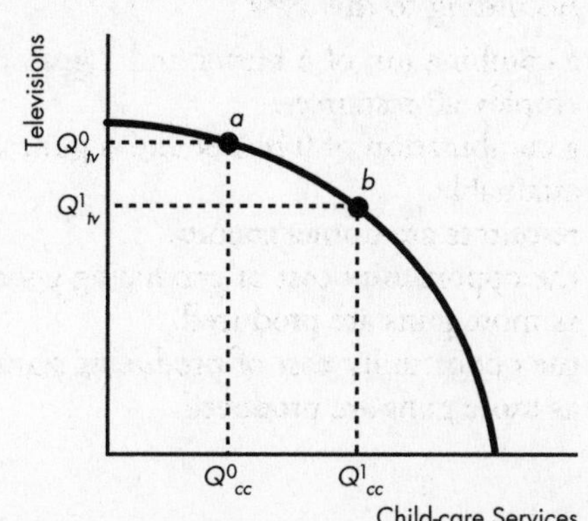

c The increased demand for child-care services puts upward pressure on the price of child-care services, making it more profitable to produce them. The higher price serves as a signal to firms to shift additional resources to producing child-care services.

Those additional resources come from the television market. The decreased demand for televisions puts downward pressure on the price of televisions, making it less profitable to produce them. The lower price serves as a signal to firms to shift resources to more profitable uses (in child-care).

Thus the market economy responds to the changing demands of households by reallocating resources into child-care services from television production. Prices are the signals that coordinate the demand decisions of households with the resource allocation decisions of firms. The market—operating through a combination of price signals, self-interest, and competition—acts like an "invisible hand" to guide resources to the uses that households desire.

d The distance of the *PPF* from the origin is determined by the quantities of resources and the technology in the economy. The *PPF* shows maximum combinations of outputs (goods and services) that can be produced with given resources and technology.

The precise point on the *PPF* at which the economy operates (for example, the combination at point *a* of child-care services and televisions) is determined by the demands of households.

The true cost of moving from point *a* to point *b* is the televisions that must be forgone as scarce resources are shifted to produce more child-care services. In other words, the true cost of additional child-care is an opportunity cost—forgone televisions.

Midterm Examination

1 d **a** and **b** show scarcity, **c** shows opportunity cost. (39–41)

2 c There are two variables plus time, which could be represented by **a**, **b**, or **d**. (21–23)

3 e Give up 6 butter to get 2 guns: 6/2 = 3 butter per gun. (39–41)

4 d Opportunity cost gun between **a** and **b** = 2 butter; between **b** and **c** = 3 butter. **a** on *PPF*, **b** outside *PPF*. (39–41)

5 c **a** is a true statement (definition); **d** and **b** are positive statements that can be tested. (12–13)

6 d As x increases, y decreases. (25–26)

7 d For example, using points (0, 4) and (16, 16): $\Delta y = 12\ (16 - 4)$, $\Delta x = 16\ (16 - 0)$. (28–29)

8 c Unemployment decreases expected average income from working. Higher opportunity cost for men may not be fair, but is a fact. (6)

9 a To move from *b* to *a*, quantity X decreases from 8 to 6. (40–41)

10 e Definition. (40–41)

11 d Scarcity implies opportunity cost, which involves a negative relationship—to get more of *X* you must give up *Y*. (39–41)

12 e Constant opportunity cost yields constant slope *PPF*. (39–41)

13 e Definition; **c** is marginal benefit, **b** and **d** are nonsense. (7, 42–43)

14 b Definition. (24–26)

15 d Definition; **a** is *post hoc ergo propter hoc*. (14–15)

Chapter 4
Demand and Supply

KEY CONCEPTS

Price and Opportunity Cost

The **relative price** of a good is the ratio of its money price to the money price of another good. Relative price measures the *opportunity cost* of buying a good—the other goods that must be forgone. The theory of demand and supply explains relative prices and makes predictions about whether the price of a good will rise or fall *relative to* the average price of other goods and services.

Demand

The **quantity demanded** of a good is the amount consumers plan to buy during a given time period at a particular price. The law of **demand** states: "Other things remaining the same, the higher the price of a good, the smaller is the quantity demanded." Higher price reduces quantity demanded for two reasons:

- *Substitution effect*—with an increase in the relative price of a good, people buy less of it and more of substitutes for the good.
- *Income effect*—with an increase in the relative price of a good and unchanged incomes, people have less money to spend on all goods, including the good whose price increased.

The **demand curve** represents the inverse relationship between quantity demanded and price, *ceteris paribus.* The demand curve also is a willingness-and-ability-to-pay curve, which measures marginal benefit.

- A change in price causes movement along the demand curve. This is called a **change in the quantity demanded**. The higher the price of a good, the lower the quantity demanded.
- A shift of the demand curve is called a **change in demand.** The demand curve shifts from changes in
  - prices of related goods.
  - expected future prices.
  - income.
  - population.
  - preferences.
- Increase in demand—demand curve shifts right.
- Decrease in demand—demand curve shifts left.
- For an increase in
  - price of a **substitute**—demand shifts right.
  - price of a **complement**—demand shifts left.
  - expected future prices—demand shifts right.
  - income (**normal good**)—demand shifts right.
  - income (**inferior good**)—demand shifts left.
  - population—demand shifts right.
  - preferences—demand shifts right.

Supply

The **quantity supplied** of a good is the amount producers plan to sell during a given time period at a particular price. The law of **supply** states: "Other things remaining the same, the higher the price of a good, the greater is the quantity supplied." Higher price increases quantity supplied because marginal cost increases with increasing quantities. Price must rise for producers to be willing to increase production and incur higher marginal cost.

The **supply curve** represents the positive relationship between quantity supplied and price, *ceteris paribus.* The supply curve is also a minimum-supply-price curve, showing the lowest price at which a producer can profitably sell another unit.

- A change in price causes movement along the supply curve. This is called a **change in the quantity supplied**. The higher the price of a good, the greater the quantity supplied.

- A shift of the supply curve is called a **change in supply**. The supply curve shifts from changes in
  - prices of productive resources.
  - prices of related goods produced.
  - expected future prices.
  - number of suppliers.
  - technology.
- Increase in supply—supply curve shifts right.
- Decrease in supply—supply curve shifts left.
- For an increase in
  - prices of productive resources—supply shifts left.
  - price of a *substitute in production*—supply shifts left.
  - price of a *complement in production*—supply shifts right.
  - expected future prices—supply shifts left.
  - number of suppliers—supply shifts right.
  - technology—supply shifts right.

Market Equilibrium

The **equilibrium price** is where the demand and supply curves intersect, where quantity demanded equals quantity supplied.

- Above the equilibrium price, there is a surplus (quantity supplied > quantity demanded), and price will fall.
- Below the equilibrium price, there is a shortage (quantity demanded > quantity supplied), and price will rise.
- Only in equilibrium is there no tendency for the price to change. The **equilibrium quantity** is the quantity bought and sold at the equilibrium price.

Predicting Changes in Price and Quantity

For a single change *either* in demand *or* in supply, *ceteris paribus*, when

- demand increases, P rises and Q increases.
- demand decreases, P falls and Q decreases.
- supply increases, P falls and Q increases.
- supply decreases, P rises and Q decreases.

When there is a simultaneous change *both* in demand *and* supply, we can determine the effect on either price or quantity. But without information about the relative size of the shifts of the demand and supply curves, the effect on the other variable is ambiguous. *Ceteris paribus*, when

- both demand and supply increase, P may rise/fall/remain constant and Q increases.
- both demand and supply decrease, P may rise/fall/remain constant and Q decreases.
- demand increases and supply decreases, P rises and Q may rise/fall/remain constant.
- demand decreases and supply increases, P falls and Q may rise/fall/remain constant.

HELPFUL HINTS

1 When you are first learning about demand and supply it is useful to think in terms of concrete examples to help build an intuitive understanding. Have some favourite examples in the back of your mind. For example, in analysing complementary goods, think about hamburgers and french fries; in analysing substitute goods, think of hamburgers and hot dogs. This will help reduce the "abstractness" of the economic theory.

2 The statement that "price is determined by demand and supply" is a shorthand way of saying that price is determined by all of the factors affecting demand (prices of related goods, expected future prices, income, population, preferences) and all of the factors affecting supply (prices of productive resources, prices of related goods produced, expected future prices, number of suppliers, technology). The benefit of using demand and supply curves is that they allow us to sort out the influences on price of each of these separate factors systematically. Changes in the factors affecting demand shift the demand curve and move us up or down the given supply curve. Changes in the factors affecting supply shift the supply curve and move us up or down the given demand curve.

Any demand and supply problem requires you to sort out these influences carefully. In so doing, *always draw a graph*, even if it is just a small graph in the margin of a true/false/uncertain or multiple-choice problem. Graphical representation is a very efficient way to "see" what happens. As you become comfortable with graphs, you will find that they are effective and powerful tools for systematically organizing your thinking.

Do not make the common mistake of thinking that a problem is so easy that you can do it in your head, without drawing a graph.

This mistake will cost you dearly on examinations. Also, when you do draw a graph, be sure to label the axes. As the course progresses, you will encounter many graphs with different variables on the axes. It is very easy to become confused if you do not develop the habit of labelling the axes.

3 Another very common mistake among students is failing to *distinguish* correctly between *a shift in a curve* and *a movement along a curve.* This distinction applies both to demand and to supply curves. Many questions in the Self-Test are designed to test your understanding of this distinction, and you can be sure that your instructor will test you heavily on this. The distinction between "shifts in" versus "movements along" a curve is crucial for systematic thinking about the factors influencing demand and supply, and for understanding the determination of equilibrium price and quantity.

Consider the example of the demand curve. The quantity of a good demanded depends on its own price, the prices of related goods, expected future prices, income, population, and preferences. The term "demand" refers to the relationship between the price of a good and the quantity demanded, holding constant all of the other factors on which the quantity demanded depends. This demand relationship is represented graphically by the demand curve. Thus the effect of a change in price on quantity demanded is already reflected in the slope of the demand curve; the effect of a change in the price of the good itself is given by a movement along the demand curve. This is referred to as a **change in quantity demanded**.

On the other hand, if one of the other factors affecting the quantity demanded changes, the demand curve itself will shift; the quantity demanded at each price will change. This shift of the demand curve is referred to as a **change in demand**. The critical thing to remember is that a change in the price of a good will not shift the demand curve; it will only cause a movement along the demand curve. Similarly, it is just as important to distinguish between shifts in the supply curve and movements along the supply curve.

To confirm your understanding, consider the effect (draw a graph!) of an increase in household income on the market for compact discs (CDs). First note that an increase in income affects the demand for CDs and not supply. Next we want to determine whether the increase in income causes a shift in the demand curve or a movement along the demand curve. Will the increase in income increase the quantity of CDs demanded even if the price of CDs does not change? Since the answer to this question is yes, we know that the demand curve will shift to the right. Note further that the increase in the demand for CDs will cause the equilibrium price to rise. This price increase will be indicated by a movement along the supply curve (an increase in the quantity supplied) and will not shift the supply curve itself.

Remember: It is shifts in demand and supply curves that cause the market price to change, not changes in the price that cause demand and supply curves to shift.

4 When analysing the shifts of demand and supply curves in related markets (for substitute goods like beer and wine), it often seems as though the feedback effects from one market to the other can go on endlessly. To avoid confusion, stick to the rule that each curve (demand and supply) for a given market can shift a maximum of once. (See Short Answer Problems **4** and **6** on page 46 for further explanation and examples.)

5 The relationships between price and quantity demanded and supplied can be represented in three equivalent forms: demand and supply schedules, curves, and equations. Text Chapter 4 illustrates schedules and curves, but demand and supply equations are also powerful tools of economic analysis. The Mathematical Note to Chapter 4 provides the general form of these equations. The purpose of this Helpful Hint and the next is to further explain the equations and how they can be used to determine the equilibrium values of price and quantity.

Fig. 4.1 presents a simple demand and supply example in three equivalent forms: (a) schedules, (b) curves, and (c) equations. The demand and supply schedules in (a) are in the same format as Text Fig. 4.8. The price-quantity combinations from the schedules are plotted on the graph in (b), yielding linear demand and supply curves. What is new about this example is the representation of those curves by the equations in (c).

If you recall (Chapter 2) the formula for the equation of a straight line ($y = a + bx$), you can see that the demand equation is the equation of a straight line. Instead of y, P is the dependent variable on the vertical axis, and, instead of x, Q_D is the independent variable on the horizontal axis. The intercept on the vertical axis a is +5, and the slope b is –1. The supply equation is also linear and graphed in the same way, but with Q_S as the independent variable. The supply curve intercept on the vertical axis is +1, and the slope is +1. The negative slope of the demand curve reflects the law of demand, and the positive slope of the supply curve reflects the law of supply.

You can demonstrate the equivalence of the demand schedule, curve, and equation by substituting various values of Q_D from the schedule into the demand equation, and calculating the associated prices. These combinations of quantity demanded and price are the coordinates (Q_D, P) of the points on the demand curve. You can similarly demonstrate the equivalence of the supply schedule, curve, and equation.

FIGURE **4.1**

(a) Demand and Supply Schedules

Price ($)	Q_D	Q_S	Shortage (–)/ Surplus (+)
1	4	0	–4
2	3	1	–2
3	2	2	0
4	1	3	+2
5	0	4	+4

(b) Demand and Supply Curves

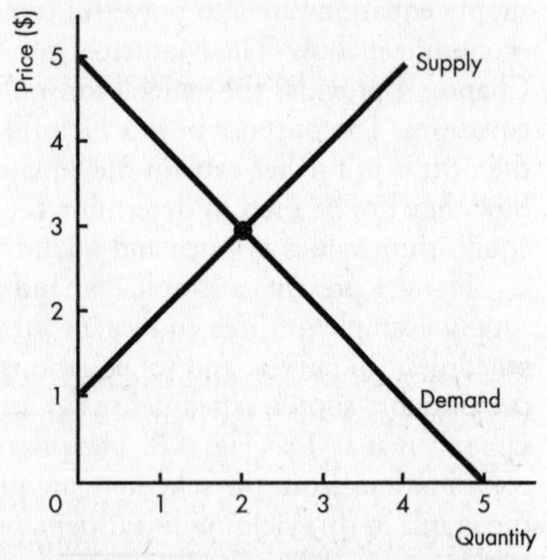

(c) Demand and Supply Equations

Demand: $P = 5 - 1Q_D$
Supply: $P = 1 + 1Q_S$

The demand and supply equations are very useful for calculating the equilibrium values of price and quantity. As the schedules and curves both show, two things are true in equilibrium: (1) the price is the same for consumers (the highest price they are willing to pay for the last unit) and producers (the lowest price they are willing to accept for the last unit) and (2) the quantity demanded equals the quantity supplied, so that there are no surpluses or shortages. In terms of the demand and supply equations, this means that, *in equilibrium,*

(1) the price in both equations is the same. We will denote the equilibrium price as P^*.
(2) $Q_D = Q_S$ = the equilibrium quantity bought and sold. We will denote the equilibrium quantity as Q^*.

In equilibrium, the equations become

Demand: $P^* = 5 - 1Q^*$
Supply: $P^* = 1 + 1Q^*$

These equilibrium equations constitute a simple set of simultaneous equations. Since there are two equations (demand and supply) and two unknowns (P^* and Q^*), we can solve for the unknowns.

Begin the solution by setting demand equal to supply:

$$5 - 1Q^* = 1 + 1Q^*$$

Collecting like terms, we find

$$4 = 2Q^*$$
$$2 = Q^*$$

Once we have Q^* (equilibrium quantity), we can solve for the equilibrium price using either the demand or the supply equations. Look first at demand:

$$P^* = 5 - 1Q^*$$
$$P^* = 5 - 1(2)$$
$$P^* = 5 - 2$$
$$P^* = 3$$

Alternatively, substituting Q^* into the supply equation yields the same result:

$$P^* = 1 + 1Q^*$$
$$P^* = 1 + 1(2)$$
$$P^* = 1 + 2$$
$$P^* = 3$$

Once you have solved for Q^*, the fact that substituting it into either the demand or the supply equation yields the correct P^* provides a valuable check on your calculations. If you make a mistake in your calculations, when you substitute Q^* into the demand and supply equations, you will get two different prices. If that happens, you know to recheck your calculations. If you get the same price when you substitute Q^* into the demand and supply equations, you know your calculations are correct.

6 Economists have developed the convention of graphing quantity as the independent variable and price as the dependent variable, and the foregoing equations reflect this. Despite this convention, economists actually consider real-world prices to be the independent variables and quantities the dependent variables. In that case, the equations would take the form

$$\text{Demand: } Q_D = 5 - 1P$$
$$\text{Supply: } Q_S = -1 + 1P$$

You can solve these equations for yourself to see that they yield exactly the same values for P^* and Q^*. (*Hint:* First solve for P^* and then for Q.) Whichever form of the equations your instructor may use, the technique for solving the equations will be similar and the results identical.

SELF-TEST

True/False/Uncertain and Explain

1 The law of demand tells us that as the price of a good rises, demand decreases.

T

2 A decrease in income will shift the demand curve to the left.

T

3 A supply curve shows the maximum price at which the last unit will be supplied.

F

4 If A and B are substitutes, an increase in the price of A will shift the supply curve of B to the left.

5 When a cow is slaughtered for beef, its hide becomes available to make leather. Thus beef and leather are substitutes in production.

6 If the price of beef rises, there will be an increase in both the supply of leather and the quantity of beef supplied.

7 When the actual price is above the equilibrium price, a shortage occurs.

8 If the expected future price of a good increases, there will be an increase in equilibrium price and a decrease in equilibrium quantity.

9 Suppose new firms enter the steel market. The equilibrium price of steel will fall and the quantity will rise.

10 Suppose the demand for personal computers increases while the cost of producing them decreases. The equilibrium quantity of personal computers will rise and the price will fall.

Multiple-Choice

Price and Opportunity Cost

1 A relative price is
- **a** the ratio of one price to another.
- **b** an opportunity cost.
- **c** a quantity of a "basket" of goods and services forgone.
- **d** determined by demand and supply.
- **e** all of the above.

Demand

2 If an increase in the price of good A causes the demand curve for good B to shift to the left, then
- **a** A and B are substitutes in consumption.
- **b** A and B are complements in consumption.
- **c** A and B are complements in production.
- **d** B is an inferior good.
- **e** B is a normal good.

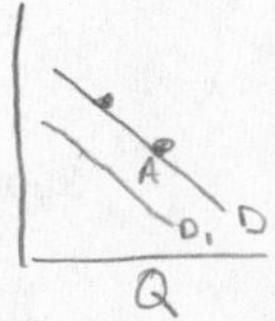

3 Which of the following could *not* cause an increase in demand for a commodity?
- **a** an increase in income
- **b** a decrease in income
- **c** a decrease in the price of a substitute
- **d** a decrease in the price of a complement
- **e** an increase in preferences for the commodity

4 Some sales managers are talking shop. Which of the following quotations refers to a movement along the demand curve?

- **a** "Since our competitors raised their prices our sales have doubled."
- **b** "It has been an unusually mild winter; our sales of wool scarves are down from last year."
- **c** "We decided to cut our prices, and the increase in our sales has been remarkable."
- **d** "The Green movement has sparked an increase in our sales of biodegradable products."
- **e** none of the above

5 If Hamburger Helper is an inferior good, then, *ceteris paribus*, a decrease in income will cause

- **a** a leftward shift of the demand curve for Hamburger Helper.
- **b** a rightward shift of the demand curve for Hamburger Helper.
- **c** movement up along the demand curve for Hamburger Helper.
- **d** movement down along the demand curve for Hamburger Helper.
- **e** none of the above.

6 A decrease in quantity demanded is represented by a

- **a** rightward shift of the supply curve.
- **b** rightward shift of the demand curve.
- **c** leftward shift of the demand curve.
- **d** movement upward and to the left along the demand curve.
- **e** movement downward and to the right along the demand curve.

7 Which of the following "other things" are *not* held constant along a demand curve?

- **a** income
- **b** prices of related goods
- **c** the price of the good itself
- **d** preferences
- **e** all of the above

Supply

8 The fact that a decline in the price of a good causes producers to reduce the quantity of the good supplied illustrates

- **a** the law of supply.
- **b** the law of demand.
- **c** a change in supply.
- **d** the nature of an inferior good.
- **e** technological improvement.

9 A shift of the supply curve for rutabagas will be caused by

- **a** a change in preferences for rutabagas.
- **b** a change in the price of a related good that is a substitute in consumption for rutabagas.
- **c** a change in income.
- **d** a change in the price of rutabagas.
- **e** none of the above.

10 If a resource can be used to produce either good *A* or good *B*, then *A* and *B* are

- **a** substitutes in production.
- **b** complements in production.
- **c** substitutes in consumption.
- **d** complements in consumption.
- **e** normal goods.

11 Which of the following will shift the supply curve for good *X* leftward?

- **a** a decrease in the wages of workers employed to produce *X*
- **b** an increase in the cost of machinery used to produce *X*
- **c** a technological improvement in the production of *X*
- **d** a situation where quantity demanded exceeds quantity supplied
- **e** all of the above

12 Some producers are chatting over a beer. Which of the following quotations refers to a movement along the supply curve?

- **a** "Wage increases have forced us to raise our prices."
- **b** "Our new, sophisticated equipment will enable us to undercut our competitors."
- **c** "Raw material prices have skyrocketed; we will have to pass this on to our customers."
- **d** "We anticipate a big increase in demand. Our product price should rise, so we are planning for an increase in output."
- **e** "New competitors in the industry are causing prices to fall."

13 If an increase in the price of good *A* causes the supply curve for good *B* to shift to the right, then

- **a** *A* and *B* are substitutes in consumption.
- **b** *A* and *B* are complements in consumption.
- **c** *A* and *B* are substitutes in production.
- **d** *A* and *B* are complements in production.
- **e** *A* is a factor of production for making *B*.

Market Equilibrium

14 If the market for Twinkies is in equilibrium, then

a Twinkies must be a normal good.
b producers would like to sell more at the current price.
c consumers would like to buy more at the current price.
d there will be a surplus.
e equilibrium quantity equals quantity demanded.

15 The price of a good will tend to fall if

a there is a surplus at the current price.
b the current price is above equilibrium.
c the quantity supplied exceeds the quantity demanded at the current price.
d all of the above are true.
e none of the above is true.

16 A surplus can be eliminated by

a increasing supply.
b government raising the price.
c decreasing the quantity demanded.
d allowing the price to fall.
e allowing the quantity bought and sold to fall.

17 A shortage is the amount by which quantity

a demanded exceeds quantity supplied.
b supplied exceeds quantity demanded.
c demanded increases when the price rises.
d demanded exceeds the equilibrium quantity.
e supplied exceeds the equilibrium quantity.

Predicting Changes in Price and Quantity

18 Which of the following will definitely cause an increase in the equilibrium price?

a an increase in both demand and supply
b a decrease in both demand and supply
c an increase in demand combined with a decrease in supply
d a decrease in demand combined with an increase in supply
e none of the above

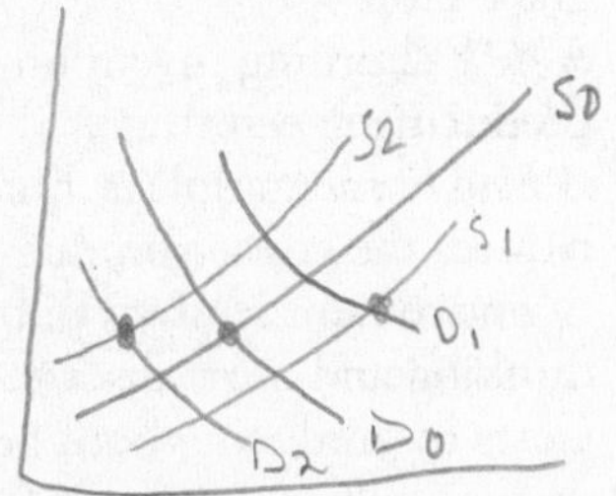

19 Coffee is a normal good. A decrease in income will

a increase the price of coffee and increase the quantity demanded of coffee.
b increase the price of coffee and increase the quantity supplied of coffee.
c decrease the price of coffee and decrease the quantity demanded of coffee.
d decrease the price of coffee and decrease the quantity supplied of coffee.
e cause none of the above.

20 An increase in the price of Pepsi (a substitute for coffee) will

a increase the price of coffee and increase the quantity demanded of coffee.
b increase the price of coffee and increase the quantity supplied of coffee.
c decrease the price of coffee and decrease the quantity demanded of coffee.
d decrease the price of coffee and decrease the quantity supplied of coffee.
e cause none of the above.

21 A technological improvement lowers the cost of producing coffee. At the same time, preferences for coffee decrease. The *equilibrium quantity* of coffee will

a rise.
b fall.
c remain the same.
d rise or fall depending on whether the price of coffee falls or rises.
e rise or fall depending on the relative shifts of demand and supply curves.

22 Since 1980, there has been a dramatic increase in the number of working mothers. Based on this information alone, we can predict that the market for child-care services has experienced a(n)

a increase in demand.
b decrease in demand.
c increase in quantity demanded.
d decrease in quantity supplied.
e increase in supply.

23 If *A* and *B* are complementary goods (in consumption) and the cost of a resource used in the production of *A* decreases, then the price of

a both *A* and *B* will rise.
b both *A* and *B* will fall.
c *A* will fall and the price of *B* will rise.
d *A* will rise and the price of *B* will fall.
e *A* will fall and the price of *B* will remain unchanged.

24 The demand curve for whatnots is $P = 75 - 6Q_D$ and the supply curve for whatnots is $P = 35 + 2Q_S$. What is the equilibrium price of a whatnot?

- a $5
- b $10
- c $40
- d $45
- e none of the above

25 The demand curve for tribbles is $P = 300 - 6Q_D$. The supply curve for tribbles is $P = 20 + 8Q_S$. If the price of a tribble was set at $120, the tribble market would experience

- a equilibrium.
- b excess demand causing a rise in price.
- c excess demand causing a fall in price.
- d excess supply causing a rise in price.
- e excess supply causing a fall in price.

Short Answer Problems

1 Explain the difference between wants and demands.

2 The price of personal computers has continued to fall even in the face of increasing demand. Explain.

ⓒ 3 A tax on crude oil would raise the cost of the primary resource used in the production of gasoline. A proponent of such a tax has claimed that it will not raise the price of gasoline using the following argument. While the price of gasoline may rise initially, that price increase will cause the demand for gasoline to decrease, which will push the price back down. What is wrong with this argument?

4 Brussels sprouts and carrots are substitutes in consumption and, since they can both be grown on the same type of land, substitutes in production too. Suppose there is an increase in the demand for brussels sprouts. Trace the effects on price and quantity traded in both the brussels sprout and carrot markets. (Keep in mind Helpful Hint 4.)

5 The information given in Table 4.1 is about the behaviour of buyers and sellers of fish at the market on a particular Saturday.

TABLE **4.1** DEMAND AND SUPPLY SCHEDULES FOR FISH

Price (per fish)	Quantity Demanded	Quantity Supplied
$0.50	280	40
$1.00	260	135
$1.50	225	225
$2.00	170	265
$2.50	105	290
$3.00	60	310
$3.50	35	320

- a On graph paper, draw the demand curve and the supply curve. Be sure to label the axes. What is the equilibrium price?
- b We will make the usual *ceteris paribus* assumptions about the demand curve so that it does not shift. List five factors that we are assuming do not change.
- c We will also hold the supply curve constant by assuming that five factors do not change. List them.
- d Explain briefly what would happen if the price was initially set at $3.00.
- e Explain briefly what would happen if the price was initially set at $1.00.
- f Explain briefly what would happen if the price was initially set at $1.50.

6 The market for wine in Canada is initially in equilibrium with supply and demand curves of the usual shape. Beer is a close substitute for wine; cheese and wine are complements. Use demand and supply diagrams to analyse the effect of each of the following (separate) events on the equilibrium price and quantity in the Canadian wine market. Assume that all of the *ceteris paribus* assumptions continue to hold except for the event listed. For both equilibrium price and quantity you should indicate in each case whether the variable rises, falls, remains the same, or moves ambiguously (may rise or fall).

- a The income of consumers falls (wine is a normal good).
- b Early frost destroys a large part of the world grape crop.
- c A new churning invention reduces the cost of producing cheese.
- d A new fermentation technique is invented that reduces the cost of producing wine.
- e A government study is published that links wine drinking and heart disease.
- f Costs of producing both beer and wine increase dramatically.

ⓒ 7 A newspaper reported that "Despite a bumper crop of cherries this year, the price drop for cherries won't be as much as expected because of short supplies of plums and peaches."

a Use a demand and supply graph for the cherry market to explain the effect of the bumper crop alone.

b On the same graph, explain the impact on the cherry market of the short supplies of plums and peaches.

8 Table 4.2 lists the demand and supply schedules for cases of grape jam.

TABLE **4.2** DEMAND AND SUPPLY SCHEDULES FOR GRAPE JAM PER WEEK

Price (per case)	Quantity Demanded (cases)	Quantity Supplied (cases)
$70	20	140
$60	60	120
$50	100	100
$40	140	80
$30	180	60

a On the graph in Fig. 4.2, draw the demand and supply curves for grape jam. Be sure to properly label the axes. Label the demand and supply curves D_0 and S_0 respectively.

FIGURE **4.2**

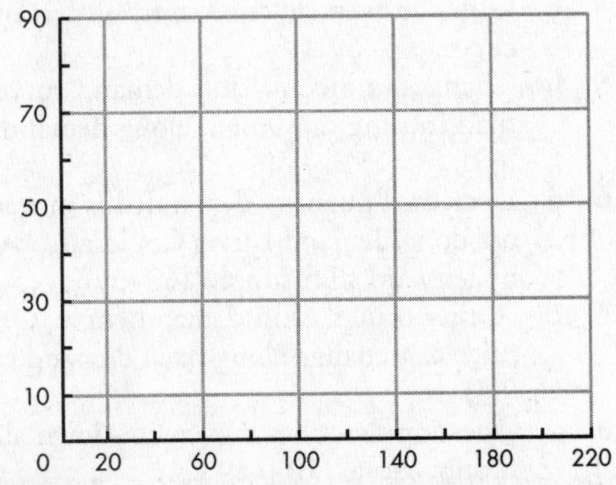

b What are the equilibrium price and quantity in the grape jam market? On your diagram, label the equilibrium point *a.*

c Is there a surplus or shortage at a price of $40? How much?

d The demand and supply schedules can also be represented by the following demand and supply equations:

Demand: $P = 75 - 0.25Q_D$
Supply: $P = 0.5Q_S$

Use these equations to solve for the equilibrium quantity (Q^*); equilibrium price (P^*). [*Hint:* Your answers should be the same as those in **8b**.]

e Suppose the population grows sufficiently that the demand for grape jam increases by 60 cases per week at every price.

i Construct a table (price, quantity demanded) of the new demand schedule.

ii Draw the new demand curve on your original graph and label it D_1.

iii Label the new equilibrium point *b.* What are the new equilibrium price and quantity?

iv What is the new demand equation? [*Hints:* What is the new slope? What is the new price-axis intercept?]

9 The demand equation for dweedles is

$$P = 8 - 1Q_D$$

The supply equation for dweedles is

$$P = 2 + 1Q_S$$

where P is the price of a dweedle in dollars, Q_D is the quantity of dweedles demanded, and Q_S is the quantity of dweedles supplied. The dweedle market is initially in equilibrium and income is $300.

a What is the equilibrium quantity (Q^*) of dweedles?

b What is the equilibrium price (P^*) of a dweedle?

c As a result of an increase in income to $500, the demand curve for dweedles shifts (the supply curve remains the same). The new demand equation is

$$P = 4 - 1Q_D$$

Use this information to calculate the new equilibrium quantity of dweedles; calculate the new equilibrium price of a dweedle.

d On the graph in Fig. 4.3, draw and label: (1) the supply curve, (2) the initial demand curve, (3) the new demand curve.

e Are dweedles a normal or inferior good? How do you know?

FIGURE **4.3**

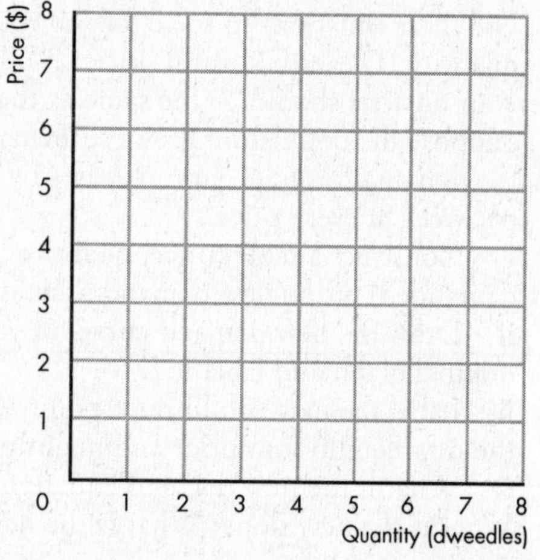

10 The demand equation for flubits is

$$P = 80 - 2Q_D$$

The supply equation for flubits is

$$P = 50 + 1Q_S$$

where P is the price of a flubit in dollars, Q_D is the quantity of flubits demanded, and Q_S is the quantity of flubits supplied. Assume that there are no changes in *ceteris paribus* assumptions.

a If the price of flubits was set at \$56, calculate the exact surplus or shortage of flubits.
b Explain the adjustment process that will bring the situation above to equilibrium.
c What is the equilibrium quantity (Q^*) of flubits?
d What is the equilibrium price (P^*) of a flubit?
e Now assume that as a result of technological advance, the supply curve for flubits shifts (the demand curve remains the same). The new supply equation is

$$P = 20 + 1Q_S$$

Use this information to calculate the new equilibrium quantity of flubits; calculate the new equilibrium price of a flubit.

ANSWERS

True/False/Uncertain and Explain

1 F As price rises, quantity demanded decreases. (65)
ⓒⓣ **2 U** Leftward shift for normal good, rightward shift for inferior good. (68)
3 F Supply curve shows minimum price at which last unit supplied. (71)
ⓒⓣ **4 U** True if *A* and *B* substitutes in production, but false if substitutes in consumption. (71–72)
ⓒⓣ **5 F** Beef and leather complements in production because produced together of necessity. (71–72)
6 T For complements in production, higher price for one good causes increased quantity supplied and increase in supply of other good. (71–72)
7 F At $P >$ equilibrium P, there is surplus (quantity supplied > quantity demanded). (74–75)
8 U Higher expected future prices cause rightward shift demand and leftward shift supply. Price rises, but Δ quantity depends on relative magnitude shifts. (67–68, 72, 79)
9 T Increased number firms causes rightward shift supply leading to fall in price and increased quantity. (77)
10 U Quantity will increase but Δ price depends on relative magnitude shifts in demand and supply. (78)

Multiple-Choice

1 e Definitions. (64)
2 b For example, higher-price french fries causes decreased demand for hamburgers. (67)
ⓒⓣ **3 c** Both income answers could be correct if commodity were normal (**a**) or inferior (**b**). (67–68)
4 c Other answers describe shifts of demand curve. (65–69)
5 b Changes in income shift demand curve rather than causing movement along demand curve. (68)
6 d Decreased quantity demanded is movement up along demand curve. Could also be caused by leftward shift supply. (68–69)
7 c "Other things" shift demand curve. Only price can change along fixed demand curve. (65)
8 a Question describes movement down along supply curve. (70–71)
9 e Answers **a**, **b**, and **c** shift demand, while **d** causes movement along supply curve. (71–72)
10 a Definition of substitute in production. (71–72)
11 b Higher price productive resource shifts supply leftward. (71–72)
12 d Other answers describe shifts of supply curve. (72–73)

13 d Definition complements in production. Price changes of related goods in consumption shift demand. (71–72)

14 e At equilibrium price, plans producers and consumers match; quantity demanded = quantity supplied. (74–75)

15 d All answers describe price above equilibrium price. (74–75)

16 d Other answers make surplus (excess quantity supplied) larger. (74–75)

17 a Shortage is horizontal distance between demand and supply curves at price below equilibrium price. (74–75)

18 c Answers **a** and **b** have indeterminate effect on price, while **d** causes lower price. (78–79)

19 d Demand shifts left. (76–77)

20 b Demand shifts right. (76–77)

21 e Supply shifts right, and demand shifts left. (79)

22 a More working mothers increases preferences for child care, causing increased demand for child-care services. (76–79)

ⓒⓣ **23 c** Supply *A* shifts right causing lower price of *A*. This increases demand for *B*, causing higher price of *B*. (76–79)

ⓒⓣ **24 d** See Helpful Hint 5. Set demand equal to supply, solve for $Q^* = 5$. Substitute $Q^* = 5$ into either demand or supply equation to solve for P^*. (84–85)

ⓒⓣ **25 b** At $P = \$120$, $Q_D = 30$, and $Q_S = 12.5$. Excess demand so price will rise. (75, 84–85)

Short Answer Problems

1 Wants are our unlimited desires for goods and services without regard to our ability or willingness to make the sacrifices necessary to obtain them. The existence of scarcity means that many of those wants will not be satisfied. On the other hand, if we demand something, then we want it, can afford it, and have made a definite plan to buy it. Demands reflect decisions about which wants to satisfy.

2 Due to the tremendous pace of technological advance, not only has the demand for personal computers been increasing, but the supply has been increasing as well. Indeed, supply has been increasing much more rapidly than demand, which has resulted in falling prices. Thus *much* (but not all) of the increase in sales of personal computers reflects a movement down along a demand curve rather than a shift in demand.

ⓒⓣ **3** This argument confuses a movement along an unchanging demand curve with a shift in the demand curve. The proper analysis is as follows. The increase in the price of oil (the primary resource in the production of gasoline) will shift the supply curve of gasoline leftward. This will cause the equilibrium price of gasoline to increase and thus decrease the quantity demanded of gasoline. Demand itself will not decrease—that is, the demand curve will not shift. The decrease in supply causes a movement along an unchanged demand curve.

4 The answer to this question requires us to trace through the effects on the two graphs in Fig. 4.4: (a) for the brussels sprout market and (b) for the carrot market. The sequence of effects occurs in order of the numbers on the graphs.

Look first at the market for brussels sprouts. The increase in demand shifts the demand curve rightward from D_0 to D_1 (1), and the price of brussels sprouts rises. This price rise has two effects (2) on the carrot market. Since brussels sprouts and carrots are substitutes in consumption, the demand curve for carrots shifts rightward from D_0 to D_1. And, since brussels sprouts and carrots are substitutes in production, the supply curve of carrots shifts leftward from S_0 to S_1. Both of these shifts in the carrot market raise the price of carrots, causing feedback effects on the brussels sprout market. But remember the rule (Helpful Hint 4) that each curve (demand and supply) for a given market can shift a maximum of *once*. Since the demand curve for brussels sprouts has already shifted, we can only shift the supply curve from S_0 to S_1 (3) because of the substitutes in production relationship. Each curve in each market has now shifted once and the analysis must stop. We can predict that the net effects are increases in the equilibrium prices of both brussels sprouts and carrots, and indeterminate changes in the equilibrium quantities in both markets.

FIGURE 4.4

(a) Brussel Sprout Market

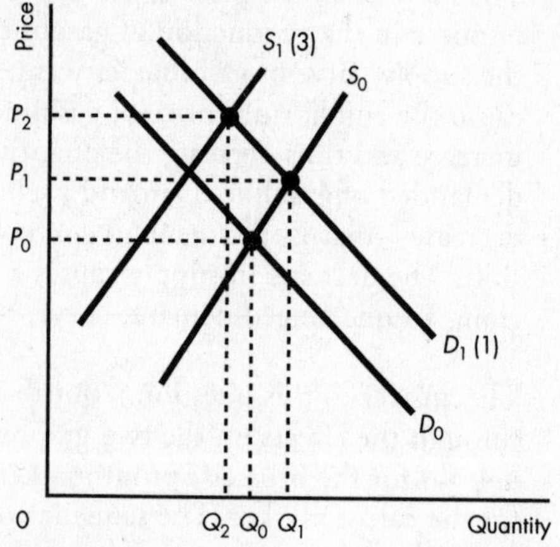

(b) Carrot Market

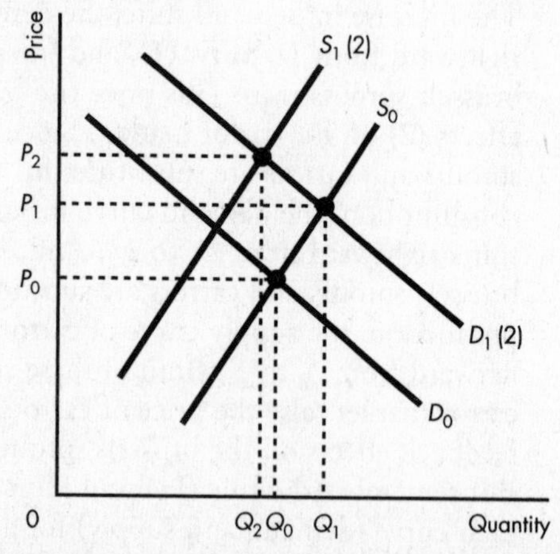

5 a The demand and supply curves are shown in Fig. 4.5. The equilibrium price is $1.50 per fish.

FIGURE 4.5

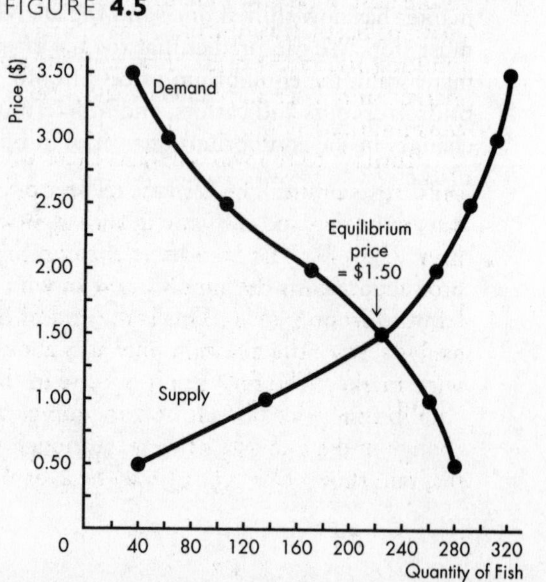

b Prices of related goods; expected future prices; income; population; preferences.

c Prices productive resources; prices of related goods produced; expected future prices; number of suppliers; technology.

d At a price of $3.00, quantity supplied (310) exceeds quantity demanded (60). Fish sellers find themselves with surplus fish. Rather than be stuck with unsold fish (which yields no revenue), some sellers cut their price in an attempt to increase the quantity of fish demanded. Competition forces other sellers to follow suit, and the price falls until it reaches the equilibrium price of $1.50, while quantity demanded increases until it reaches the equilibrium quantity of 225 units.

e At a price of $1.00, the quantity demanded (260) exceeds the quantity supplied (135)—there is a shortage. Unrequited fish buyers bid up the price in an attempt to get the "scarce" fish. As prices continue to be bid up as long as there is excess demand, quantity supplied increases in response to higher prices. Price and quantity supplied both rise until they reach the equilibrium price ($1.50) and quantity (225 units).

f At a price of $1.50, the quantity supplied exactly equals the quantity demanded (225). There is no excess demand (shortage) or excess supply (surplus), and therefore no tendency for the price or quantity to change.

6 The demand and supply diagrams for parts **a** to **e** are shown in Fig. 4.6.

FIGURE **4.6**

(a)

Price
D_0
S
D_1
P_0
↓
P_1
↓ Price
↓ Quantity
0
$Q_1 \leftarrow Q_0$
Quantity

(b)

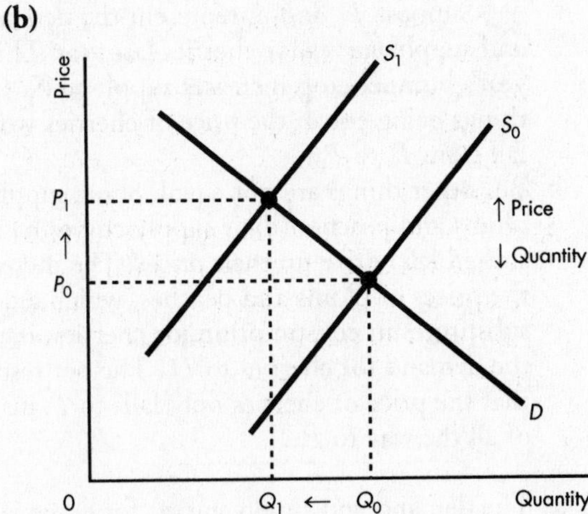

(c)

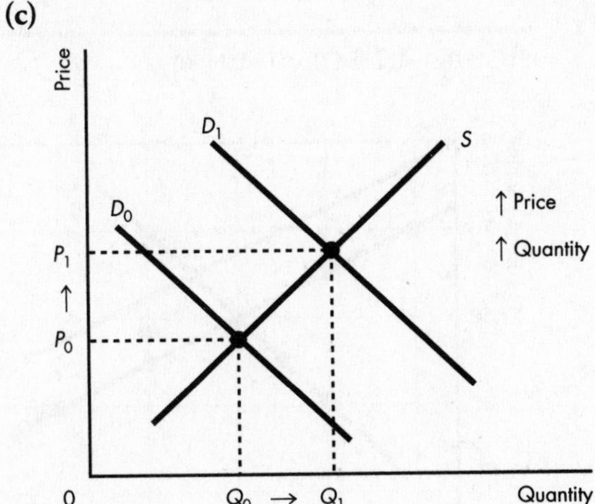

(d)

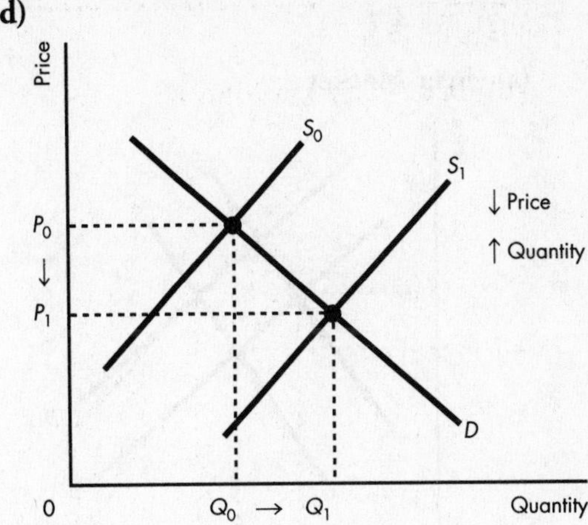

(e)

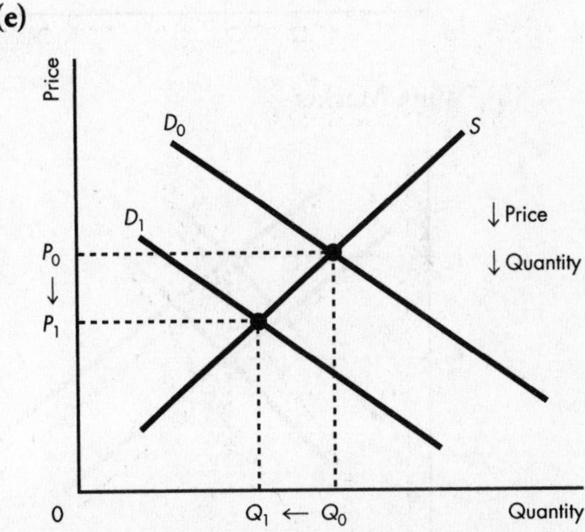

f Questions like this require the examination of two separate but related markets—the beer and wine markets. Since this kind of question often causes confusion for students, Fig. 4.7 gives a more detailed explanation of the answer.

Look first at the beer market. The increase in the cost of beer production shifts the supply curve of beer leftward from S_0 to S_1. The resulting rise in the price of beer affects the wine market since beer and wine are substitutes (in consumption).

Turning to the wine market, there are two shifts to examine. The increase in beer prices causes the demand for wine to shift rightward from D_0 to D_1. The increase in the cost of wine production shifts the supply curve of wine leftward from S_0 to S_1. This is the end of the analysis, since the question only asks about the wine market. The final result is a rise in the equilibrium price of wine and an ambiguous change in the quantity of wine. Although the diagram shows $Q_1 = Q_0$, Q_1 may be $\geq$ or $\leq Q_0$.

FIGURE **4.7**

(a) Beer Market

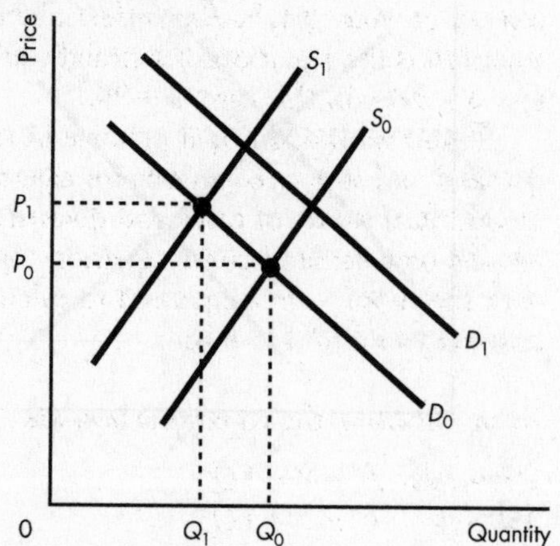

(b) Wine Market

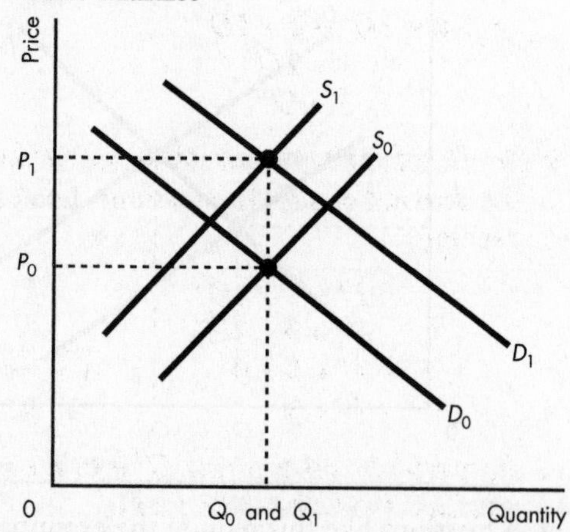

Many students rightfully ask, "But doesn't the rise in wine prices then shift the demand curve for beer rightward, causing a rise in beer prices and an additional increase in the demand for wine?" This question, which is correct in principle, is about the dynamics of adjustment, and these graphs are only capable of analysing once-over shifts of demand or supply. We could shift the demand for beer rightward, but the resulting rise in beer prices would lead us to shift the demand for wine a *second time.* In practice, stick to the rule that each curve (demand and supply) for a given market can shift a maximum of *once.*

ⓒ **7 a** The demand and supply curves for the cherry market are shown in Fig. 4.8.

FIGURE **4.8**

Cherry Market

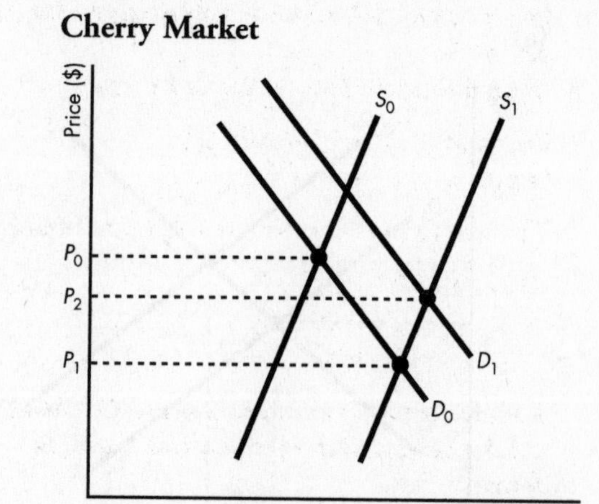

Suppose D_0 and S_0 represent the demand and supply curves for cherries last year. This year's bumper crop increases supply to S_1. Other things being equal, the price of cherries would fall from P_0 to P_1.

b But other things are not equal. Short supplies of plums and peaches (their supply curves have shifted left) drive up their prices. The increase in the prices of plums and peaches, which are substitutes in consumption for cherries, increases the demand for cherries to D_1. The net result is that the price of cherries only falls to P_2 instead of all the way to P_1.

8 a The demand and supply curves for grape jam are shown in Fig. 4.2 Solution.

FIGURE **4.2** SOLUTION

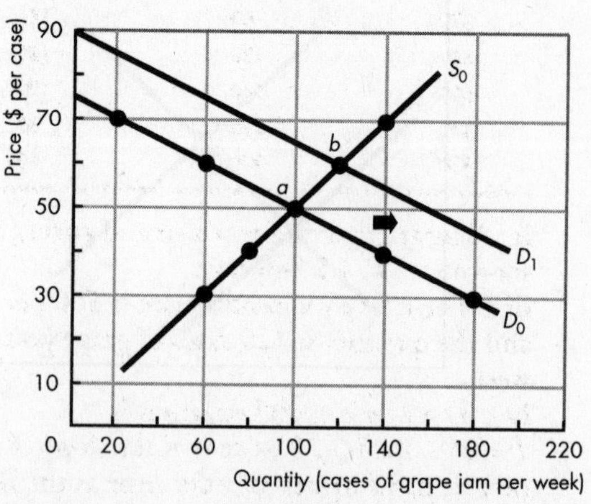

b The equilibrium is given at the intersection of the demand and supply curves (labelled point *a*). The equilibrium price is $50 per case and the equilibrium quantity is 100 cases per week.

c At a price of $40 there is a shortage of 60 cases per week.

d In equilibrium, the equations become:

Demand: $P^* = 75 - 0.25Q^*$
Supply: $P^* = 0.5Q^*$

To solve for Q^*, set demand equal to supply:

$$75 - 0.25Q^* = 0.5Q^*$$
$$75 = 0.75Q^*$$
$$100 = Q^*.$$

To solve for P^*, we can substitute Q^* into either the demand or supply equations. Look at demand first:

$$P^* = 75 - 0.25Q^*$$
$$P^* = 75 - 0.25(100)$$
$$P^* = 75 - 25$$
$$P^* = 50$$

Alternatively, substituting Q^* into the supply equation yields the same result:

$$P^* = 0.5Q^*$$
$$P^* = 0.5(100)$$
$$P^* = 50$$

e i Table 4.3 also contains the (unchanged) quantity supplied, for reference purposes.

TABLE **4.3** DEMAND AND SUPPLY SCHEDULES FOR GRAPE JAM PER WEEK

Price (per case)	Quantity Demanded (cases)	Quantity Supplied (cases)
$70	80	140
$60	120	120
$50	160	100
$40	200	80
$30	240	60

ii The graph of the new demand curve, D_1, is shown in Fig. 4.2 Solution.

iii The new equilibrium price is $60 per case and the quantity is 120 cases of grape jam per week.

iv The new demand equation is $P = 90 - 0.25Q_D$. Notice that the slope of the new demand equation is the same as the slope of the original demand equation. An increase in demand of 60 cases at every price results in a rightward *parallel* shift of the demand curve. Since the two curves are parallel, they have the same slope. The figure of 90 is the price-axis intercept of the new demand curve, which you can see on your graph. *Remember:* The demand equation is the equation of a straight line ($y = a + bx$)—in this case, $a = 90$.

If you want additional practice in the use of demand and supply equations for calculating equilibrium values of price and quantity, you can use the new demand curve equation together with the supply curve equation to calculate the answers you found in **e iii**.

9 In equilibrium, the equations become

Demand: $P^* = 8 - 1Q^*$
Supply: $P^* = 2 + 1Q^*$

a To solve for Q^*, set demand equal to supply:

$$8 - 1Q^* = 2 + 1Q^*$$
$$6 = 2Q^*$$
$$3 = Q^*$$

b To solve for P^*, we can substitute Q^* into either the demand or supply equations. Look first at demand:

$$P^* = 8 - 1Q^*$$
$$P^* = 8 - 1(3)$$
$$P^* = 8 - 3$$
$$P^* = 5$$

Alternatively, substituting Q^* into the supply equation yields the same result:

$$P^* = 2 + 1Q^*$$
$$P^* = 2 + 1(3)$$
$$P^* = 2 + 3$$
$$P^* = 5$$

c In equilibrium, the equations are

Demand: $P^* = 4 - 1Q^*$
Supply: $P^* = 2 + 1Q^*$

To solve for Q^*, set demand equal to supply:

$$4 - 1Q^* = 2 + 1Q^*$$
$$2 = 2Q^*$$
$$1 = Q^*$$

To solve for P^*, we can substitute Q^* into either the demand or supply equations. Look first at demand:

$$P^* = 4 - 1Q^*$$
$$P^* = 4 - 1(1)$$
$$P^* = 4 - 1$$
$$P^* = 3$$

Alternatively, substituting Q^* into the supply equation yields the same result:

$$P^* = 2 + 1Q^*$$
$$P^* = 2 + 1(1)$$
$$P^* = 2 + 1$$
$$P^* = 3$$

d The supply curve, initial demand curve, and new demand curve for dweedles are shown in Fig. 4.3 Solution.

FIGURE **4.3** SOLUTION

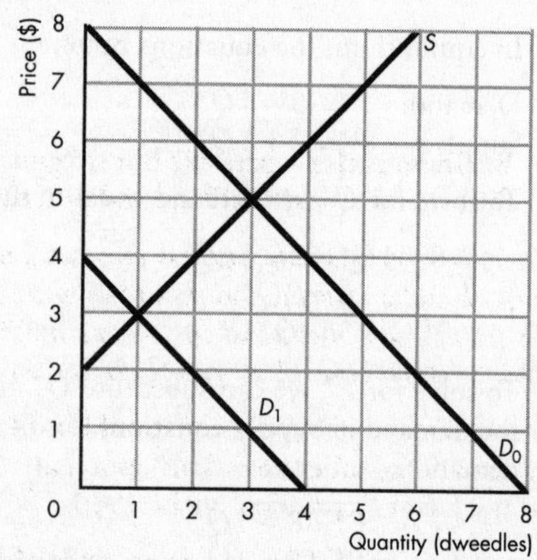

e Dweedles are an inferior good. An increase in income (from $300 to $500) caused a decrease in demand—the demand curve for dweedles shifted leftward.

10 a Substitute the price of $56 into the demand and supply equations to calculate the quantities demanded and supplied at that price. This is the mathematical equivalent of what you do on a graph when you identify a price on the vertical axis, move your eye across to the demand (or supply) curve, and then move your eye down to read the quantity on the horizontal axis.

Substituting into the demand equation, we find

$$P = 80 - 2Q_D$$
$$56 = 80 - 2Q_D$$
$$2Q_D = 24$$
$$Q_D = 12.$$

Substituting into the supply equation,

$$P = 50 + 1Q_S$$
$$56 = 50 + 1Q_S$$
$$6 = Q_S$$

Quantity demanded exceeds quantity supplied by 6 (12 – 6), so there is a shortage of 6 flubits.

b A shortage means the price was set below the equilibrium price. Competition between consumers for the limited number of flubits will bid up the price and increase the quantity supplied until we reach the equilibrium price and quantity.

c In equilibrium, the equations are

Demand: $P^* = 80 - 2Q^*$
Supply: $P^* = 50 + 1Q^*$

To solve for Q^*, set demand equal to supply:

$$80 - 2Q^* = 50 + 1Q^*$$
$$30 = 3Q^*$$
$$10 = Q^*$$

d To solve for P^*, substitute Q^* into the demand equation:

$$P^* = 80 - 2Q^*$$
$$P^* = 80 - 2(10)$$
$$P^* = 80 - 20$$
$$P^* = 60$$

You can check this answer yourself by substituting Q^* into the supply equation.

e The new equilibrium equations are

Demand: $P^* = 80 - 2Q^*$
Supply: $P^* = 20 + 1Q^*$

To solve for Q^*, set demand equal to supply:

$$80 - 2Q^* = 20 + 1Q^*$$
$$60 = 3Q^*$$
$$20 = Q^*$$

To solve for P^*, substitute Q^* into the supply equations:

$$P^* = 20 + 1Q^*$$
$$P^* = 20 + 1(20)$$
$$P^* = 20 + 20$$
$$P^* = 40$$

You can check this answer yourself by substituting Q^* into the demand equation.

Chapter 21
A First Look at Macroeconomics

KEY CONCEPTS

Origins and Issues of Macroeconomics

Modern macroeconomics was born during the **Great Depression** (a decade of high unemployment).

- ◆ Keynes' focus was the short-term problems of the depression, which he thought were caused by too little spending, implying a need for increased government spending.
- ◆ Once out of depression, long-term problems of inflation, etc. become central, implying government spending must be moderated. The events of the 1960s–70s showed the importance of these long-term problems.
- ◆ Recently, macroeconomics has merged the short-term and long-term issues in a broad study of unemployment, economic growth, inflation, and deficits. Our goal is to understand these theories.

Economic Growth

Economic growth increases economy's capacity to produce goods and services, measured by rise in real domestic product (real GDP).

- ◆ **Real GDP**—value of total production, measured in the prices of a single year.
- ◆ **Potential GDP**—real GDP when labour, capital, land, and entrepreneurial ability are fully employed.
- ◆ Economic growth in Canadian history has two features.
  - Long-term economic growth, as measured by potential GDP, grew rapidly in the 1960s, but output per person has grown much less rapidly since then due to a **productivity growth slowdown**.
  - **Business cycles**—periodic but irregular fluctuation of real GDP around potential.
- ◆ Each cycle is irregular, but has two turning points (a *peak* and a *trough*), and two phases (a **recession** when real GDP decreases for two or more periods, and an **expansion** when real GDP increases).
- ◆ The recession of 1990–91 was mild but long compared to earlier recessions, especially compared to the Great Depression of the 1930s.
- ◆ Examining real GDP per person since 1960 for Canada versus the world's largest economies shows
  - similar business cycles and productivity slowdowns.
  - faster growth of potential GDP than United States or Germany, but slower growth than Japan.
- ◆ Benefit of economic growth—increased consumption possibilities of individuals and governments. Slower recent growth has meant lost consumption possibilities.
- ◆ Costs of economic growth—lost consumption as a result of resources devoted to growth rather than consumption, perhaps more rapid resource depletion and environmental pollution, more frequent job changes.

Jobs and Unemployment

Each year in Canada, many jobs are created and destroyed. Average net effect is 200,000 new jobs, but when production is falling, then more jobs destroyed than created, and vice versa when production is rising.

- ◆ **Unemployment** occurs when qualified workers seeking jobs cannot find any.
  - **Unemployment rate**—percentage of labour force unemployed.
  - **Labour force**—sum of unemployed and employed.

- Measured unemployment is flawed due to exclusion of **discouraged workers** (those who wish to work but give up searching) and part-time workers who desire full-time work.

◆ Unemployment has fluctuated greatly in Canadian history, with peaks occurring in 1930s, early 1980s, and early 1990s, average of 6.7 percent since World War II.

◆ Canadian unemployment moves with U.S. unemployment, but recently has risen to higher levels.

◆ Unemployment rises in recessions and falls in expansions.

◆ Costs of unemployment are lost production and income of unemployed and deterioration of job prospects due to lost human capital.

Inflation

Inflation is an increase in average level of prices (or **price level**), measured by the inflation rate (percentage change in price level).

◆ **Deflation**—inflation rate is negative.

◆ Inflation in Canada was less than 3 percent in 1960s, rose to around 10 percent through 1970s, down since then to almost zero in response to the actions of the Bank of Canada.

◆ Canada's inflation rate is historically similar to that of other industrial countries, but recently is lower.

◆ Unpredictable inflation
- creates winners/losers by creating unpredictable changes in the value of money.
- leads to resources getting diverted from productive activities to predicting inflation.

◆ Getting rid of inflation is costly, since it usually involves more unemployment.

Surpluses and Deficits

◆ **Government budget surpluses** occur when tax revenues exceed spending.

◆ **Government budget deficits** occur when government spending exceeds tax revenues, a common occurrence until recently.

◆ Canada's international deficit occurs when our imports exceed our exports, as in recent years.

◆ Deficits mean governments and nations must borrow, and pay interest on debts. This borrowing is a problem if it was for consumption, but not if it was to buy assets that would generate additional income that can repay the debt.

Macroeconomic Policy Challenges and Tools

Keynes was the first to argue the government needed to fix the economy and maintain full employment.

◆ Five main policy challenges are to reduce unemployment, increase economic growth, stabilize the business cycle, keep inflation low, lower government and international deficits.

◆ Two main policy tools are
- **fiscal policy**—the government changing its taxes and spending programs.
- **monetary policy**—the Bank of Canada changing interest rates and the amount of money in the economy.

HELPFUL HINTS

1 Note that to be unemployed, as officially measured by the Canadian Labour Force Survey, it is not enough to be without a job. One must also be "actively" seeking a job. Most university students are without jobs but they are not counted as unemployed since they are not looking for jobs while they are attending school.

2 The variables we study in this chapter are interdependent—they affect and are affected by each other in economic interrelationships that we will learn about in subsequent chapters.

The most important relationship is the effect of the business cycle on other variables. Business cycles significantly affect the unemployment rate. In a recession, the unemployment rate rises, reaching its highest level when the economy is in the trough of the cycle. In an expansion, the unemployment rate falls, reaching its lowest level at the peak.

Government deficits are also affected strongly by business cycles. In a recession, real GDP falls and taxes collected fall, while government payments such as employment insurance and social assistance rise, creating a larger deficit. The opposite effects occur during an expansion.

There is also a strong relationship between business cycles and the current account. When exports are rising and we have a current account surplus, the surplus creates expansionary pressures on real GDP. On the other hand, as the economy expands, Canadians tend to buy more imported goods, pushing the current account towards a deficit.

3 The inflation rate is calculated as the percentage change in prices using the formula

$$\text{Inflation rate} = \frac{\text{Current year's price level} - \text{Last year's price level}}{\text{Last year's price level}} \times 100.$$

For example, the average 1997 price level was 107.6, and the average 1996 price level was 105.9, allowing us to calculate the inflation rate for 1997:

$$\text{Inflation rate} = \frac{107.6 - 105.9}{105.9} \times 100 = 1.6\%.$$

4 Inflation creates problems because it creates unpredictable changes in the value of money. The *value of money* is the quantity of goods and services that can be bought with a given amount of money. When an economy experiences inflation, the value of money falls—you cannot buy as many goods with a dollar this year as you could last year.

To illustrate this point, consider the data in Table 21.1 on the price of a chocolate bar in Canada over the past 46 years:[1]

TABLE **21.1**

Year	Price of Chocolate Bar (¢)	Number of Bars $1 Buys
1950	10	10.00
1966	15	6.67
1976	30	3.33
1986	75	1.33
1999	100	1.00

The table shows us the strong cumulative impact of inflation over this time period, as well as the result that the value of a dollar has fallen enormously over this time period—it buys about 1/10th as many chocolate bars as it did in 1950. When your grandfather tells you "A dollar ain't worth what it used to be," he's telling the truth!

[1] *Source:* Statistics Canada, *The Consumer Price Index*, with calculations and extrapolation from 1989 by H. King.

SELF-TEST

True/False/Uncertain and Explain

1 Macroeconomics focuses only on short-term problems such as unemployment.

2 Higher economic growth is good for an economy.

3 In the recession phase of a business cycle, the unemployment rate is rising.

4 Discouraged workers are counted as unemployed but probably should not be.

5 Canadian unemployment is virtually identical to U.S. unemployment.

6 If the price level was 130 in 1998 and 110 in 1997, the inflation rate in 1998 was 20 percent.

7 Since inflation is costly, getting rid of it is a good idea.

8 If Canada sells more to the rest of the world than it buys from the rest of the world, Canada will have an international deficit.

9 A government budget deficit will create problems for the government.

10 In Canada, fiscal policy is implemented by the federal government.

Multiple-Choice

Origins and Issues of Macroeconomics

1 Modern macroeconomics

a was born during the 1960s–70s.
b initially focused on long-term problems.
c focuses only on short-term problems.
d now merges both short-term and long-term problems.
e focuses only on long-term problems.

2 Which of the following statements about long-term economic problems is *true*?

a Keynes ignored them.
b Keynes said they could be cured by increased government spending.
c Economists consider them much less important than short-term problems.
d They include inflation and slow economic growth.
e The biggest one is business cycles.

Economic Growth

3 Comparing Canada's economic growth with the major industrial economies' growth shows that

a Canada experienced a slowdown in productivity, but they did not.
b Canada and the United States experienced a slowdown in productivity, but Japan and Germany did not.
c Canada did not experience the slowdown in productivity that the others did.
d Canada always had a lower level of productivity and economic growth.
e All four countries experienced a slowdown in productivity at about the same time.

4 Increasing potential GDP is

a always beneficial since living standards rise.
b always too costly since pollution and resource depletion rise.
c beneficial only if pollution rises at 5 percent a year.
d beneficial if the benefits of rising living standards outweigh the costs of higher pollution and resource depletion.
e none of the above.

5 Which of the following politicians is talking about the business cycle?

a "Canadian unemployment is falling due to the upturn in the economy."
b "Crime rates increase every spring as the school year ends."
c "An average of 200,000 new jobs are created each year in Canada."
d "More capital investment will create more jobs."
e "Business always rises just before Christmas."

6 Real GDP is defined as the yearly value of

a all goods produced in an economy.
b all goods and services produced in an economy.
c the goods and services produced in households.
d production when resources are full employed.
e all goods and services produced in an economy, controlling for inflation.

7 The correct order of the sequence of business cycle phases is

a expansion, peak, recession, trough.
b expansion, peak, trough, deviation.
c expansion, trough, recession, peak.
d expansion, recession, trough, peak.
e expansion, deviation, recession, trough.

Jobs and Unemployment

8 Compared to the U.S. unemployment rate, the Canadian unemployment rate moves

a independently of the U.S. rate.
b with the U.S. rate, but at a lower level recently.
c in the opposite direction to the U.S. rate.
d with the U.S. rate, but at a higher level recently.
e with the U.S. rate, and at the same level.

9 The economic costs of unemployment include

a workers quitting and going to university.
b political problems for government.
c lost job prospects of the unemployed.
d the fast pace of job changes.
e the diversion of resources from productive activities to predicting unemployment.

10 In which of the following years was the unemployment rate in Canada almost 20 percent?

a 1982
b 1976
c 1959
d 1933
e 1926

11 In a country with a population of 20 million, there are 9 million employed and 1 million unemployed. What is the labour force?

- **a** 20 million
- **b** 10 million
- **c** 9 million
- **d** 8 million
- **e** 1 million

12 In a country with a population of 20 million, there are 9 million employed and 1 million unemployed. What is the unemployment rate?

- **a** 11 percent
- **b** 10 percent
- **c** 8 percent
- **d** 5 percent
- **e** 1 percent

13 Including discouraged workers in the measured unemployment rate would

- **a** not change the measured unemployment rate.
- **b** lower the measured unemployment rate.
- **c** lower the labour force.
- **d** raise the measured unemployment rate only if there are no part-time workers.
- **e** raise the measured unemployment rate.

Inflation

14 If the inflation rate is positive, the price level in an economy is

- **a** falling rapidly.
- **b** rising.
- **c** constant.
- **d** falling slowly.
- **e** zero.

15 An unpredictable inflation causes problems because

- **a** it increases the variability of business cycles.
- **b** the stock market falls in value.
- **c** the value of money starts rising.
- **d** resources are diverted from productive activities to tax evasion.
- **e** resources are diverted from productive activities to forecasting inflation.

16 Which of the following statements about Canada's inflation rate is *false*?

- **a** It is currently lower than that of most other industrial countries.
- **b** It was low in the 1960s.
- **c** It rose in the 1970s.
- **d** It fell in the 1980s due to the actions of the Bank of Canada.
- **e** Historically, it has always been higher than that of other industrial countries until recently.

17 If a price index was 128 at the end of 1987 and 136 at the end of 1988, what was the rate of inflation for 1988?

- **a** 4.2 percent
- **b** 5.9 percent
- **c** 6.25 percent
- **d** 8 percent
- **e** 9.4 percent

18 If the price index in 1997 is equal to 130, and the inflation rate between 1997 and 1998 is 5 percent, what is the price index in 1998?

- **a** 136.5
- **b** 135
- **c** 125
- **d** 123.5
- **e** 105

19 A predictable inflation is

- **a** costly because higher inflation causes unemployment.
- **b** costly because people shift resources from production to predicting inflation.
- **c** costly because people do not alter their behaviour.
- **d** costly because it causes lost output.
- **e** none of the above.

Surpluses and Deficits

20 The government deficit will rise if

- **a** we buy more from other countries than we sell to them.
- **b** we sell more to other countries than we buy from them.
- **c** government revenues rise.
- **d** unemployment rises.
- **e** the baby boomers continue to run the country.

21 Most of the time since 1970, the current account

a deficit has been large.
b surplus has been large.
c deficit has been small.
d surplus has been small.
e has had alternating surpluses and deficits.

22 Deficits are a problem

a if they are caused by economic growth.
b only if they are international deficits, not government budget deficits.
c only if they are government budget deficits, not international deficits.
d only when they are caused by borrowing for consumption purposes.
e only when they are caused by borrowing to buy income-generating assets.

23 Which of the following will *increase* the Canadian current account deficit?

a Japan buys wheat from farmers in Canada.
b Japan buys wheat from farmers in Australia.
c Japan buys Canada Savings Bonds.
d Canada buys Toyotas from Japan.
e Canada sells coal to Japan.

Macroeconomic Policy Challenges and Tools

24 An example of fiscal policy is changing the

a interest rate.
b money supply.
c exchange rate.
d tax rate.
e all of the above.

25 Which of the following is *not* a policy challenge?

a lowering unemployment
b stabilizing the business cycle
c keeping inflation low
d stopping economic growth
e lowering government deficits

Short Answer Problems

1 What are the economic costs of unemployment?

2 Go to the Statistics Canada World Wide Web site (**http://www.statcan.ca**) or the Statistics Canada publication *The Consumer Price Index*, and find out the price level in December of the most recent year available, as well as the previous year, and calculate the inflation rate over that year.

3 What is meant by the value of money? Why does the value of money fall when there is inflation?

ⓒⓣ **4** The federal government gives full-time students a tax credit per month of studies. In 1980, Tracy received this credit, which was worth $50 per month, whereas in 1992 Jennifer received a credit worth $60 per month. In 1980, the price level was 62.3, and in 1992 it was 130. Is the value of the tax credit money worth more to Jennifer or Tracy? (Ignore any changes in taxes, tuition, etc.)

5 What is the current account? What has its recent history been like?

6 During each of the four parts of the business cycle, what happens to real GDP compared to potential GDP, and to the unemployment rate?

7 Workers and managers in the ABC Company have negotiated a wage agreement under the expectation that the inflation rate will be zero over the period of the contract. In order to protect workers against unpredictable inflation, however, the contract states that at the end of each year, the wage rate will increase by the same percentage as the increase in the consumer price index (CPI). At the beginning of the contract the CPI is 214 and the wage rate is set at $10 an hour. At the end of the first year the CPI is 225, and at the end of the second year the CPI is 234. What will the new wage rate become at the end of the first year? the second year?

8 Consider the following information about an economy: Population—25 million, employment—10 million, unemployment—1 million.

a What is the labour force in this economy?
b What is the unemployment rate?

9 Consider the following data on unemployment and the growth rate of real GDP from the country of Dazedland:

Year	Percentage Change in Real GDP	Unemployment Rate
1	2.0	7.0
2	3.0	6.0
3	1.0	7.8
4	0.0	9.0
5	–2.0	11.5
6	–0.3	9.5
7	3.0	6.5
8	1.5	7.5

a Identify the peaks and troughs of the business cycle for this economy.
b In what years is this economy in recession?
c What is the relation between unemployment and the business cycle for this economy?

ⓒ **10** Is more economic growth good or bad for a society?

ANSWERS

True/False/Uncertain and Explain

1 F Recently macroeconomics has merged the short-term and long-term issues into a broad study. (456)
2 U It depends on the benefits versus the costs of the higher growth. (461)
3 T As economy moves in recession, real GDP growth becomes negative, some workers become unemployed. (463)
4 F They are not counted as unemployed, but probably should be. (463)
5 F Canadian and U.S. unemployment move together, but recently Canadian unemployment > U.S. unemployment. (464)
6 F Inflation = [(130 – 110)/110] × 100 = 18.2%. (465)
7 U Inflation is costly, but so is getting rid of it, which increases unemployment. It depends on the relative size of the costs. (466–467)
8 F Sales > purchases implies international *surplus.* (467)
9 U It depends whether or not the government borrows to increase consumption (bad) or investment (good). (467)
10 T It chooses spending, taxation, and deficit which is fiscal policy. (469)

Multiple-Choice

1 d It was born during the Great Depression, when it focused on short-term problems, but recently it has merged studies of both. (456)
2 d Keynes did worry about them, noting they could be caused by too much government spending. Economists now study them and short-term problems together. **e** is short-term. (456)
3 e See Text Fig. 21.4—all four countries had a substantial fall in their growth rates around 1970. (460)
4 d To decide, must weigh both costs and benefits and see which is higher. (461–462)
5 a Upturn implies expansion implies unemployment falls. **b** and **e** are irrelevant, **c** is the average over the cycle, **d** is growth in potential GDP. (458)
6 e Definition. (457)
7 a Definition. (458)
8 d See Text Fig. 21.7 and its discussion. (464)
9 c **a** is a gain, **b** is cost to government, **d** is cost of growth, **e** is not a cost, just an outcome. (464)
10 d During the Great Depression of the 1930s. (463)
11 b Labour force = unemployed + employed. (462–463)
12 b Unemployment rate = unemployed/labour force = 1/10. (463)
13 e It would add extra unemployed workers to the measured rate. (463)
14 b Positive inflation implies current price level – past price level > 0 by definition. (465)
15 e Forecasting inflation becomes important because unpredictable inflation leads to unpredictable winners and losers because the value of money *falls.* (466)
16 e Historically, it was about the same as other countries until recently. (465–466)
17 c 6.25% = [(136 – 128)/128] _ 100. (465)
18 a Solve by inverting formula inflation rate = $((P_{1998} - P_{1997})/P_{1997}) \times 100$. (465)
19 e See Text discussion. (466)
20 d **a, b, e** are irrelevant, while **c** lowers deficit. Unemployment increasing implies more government outlays and less tax revenues. (467)
21 a See Text Fig. 21.10. (468)
22 d Both types of deficits can be problems, if they are for consumption, because they do not generate profits/income to help repay the resulting debts. **a** is irrelevant. (468)
23 d **a** and **e** lower the deficit, **b** and **c** are irrelevant. (467–468)

24 d **a** and **b** are monetary policy, **c** is neither. (469)

25 d Raising economic growth is a policy challenge. (469)

Short Answer Problems

1 The biggest cost of unemployment is the lost production and income. In addition, when workers are unemployed for long periods of time, their skills and abilities deteriorate, and so do their job prospects.

2 You should have used the following formula:

$$\text{Inflation rate} = \frac{\text{Current year's price level} - \text{Last year's price level}}{\text{Last year's price level}} \times 100.$$

3 The value of money is the quantity of goods and services that can be purchased with one unit of money. Since inflation means that prices are rising on average, it means that one unit of money will buy less. Thus the value of money falls when there is inflation.

4 There are two ways to answer this question. First, between 1980 and 1992 the tax credit has risen in value by 20 percent (= 10/50 × 100), while the price level has risen by 109 percent (= (130 – 62.3) × 100). Clearly prices have risen faster than the dollar value of the credit, lowering the value of this money, so Jennifer gains less from it. Second, you could calculate the purchasing power of the tax credit in terms of how many goods it can purchase (remember the price index measures the cost of a typical family's purchases). For Tracy the credit purchased 0.8 of a typical family's purchases (= 50/62.3), whereas for Jennifer it purchased 0.46 (= 60/130). Clearly Tracy gained more from the credit.

5 The current account includes our exports minus our imports and also takes interest payments paid to and received from the rest of the world into account. As Text Fig. 21.10 shows, Canada's current account has fluctuated since 1960, but since the late 1980s it has been persistently around 4 percent of GDP.

6 During the recession phase of the business cycle, the rate of growth of real GDP slows down and becomes negative, and real GDP falls below potential GDP. During this phase the unemployment rate is rising. At the trough, real GDP reaches its lowest point below potential GDP, and the unemployment rate is at its highest point over the cycle. The trough is a turning point between the recession phase and the expansion phase during which the rate of growth of real GDP increases and the unemployment rate falls. At the end of an expansion, the economy reaches the peak of the business cycle. The peak is characterized by real GDP at its highest point above potential GDP and the rate of unemployment is at its lowest point over the business cycle.

7 In order to determine the new wage rate at the end of the first year, we must determine the percentage increase in the CPI and apply that percentage change to the initial wage rate of $10 an hour. The percentage change in the CPI is [(225 – 214)/214] × 100, or 5.1 percent. Therefore the new wage rate at the end of the first year will be $10 × 1.051 = $10.51. During the second year, the increase in the CPI is 4 percent. Thus the new wage rate at the end of the second year will be $10.51 × 1.04 = $10.93.

8 a The labour force is 11 million, the sum of employment and unemployment.

b The unemployment rate is 9.1 percent, the number of unemployed as a percentage of the labour force.

9 a Peaks occur when the percentage change in real GDP turns from positive to negative, year 4. Troughs occur when the percentage change in real GDP turns from negative to positive, between years 6 and 7.

b The economy is in recession when the growth rate of real GDP is negative, years 5 and 6.

c There is a rough inverse relationship between the two variables—when real GDP is rising, the unemployment rate is falling (between years 1 and 2), and when real GDP is falling, the unemployment rate is rising (between years 4 and 5).

10 There is no correct answer to this question, since it depends on the balance of the costs versus the benefits of more growth—it is a normative question. However, a society would need to weigh the costs (lost consumption because of resources devoted to growth rather than consumption, potentially more rapid resource depletion and environmental pollution, and an increase in the frequency of job changes) against the benefits (an increase in consumption possibilities of individuals and governments) and make a judgement.

Chapter 22

Measuring GDP, Inflation, and Economic Growth

KEY CONCEPTS

Gross Domestic Product

Gross domestic product (GDP) is value of total production of goods and services in a year, and is a **flow** (quantity per unit of time). A **stock** is a quantity at a point in time.

- Key stock is **capital** (plant, equipment, buildings, and inventories used to produce goods and services).
  - Investment (I) = purchase of *new* capital.
  - Δ capital stock = **net investment.**
  - **Depreciation** = fall in stock of capital because of wear and tear.
  - **Gross investment** = net investment + replacing depreciated capital.
- Another key stock is **wealth** (value of all things people own), and Δ wealth = saving.
  - **Saving** (S) = income – consumption.
  - **Consumption expenditure** (C) = amount spent on consumption goods and services.

Flows of investment and saving interact with flows of income and consumption in the *circular flow* to determine total production = aggregate income = aggregate expenditure.

- Four economic sectors (firms, households, governments, rest of world) operate in three key markets (goods markets, resource markets, financial markets).
- Households sell resource services to firms in return for income – total household income = aggregate income (Y).
- Households place their S in financial markets, where it is borrowed by firms (to finance I), governments (to cover budget deficits), and rest of the world.
- Firms produce goods and services and sell them:
  - C to households
  - I to other firms
  - **Government expenditures** (G) to governments
  - **Net exports** (NX) = exports (X) – imports (M) to rest of world
- Governments buy goods and services, collect taxes from households and firms, give them transfer payments (**net taxes** [NT] = taxes – transfer payments – government debt interest payments), and borrow.
- Rest of world buys our exports and sells us imports, and borrows and lends to us in financial markets.

Circular flow shows how to value GDP.

- Firms' production of goods and services is purchased by economic decision makers (production = expenditure).
- Money earned by sales is used to pay incomes, rents, profits, etc. (expenditure = income).
- Result: aggregate income = aggregate production = aggregate expenditure ($Y = C + I + G + NX$).

Injections from circular flow (expenditures that did not originate with households) = **leakages** (income not spent on domestically produced goods).

- Household income (Y) = $C + S + NT$.
- Also, $Y = C + I + G + X - M$.
- Subtracting second equation from first and rearranging yields $I + G + X = S + NT + M$, or injections = leakages.

Circular flow shows how I is financed by national saving + borrowing from rest of world.

- **National saving** = household/firm saving + government saving.
- Government saving = $NT - G$ (if $NT > G$, government can lend some of its surplus, etc.), so national saving = $S + (NT - G)$, and $I = S + (NT - G)$.
- If foreigners sell Canadians more goods than they buy from us ($M > X$), we must borrow this amount from them to finance it, so part of their savings flows to us for investment purposes.
- If foreigners buy more from us than they sell to us ($M < X$), they must borrow from us to finance it, so part of our savings flows to them.

Measuring Canadian GDP

Statistics Canada measures GDP two ways on the basis of income = production = expenditure equality:

- *Expenditure approach* measures $C + I + G + NX$.
- Items not measured in GDP include
  - **intermediate goods and services** (bought by firms from each other and used as inputs in production)
  - used goods
  - financial assets
- *Income approach* adds up all incomes paid from firms to households, and makes adjustments.
  - Net domestic income at factor cost = wages, etc. + profits + interest/investment income + farm income + nonfarm unincorporated business income.
  - Net domestic product at market prices = net domestic income + indirect taxes – subsidies.
  - GDP = net domestic product + depreciation.
- To value production of an industry/firm, use value added of each sector, where **value added** = value of firms' production – value of intermediate goods bought from other firms.

The Price Level, Inflation, and Real GDP

There are two price indexes used to measure the price level:

- **Consumer Price Index** (CPI) measures current cost of typical urban family's base-period basket of consumer goods and services relative to base-period cost =

$$\frac{\text{Current-period's value of basket}}{\text{Base-period's value of basket}} \times 100.$$

- **GDP deflator** measures current cost of current-period basket of all produced goods and services relative to base-period cost =

$$\frac{\text{Nominal GDP}}{\text{Real GDP}} \times 100.$$

  - **Nominal GDP** uses current prices, and includes impact of inflation and changes in quantity of goods and services.
  - **Real GDP** uses base-period prices, and shows only quantity of goods and services.

The Biased CPI

- The CPI overstates inflation rate (biased upwards) because:
  - new goods replace old goods.
  - quality improvements create some part of price rises.
  - consumers change consumption towards cheaper goods not reflected in fixed-basket price index.
  - consumers substitute towards discount outlets not covered in CPI surveys.
- Magnitude of bias probably low in Canada, but it will lead to distorted contracts, more government outlays, and incorrect wage bargaining.

The Limitations of Real GDP

Real GDP is used to assess **economic welfare** (measure of economic well-being), make international comparisons and assess business cycles.

- Real GDP as a measure of economic welfare is flawed because:
  - price indexes overadjust for inflation.
  - real GDP does not include some items that increase economic welfare—household production, underground economy, leisure time, health and life expectancy, political freedoms.
  - real GDP does not include some items that lower economic welfare—depletion of resources, pollution.
- Comparing real GDP per capita between countries can be difficult due to price variation.
- Despite flaws, real GDP reasonably accurate indicator of recessions/expansions, but probably overstates fluctuations in economic welfare by ignoring household production and leisure time.

HELPFUL HINTS

1 Studying the circular flow and the national accounts may seem boring, but it is useful for several reasons. First, they provide crucial equalities that are the starting point for our economic model—studying this material will help you pass the course! Second, many current debates involve tradeoff between economic growth and environmental damage. Understanding what GDP does and does not measure is crucial to this debate. Third, in macroeconomics we study how several markets operate simultaneously in a joint, interrelated equilibrium—the circular flow gives us our first taste of this interrelation.

2 One of the key equations in this and future chapters is the identity:

$$Y = C + I + G + NX$$

This equation can be understood by carefully examining the circular flow. The circular flow shows a stylized view of the economy, which the equation attempts to measure. Macroeconomics tries to understand what affects GDP, and we start in this chapter by measuring production (GDP). However, we cannot directly measure production that easily. The circular flow helps us measure it indirectly. In the circular flow, production is purchased by the four economic decision makers (measured by expenditure), and the money earned from these sales is used to pay incomes. Therefore production can be measured in three equivalent ways: income = expenditure = value of production (GDP). This equation and the circular flow give us the crucial identity:

$$Y = C + I + G + NX$$

This equation underlies Chapters 25 and 26.

3 Be sure to distinguish carefully between intermediate goods and investment goods. Both are goods sold by one firm to another, but they differ in terms of their use. Intermediate goods are processed and then resold, while investment goods are final goods. Also note that the national income accounts include purchases of residential housing as investment because housing, like business capital stock, provides a continuous stream of value over time.

4 Note the difference between government expenditures on goods and services (G) and government transfer payments. Both involve payments by the government, but transfer payments are not payments for currently produced goods and services. Instead, they are simply a flow of money, just like taxes. Think of transfer payments as negative taxes. We define net taxes (NT) as taxes minus transfer payments – interest payments on government debt.

5 A price index for the current year is computed as the ratio of the value of a basket of goods in the current year to the value of the same basket of goods in a base year, multiplied by 100. It calculates the cost of purchasing the same choice of goods in two different years. There are two major differences between the price indexes presented in this chapter.

a Kinds of goods included in the basket. The goods used to calculate the CPI are purchased by a typical urban Canadian family. The goods used to calculate the GDP deflator, are *all* the goods and services in GDP, including capital goods.

b Basket year. The CPI basket uses commodities purchased in the *base* year. The GDP deflator basket uses goods purchased in the *current* year. Thus the CPI uses a fixed basket of goods (as long as the base year is fixed), while the basket of goods used to compute the GDP deflator changes each year.

6 It is very important to understand the difference between real and nominal GDP. Nominal GDP is the value, *in current prices,* of the output of final goods and services in the economy in a year. Real GDP evaluates those final goods and services *in the prices prevailing in a base year.*

Nominal GDP can rise from one year to the next either because prices rise or because the output of goods and services rises. A rise in real GDP, however, means that the output of goods and services has risen. Consider, for example, a simple economy that produces only pizzas. In most cases, we are more interested in real GDP—the number of pizzas we can eat!

SELF-TEST

True/False/Uncertain and Explain

1 Wage payments to households are an example of a real flow from firms to households.

2 A higher government deficit lowers investment, other things being equal.

3 Net investment gives the net addition to the capital stock.

4 In the aggregate economy, income is equal to expenditure and to GDP.

5 Goods that are produced this year but not sold this year do not add to this year's GDP.

6 If there were only households and firms and no government, market price and factor cost would be equal for any good.

7 If you are interested in knowing whether the economy is producing more output, you would look at real GDP rather than nominal GDP.

8 The GDP deflator is real GDP divided by nominal GDP, multiplied by 100.

9 The CPI overstates the inflation rate because it ignores substitution towards lower-quality goods by households.

10 If two economies have the same real GDP per person, then the standard of living is the same in each economy.

Multiple-Choice

Gross Domestic Product

1 The capital stock in the year 2000 would equal the capital stock in the year 1999

- **a** minus depreciation.
- **b** plus net investment plus depreciation.
- **c** plus gross investment.
- **d** plus net investment.
- **e** plus net investment minus depreciation.

2 Which of the following is a *real* flow from households to firms?

- **a** goods and services
- **b** resource services
- **c** payments for goods and services
- **d** payments for resource services
- **e** loans

3 Which of the following is a leakage from the circular flow of income?

- **a** exports
- **b** investment
- **c** saving
- **d** subsidies
- **e** government expenditures

4 For the aggregate economy, income equals

- **a** expenditure, but these are not generally equal to GDP.
- **b** GDP, but expenditure is generally less than these.
- **c** expenditure equals GDP.
- **d** expenditure equals GDP only if there is no government or foreign sectors.
- **e** expenditure equals GDP only if there is no depreciation.

5 Which of the following is *false*?

- **a** $Y = C + I + G + M - X$
- **b** $I + G + X = S + NT + M$
- **c** $Y = C + S + NT$
- **d** $Y + M = C + I + G + X$
- **e** $Y = C + I + G + NX$

6 The capital stock does *not* include the

a house owned by the Smith family.
b Smith family holdings of stock in the Smith Pickle Company.
c pickle factory building owned by the Smith family.
d pickle-packing machine in the pickle factory building owned by the Smith family.
e pickle inventories in the pickle factory building owned by the Smith family.

7 Saving can be measured as income minus

a taxes.
b transfer payments.
c consumption expenditure.
d net taxes minus consumption expenditure.
e net taxes plus subsidies.

Measuring Canadian GDP

8 The difference between the value of a firm's production and value of intermediate goods bought from other firms is

a net exports.
b investment in inventories.
c net taxes.
d transfer payments.
e value added.

9 To obtain the factor cost of a good from its market price

a add indirect taxes and subtract subsidies.
b subtract indirect taxes and add subsidies.
c subtract both indirect taxes and subsidies.
d add both indirect taxes and subsidies.
e subtract depreciation.

10 Interest plus miscellaneous investment income is a component of which approach to measuring GDP?

a income approach
b expenditure approach
c injections approach
d output approach
e opportunity cost approach

11 From the data in Table 22.1, what is net investment in Eastland?

a –$160
b $160
c $240
d $400
e $500

TABLE **22.1** DATA FROM EASTLAND

Amount	Item ($)
Wages, salaries, and supplementary labour income	800
Farmers' income	80
Government purchases of goods and services	240
Capital consumption	240
Gross private domestic investment	400
Personal income taxes net of transfer payments	140
Indirect taxes	120
Net exports	80
Consumption expenditures	640
Interest and miscellaneous investment income	100

12 From Table 22.1, what additional data are needed to compute net domestic income at factor cost?

a income of nonfarm unincorporated businesses
b the statistical discrepancy
c subsidies
d depreciation
e value added

13 From the data in Table 22.1, what is GDP in Eastland?

a $1,120
b $1,180
c $1,360
d $1,420
e Not calculable with the given information

The Price Level and Inflation

14 From the data in Table 22.2, compute Southton's nominal GDP in the current year.

a $197
b $208
c $209
d $226
e It cannot be calculated given the data.

TABLE **22.2** DATA FROM SOUTHTON

Item	Price ($) Base	Price ($) Current	Quantity Base	Quantity Current
Rubber ducks	1.00	1.25	100	100
Beach towels	9.00	6.00	12	14

15 From the data in Table 22.2, what is Southton's consumer price index for the current year?

a 112
b 105.6
c 100.5
d 100
e 94.7

16 From the data in Table 22.3, what is Northton's GDP deflator in 2000?

a 250
b 200
c 160
d 125
e 80

TABLE **22.3** DATA FROM NORTHTON

Year	Nominal GDP	Real GDP	GDP Deflator (1991 = 100)
1991	125	125	100
2000	250	200	
2001	275		122.22

17 Use the Northton data in Table 22.3. What is real GDP in 2001?

a 336.2
b 275
c 225
d 220
e 110

18 Consider the data in Table 22.4. There are only two goods in this economy. What is current nominal GDP?

a 192,000
b 189,900
c 95,000
d 93,000
e none of the above

TABLE **22.4** DATA FROM WESTLAND

	Price ($) Base Year	Price ($) Current Year	Quantity Base Year	Quantity Current Year
Bread	1.00	2.10	70,000	75,000
Computer disks	1.00	1.80	25,000	18,000

19 Consider the data in Table 22.4. There are only two goods in this economy. What is current real GDP?

a 192,000
b 189,900
c 95,000
d 93,000
e none of the above

20 Consider the data in Table 22.4. There are only two goods in this economy. What is the current value of the GDP deflator?

a 206
b 204
c 200
d 49
e none of the above

The Biased CPI

21 Which of the following is *not* a reason the Consumer Price Index overstates inflation?

a New goods of higher quality and prices replace old goods.
b Quality improvements create some part of price rises in existing goods and services.
c Consumers change consumption basket towards cheaper goods not reflected in fixed-basket price index.
d Consumers substitute towards using discount outlets not covered in CPI surveys.
e It does not measure the underground economy.

The Limitations of Real GDP

22 The underground economy is all economic activity that

a produces intermediate goods or services.
b is not taxed.
c is legal but unreported or is illegal.
d has negative social value.
e is conducted underground.

23 Given that pollution is a by-product of some production processes,

a GDP accountants adjust GDP downward.
b GDP accountants adjust GDP upward.
c GDP accountants do not adjust GDP unless pollution is a serious problem, as in the former East Germany.
d GDP tends to overstate economic welfare.
e GDP tends to understate economic welfare.

24 Which of the following is *not* a reason for GDP incorrectly measuring the value of total output?

a leisure time
b nonmarket activities
c the underground economy
d capital consumption
e externalities such as pollution

25 Real GDP

a overestimates welfare if there is an underground economy.
b is an accurate measure of welfare.
c corrects nominal GDP with purchasing power parity prices.
d overestimates welfare if there is pollution.
e overestimates welfare because it implies economists provide useful services.

Short Answer Problems

ⓒⓣ **1** How can we measure gross domestic product by using either the expenditure or the income approach, when neither of these approaches actually measures production?

2 Suppose nominal GDP rises by 75 percent between year 1 and year 2.

a If the average level of prices has also risen by 75 percent between year 1 and year 2, what has happened to real GDP?
b If the average level of prices has risen by less than 75 percent between year 1 and year 2, has real GDP increased or decreased?

3 What *productive* activities are *not* measured and thus are *not* included in GDP? Is this lack of measurement a serious problem?

ⓒⓣ **4** Economic analysts who studied the former Soviet economy in the late 1980s noted that the Soviet Union produced many natural resources that it did not sell on the world market, but instead turned into consumption and investment goods. Calculations showed that the market value of the Soviet natural resources on the world market was greater than the market value of the Soviet processed goods.

a What can you say about the value added of these goods?
b Many politicians in Canada argue that we would be better off if we did not sell our unprocessed resources, but worked to process the goods first instead (this argument is often made about log shipments out of British Columbia or farm products on the Prairies). Was the former Soviet Union made better off by processing its resources? Is it always better to process goods before exporting them?

5 Use the data for Northland given in Table 22.5 to compute the following:

TABLE **22.5** DATA FROM NORTHLAND

Amount	Item (billions of $)
Consumption expenditure (*C*)	600
Taxes (*Tax*)	400
Transfer payments (*TR*)	250
Exports (*X*)	240
Imports (*M*)	220
Government spending on goods and services (*G*)	200
Gross investment (*I*)	150
Depreciation (*Depr*)	60

a GDP
b net investment
c net exports
d after-tax income
e saving
f total leakages from and total injections into the circular flow of income (Are they equal?)
ⓒⓣ **g** the value of each of the three sources of financing for investment

6 Use the data for the same economy given in Table 22.6 to compute:

TABLE **22.6** DATA FOR NORTHLAND

Amount	Item (billions of $)
Wages, salaries, and supplementary labour income	550
Indirect taxes	120
Subsidies	20
Farmers' income	20
Corporate profits	80
Interest and miscellaneous investment income	90
Depreciation	60
Income of nonfarm unincorporated businesses	70

a net domestic income at factor cost
b net domestic product at market prices
c GDP

7 Table 22.7 gives data for Southland, where there are three consumption goods: bananas, coconuts, and grapes.

TABLE **22.7** DATA FOR SOUTHLAND

		Base Period		Current Period	
Goods	Quantity in Base-Period Basket	Price ($)	Expenditure ($)	Price ($)	Expenditure ($)
Bananas	120	6		8	
Coconuts	60	8		10	
Grapes	40	10		9	

a Complete the table by computing expenditures for the base period and expenditures for the same quantity of each good in the current period.
b What is the value of the basket of consumption goods in the base period? in the current period?
c What is the consumer price index for the current period?
ⓒⓣ **d** On the basis of the data in this table, would you predict consumers would make any substitutions between goods between the base period and the current period? If so, what kind of problems would this create for your measurement of the CPI?

8 Table 22.8 gives data for Easton, where there are three final goods included in GDP: pizzas, beer, and CDs.
a Complete the table by computing expenditure on each good evaluated at base-period prices.
b What is the value of nominal GDP in the current period?
c What is the value of real GDP in the current period?
d What is the GDP deflator in the current period?

TABLE **22.8**

		Current Period		Base Period	
Goods	Current-Year Output	Price ($)	Expenditure ($)	Price ($)	Expenditure ($)
Pizza	110	8	880	6	
Beer	50	10	500	8	
CDs	50	9	450	10	

9 Table 22.9 gives data for the country of Weston.

TABLE **22.9** DATA FOR WESTON

Year	Nominal GDP	Real GDP	GDP Deflator
1995	3,055		94
1996		3,170	100
1997	3,410	3,280	
1998		3,500	108

a Complete Table 22.9.
b What is the base year for the GDP deflator?
c Calculate the percentage change in nominal GDP, real GDP, and the GDP deflator between 2000 and 2001. Was the increase in nominal GDP due mostly to an increase in real GDP or to an increase in the price level?

10 Figure 22.1 shows the circular flow for Northweston. All amounts are in thousands of dollars.

FIGURE **22.1**

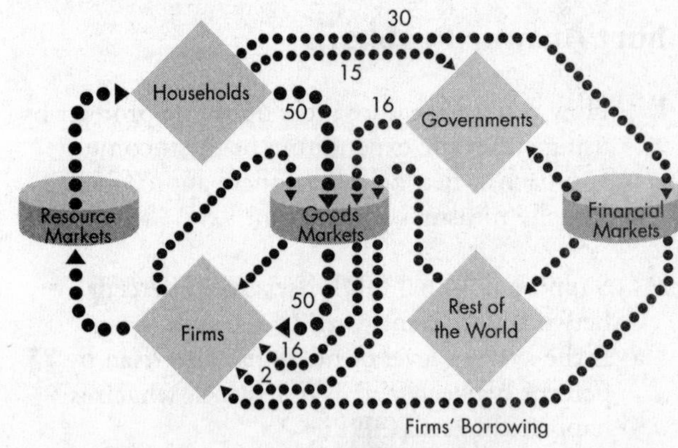

Use Fig. 22.1 to calculate for Northweston:
a GDP
b aggregate expenditure

c investment
d aggregate income
e household saving
f government borrowing or saving
g foreign borrowing or saving
h firms' borrowing

ANSWERS

True/False/Uncertain and Explain

1 F It is an example of money flow in payment for real flow. (477)
2 T Higher deficit implies lower $(NT - G)$, which implies lower $I = S + (NT - G)$. (480)
3 T Net investment nets out depreciation (replacement of worn-out capital), leaving only new capital additions. (476)
4 T From circular flow, firm production is sold (expenditure) and earnings used to pay out incomes. (479)
5 F GDP measures production in current year. (482)
6 T Market price = factor cost + taxes – subsidies. (483)
7 T Real GDP measures amount of goods and services, while nominal measures current dollar value and includes inflation's impact. (486)
8 F GDP deflator = [(nominal GDP)/(real GDP)] × 100. (486)
9 F It overstates substitution towards cheaper goods, or the presence of higher-quality goods with higher prices. (488–489)
10 U Real GDP is imperfect measure of standard of living; answer depends on factors such as prices in each country. (492–493)

Multiple-Choice

1 d Definition. (476)
2 b **a** is in opposite direction, others are money flows. (477)
3 c Definition – income *not* spent on domestic goods. (480)
4 c Expenditure = money earned by sales of produced goods which is used to pay incomes (including profits). (479)
5 a Should be $X - M$ and not $M - X$. (479–480)
6 b Equity is financial asset, not capital. (476)
7 d From $S = (Y - NT) - C$. (480)
8 e Definition. (483–484)
9 b Market price = factor cost + indirect taxes – subsidies. (483)
10 a Definition. (482)
11 b Net investment = gross investment – capital consumption. (476)
12 a Table lists other four components of resource incomes. (482–483)
13 c $Y = C + I + G + NX = 640 + 400 + 240 + 80 = 1{,}360$. (481)
14 c Nominal GDP = sum of dollar value (= current price × current quantity) of all goods. (486–487)
ⓔ **15 e** CPI = [(sum of current prices × base quantities)/(sum of base prices × base quantities)] × 100. (485)
16 d GDP deflator = [(nominal GDP)/(real GDP)] × 100. (486)
17 c Real GDP = [(nominal GDP)/(GDP deflator)] × 100. (486)
ⓔ **18 b** Nominal GDP = sum of current expenditures on all goods. (486)
ⓔ **19 d** Real GDP = sum of current quantities at base prices. (486)
ⓔ **20 b** GDP deflator = [(nominal GDP)/(real GDP)] × 100. (486)
21 e This answer is problem with real GDP. (488–491)
22 c Definition. (490–491)
23 d No such adjustment occurs, so GDP overstates economic welfare. (491)
24 d Capital consumption is depreciation and is part of GDP. (490–492)
25 d **a** is backwards, **b** is not true, **c** and **e** are nonsense. (490–492)

Short Answer Problems

ⓔ **1** The analysis of the circular flow showed that firms produce goods and services (what we wish to measure), sell them (what the expenditure approach measures), and then use the proceeds to pay for incomes, rents, profits, etc. (what the income approach measures). Therefore expenditure = production = income.

2 a Real GDP is unchanged. The increased value of goods and services is only because of increased prices.
b The fact that prices have risen less in proportion to the increase in nominal GDP means that real GDP has increased.

3 Activities that produce goods and services that are not included in GDP are production in the underground economy and household production. The first of these is not reported because the activities themselves are illegal or are legal but are not reported to circumvent taxes or government regulations. The second includes productive activities that households perform for themselves. Because they do not hire someone else to mow the lawn or wash the car, it is not included in GDP. The seriousness of the problem depends on the actual size of activity. The underground economy is usually estimated as about 5 to 15 percent of the Canadian economy.

ⓒ **4 a** The value added was negative, since the value of produced goods was less than the value of intermediate products.

b If we use the measure of real GDP, the former Soviet Union was not made better off—the action of processing lowered real GDP compared to just selling the resources on the world market. Clearly, it is *not* always better to process goods before export; it may lower GDP.

5 a GDP = $C + I + G + (X - M)$ = \$970 billion.

b Net $I = I - Depr$ = \$90 billion.

c $NX = X - M$ = \$20 billion.

d After-tax income = GDP + $TR - Tax$ = \$820 billion.

e Saving = after-tax income – C = \$220 billion.

f Total leakages = $(Tax - TR) + M + S$ = \$590 billion. Total injections = $I + G + X$ = \$590 billion. So, total leakages = total injections.

ⓒ **g** $I = S + (NT - G) + (M - X)$ or 150 = 220 + (150 – 200) + (220 – 240). Saving contributes \$220 billion, the government budget deficit reduces investment by \$50 billion, and the net export surplus reduces investment by \$20 billion.

6 a Net domestic income at factor cost = wages, salaries, and supplementary labour income + interest and miscellaneous investment income + corporate profits + farmers' income + income of nonfarm unincorporated business = \$810 billion.

b Net domestic product at market prices = net domestic product at factor cost + indirect taxes – subsidies = \$910 billion.

c GDP = net domestic product at market prices + depreciation = \$970 billion.

7 a Table 22.7 is completed here as Table 22.7 Solution. Note that the base-period quantities are evaluated at current prices to find the value of quantities in the current period.

TABLE **22.7** SOLUTION

Goods	Quantity in Base-Period Basket	Base Period Price ($)	Base Period Expenditure ($)	Current Period Price ($)	Current Period Expenditure ($)
Bananas	120	6	720	8	960
Coconuts	60	8	480	10	600
Grapes	40	10	400	9	360

b The value of the basket of consumption goods in the base period is the sum of the expenditures in that period: \$1,600. The value of the basket of consumption goods in the current period is obtained as the sum of the values of quantities in that period: \$1,920.

c The Consumer Price Index is the ratio of the value of quantities in the current period to the base period expenditure, times 100:

$$\text{CPI} = (1{,}920/1{,}600) \times 100 = 120.$$

ⓒ **d** Since the price of grapes has fallen relative to the prices of bananas and coconuts, we would expect that consumers would substitute towards the cheaper grapes and away from bananas and coconuts. This substitution means that our CPI measure will be biased upwards.

8 a Table 22.8 is completed here as Table 22.8 Solution. Base-period expenditure for each item is obtained by evaluating the current-period quantity at the base-year price.

TABLE **22.8** SOLUTION

Goods	Current-Year Output	Current Period Price ($)	Current Period Expenditure ($)	Base Period Price ($)	Base Period Expenditure ($)
Pizza	110	8	880	6	660
Beer	50	10	500	8	400
CDs	50	9	450	10	500

b The value of nominal GDP in the current period is the sum of expenditures in the current period: \$1,830.

c The value of real GDP in the current period is the sum of the current-period quantities evaluated at base-period prices; in other words, what the expenditures would have been at base-year prices: \$1,560.

d The GDP deflator for the current period is the ratio of nominal GDP to real GDP, times 100: GDP deflator = $(1{,}830/1{,}560) \times 100 = 117.3$.

9 a Table 22.9 is completed here as Table 22.9 Solution. The following equation is used: GDP deflator = (nominal GDP/real GDP) × 100.

TABLE **22.9** SOLUTION

Year	Nominal GDP	Real GDP	GDP Deflator
1995	3,055	3,250	94
1996	3,170	3,170	100
1997	3,410	3,280	104
1998	3,780	3,500	108

b The base year is 1999—GDP deflator is 100.

c Percentage change in nominal GDP = [(3,780 – 3,410)/3,410] × 100 = 10.9%. Percentage change in real GDP = [(3,500 – 3,280)/3,280] × 100 = 6.7%. Percentage change in GDP deflator = [(108 – 104)/104] × 100 = 3.8%. Since the percentage change in real GDP is higher than the percentage change in the GDP deflator, most of the increase in nominal GDP is due to an increase in real GDP.

10 a GDP can be calculated from how households spend their income: $Y = C + S + NT = 50 + 30 + 15 = \$95{,}000$.

b Aggregate expenditure = GDP = $95,000.

c Investment is the only missing component of aggregate expenditure, and can be deduced from the equation $Y = C + I + G + NX$ or $95 = 50 + I + 16 + 2$, implying $I = \$27{,}000$. (Note that the components of aggregate expenditure must all flow through the goods market.)

d Aggregate income paid to households must equal aggregate expenditure earned by firms, so it equals $95,000.

e Household saving goes from households to financial markets, and equals $30,000.

f Government borrowing or saving = $NT - G = 15 - 16 = -\$1{,}000$, borrowing.

g From examining the goods market, foreign borrowing or saving = $X - M = \$2{,}000$ of borrowing.

h Firms' borrowing comes from the fact that saving = firms' borrowing + government borrowing + foreign borrowing, or 30 = firms' borrowing + 1 + 2, so that firms' borrowing = $27,000.

Chapter 23

Measuring Employment and Unemployment

KEY CONCEPTS

Employment and Wages

Real GDP supplied depends on the level of employment. Statistics Canada surveys households to estimate job status.

- **Working-age population** = number of people 15 years and over.
- **Labour force** = employed + unemployed
  - Employed = those with full-time and part-time jobs.
  - Unemployed = without work, actively seeking within last 4 weeks, waiting to be called back after layoff, or waiting to start new job within 4 weeks.
  - Some part-time workers are involuntary as they want a full-time job.
- **Unemployment rate** = percentage of labour force who are unemployed. It increases in recessions, but has no trend recently.
- Involuntary part-time rate = percentage of labour force who are part-time but want full-time. It has an upward trend recently, and increases in recessions.
- **Labour force participation rate** = percentage of working-age population who are in labour force. It has strong upward trend, but decreases in recessions because of **discouraged workers** (people who temporarily leave labour force in a recession).
- **Employment-to-population ratio** = percentage of working-age population with jobs. It has increased overall since 1960s (many new jobs created), but decreases in recessions.
- Participation and employment rates down for men and up (strongly) for women since 1960s, creating increase in overall rate.
- To see quantity of labour employed, examine **aggregate hours** = total hours worked.
  - Has upward trend, decreases in recessions.
  - Hours per worker decreased until earlier 1990s, with faster decreases in recessions.
- **Real wage rate** = quantity of goods an hour's work can buy = **money wage rate** (dollars per hour)/price level. Has upward trend, but at a slower rate since early 1970s.

Unemployment and Full Employment

- People become unemployed when they
  - are laid off (**job losers**).
  - voluntarily quit (**job leavers**).
  - enter (**entrants**) or re-enter (**re-entrants**) the labour force.
- People end unemployment when they are hired, recalled, or withdraw from the labour force.
- Primary source of unemployment is job loss, which fluctuates strongly with business cycle.
- There is a wide range of duration of unemployment. Duration is higher in recessions.
- Unemployment rate higher for younger people because
  - they try different types of jobs more frequently.
  - firms hire them on a trial basis.
  - more of them are out of labour force, and so unemployment rate is high for those in labour force, but low for group as a whole.

The types of unemployment are frictional, structural, seasonal, and cyclical.

- **Frictional unemployment** is due to normal turnover, people searching for good job matches, and is healthy part of dynamic economy. It depends on the number of entrants/re-entrants and job creation/destruction. It is higher in Canada than in the United States due to Canada's employment insurance generosity.
- **Structural unemployment** is job losses in industries/regions declining due to technological change, and tends to last longer than frictional unemployment. It was high around 1980 due to oil price hikes and increasing international competition.
- **Seasonal unemployment** occurs when number of jobs decreases in certain seasons (for example, it increases in Atlantic provinces in winter).
- **Cyclical unemployment** is the fluctuations in unemployment over the business cycle. It increases in recession, decreases in expansion.

Natural rate of unemployment—only frictional, structural, and seasonal unemployment occurring, or no cyclical unemployment.

- Actual unemployment rate fluctuates around the natural rate, as real GDP fluctuates around potential GDP.
  - When real GDP $<$ potential GDP, unemployment rate $>$ natural rate.
  - When real GDP $>$ potential GDP, unemployment rate $<$ natural rate.
- **Full employment** occurs when unemployment rate = natural rate.

HELPFUL HINTS

1 In a dynamic economy, some unemployment is efficient. There are economic benefits of frictional unemployment to the individual and society. Younger workers typically experience periods of unemployment trying to find jobs that match their skills and interests. The benefit of the resulting frictional unemployment is a more satisfying and productive work life. Society benefits because the frictional unemployment that accompanies such a job-search process allows workers to find jobs in which they are more productive. As a result, the total production of goods and services in the economy increases. (Compare this case with the case for graduates in the Republic of China up until the 1990s. They were assigned jobs upon graduation, with very little personal input about type of job or location.)

On the other hand, structurally unemployed workers will not get a new job without retraining or relocation. This fact means a much greater cost to the worker and society—for example, structurally unemployed workers are typically unemployed for much longer time periods. These workers bear the brunt of the cost of restructuring industries in our economy, although society gains in the long run from the shift of resources to the new industries.

2 The term "full employment," or its equivalent "the natural rate of unemployment," does not mean that everyone has a job. Rather, it means that the only unemployment is frictional, structural, and seasonal—there is no cyclical unemployment. (Note this definition implies the natural rate is higher in the wintertime!)

It is possible for the actual rate of unemployment to be less than the natural rate of unemployment, because it is possible for the level of employment to exceed full employment. In these situations, people are spending too little time searching for jobs, and therefore less-productive job matches are being made.

3 There are four different types of unemployment, but defining these types does not explain them. Explanations of how unemployment occurs is a goal of the remaining chapters in the textbook!

SELF-TEST

True/False/Uncertain and Explain

1 The employment-to-population ratio is the percentage of working-age population in the labour force.

2 If the employment-to-population ratio increases, unemployment decreases.

3 If the number of discouraged workers decreases, the employment-to-population ratio decreases as they begin to look for jobs.

4 George was laid off last month, and is waiting to be recalled to his old job, so he is not actively seeking work. George is *not* counted as unemployed.

5 The real wage rate has an upward trend since the 1970s.

6 Being unemployed for a few months after graduating from university hurts the graduate.

7 A decline in the number of jobs in the automobile sector matched by an equal increase in the number of jobs in the banking sector will not alter the unemployment rate.

8 At full employment, there is no unemployment.

9 Bill has just graduated from high school and is looking for his first job. Bill is frictionally unemployed.

10 Fluctuations in unemployment over the business cycle create frictional unemployment.

Multiple-Choice

Employment and Wages

1 Including discouraged workers in the measured unemployment rate would

- **a** not change the measured unemployment rate.
- **b** lower the measured unemployment rate.
- **c** raise the natural rate of unemployment.
- **d** raise the full employment rate.
- **e** raise the measured unemployment rate.

2 In a country with a working-age population of 20 million, 13 million are employed, 1.5 million are unemployed, and 1 million of the employed are working part-time, half of whom wish to work full-time. The size of the labour force is

- **a** 20 million.
- **b** 15.5 million.
- **c** 14.5 million.
- **d** 13 million.
- **e** 11.5 million.

3 In a country with a working-age population of 20 million, 13 million are employed, 1.5 million are unemployed, and 1 million of the employed are working part-time, half of whom wish to work full-time. The size of the labour force participation rate is

- **a** 75.5 percent.
- **b** 72.5 percent.
- **c** 65 percent.
- **d** 57.5 percent.
- **e** none of the above.

4 In a country with a working-age population of 20 million, 13 million are employed, 1.5 million are unemployed, and 1 million of the employed are working part-time, half of whom wish to work full-time. The unemployment rate is

- **a** 10 percent.
- **b** 10.3 percent.
- **c** 11.5 percent.
- **d** 15.4 percent.
- **e** none of the above.

5 In a recession, typically

- **a** unemployment decreases.
- **b** participation rates increase.
- **c** employment-to-population ratios decrease.
- **d** employment-to-population ratios increase.
- **e** none of the above.

6 Who of the following would be counted as unemployed in Canada?

- **a** Doris only works five hours a week but is looking for a full-time job.
- **b** Kanhaya has stopped looking for work since he was unable to find a suitable job during a two-month search.
- **c** Sharon is a college student with no job.
- **d** Maurice has been laid off from his job for 20 weeks but expects to be called back soon.
- **e** Bogdan has been laid off from his job but does not expect to be called back, and is not looking.

7 In the past 20 years in the labour market

a real wages have decreased in all industries.
b real wages have increased in all industries.
c employment has decreased strongly.
d the unemployment rate has risen on average.
e the unemployment rate has fluctuated without any trend.

8 If the number of discouraged workers increases, all else unchanged, then the

a unemployment rate will increase.
b employment-to-population ratio will decrease.
c labour force participation rate will increase.
d labour force participation rate will decrease.
e employment-to-population ratio will increase.

9 Initially the money wage rate is $10 per hour, and the price level is 100. If the money wage rate increases to $20 per hour and the price level increases to 125, what happens to the real wage rate?

a It stays the same.
b It doubles in value.
c It decreases in value.
d It increases in value, but by less than double.
e It increases in value, by more than double.

10 If the employment-to-population ratio increases, then

a the unemployment rate *must* decrease.
b the labour force participation rate *must* increase.
c the labour force participation rate will be unaffected.
d aggregate hours worked *must* increase.
e none of the above.

11 The recent increase in the Canadian labour force participation rate is largely due to the

a increase in female labour force participation.
b increase in male labour force participation.
c decrease in the number of baby boomers.
d increase in youth labour force participation.
e decrease in the number of discouraged workers.

12 The labour force participation rate fluctuates with the business cycle due to fluctuations in

a cyclical unemployment.
b discouraged workers.
c natural unemployment.
d real wage rates.
e the involuntary part-time rate.

Unemployment and Full Employment

13 Which of the following events would raise cyclical unemployment?

a real GDP growth slows down or turns negative
b an increase in unemployment benefits
c an increase in the pace of technological change
d an increase in both job destruction and job creation
e all of the above

14 Unemployment will increase if there is an increase in the number of people

a retiring.
b withdrawing from the labour force.
c recalled from layoffs.
d leaving jobs to go to school.
e leaving school to find jobs.

15 Who of the following would be considered structurally unemployed?

a a Saskatchewan farmer who has lost her farm and is unemployed until retrained
b a Nova Scotia fishery worker who is searching for a better job closer to home
c a steelworker who is laid off but who expects to be called back soon
d an office worker who has lost her job because of a general slowdown in economic activity
e none of the above

16 Who of the following would be considered cyclically unemployed?

a a Saskatchewan farmer who has lost her farm and is unemployed until retrained
b a Nova Scotia fishery worker who is searching for a better job closer to home
c a steelworker who is laid off but who expects to be called back soon
d an office worker who has lost her job because of a general slowdown in economic activity
e none of the above

17 Who of the following would be considered frictionally unemployed? A steelworker who

a loses her job because of technological change.
b is laid off but expects to be called back very soon.
c gives up her job because she retires.
d decides to leave the labour force and become a full-time ballet student.
e becomes discouraged and stops looking for a job.

18 If the economy is at full employment, then the
- **a** entire population is employed.
- **b** entire labour force is employed.
- **c** only unemployment is frictional unemployment plus discouraged workers.
- **d** unemployment rate is less than 3 percent.
- **e** only unemployment is frictional, structural, and seasonal unemployment.

19 In a recession, what is the largest source of the increase in unemployment?
- **a** job leavers
- **b** job losers
- **c** new entrants to the labour force
- **d** re-entrants to the labour force
- **e** involuntary part-time workers

20 At full employment, there is no
- **a** natural unemployment.
- **b** unemployment.
- **c** cyclical unemployment.
- **d** structural unemployment.
- **e** frictional unemployment.

21 Unemployment caused by permanently decreased demand for horse-drawn carriages is an example of
- **a** cyclical unemployment.
- **b** seasonal unemployment.
- **c** frictional unemployment.
- **d** structural unemployment.
- **e** discouraged unemployment.

22 The participation rate for those 15–24 years old fell from 70.6 percent in 1989 to 61.5 percent by 1996. The fall in the participation rate was likely due to
- **a** many young people getting jobs.
- **b** many young discouraged workers now being counted as unemployed.
- **c** young people quitting jobs to go to school.
- **d** unemployed young people giving up on searching for jobs.
- **e** a fall in the number of young people.

23 The natural rate of unemployment is
- **a** the rate at which unemployment equals 0 percent.
- **b** the same as cyclical unemployment.
- **c** the rate at which cyclical unemployment equals 6 percent.
- **d** the rate at which cyclical unemployment equals 0 percent.
- **e** none of the above.

24 People end unemployment when they
- **a** graduate from school.
- **b** are laid off.
- **c** enter the labour force.
- **d** quit their job.
- **e** are recalled from a layoff.

25 The duration of a spell of unemployment typically
- **a** decreases in a recession and increases in an expansion.
- **b** decreases in a recession and in an expansion.
- **c** increases in a recession and in an expansion.
- **d** increases in a recession and decreases in an expansion.
- **e** does not change during recessions and expansions.

Short Answer Problems

ⓒⓣ **1** Explain why an economy does not have 0 percent unemployment when it has full employment.

ⓒⓣ **2** Should the government try to force the unemployment rate down as close to zero as possible? Discuss some problems such a policy might create.

3 Consider the following information about an economy: working-age population—20 million; full-time employment—8 million; part-time employment—2 million (1 million of whom wish they had full-time jobs); unemployment—1 million.
- **a** What is the labour force in this economy? What is the labour force participation rate?
- **b** What is the unemployment rate?
- **c** What is the involuntary part-time rate?
- **d** What is the employment-to-population ratio?
- **e** If 0.6 million of those unemployed are frictionally, structurally, and seasonally unemployed, what is the natural rate of unemployment?
- **f** What is the amount of cyclical unemployment?

4 Consider the economy described in Short Answer Problem **3**. Over the next year, there is no change in the working-age population, but the number of unemployed rises to 1.5 million, while the number of full-time employed rises to 8.5 million. There are no changes in part-time employment.
- **a** Calculate the new labour force participation rate, the new employment-to-population ratio, and the new unemployment rate.

b How is it possible that all three of these rates rose at the same time? Explain briefly. (*Hint:* what do you think has happened to the number of discouraged workers over this time period?)

5 In Chapter 21 we learned about the costs of unemployment. Are they more severe for frictional or structural unemployment?

6 Explain the difference between cyclical and structural unemployment. How would you tell a cyclically unemployed person from a structurally unemployed person?

ⓒ **7** The recent reforms to employment insurance reduce the compensation received while unemployed, reduce the total period you can get compensation, and make it more difficult to get compensation if you quit or are fired for "just cause." Explain what these reforms might do to the four types of unemployment. Are these reforms a good idea from the unemployment viewpoint?

8 Examine each of the following changes in John Carter's labour market activity, and explain whether they constitute unemployment, employment, or being out of the labour force. If unemployment, which of the four types of unemployment is represented?

a John graduates from Barsoom High and starts looking for a job.
b John has no luck finding the full-time job he wants and takes a part-time job cleaning out the canals.
c Canal-cleaning doesn't work out for John because of unforeseen allergies, so he quits.
d Discouraged by the lack of work, John stops looking and stays home watching his favourite soap opera, *As Mars Turns.*
e John sees an advertisement on TV for the Barsoom Swordfighter School, and enrolls to get his B.S.F.
f John graduates at the top of his class and joins up with Princess Dejah Thoris' guard.
g An inventor at Barsoom University comes up with a new laser personal defence system, and the Princess disbands her guard—John spends a long time looking for work.
h John gets a job cleaning up after the sandstorms, but once the wet season comes along, he is laid off.
i John sees an advertisement seeking someone to help explore the ruins of the lost city of Rhiannon and signs up as security—the six-armed tribes are particularly ferocious there.

ⓒ **9** Consider the data from 1995 in Table 23.1 on Canada as a whole and Newfoundland specifically.

TABLE **31.2**

Economy	Labour Force Participation Rate	Unemployment Rate	Employment-to-Population Ratio
Canada	64.8	9.5	58.6
Newfoundland	53.1	18.3	43.3

Newfoundland has twice the unemployment of Canada, as well as a radically lower employment-to-population ratio and labour force participation rate. By examining these, can you get any insight into the impact of such a high unemployment rate on the labour market in Newfoundland? Why is the gap in the employment-to-population ratio (15.3 points) so much bigger than the unemployment gap (8.8 points)?

ⓒ **10** It has been argued that one of the reasons Canada has a higher unemployment rate than the United States is that our more generous employment insurance system keeps people measured as unemployment in Canada who would be out of the labour force in the United States. Is this generosity good or bad?

ANSWERS

True/False/Uncertain and Explain

1 F Percentage with jobs. (502)
2 U True if participation decreases or does not increase by much, otherwise false. (502)
3 F This change will only change labour force participation. (502)
4 F Since waiting for recall, he is counted. (500)
5 T See text discussion. (504)
6 U It depends on whether time unemployed leads to better job. (507)
7 F Workers retrain/relocate leading to more structural unemployment. (508)
8 F Full employment = frictional, structural, and seasonal unemployment. (509)
9 T Searching for jobs = frictionally unemployed. (507)
10 F They create *cyclical* unemployment. (508)

Multiple-Choice

1 **e** It would add extra unemployed workers to the measured rate. (502)
2 **c** Employed + unemployed. (500)
3 **b** Labour force/working-age population = 14.5/20 = 72.5 percent. (502)
4 **b** Unemployed/labour force = 1.5/14.5 = 10.3 percent. (501)
5 **c** Since job losses have increased. (501–503)
6 **d** Doris is employed, Kanhaya should be looking for work, Sharon is out of labour force, Bogdan does not expect to be called back. (500)
7 **e** See text discussion. (504)
8 **d** Discouraged workers were unemployed, but stop looking and exit labour force, so unemployment rate decreases, labour force participation decreases, employment-to-population ratio unchanged. (502)
9 **d** Money wage doubles, but since the price level increases by 25 percent, real wage doesn't double. (504)
10 **e** Any of **a** to **d** *could* occur, but they do not *have to* occur. (502–503)
11 **a** See Text Fig. 23.3 and discussion. (502)
12 **b** In recessions, they quit looking for jobs and exit the labour force, and in expansions they re-enter the labour force and start looking for jobs. (502)
13 **a** **b** to **d** raise frictional or structural unemployment, but if real GDP growth slows down, cyclical unemployment increases. (508)
14 **e** Others all lower unemployment. (505)
15 **a** Structural unemployment includes having wrong skills. Others are frictional or cyclical unemployment. (508)
16 **d** Cyclical unemployment is due to economy-wide slowdowns. (508)
17 **b** **a** is structural, rest are not officially unemployed. (508)
18 **e** Definition. (509)
19 **b** See text discussion. (505)
20 **c** Definition. (509)
21 **d** Definition—unemployment caused by structural change. (507–508)
22 **d** **a** and **b** would raise participation rate, **c** is unlikely, **e** would not affect *rate.* (506–507)
23 **d** Definition. (508)
24 **e** Others are examples of entering unemployment. (505)
25 **d** See Text Fig. 23.8. (506)

Short Answer Problems

ⓒⓣ **1** An economy always has some unemployment, of people searching for jobs—frictional, structural, and seasonal unemployment. We define full unemployment as when there is only frictional, structural, and seasonal unemployment.

ⓒⓣ **2** Pushing down the unemployment rate would entail stopping frictional unemployment, which would reduce the number of good job matches, and stopping structural unemployment, which would likely prevent the kind of structural readjustment the economy needs. Therefore it does not seem like a good idea to get unemployment as close to zero as possible!

3 **a** The labour force is 11 million, the sum of employment and unemployment. The labour force participation rate = percentage of working-age population who are in the labour force = 11/20 or 55 percent.

b The unemployment rate is 9.1 percent, the number of unemployed as a percentage of the labour force.

c It is 9.1 percent, the percentage of the labour force who are part-time and want full-time.

d It is 50 percent, percentage of working-age population with a job.

e The natural rate of unemployment is frictional plus structural plus seasonal unemployment. In our case, it is the rate of unemployment if unemployment were only 0.6 million. Thus the natural rate of unemployment is 5.45 percent.

f Cyclical unemployment is actual unemployment minus natural unemployment, or 0.4 million.

4 **a** The labour force participation rate = percentage of working-age population who are employed + unemployed = (1.5 + 8.5 + 2)/20 = 60 percent. The employment-to-population ratio is the percentage of the population with a job = 52.5 percent. The unemployment rate is the percentage of the labour force without a job = 12.5 percent.

b One million more people entered the labour force (participation rate increases), half of whom found a job (employment-to-population ratio increases) and half of whom did not (unemployment rate increases). It seems likely this change is due to discouraged workers now retrying to find jobs because the overall economy is improving.

5 The costs of unemployment include the lost output of the unemployed, and the deterioration of skills and abilities; in other words, human capital erodes. These costs will be higher for structural unemployment because it lasts longer, and often the workers' human capital becomes worthless in the marketplace.

6 Cyclical unemployment is caused by a downturn in the economy, when there is a decrease in demand for all products. Structural unemployment is caused by structural changes in a specific industry or region, and there is a decrease in demand for a certain type of labour whose skills are no longer desired.

Cyclical unemployment will end when the economy turns up. Structural unemployment will end when the workers retrain or move.

ⓒ **7** As a result of the reforms, people will be quicker to take a job when offered one, since the value of further search is now lower due to the lower compensation—this change will reduce frictional unemployment for sure, but will not create new jobs under seasonal, structural, or cyclical. However, presumably workers under these four types will be more likely to take a low-wage or different job because of the lower unemployment compensation, if they can find one, reducing these types of unemployment (least effect on cyclical). As well, people who quit jobs have a harder time getting coverage so they will be less likely to quit; frictional unemployment will be lower for this reason.

These reforms will reduce natural unemployment, which may be good. However, people will be less able to spend time searching for the optimal job match and will settle for "inappropriate" jobs more frequently, which is not optimal from society's viewpoint. It is hard to say if the previous levels were too generous or not without further information.

8
- **a** He is an entrant, and is frictionally unemployed.
- **b** He is now employed, although he is also involuntarily part-time.
- **c** He is a job leaver, and is frictionally unemployed.
- **d** He is a discouraged worker, but technically out of the labour force.
- **e** He is still out of the labour force.
- **f** He is employed.
- **g** He is structurally unemployed.
- **h** He is initially employed, but then is seasonally unemployed.
- **i** He is employed again.

ⓒ **9** The higher unemployment rate in Newfoundland has pushed many workers out of the labour force—they have become discouraged workers and are not even attempting to find work. (We can see this in the lower participation rate.) The bigger gap in the employment-to-population ratio reflects this exiting, because it includes the measured unemployed and the discouraged workers.

10 There is no correct answer—this answer depends on value judgements. The generosity encourages people to stay in the labour force who have no intention of getting a job, thus raising the unemployment rate needlessly, and wasting taxpayers' money. On the other hand, in the United States some workers become discouraged and stop looking, and stop being measured as unemployed since they do not register for insurance, even though they want a job and should be measured. Finally, the generous unemployment insurance will keep people looking for a better job for a longer time period, leading to better job matches.

Chapter 24

Aggregate Supply and Aggregate Demand

KEY CONCEPTS

Aggregate Supply

The *AS-AD* model enables us to understand how equilibrium, real GDP and the price level are determined.

Quantity of real GDP supplied (Y) depends on quantities of labour (*L*), capital (*K*), and technology (*T*) as described by **aggregate production function**: $Y = F(L, K, T)$.

- At a given time, only quantity of labour can vary.
  - Quantity of labour depends on demand and supply of labour.
  - **Full employment** occurs at the wage rate where quantity of labour demanded = quantity of labour supplied.
  - Even at full employment there is some unemployment due to labour market turnover.
  - Unemployment rate at full employment is **natural rate of unemployment**.
- **Potential GDP** is quantity of real GDP supplied at full employment.
  - Over business cycle, employment fluctuates around full employment as real GDP fluctuates around potential GDP.

Two separate *AS* concepts: short-run (*SAS*) and long-run (*LAS*).

- **Macroeconomic long run** is long enough time frame so that real GDP = potential GDP. **Macroeconomic short run** is a period during which real GDP is above or below potential GDP.
- **Long-run aggregate supply (*LAS*)** is relationship between quantity of real GDP supplied and price level when real GDP = potential.
  - *LAS* curve is vertical at potential GDP.
  - Increase in *P* leads to equivalent percentage increase in resource prices, which means real wages remain constant—no Δ employment, no Δ quantity supplied *Y*.
- **Short-run aggregate supply (*SAS*)** is relationship between quantity of real GDP supplied and price level when wages and other resource prices are held constant.
  - *SAS* curve is upward-sloping.
  - Increase in *P* leads to an increase in employment and an increase in quantity supplied *Y*.
- *LAS* shifts rightward when potential GDP increases, due to increase in full employment quantity of labour, increase in capital stock (including human capital), technological advance.
- *SAS* shifts along with *LAS*, but also shifts if Δ resource prices.
- Δ resource prices do not shift *LAS* since no change in underlying supply variables.

Aggregate Demand

Quantity of real GDP demanded is total amount of final goods and services produced in Canada that economic agents plan to buy. It depends on price level, expectations, fiscal/monetary policy, and world economy.

- **Aggregate demand (*AD*)** is total quantity real GDP (*Y*) demanded at given price level (*P*).
- Increase in *P* decreases quantity real GDP demanded, represented by movement up along *AD* curve because of
  - *wealth effect*—as *P* increases, decrease in real value of financial assets increases saving and decreases spending.

- *substitution effects*—as *P* increases, people substitute towards relatively cheaper foreign goods (lowering *NX*), and as *P* increases, interest rates increase so *S* increases and *C* decreases.

◆ Changes in other factors *shift AD* curve.

- If **fiscal policy** increases taxes or decreases government expenditure, then *AD* decreases.
- If **monetary policy** decreases interest rates or increases money supply, then *AD* increases.
- If exchange rate increases or foreign income decreases, then *AD* decreases.
- Increase in expectations of future income or future inflation or future profits increases *AD*.

Macroeconomic Equilibrium

There are two different types of macroeconomic equilibriums—long-run equilibrium is state towards which economy is heading, short-run equilibrium occurs at each point in time along path to long-run equilibrium.

◆ **Short-run macroeconomic equilibrium** occurs where *AD* = *SAS*, with *P* adjusting to achieve equilibrium.

◆ **Long-run macroeconomic equilibrium** occurs when real GDP = potential GDP—when *AD* = *SAS* = *LAS*.

◆ Economic growth results from *LAS* shifting rightward on average, due to increase in underlying supply variables.

◆ Persistent inflation occurs when *AD* grows faster than *LAS*.

◆ Growth in *Y* is not steady, but goes in cycles because *AD* and *SAS* do not shift at same pace.

◆ Over the business cycle, short-run equilibrium may occur at

- long-run equilibrium.
- **below full-employment equilibrium**—*AD* = *SAS* left of *LAS*, real GDP < potential by amount of **recessionary gap**.
- **above full-employment equilibrium**—*AD* = *SAS* right of *LAS*, real GDP > potential by amount of **inflationary gap**.

◆ Economy fluctuates in short run because of fluctuations in *AD* and *SAS*.

- If *AD* increases so *Y* > potential, economy does not stay in above-full equilibrium—upward pressures on wages shift *SAS* leftward towards long-run equilibrium.
- If resource prices increase so *SAS* shifts leftward and *Y* < potential, then *stagflation* results (*P* higher, *Y* lower). Slow adjustment back to long-run equilibrium via decreasing resource prices (*SAS* shifts rightward).

Growth, Inflation, and Cycles in the Canadian Economy

Levels of *Y* and *P* have changed dramatically over time in Canadian economy with economic growth, inflation, and business cycles.

◆ In 1970s, inflation increased and growth decreased due to massive increase in oil prices, and increase in quantity of money.

◆ Central banks responded by restraining *AD*, leading to deep recession in 1981–82.

◆ Through 1980s, steady growth and inflation as *LAS* shifted rightward.

◆ In 1991, decreasing *AD* led to recession. Since then, economic growth, low inflation, return to full employment.

HELPFUL HINT

1 The aggregate demand and aggregate supply model introduced in this chapter (and developed in detail throughout this book) is an insightful method of analysing complex macroeconomic events. In order to help yourself sort out these complex events, it will be helpful if *you always draw a graph*—even if it is a small graph in the margin of a multiple-choice question. Graphs are powerful and effective tools for analysing economic events, and you should become familiar with using them as soon as possible.

2 When using graphs, two factors often confuse students:

a Sometimes graphs are based on explicit numerical or algebraic models, where the intercepts, slopes, sizes of shifts, etc. have explicit values. Often these numbers are based on real-world values, but sometimes they are just "made-up" numbers that the instructor has picked to illustrate the point (although they are still economically logical). Do *not* get caught up in the exact values of the numbers. Concentrate on the basic economic results—for example, an increase in *AD* leads to an increase in the price level and real GDP.

b One common student mistake is failing to *distinguish between a shift in a curve versus a movement along a curve.* This distinction is crucial in understanding the factors that influence *AD* and *AS*, and you can be sure that your instructor will test you on it! The slope of the *AD* curve reflects the impact of a change in the price level on aggregate demand. A change in the price level produces a *movement along* the *AD* curve. A change in one of the factors affecting the *AD* curve other than price is reflected by a *shift* in the entire *AD* curve. Similarly, a change in price produces a *movement along* the *SAS* or the *LAS* curve and does not lead to a shift in the curves.

3 A change in price will not shift the *AD* or the *AS* curves. To cement the previous point, consider Fig. 24.1. The initial long-run equilibrium is at the point *a*.

What happens in our model when there is a decrease in expected future income and profits (such as happened in the recent recession)? This decrease in expected income and profits leads to a decrease in consumption and investment, and a decrease in aggregate demand, shown as the shift from AD_0 to AD_1.

We can best understand what happens next by imagining that the curve AD_0 can be peeled off the page, that it no longer exists—after all, the factors that created it no longer exist! This removal leaves us with the curves SAS_0 and AD_1, and with a price level of P_0. At P_0, there is a surplus of goods and services (the quantity of real GDP supplied is equal to Y_0 [at *a*], greater than the quantity of real GDP demanded of Y_c [at *c*]), so that firms find their inventories piling up. In this case, they cut prices and decrease production. This decrease in price eliminates the surplus in two ways. First, as price decreases, firms supply fewer goods and services: a movement along the *SAS* curve from *a* to *b*. (Be careful, the price change does *not* shift the *SAS* curve.) Second, the decrease in price leads to an increase in the quantity demanded: a movement along AD_1 from *c* to *b*. (Note there is no shift in the *AD* curve as price changes.)

FIGURE **24.1**

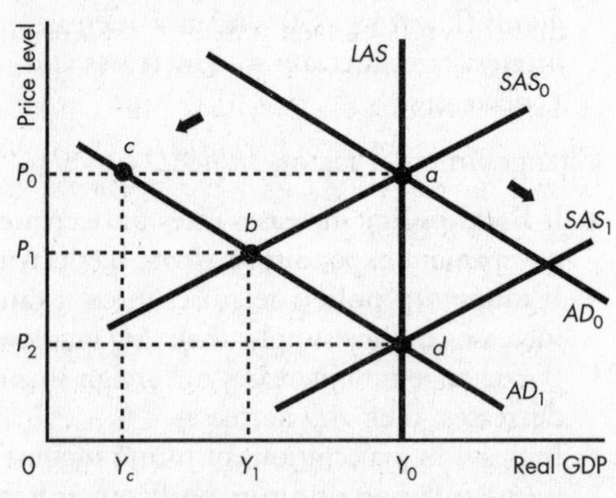

The end result is the new below full-employment equilibrium at *b*, with a lower price level and a lower level of real GDP.

4 In Fig. 24.1, point *b* is a short-run below full-employment equilibrium, but it is not a long-run equilibrium since $Y_1 < Y_0$ (potential). There are two possible adjustments back from Y_1 to Y_0. First, the government or central bank could intervene with an expansionary fiscal or monetary policy, raising *AD* back to AD_0—the economy will move back to a full-employment, long-run equilibrium at *a* with $Y = Y_0$ (potential). Second, if the government does nothing, then the unemployment at *b* will lead to downward pressures on wages and other resource prices (although this adjustment can be very slow). As wages decrease, the *SAS* curve shifts slowly rightward, eventually reaching SAS_1, with a full-employment, long-run equilibrium at *d* with $Y = Y_0$ (potential).

5 On the supply side, a crucial (and often hard to understand) distinction occurs between suppliers' behaviour in the short run and the long run. The short run and long run are not lengths of calendar time, but are defined in terms of whether or not resource prices change. In the short run, the prices of productive resources do not change; in the long run, they do change.

To see what this difference implies for the supply decision, consider what happens when the price level increases. In the short run, resource prices stay unchanged. As a result, per-unit revenues are increasing, while per unit costs are unchanged. Therefore profit-maximizing firms react by hiring more productive resources and supplying more real GDP as the price level increases—the short-run aggregate supply curve is upward-sloping.

In the long run, resource prices adjust by the same amount as the price level, which means that the costs of each unit of production have increased by the same percentage as the revenue. These two effects offset each other, and firms do not change their supply decision as the price level increases—the long-run aggregate supply curve is vertical.

This distinction between the short run and the long run also applies to the influences that affect the short-run and long-run aggregate supply curves. Since prices of productive resources are held constant for the short-run aggregate supply curve but not for the long-run aggregate supply curve, a change in the prices of productive resources will shift *SAS* but not *LAS*.

SELF-TEST

True/False/Uncertain and Explain

1 As the price level increases, the aggregate quantity of goods and services supplied increases.

2 Any factor that shifts the short-run aggregate supply curve rightward will also shift the long-run aggregate supply curve rightward.

3 If there is a significant technological advance (other things remaining unchanged), the long-run aggregate supply curve will shift rightward but the short-run aggregate supply curve will not shift.

4 An increase in the foreign exchange value of the dollar will increase aggregate demand in Canada.

5 An increase in the expected rate of inflation will decrease aggregate demand.

6 A shift rightward in the aggregate demand curve leads to an increase in the price level, which in turn shifts the short-run aggregate supply curve rightward in the short run.

7 If the aggregate demand curve and the short-run aggregate supply curve both shift rightward at the same time, then the price level increases.

8 An economy is initially in short-run equilibrium and then expected future profits decrease. The new short-run equilibrium will be a below full-employment equilibrium.

9 Increases in long-run aggregate supply are the main force generating the underlying tendency of real GDP to expand over time.

10 If the economy is in an above full-employment equilibrium, the long-run aggregate supply curve will shift rightward until the economy is in a full-employment equilibrium.

Multiple-Choice

Aggregate Supply

1 A technological improvement will shift
- **a** both *SAS* and *AD* rightward.
- **b** both *SAS* and *LAS* leftward.
- **c** *SAS* rightward but leave *LAS* unchanged.
- **d** *LAS* rightward but leave *SAS* unchanged.
- **e** both *SAS* and *LAS* rightward.

2 An increase in wages will shift
- **a** both *SAS* and *LAS* rightward.
- **b** both *SAS* and *LAS* leftward.
- **c** *SAS* leftward, but leave *LAS* unchanged.
- **d** *LAS* rightward, but leave *SAS* unchanged.
- **e** *SAS* rightward, but leave *LAS* unchanged.

3 Long-run aggregate supply will increase for all of the following reasons *except*

- **a** a fall in wages.
- **b** a rise in human capital.
- **c** the introduction of new technology.
- **d** more aggregate labour hours.
- **e** more capital stock.

4 Potential GDP is the level of real GDP at which

- **a** aggregate demand equals short-run aggregate supply.
- **b** there is full employment.
- **c** there is a recessionary gap.
- **d** there is over full employment.
- **e** prices are sure to increase.

5 The short-run aggregate supply curve is the relationship between the price level and the quantity of real GDP supplied, holding constant the

- **a** wage rate only.
- **b** quantities of productive resources.
- **c** level of government expenditures.
- **d** price level.
- **e** prices of productive resources.

6 Consider Fig. 24.2. Which graph illustrates what happens when resource prices decrease?

- **a** (a)
- **b** (b)
- **c** (c)
- **d** (d)
- **e** none of the above

FIGURE **24.2**

(a)

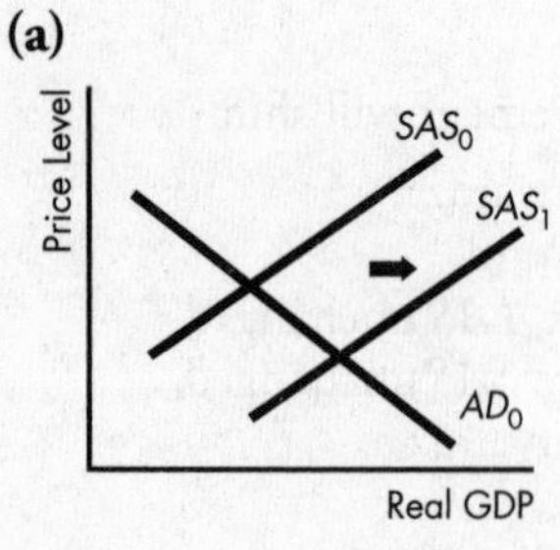

(b)

Price Level
SAS_1
SAS_0
AD_0
Real GDP

(c)

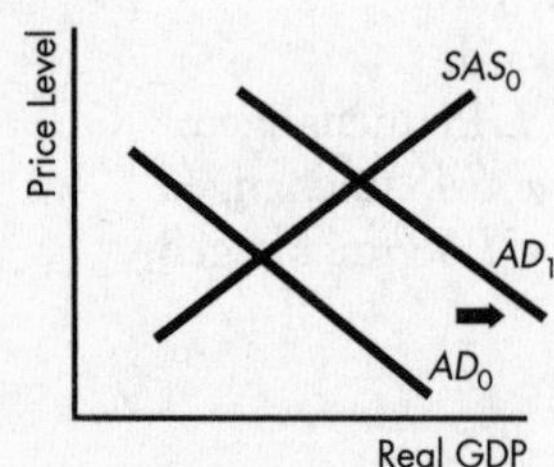

(d)

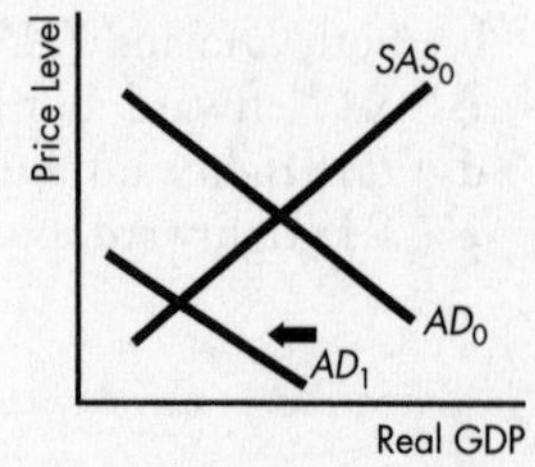

Aggregate Demand

7 Consider Fig. 24.2. Which graph illustrates what happens when government expenditures increase?

- **a** (a)
- **b** (b)
- **c** (c)
- **d** (d)
- **e** none of the above

8 Consider Fig. 24.2. Which graph illustrates what happens when the money supply decreases?

- **a** (a)
- **b** (b)
- **c** (c)
- **d** (d)
- **e** none of the above

9 Consider Fig. 24.2. Which graph illustrates what happens when expected future income increases?

- **a** (a)
- **b** (b)
- **c** (c)
- **d** (d)
- **e** none of the above

10 Which of the following is a reason for the downward slope of the aggregate demand curve?

- **a** the wealth effect
- **b** the expectations effect
- **c** the expected inflation effect
- **d** the nominal balance effect
- **e** none of the above

11 Which of the following will cause the aggregate demand curve to shift rightward?

- **a** an increase in interest rates (at a given price level)
- **b** an increase in expected inflation
- **c** an increase in taxes
- **d** a decrease in the price level
- **e** an increase in the price level

Macroeconomic Equilibrium

12 We observe an increase in the price level and a decrease in real GDP. Which of the following is a possible explanation?

- **a** The expectation of future profits has increased.
- **b** The expectation of future income has increased.
- **c** The price of raw materials has increased.
- **d** The stock of capital has increased.
- **e** The money supply has increased.

13 Short-run macroeconomic equilibrium *always* occurs when the

a economy is at full employment.
b economy is below full employment.
c economy is above full employment.
d quantity of real GDP demanded equals the quantity of real GDP supplied.
e *AD* curve intersects the *LAS* curve.

14 Consider the economy represented in Table 24.1. In short-run macroeconomic equilibrium, the price level is ________ and the level of real GDP is ________ billion dollars.

a 120; 600
b 120; 500
c 125; 550
d 130; 600
e 130; 500

TABLE **24.1**

Price Level	Aggregate Demand (billions of 1992 $)	Short-Run Aggregate Supply (billions of 1992 $)	Long-Run Aggregate Supply (billions of 1992 $)
100	800	300	600
110	700	400	600
120	600	500	600
130	500	600	600
140	400	700	600

15 Consider the economy represented in Table 24.1. The economy is in a(n)

a long-run equilibrium and resource prices will not change.
b above full-employment equilibrium, and resource prices will increase.
c above full-employment equilibrium, and resource prices will decrease.
d below full-employment equilibrium, and resource prices will decrease.
e below full-employment equilibrium, and resource prices will increase.

16 Consider the economy represented in Table 24.1. There is

a an inflationary gap equal to $100 billion.
b an inflationary gap equal to $50 billion.
c a recessionary gap equal to $50 billion.
d a recessionary gap equal to $100 billion.
e no gap, the economy is at full employment.

17 The economy cannot remain at a level of real GDP above long-run aggregate supply (*LAS*) because prices of productive resources will

a decrease, shifting *LAS* rightward.
b decrease, shifting *SAS* rightward.
c increase, shifting *LAS* leftward.
d increase, shifting *SAS* leftward.
e increase, shifting *SAS* rightward.

18 Consider an economy starting from a position of full employment. Which of the following changes does *not* occur as a result of a decrease in aggregate demand?

a The price level decreases.
b The level of real GDP decreases in the short run.
c A recessionary gap arises.
d Resource prices will decrease in the long run, shifting the short-run aggregate supply curve rightward.
e The long-run aggregate supply curve shifts leftward to create the new long-run equilibrium.

19 If prices of productive resources remain constant, an increase in aggregate demand will cause a(n)

a increase in the price level and an increase in real GDP.
b increase in the price level and a decrease in real GDP.
c decrease in the price level and an increase in real GDP.
d decrease in the price level and a decrease in real GDP.
e increase in the price level, but no change in real GDP.

20 Which of the graphs in Fig. 24.3 illustrates a below full-employment equilibrium?

a (a) only
b (b) only
c (c) only
d (d) only
e both (c) and (d)

FIGURE **24.3**

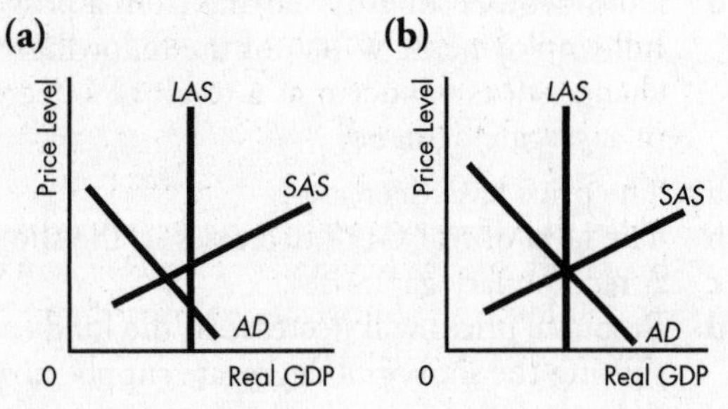

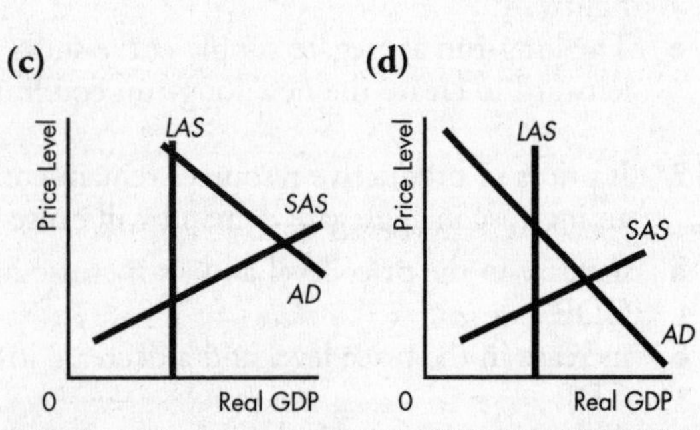

21 Which of the graphs in Fig. 24.3 illustrates an above full-employment equilibrium?

a (a) only
b (b) only
c (c) only
d (d) only
e both (c) and (d)

22 If real GDP is greater than potential GDP, the economy is

a not in short-run equilibrium.
b in a recessionary equilibrium.
c in an above full-employment equilibrium.
d in a below full-employment equilibrium.
e in long-run equilibrium.

23 Which one of the following newspaper quotations best describes a movement along an *SAS* curve?

a "The decrease in consumer spending may lead to a recession."
b "The increase in consumer spending is expected to lead to inflation, without any increase in real GDP."
c "Recent higher wage settlements are expected to cause higher inflation this year."
d "Growth has been unusually high the last few years due to more women entering the workforce."
e "The recent tornadoes destroyed many factories in Calgary and Edmonton."

Growth, Inflation, and Cycles in the Canadian Economy

24 The fact that the short-run aggregate supply and aggregate demand curves do not shift at a fixed, steady pace explains why we observe

a persistent inflation.
b business cycles.
c economic growth.
d large government budget deficits.
e persistent unemployment.

25 *Persistent* inflation is caused by

a shifts rightward in aggregate demand.
b shifts rightward in short-run aggregate supply.
c the tendency for long-run aggregate supply to increase faster than aggregate demand.
d shifts rightward in short-run aggregate supply accompanied by shifts leftward in aggregate demand.
e the tendency for aggregate demand to increase faster than long-run aggregate supply.

Short Answer Problems

1 The substitution effects imply that an increase in the price level will lead to a decrease in the aggregate quantity of goods and services demanded. Explain.

2 Why is the *LAS* curve vertical?

3 Why is the *SAS* curve positively sloped?

4 What are the most important factors in explaining the steady and persistent increases in the price level over time in Canada?

5 Suppose the economy is initially in long-run equilibrium. Graphically illustrate the short-run effects of an increase in wages. What happens to the price level and the level of real GDP?

6 Consider an economy that is in above full-employment equilibrium due to an increase in *AD*. Prices of productive resources have not changed. With the help of a graph, discuss how the economy returns to long-run equilibrium, with no government intervention.

7 Suppose that the economy is initially in long-run equilibrium. Next, suppose that investors' confidence in the future decreases (they expect future profits to decrease).

a Explain (with the aid of a graph) what this shock does to *AD*, the price level, real GDP, and *AS* in the short run.

b Suppose that the government does not take any action and that investor confidence stays low. What kind of adjustments occur in the long run? Explain what happens to the price level, real GDP, *AD*, and *AS* during this adjustment, illustrating the changes on your graph.

8 With the aid of a graph, illustrate the case of an economy that has persistent inflation and positive economic growth over a three-year period.

ⓒⓣ 9 Consider an economy where economists have estimated that last year's real GDP was $800 billion, equal to potential GDP. The price level was 105. Suppose that this year the economists estimate that potential GDP has increased by 10 percent. However, actual real GDP has decreased by 5 percent, while the price level has also decreased by 5 percent.

Draw an *AD-AS* graph that shows last year's equilibrium, as well as last year's aggregate demand, aggregate supply (short-run and long-run), price level, and real GDP level. Next, given the information above, show what has happened to the price level and the level of real GDP this year (show this year's equilibrium), plus what has happened to aggregate demand, short-run aggregate supply, and long-run aggregate supply since last year.

ⓒⓣ 10 In 1996, the Saguenay region of Quebec suffered some of the worst floods in memory, with many roads, towns, and buildings destroyed.

a Assuming that the economy was originally in long-run equilibrium, explain what has happened to the *LAS* and *SAS* curves in the local economy as a result of the destruction of the capital stock.

b Assuming that the *AD* curve is constant, what might happen to the price level and real GDP in the short run as a result of the changes you have described in part **a**? Show this result on an *AD-SAS* graph.

c Several observers, especially those in the construction industry, argued that the rebuilding of the destroyed capital stock would strongly stimulate the local economy. What component of aggregate demand is affected by this rebuilding? What will happen to aggregate demand as a result of this rebuilding?

d Some observers implied the local economy was better off, in a purely economic sense, as a result of the floods and the resulting rebuilding process. Do you agree?

ANSWERS

True/False/Uncertain and Explain

1 U Answer is **T** if it is short-run, and **F** if it is long-run. (516–518)

2 F Changes in resource prices shift only *SAS* and not *LAS*. (519–520)

3 F Anything that shifts *LAS* also shifts *SAS*. (519–520)

4 F Increase in value of dollar makes Canadian exports more expensive and imports cheaper, leading to decrease in demand for Canadian goods. (523)

5 F If individuals expect increased inflation rate, they will spend more today to avoid higher future prices. (524)

6 F Increase in *P* leads to movement along *SAS* curve, not shift in it. (528–529)

7 U It depends on relative size of two shifts—try drawing a graph. (528–530)

ⓒⓣ **8 U** It depends on where initial equilibrium is and on size of decrease in *AD* that results from decrease in future profits—try drawing a graph or two. (528–530)

9 T Increase in population or capital stock or human capital, and new technology shift *LAS* rightward over time. (530–531)

10 F *SAS* shifts in this type of situation, not *LAS*. (528–530)

Multiple-Choice

1 e Technological improvements means same inputs can produce more output, leading to increase in quantity supplied in both short and long run. (516–524)

2 c Wages are held constant along given *SAS*; if wages increase, production is less at every price level leading to *SAS* shifting leftward. (518–520)

3 a Changes in wages change *SAS* only, not *LAS*. (518–520)

4 b Definition. (516)

5 e Short run is defined as time period within which resource prices are constant. (517)

6 a When resource prices decrease, firms produce more at every price level shifting *SAS* rightward. (520)

7 c Increase in government expenditures leads to increase in aggregate spending, shifting *AD* rightward. (522–523)

8 d Decrease in money supply leads to decrease in aggregate spending, shifting *AD* leftward. (523)

9 c Increase in expected future income leads to increase in household consumption, shifting *AD* rightward. (524)

10 a **b** and **c** shift *AD* curve, and **d** doesn't exist. (521–524)

11 b Answers **a** and **c** cause it to shift leftward, while **d** and **e** are movements along *AD* curve. (521–524)

ct **12 c** Answers **a**, **b**, and **e** increase *AD* leading to increase in real GDP, while **d** shifts *LAS* rightward, leading to increase in real GDP. **c** shifts *SAS* leftward leading to increase in *P*, decrease in real GDP (try drawing a graph). (528–529)

13 d Short-run macroeconomic equilibrium always occurs where *AD* = *SAS*; equilibrium *may* occur at answers **a–c** and **e**, but it doesn't *always* occur there. (524–527)

14 c Short-run equilibrium occurs where *AD* = *SAS*, which occurs at *P* = 125 and real GDP = 550—halfway between *P* = 120 and *P* = 130. (524)

ct **15 d** Real GDP = 550 billion < potential GDP of 600 billion which is below full-employment equilibrium, so unemployed workers eventually offer to work for less. (526–529)

16 c Actual real GDP = 550 billion, which is 50 billion less than potential GDP of 600 billion. (526)

17 d Above long-run aggregate supply, extra demand for resources leads to increase in their prices leading to increase in cost of production leading to *SAS* shifting leftward. (528–529)

18 e Decrease in *AD* creates recession, leading to decrease in resource prices, shifting *SAS* rightward, pushing economy back to *LAS*. (528–529)

19 a Increase in *AD* leads to shortages leading to increase in prices leading to increase in aggregate quantity supplied in short run, so increase in *P* and increase in real GDP. (528–529)

20 a Below full-employment equilibrium occurs when *AD* = *SAS* to left of *LAS*. (524–527)

21 e Above full-employment equilibrium occurs when *AD* = *SAS* to right of *LAS*. (526–527)

22 c Equilibrium is with *AD* = *SAS*; if *Y* is > *LAS* then an above full-employment equilibrium. (526–527)

ct **23 a** Decrease in consumer spending leads to shift leftward in *AD* leading to movement down an *SAS* curve in short-run leading to decrease in *P* and decrease in *Y*. (524–529)

24 b Sometimes curves shift leftward (creating recession) and sometimes rightward (creating boom). (530–531)

25 e Combination of these shifts leads to shortages leading to increase in *P*. **a**, **b**, and **c** may lead to increase in *P*, while **d** leads to decrease in *P*. (530–531)

Short Answer Problems

1 There are two substitution effects. First, if the prices of domestic goods increase and foreign prices remain constant, domestic goods become relatively more expensive, and so households will buy fewer domestic goods and more foreign goods. This decline in spending means that there will be a decrease in the quantity of real GDP demanded. Thus an increase in the price level (the prices of domestic goods) will lead to a decrease in the aggregate quantity of (domestic) goods and services demanded.

Second, the increase in the price level increases the rate of interest, which increases saving and decreases spending. This decline in spending also means that there will again be a decrease in the quantity of real GDP demanded.

2 Long-run aggregate supply is the level of real GDP supplied when there is full employment. Since this level of real GDP is independent of the price level, the long-run aggregate supply curve is vertical. This level of real GDP is that attained when prices of productive resources are free to adjust so as to clear resource markets.

3 The short-run aggregate supply curve is positively sloped because it holds prices of productive resources constant. When the price level increases, firms see the prices of their output (revenues) increasing, but the prices of their input (costs) remain unchanged. Each firm is then induced to increase output and so aggregate output increases.

4 The price level can increase as the result of either an increase in aggregate demand or as the result of a decrease in aggregate supply. Both of these forces have contributed to periods of an increasing price level. The steady and persistent increases in the price level, however, have been the result of a tendency for aggregate demand to increase faster than aggregate supply.

5 In Fig. 24.4, the economy is initially at point *a* on the SAS_0 curve. An increase in wages will shift the *SAS* curve leftward to SAS_1. At the new equilibrium, point *b*, the price level has increased and the level of real GDP has decreased.

FIGURE **24.4**

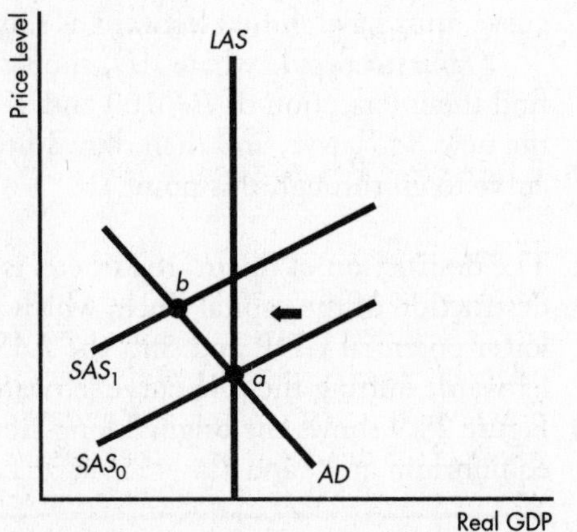

6 In Fig. 24.5 shown here, the increase in *AD* from AD_0 to AD_1 results in the above-full-employment equilibrium at point *b* and causes the price level to increase. Since wages have not changed, the real cost of labour to firms has decreased, and thus output is stimulated as indicated by the movement along the SAS_0 curve from point *a* to point *b*. Furthermore, the purchasing power of workers' wages has decreased. Eventually, workers will demand higher wages and firms will be willing to pay them. In a similar way, other prices of productive resources will increase as well. This long-run increase in prices of productive resources will shift the *SAS* curve leftward, which results in a new equilibrium. There will continue to be pressure for wages and other prices of productive resources to increase until the *SAS* curve shifts all the way to SAS_1, where the purchasing power of wages and other prices of productive resources has been restored and the economy is again at full employment, point *c*.

FIGURE **24.5**

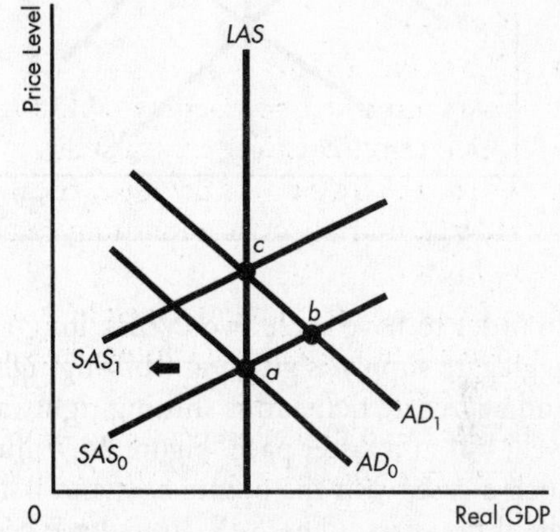

7 a Lower investor confidence leads to lower aggregate spending, shifting the *AD* curve leftward in Fig. 24.6 to AD_1. This decrease in aggregate demand creates a surplus at the original price level, leading to firms cutting prices, which leads to a decrease in quantity produced, represented by the movement along SAS_0 to the new equilibrium at point *b*, leading to a lower level of real GDP.

b The economy is in a below-full-employment equilibrium, and eventually unemployed resources start offering to work for lower resource prices, which shifts the *SAS* curve rightward to SAS_1, raising aggregate supply, lowering prices even more, and leading to a new long-run equilibrium at point *c*, with a higher level of real GDP than at point *b*. There is no shift in *AD*.

FIGURE **24.6**

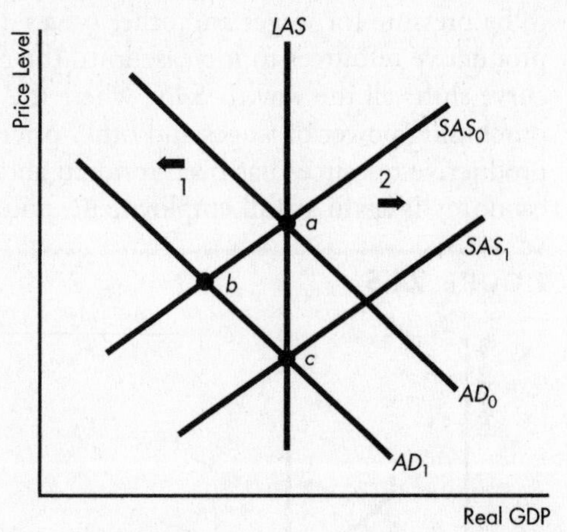

8 In order to have these two events, long-run aggregate supply is growing (shifting rightward), and aggregate demand is shifting rightward as well, but at a faster pace. Figure 24.7 illustrates such a case, with the points *a*, *b*, and *c* showing the three years. (The *SAS* curves have been omitted from the graph for simplicity.)

FIGURE **24.7**

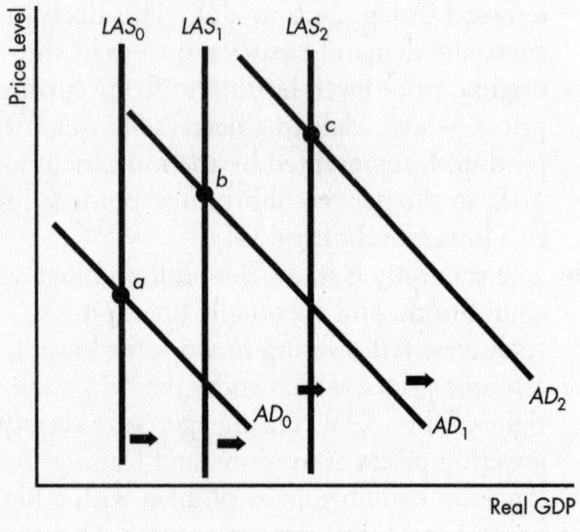

9 Figure 24.8 shows the original full-employment equilibrium, at last year's equilibrium price level of 105 and income level of 800.

FIGURE **24.8**

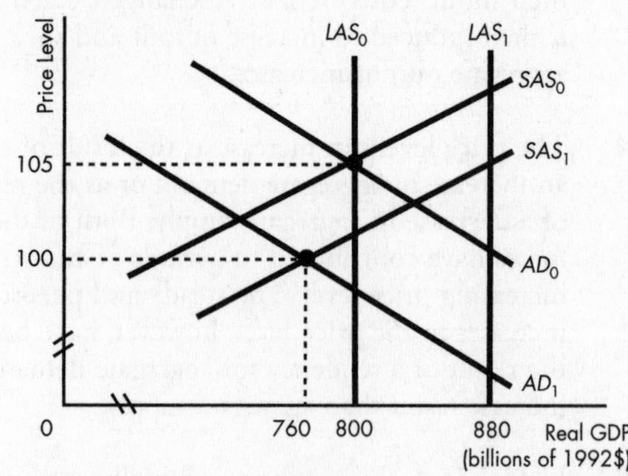

For the current year, the *LAS* curve has shifted rightward to LAS_1, a value of 880, and the *SAS* curve shifts with it to SAS_1, all else equal. The new short-run equilibrium must be along the intersection of SAS_1 and an *AD* curve. Since prices are 5 percent lower at 100, and real GDP is 5 percent lower at 760, the new *AD* curve must have shifted leftward as shown.

(*Hint:* to decide where AD_1 should be, first find the intersection of $P = 100$ and $Y = 760$ on the new *SAS* curve, and then draw in the *AD* curve to go through this point.)

10 a The destruction of towns, roads, etc. is a destruction of the capital stock, which would lower potential GDP, and shift the *LAS* curve leftward, shifting the *SAS* curve leftward as well.

b Figure 24.9 shows the original long-run equilibrium at Y_0 and P_0.

FIGURE **24.9**

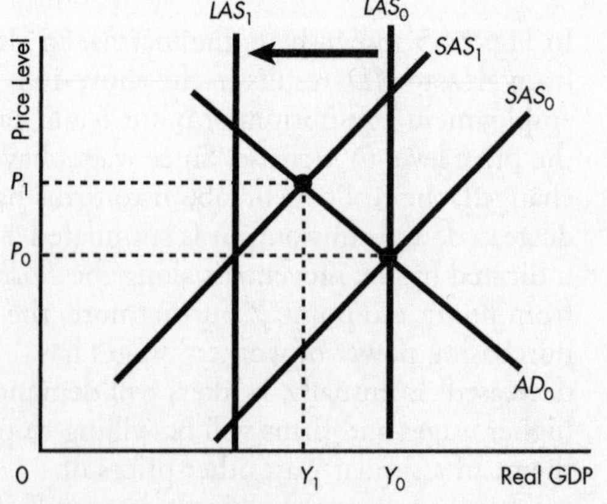

The shift leftward in the long-run aggregate supply to LAS_1 and the short-run aggregate supply to SAS_1, combined with the unchanged *AD* curve leads to stagflation—a rise in the price level to P_1, accompanied by a fall in real GDP to Y_1.

c The resulting rebuilding would stimulate investment demand, and increase aggregate demand, perhaps dramatically.

d The region is worse off—higher inflation, and a lower level of potential GDP and real GDP. This recession is followed by higher growth once the new investment starts, *but* this investment is merely replacing lost capital, and is not adding new capital stock.

Chapters
21–24

Part 7 Overview

Understanding the Issues of Macroeconomics

PROBLEM

a Consider the following data for the economy of Autoland for 2000 and 2001. Calculate the value of nominal GDP for each year.

TABLE **P7.1** 2000

Item	Amount (billions of $)
Government purchases of goods and services	60
Government transfer payments	30
Income taxes	80
Wages, etc., paid to labour	200
Export earnings	30
Consumption expenditure	180
Import payments	25
Net investment expenditure	15
Depreciation	5

TABLE **P7.2** 2001

Item	Amount (billions of $)
Wages, etc., paid to labour	200
Indirect taxes	20
Profits	20
Subsidies	5
Interest and miscellaneous investment income	5
Depreciation	10
Farmers' income	10
Income of nonfarm unincorporated business	10

b Using your data from **a**, complete the following table:

TABLE **P7.3**

Year	Nominal GDP (billions of $)	Price Level	Real GDP (billions of 1992 $)
2000		132.5	
2001		140.0	

c Draw an *AD-AS* graph that represents the Autoland economy for 2000 and 2001, based on the data in Table P7.3, and explain what has happened to the economy over this time period.

d If the economy was in long-run equilibrium in 2000, what has happened to cyclical unemployment between 2000 and 2001?

e Calculate the inflation rate, the growth rate in real GDP, and the growth rate in nominal GDP over this time period.

nGDP=

MIDTERM EXAMINATION

You should allocate 32 minutes for this examination (16 questions, 2 minutes per question). For each question, choose the one *best* answer.

1 Which of the following would be counted as employed in Canada?
- **a** Doris only works five hours a week but is looking for a full-time job.
- **b** Kanhaya has stopped looking for work since he was unable to find a suitable job during a two-month search.
- **c** Sharon is a college student with no job.
- **d** Maurice is working in his garden while looking for work.
- **e** Taylor is a homemaker.

2 Which of the following is *not* an example of investment in the expenditure approach to measuring GDP? General Motors
- **a** buys a new auto stamping machine.
- **b** adds 500 new cars to inventories.
- **c** buys Canadian government bonds.
- **d** builds another assembly plant.
- **e** replaces some worn-out stamping machines.

3 The changes represented in Fig. P7.1 must
- **a** not occur in the real world, because *AD* and *SAS* cannot change at the same time.
- **b** lead to an inflationary gap.
- **c** lead to a recessionary gap.
- **d** create inflation.
- **e** none of the above.

FIGURE **P7.1**

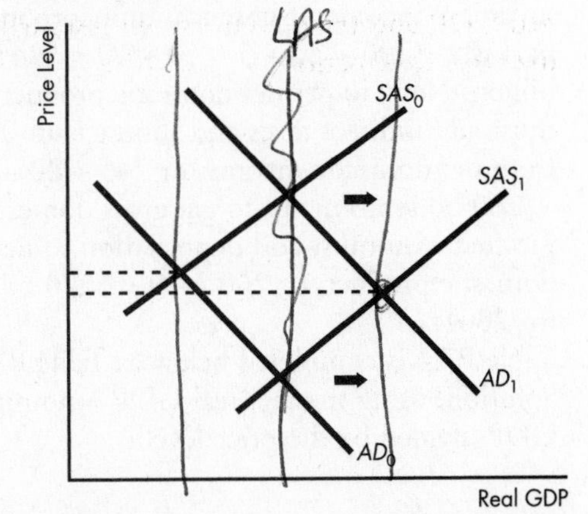

4 In a country with a working-age population of 20 million, 13 million are employed, 1.5 million are unemployed, and 1 million of the employed are working part-time, half of whom wish to work full-time. The employment-to-population ratio is
- **a** 72.5 percent.
- **b** 65 percent.
- **c** 75.5 percent.
- **d** 57.5 percent.
- **e** none of the above.

13 ÷ 20

5 In a country with a working-age population of 20 million, 13 million are employed, 1.5 million are unemployed, and 1 million of the employed are working part-time, half of whom wish to work full-time. The size of the involuntary part-time ratio is
- **a** 3.4 percent.
- **b** 3.8 percent.
- **c** 2.5 percent.
- **d** 5 percent.
- **e** none of the above.

~~500,000 ÷ 13M~~
0.5 ÷ 14.5
involuntary P/T ÷ labour force

6 Which of the following is *not* a part of the incomes approach to GDP?
- **a** net exports
- **b** wages, salaries, and supplementary labour income
- **c** corporate profits
- **d** farmers' income
- **e** income of nonfarm unincorporated businesses

7 The technique used to calculate the CPI implicitly assumes that consumers buy
- **a** relatively more of goods with relative prices that are rising.
- **b** relatively fewer goods with relative prices that are rising.
- **c** the same relative quantities of goods as in a base year.
- **d** goods and services whose quality improves at the rate of growth of real income.
- **e** more computers and CD players and fewer black-and-white TVs.

8 If a price index was 150 at the end of 2000 and 165 at the end of 2001, what was the rate of inflation for 2001?
- **a** 15 percent
- **b** 9.1 percent
- **c** 10 percent
- **d** 50 percent
- **e** 65 percent

(165 − 150) / 150 × 100

9 If wages decrease, then

a *AD* shifts rightward.
b firms hire less labour.
c only *LAS* shifts rightward.
d only *SAS* shifts rightward.
e both *SAS* and *LAS* shift rightward.

10 The aggregate demand curve (*AD*) illustrates that, as the price level decreases, the

a quantity of real GDP demanded increases.
b quantity of real GDP demanded decreases.
c quantity of nominal GDP demanded increases.
d quantity of nominal GDP demanded decreases.
e value of assets decrease.

11 We observe an increase in the price level and an increase in real GDP. A possible explanation is that the

a money supply has fallen.
b expectation of future income has decreased.
c price of raw materials has increased.
d stock of capital has increased.
e expectation of future profits has increased.

12 In the circular flow, the flows of investment and saving interact with the flows of income and consumption to determine

a total production.
b aggregate income.
c aggregate expenditure.
d all of the above.
e none of the above.

13 Which of the following would be considered seasonally unemployed?

a a Saskatchewan farmer who has lost her farm and is unemployed until retrained
b a Nova Scotia fishery worker who is laid off during the winter
c a steelworker who is laid off but who expects to be called back soon
d an office worker who has lost her job because of a general slowdown in economic activity
e none of the above

14 Unemployment caused by an economy-wide decrease in the demand for goods and services is known as

a cyclical unemployment.
b seasonal unemployment.
c frictional unemployment.
d structural unemployment.
e natural unemployment.

15 Macroeconomic policy challenges include

a keeping the deficit high if borrowing is for consumption.
b stabilizing the business cycle.
c stabilizing inflation at the current level.
d ignoring inflation if unemployment is a problem.
e none of the above.

16 A business cycle is the

a increase in real GDP for more than 2 periods.
b decrease in real GDP for more than 2 periods.
c irregular fluctuation of potential GDP around real GDP.
d increase in the economic potential to produce goods and services.
e irregular fluctuation of real GDP around potential GDP.

ANSWERS

Problem

a For 2000, calculate nominal GDP as the sum of $C + I + G + NX$. For G, you must use only expenditures on goods and services, and you need to calculate gross investment (= net investment + depreciation, or $20 billion) as well as net exports (= exports – imports, or $5 billion). Thus nominal GDP = 180 + 20 + 60 + 5 = $265 billion for 2000.

For 2001, you need to use the incomes approach. First, calculate net domestic income at factor cost = wages, etc. + profits + interest and miscellaneous investment income + farmers' income + income of nonfarm unincorporated business = 200 + 20 + 5 + 10 + 10 = $245 billion. Next, to get net domestic product you must add indirect taxes and subtract subsidies from net domestic income, or 245 + 20 – 5 =$260 billion. Finally, to get gross domestic product, you must add depreciation to net domestic product, or 260 + 10 = $270 billion for 2001.

b Table P7.3 is completed below as Table P7.3 Solution, using the fact real GDP = nominal GDP divided by the price level.

TABLE **P7.3** SOLUTION

Year	Nominal GDP (billions of $)	Price Level	Real GDP (billions of 1992 $)
2000	265	132.5	200.0
2001	270	140.0	192.9

ⓒⓣ **c** Figure P7.2 shows the Autoland economy in 2000 and 2001. The exact sizes of shifts in *AD* and *SAS* depends on assumptions about their slopes, but the relative types of shifts must be as shown in order to get the simultaneous increase in the price level and decrease in real GDP that occurred from 2000 to 2001. As the graph shows, the likely changes were a shift leftward in *SAS* and a shift leftward in *AD*, with the shift leftward in *SAS* larger (it is this shift that results in the price level increasing).

FIGURE **P7.2**

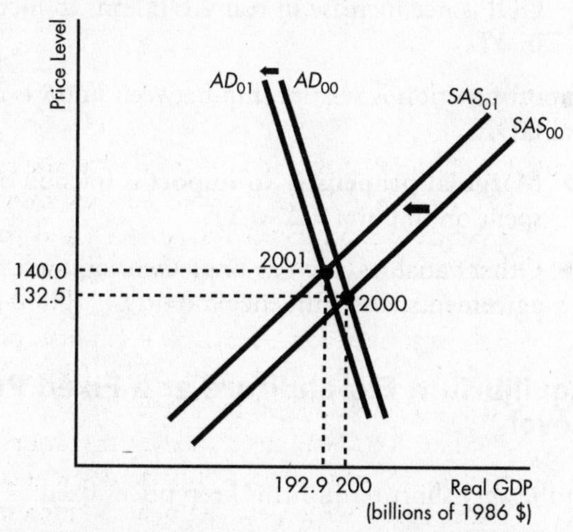

d If the economy was in long-run equilibrium in 2000, then there was zero cyclical unemployment. The decrease in real GDP to below potential GDP means that unemployment must be above the natural rate, so that cyclical unemployment has increased in 2001.

e The inflation rate is equal to

$$5.7\% = \frac{140.0 - 132.5}{132.5} \times 100$$

The growth rate of real GDP is equal to

$$-3.6\% = \frac{192.9 - 200}{200} \times 100$$

The growth rate of nominal GDP is equal to

$$1.9\% = \frac{270 - 265}{265} \times 100$$

Midterm Examination

1 a Doris is employed part-time, Kanhaya is not looking for work (discouraged worker), Sharon and Taylor are out of labour force, Maurice is unemployed. (500–504)

2 c This is purchase of financial assets, not capital stock. (480–484)

3 e These changes can occur. Whether or not there is gap cannot be determined without *LAS* curve. (524–529)

4 b Employed/working-age population = 13/20 = 65 percent. (500–504)

5 a Involuntarily part-time/labour force = 0.5/14.5 = 3.4 percent. (500–504)

6 a It is part of expenditure approach. (480–484)

7 c Because it assumes same basket of goods used for years being compared. (488–489)

8 c 10% = [(165 – 150)/150] × 100. (465–467)

9 d If wages decrease, cost of production decreases, firms hire more labour, supply more goods and services, represented by (only) *SAS* shifting rightward. (516–520)

10 a *AD* curve is downward-sloping due to three effects. It is real GDP by definition, not nominal, and asset values increase here. (521–524)

ⓒⓣ **11 e** Answer **e** shifts *AD* rightward, leading to an increase in *P* and real GDP. **a** and **b** shift *AD* leftward, while **c** shifts *SAS* leftward, leading to a decrease in *Y*, and **d** shifts *LAS* rightward, which decreases *P* (try drawing a graph). (524–529)

12 d Expenditure = money earned by sales of produced goods, and is used to pay incomes (including profits). (476–480)

13 b Job not available in winter. (505–509)

14 a Definition. (505–509)

15 b It should be reducing the deficit and keeping inflation low. (469)

16 e Definition. (457–462)

Chapter 25 Expenditure Multipliers

KEY CONCEPTS

Expenditure Plans and GDP

Components of aggregate expenditure are consumption (C), investment (I), government expenditures (G), and net exports (exports (X) – imports (M), which sum to real GDP (Y).

- In short term, I, G, X are fixed, but C, M depend on real GDP (Y).
- Increase in Y increases AE, and increase in AE increases Y—this chapter explores this feedback loop.

Consumption and saving depend primarily on **disposable income** (YD) = real GDP – net taxes (NT).

- **Consumption function** shows increase in YD leads to increase in consumption.
- **Saving function** shows increase in YD leads to increase in saving, with $\Delta C + \Delta S = \Delta YD$.
- Increase in YD by $1 leads to increase in C and increase in S, but increases in C and S are each less than $1. However, they add up to $1.
  - **Marginal propensity to consume** (MPC) = fraction of ΔYD that is consumed = $\Delta C/\Delta YD$ = slope of consumption function.
  - **Marginal propensity to save** (MPS) = fraction of ΔYD that is saved = $\Delta S/\Delta YD$ = slope of saving function.
  - $MPC + MPS = 1$.
- ΔYD creates movement along consumption and saving functions, but other influences *shift* the functions.
  - Increase in expected future income shifts S function downwards, C function upwards.
  - Increase in interest rate shifts S function upwards, C function downwards.
  - Increase in wealth shifts S function downwards, C function upwards.
- Consumption and saving are a function of real GDP since increase in real GDP leads to increase in YD.

Import function is relationship between imports and real GDP.

- **Marginal propensity to import** is fraction of ΔY spent on imports = $\Delta M/\Delta Y$.
- Other variables, such as implementing trade agreements, also influence imports.

Equilibrium Expenditure at a Fixed Price Level

In the very short term, firms keep prices fixed.

- Therefore the price level is fixed—aggregate demand determines aggregate quantity sold.
- To understand AD, we study the aggregate expenditure model.
- **Aggregate planned expenditure** (AE) = planned C + planned I + planned G + planned X – planned M.

The components of aggregate expenditure interact to determine Y, and AE is influenced by Y.

- AE can be represented by graph or schedule. Increase in Y leads to increase in AE.
- Aggregate planned expenditure has two parts:
  - **Autonomous expenditure** (A) = part of AE that does *not* vary with income.
  - **Induced expenditure** (N) = part of AE that *does* vary with income.

- Actual aggregate expenditure may not equal planned expenditure if level of real GDP is not consistent with plans.
- **Equilibrium expenditure** occurs when *AE* = real GDP.
  - On graph this point occurs when *AE* curve crosses 45° line.
  - If real GDP is above equilibrium value, *AE* < real GDP. Firms cannot sell all their production, leading to increase in unplanned inventories, so firms lower production, leading to decrease in real GDP and convergence to equilibrium.
  - If real GDP below equilibrium value, *AE* > real GDP. Firms sell all their production and more, leading to unplanned decrease in inventories, so firms increase production to restore inventories, leading to increase in real GDP and convergence to equilibrium.

The Multiplier

Multiplier is amount by which change in autonomous expenditure is multiplied to determine change in equilibrium expenditure and real GDP.

- Increase in autonomous expenditure leads to primary effect of increased aggregate planned expenditure, leading to increase in real GDP, leading to further (secondary) increase in aggregate planned expenditure, leading to further increases in real GDP, etc.
- Secondary *induced* effects means total Δ real GDP > initial Δ autonomous expenditure.
- Multiplier = (Δ real GDP)/(Δ autonomous expenditure) = 1/(1 – slope of *AE* function) > 1 because of induced effects.
  - Higher slope of *AE* function implies larger induced effects and larger multiplier.
  - Multiplier is higher if *MPC* is higher, or marginal tax rate is lower or marginal propensity to import is lower.
- Recessions and depressions begin with expenditure fluctuations magnified by multiplier effect.

The Multiplier and the Price Level

Aggregate demand curve shows relationship between real GDP demanded and price level, other things remaining the same, and can be derived from *AE* curve.

- *AE* curve shows relationship between *AE* and real GDP, other things remaining the same.
- Increase in price level shifts *AE* curve downward, lowers equilibrium real GDP, shown by movement up and to left on *AD* curve.
- Δ nonprice variables shift both *AE* and *AD* curves.
  - Increase in *A* leads to shift upward in *AE* curve, shift rightward in *AD* curve by Δ*A* × multiplier.

Real-world multipliers are smaller because of changes in price level.

- In short run, increase in *AE* leads to increase in price level, which lowers *AE* somewhat, offsetting increase in *Y* somewhat, so multiplier is smaller.
- In long run, vertical *LAS* means there is large enough increase in price level to create decrease in *AE* that totally offsets initial increase, so that multiplier = 0.

Mathematical Note to Chapter 25: The Algebra of the Multiplier

- Aggregate planned expenditure (*AE*) = sum of components planned levels:

  $AE = C + I + G + X - M$

  - Consumption = autonomous consumption (*a*) + induced, or

    $C = a + bYD = a + b(Y - NT) = a + b(1 - t)Y$

  - Imports depend on real GDP ($M = mY$).
- Substitute consumption and import functions into *AE* function:
  - $AE = a + b(1 - t)Y + I + G + X - mY$, or
  - $AE = [a + I + G + X] + [b(1 - t) - m]Y$, or
  - $AE = A + [b(1 - t) - m]Y$, where $[b(1 - t) - m]$ is slope of *AE* curve
- Equilibrium occurs when $Y = AE$ along the 45° line:

  $Y = A + [b(1 - t) - m]Y$, which can be solved for

  - $Y = \dfrac{1}{1 - [b(1 - t) - m]}A$
- ΔA creates $\Delta Y = \Delta A/(1 - [b(1 - t) - m])$, so that

$$\text{multiplier} = \frac{\Delta Y}{\Delta A} = \frac{1}{1 - [b(1 - t) - m]}$$

$$= \frac{1}{1 - \text{Slope of } AE \text{ function}}$$

HELPFUL HINTS

1 The 45° line is an important concept for understanding the consumption function and equilibrium expenditure. The 45° line is a *reference line* on a graph, showing the points where the two variables on the axes of the graph have the same value.

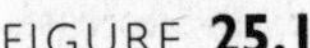

FIGURE **25.1**

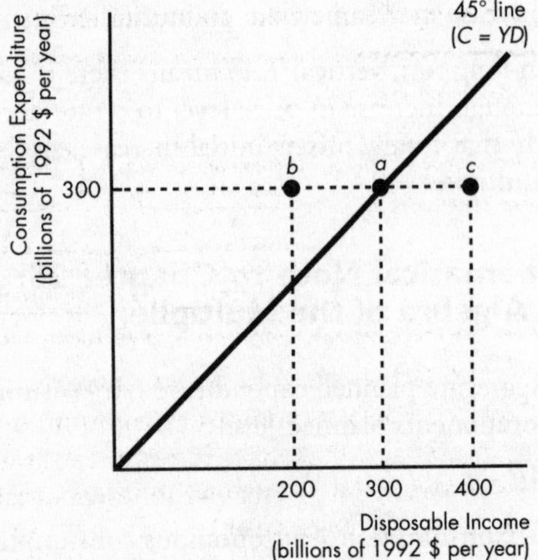

Consider the graph of consumption and disposable income illustrated in Fig. 25.1. Along the 45° line, consumption equals disposable income at all points. For example, at point *a*, $C = YD$ = \$300 billion.

Consider point *b*. Consumption is still equal to \$300 billion, but now disposable income is only \$200 billion. *To the left of the 45° line, variables measured on the vertical axis (here, consumption) are greater than variables measured on the horizontal axis (here, disposable income).*

Next, consider point *c*. Consumption is still equal to \$300 billion, but now disposable income is \$400 billion. *To the right of the 45° line, variables measured on the vertical axis are less than variables measured on the horizontal axis.*

To summarize, consider the consumption function (*CF*) shown in Fig. 25.2. Using the 45° as our reference, any point on the consumption function that is to the left of the 45° line has consumption greater than disposable income (and therefore saving (= $YD - C$) is negative). Any point on the consumption function to the right of the 45° line has consumption less than disposable income (and saving is positive).

FIGURE **25.2**

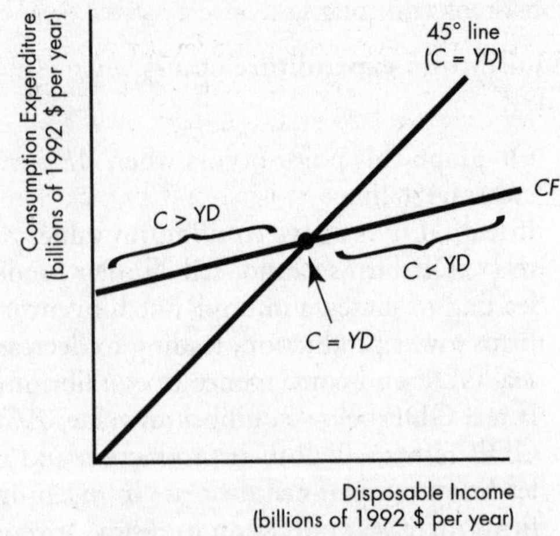

To make sure you understand, draw the graph of the aggregate expenditure function, with a 45° line, and identify the points on your graph where aggregate expenditure is greater than income, equal to income, or less than income. *Note:* For the consumption function, the 45° line is a pure reference line—it is possible in equilibrium for consumption to be greater than, less than, or equal to disposable income. However, for the aggregate expenditure function, the point on the 45° line where $AE = Y$ is more than just a reference point, it shows the point of *equilibrium expenditure.*

2 Aggregate demand is the relationship between the price level and the quantity of goods and services demanded; in other words, it is the relationship between the price level and the level of planned aggregate expenditure. One purpose of this chapter is to help you better understand the behaviour of planned aggregate expenditure by separating and examining its individual components. In particular, consumption expenditure, investment, and net exports—the three components of private aggregate expenditure—will be examined. As you put the discussion of this chapter and the next in perspective, remember that the ultimate objective is a more complete understanding of aggregate demand (and what shifts it), which combines these expenditure components with government expenditure on goods and services. This understanding of the components such as consumption will help you in later chapters to understand the potential causes of past and future recessions.

Be sure you are able to distinguish the *AD* curve from the *AE* curve—they are based on different thought experiments. Each *AE* curve holds constant the price level, and represents only a single point on an *AD* curve, while the *AD* curve allows the price level to vary. Changing the price level will shift the *AE* curve, but create a movement along the *AD* curve.

3 Unplanned changes in inventory are an important part of the story of how equilibrium expenditure is achieved, and how it changes in the face of a shock. To help you see how this effect works, suppose that you were running a retail store—for example, selling CDs or dresses. On the basis of your normal sales and the costs versus benefits of holding inventories, you would have a target optimal planned inventory of perhaps 200 dresses. Each week you might sell an average of 40 dresses, and also reorder 40 dresses from the manufacturer who supplies you. In this simple example, production of 40 dresses equals the sales (planned expenditure) of 40 dresses on average, with week-to-week fluctuations depending on the weather, etc.

Next, suppose that there is a change in planned expenditures by consumers that leads to a decrease in your sales to only 30 dresses a week. Initially, you are still ordering 40 dresses a week because you think that this change is just a temporary fluctuation that will eventually reverse itself. However, after a few weeks there has been no reversal, and you find that your inventory of dresses in the store has had an unplanned increase. You react to this information by cutting your orders to your supplier in order to shrink your inventory. In turn, the dress manufacturer cuts production, and may lay off workers, etc.—the decrease in planned expenditures by consumers has led to a decrease in real GDP.

There are two real-world complications to this simple story. First, while initially the text holds constant the price level, in the real world (and at the end of the chapter), prices do some adjusting. For example, our dress shop might cut prices to try and move excess inventory and raise sales.

Second, there are many industries where firms cannot hold inventories, and must adjust production or prices instantly when sales decrease. Most service industries fall into this category—consider the example of a law firm. A law firm cannot maintain an inventory of legal briefs. Instead, it reacts to changes in the demand for its services by an immediate change in production. As a result, lawyers and others in various service industries have frequent periods of low workloads, followed by frequent periods of high workloads—in a sense, the inventory adjustment occurs by an adjustment of the hours of work.

4 This chapter distinguishes between *autonomous* expenditure and *induced* expenditure. Autonomous expenditure is independent of changes in real GDP, whereas induced expenditure will vary as real GDP varies. In general, a change in autonomous expenditures creates a change in real GDP, which in turn creates a change in induced expenditure. As the flow graph in Fig. 25.3 illustrates, these changes are at the heart of the multiplier effect.

FIGURE **25.3**

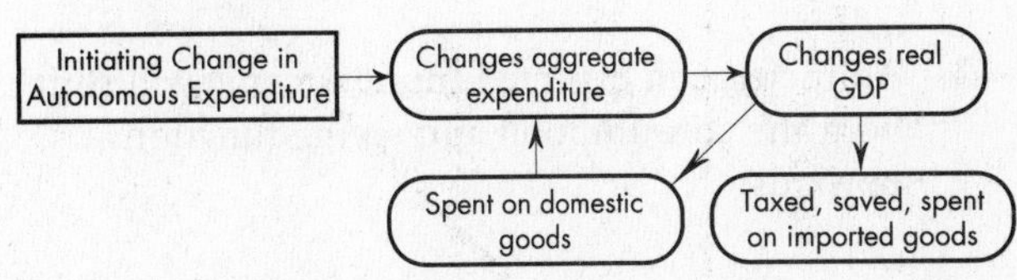

(It is important to realize, however, that even though autonomous expenditure may be independent of changes in real GDP, it will not be independent of changes in other variables, for example, the price level.)

5 The concept of the multiplier is very important. It is a result of the interaction of the components of aggregate expenditure. In particular, an initial increase in autonomous expenditure will increase real GDP directly, but that is not the end of the story. That initial increase in real GDP will generate an increase in *induced* expenditure, which further increases real GDP, and thus induces further increases in expenditure. The total effect on real GDP will be larger than the initial increase in autonomous expenditure because there is induced expenditure. You should become thoroughly familiar with both the intuition and the mathematics behind the multiplier.

6 The multiplier shows the change in equilibrium expenditure, and the change in equilibrium real GDP, price level held constant—it shows the shift rightward or leftward in the *AD* curve. However, normally the price level will change in face of a shift in the *AD* curve, with the size of the change depending on the *AS* curve. In the short run, the change in the price level creates an opposite change in aggregate expenditure, that somewhat offsets the initial change in aggregate expenditure, so that the total change in real GDP is less than the initial shift in *AD* would indicate. In the long run, this offsetting effect is 100 percent.

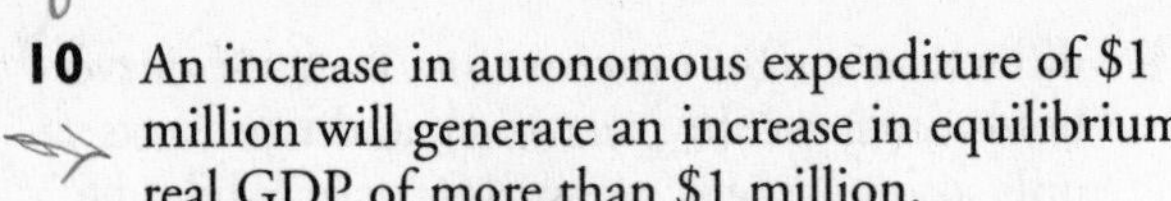

SELF-TEST

True/False/Uncertain and Explain

1 The sum of the marginal propensity to consume and the marginal propensity to save is equal to 1.

2 A change in disposable income will shift the consumption function.

3 An increase in expected future income will shift both the consumption and saving functions upwards.

4 When aggregate planned expenditure exceeds real GDP, inventories will increase more than planned.

5 Equilibrium expenditure occurs when aggregate planned expenditure equals real GDP.

6 Induced expenditure is that part of aggregate expenditure that varies as real GDP varies.

7 If the slope of the *AE* function is 0.75, the multiplier is equal to 3.

8 If the marginal tax rate increases and the marginal propensity to import decreases, the multiplier will be higher.

9 An increase in the price level will shift the aggregate expenditure curve upward.

10 An increase in autonomous expenditure of $1 million will generate an increase in equilibrium real GDP of more than $1 million.

Multiple-Choice

Expenditure Levels and Real GDP

1 The fraction of the last dollar of disposable income saved is the

a marginal propensity to consume.
b marginal propensity to save.
c marginal propensity to dispose.
d marginal tax rate.
e saving function.

2 Consider Table 25.1. Autonomous consumption is equal to

a $0.
b $65.
c $100.
d $260
e $400.

TABLE **25.1**

Disposable Income (1992 $)	Consumption Expenditure (1992 $)
0	100
100	165
200	230
300	295
400	360

3 Consider Table 25.1. The marginal propensity to consume is

a 0.35.
b 0.65.
c 1.15.
d 1.65.
e not calculable with the information given.

4 In Table 25.1, at which of the following level(s) of *YD* is there positive saving?

a 0
b 100
c 200
d 300
e All of the above levels

5 Which of the following events would shift the consumption function upward?

a An increase in disposable income
b A decrease in disposable income
c An increase in the interest rate
d A decrease in expected future income
e An increase in wealth

Equilibrium Expenditure at a Fixed Price Level

6 The aggregate expenditure curve shows the relationship between aggregate planned expenditure and

a disposable income.
b real GDP.
c the interest rate.
d consumption expenditure.
e the price level.

7 If there is an unplanned increase in inventories, aggregate planned expenditure is

a greater than real GDP and firms will increase output.
b greater than real GDP and firms will decrease output.
c less than real GDP and firms will increase output.
d less than real GDP and firms will decrease output.
e less than real GDP and firms will decrease investment.

8 If $AE = 50 + 0.6Y$ and $Y = 200$ then unplanned inventory

a increases are 75.
b increases are 30.
c decreases are 75.
d decreases are 30.
e changes are 0 and equilibrium exists.

9 Autonomous expenditure is *not* influenced by

a the interest rate.
b the foreign exchange rate.
c real GDP.
d the price level.
e any variable.

10 In Fig. 25.4, the marginal propensity to consume is

a 0.3.
b 0.6.
c 0.9.
d 1.0.
e none of the above.

FIGURE **25.4**

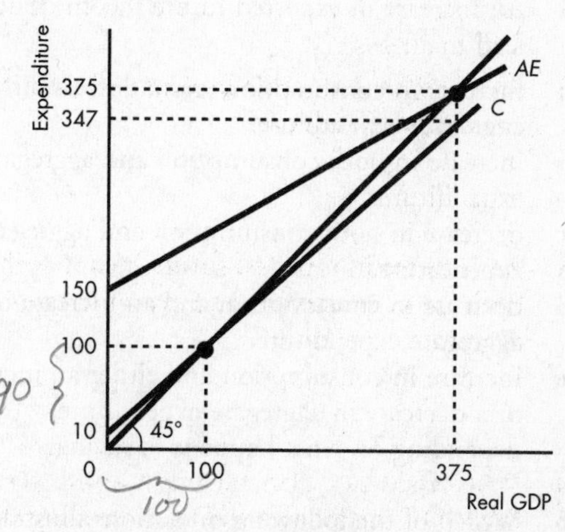

Note: There are no taxes in this economy.

11 In Fig. 25.4, *autonomous* aggregate expenditure is

a 10.
b 100.
c 150.
d 347.
e 375.

12 In Fig. 25.4, at the equilibrium level of real GDP, *induced* expenditure is

a 28.
b 150.
c 225.
d 347.
e 375.

13 In Fig. 25.4, the marginal propensity to import is

a 0.
b 0.1.
c 0.25.
d 0.3.
e 0.6.

The Multiplier

14 In Fig. 25.4, the multiplier is

a 0.25.
b 1.00.
c 1.60.
d 2.50.
e 10.

15 An increase in expected future income would lead to a(n)

a increase in consumption and a decrease in aggregate expenditure.
b increase in both consumption and aggregate expenditure.
c decrease in both consumption and aggregate expenditure.
d decrease in consumption and an increase in aggregate expenditure.
e increase in consumption and either an increase or a decrease in aggregate expenditure, depending on what happens to saving.

16 Which of the following quotations illustrates the idea of the multiplier?

a "The new stadium will generate $200 million in spinoff spending."
b "Higher expected profits are leading to higher investment spending by business, and will lead to higher consumer spending."
c "The projected cuts in government jobs will hurt the local retail industry."
d "Taking the grain elevator out of our small town will destroy 300 jobs."
e All of the above.

17 Which of the following will lead to an increase in the value of the multiplier?

a an increase in the marginal propensity to import
b an increase in the marginal tax rate
c a decrease in the marginal propensity to consume
d a decrease in the marginal propensity to save
e an increase in the marginal propensity to save

The Multiplier and the Price Level

18 An increase in the price level will

a shift the *AE* curve upward and increase equilibrium expenditure.
b shift the *AE* curve upward and decrease equilibrium expenditure.
c shift the *AE* curve downward and increase equilibrium expenditure.
d shift the *AE* curve downward and decrease equilibrium expenditure.
e have no impact on the *AE* curve.

19 A decrease in the price level will

a increase aggregate expenditure and thus produce a movement along the aggregate demand curve.
b increase aggregate expenditure and thus produce a rightward shift in the aggregate demand curve.
c increase aggregate expenditure and thus produce a leftward shift in the aggregate demand curve.
d have no effect on aggregate expenditure.
e increase aggregate expenditure, but produce no effect on the aggregate demand curve.

20 Suppose that investment increases by $10 billion. If the multiplier is 2, the *AD* curve will

a shift rightward by the horizontal distance of $20 billion.
b shift rightward by a horizontal distance greater than $20 billion.
c shift rightward by a horizontal distance less than $20 billion.
d not be affected.
e shift upward by a vertical distance equal to $20 billion.

21 Suppose the multiplier is 2 and the short-run aggregate supply curve is positively sloped. If investment increases by $10 billion, equilibrium real GDP will

a increase by $20 billion.
b increase by more than $20 billion.
c decrease by less than $20 billion.
d be unaffected.
e increase by less than $20 billion.

Mathematical Note to Chapter 25: The Algebra of the Multiplier

22 Consider Fig. 25.5. The equation of the consumption function in this figure is

- **a** $C = 200 + 0.8YD$.
- **b** $C = 200 + 800YD$.
- **c** $C = 200 + 0.75YD$.
- **d** $C = 200 + 0.25YD$.
- **e** $C = 200 + 200YD$.

FIGURE **25.5**

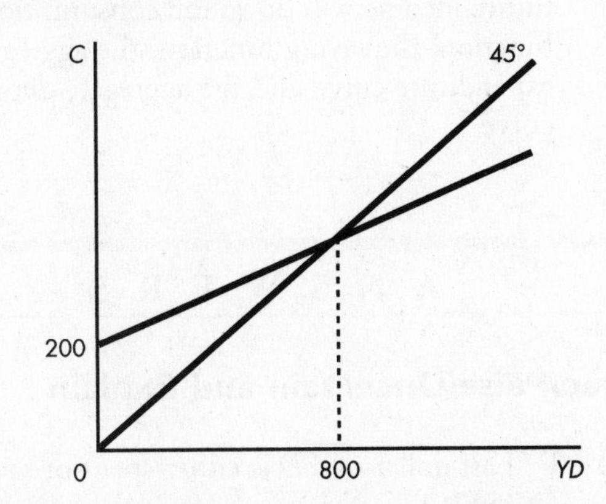

23 If the saving function is $S = -25 + 0.4YD$, then the consumption function is

- **a** indeterminate without further information.
- **b** $C = -25 + 0.4YD$.
- **c** $C = 25 - 0.4YD$.
- **d** $C = 25 + 0.6YD$.
- **e** $C = 25 - 0.4YD$.

24 Consider Fact 25.1. What is the equation for the aggregate expenditure function of this economy?

- **a** $AE = 16 + 0.7Y$
- **b** $AE = 36 - 0.7Y$
- **c** $AE = 26 + 0.8Y$
- **d** $AE = 36 + 0.9Y$
- **e** $AE = 36 + 0.7Y$

FACT **25.1**

The economy of Beverly Hills has a consumption function of $C = 10 + 0.8Y$, investment equal to 6, government expenditures on goods and services equal to 10, exports equal to 10, and an import function of $M = 0.1Y$.

25 Consider Fact 25.1. What is equilibrium real GDP in this economy?

- **a** 36
- **b** 120
- **c** 130
- **d** 360
- **e** none of the above

Short Answer Problems

1 Explain how studying the circular flow in Chapter 22 helps us to understand the multiplier process of Chapter 25.

2 Suppose aggregate planned expenditure is greater than real GDP. Explain the process by which equilibrium expenditure is achieved.

3 Define and explain what autonomous expenditure is, and what induced expenditure is, and what role each plays in the multiplier process.

4 Explain (without algebraic expressions) why the multiplier is larger if the marginal propensity to consume is higher.

5 Explain how the effects of price level changes on the *AE* curve will generate an *AD* curve.

6 Table 25.2 illustrates the consumption function for a very small economy.

TABLE **25.2**

Disposable Income (1992 $)	Consumption Expenditure (1992 $)	Saving (1992 $)
0	3,000	
3,000	5,250	
6,000	7,500	
9,000	9,750	
12,000	12,000	
15,000	14,250	

- **a** Compute the economy's saving at each level of disposable income by completing Table 25.2.
- **b** Compute the economy's *MPC* and *MPS*.
- **c** From the information given and computed, draw the economy's consumption and saving functions.
- **d** Write out the equations of the consumption and saving functions.

7 Consider an economy with the following components of aggregate expenditure:

- Consumption function: $C = 20 + 0.8Y$
- Investment function: $I = 30$
- Government expenditures: $G = 8$
- Export function: $X = 4$
- Import function: $M = 2 + 0.2Y$

(There are no taxes, so $YD = Y$.)

a What is the marginal propensity to consume in this economy?
b What is the equation of the aggregate expenditure function in this economy?
c What is the slope of the *AE* function?
d Find this economy's equilibrium aggregate expenditure and real GDP by completing the columns of Table 25.3.

TABLE **25.3**

Y	C	I	G	X	M	AE
0		30	8	4	2	
30		30	8	4		
60		30	8	4		
90		30	8	4		
120		30	8	4		
150		30	8	4		
180		30	8	4		

e Using the equation of the aggregate function you derived in **b**, solve mathematically for the equilibrium aggregate expenditure and real GDP.
f What is the multiplier for this economy?

8 Consider an economy with the following characteristics:

- Autonomous part of consumption expenditure = \$10 billion
- Investment = \$5 billion
- Government expenditures of goods and services = \$40 billion
- Exports = \$5 billion
- Slope of the *AE* function = 0.5.
- There are no autonomous imports.

(Assume that the price level is constant.)

a What is autonomous expenditure in this economy?
b What is the equation of the *AE* function?
c Draw a graph containing the *AE* curve for this economy (label it AE_0) as well as a 45° line.
d What is equilibrium expenditure?
ⓔ **e** What is induced expenditure in equilibrium?

9 Return to the economy of Short Answer Problem **8**. Now suppose that the government decides to increase its expenditures goods and services to \$60 billion.

a Using the graph from Short Answer Problem **8c**, draw the new *AE* curve and label it AE_1.
b What is the new equilibrium expenditure? Solve for this value using both the graphical approach and the mathematical approach.
c What is the multiplier?
ⓔ **d** Were there increases or decreases in autonomous expenditure, induced expenditure, consumption, imports, and investment after the increase in government expenditures?

10 Explain carefully what an increase in expected future income will do to the consumption function, the saving function, the aggregate expenditure curve and the aggregate demand curve.

ANSWERS

True/False/Uncertain and Explain

1 T Last dollar of *YD* is either spent or saved. (547)
2 F Change in *YD* leads to movement along consumption function. (547)
3 F Shifts upward the consumption function—more consumption expenditure at each level of *current YD*, but given constant current *YD*, this increase in consumption means less saving. (547)
4 F *AE* > real GDP creates excess sales, leading to falling inventories. (553)
5 T Definition. (553)
6 T Definition. (551)
7 F Multiplier = 1/(1 – slope of *AE* function) = 1/(1 – 0.75) = 1/0.25 = 4. (556)
8 U A higher marginal tax rate lowers the slope of the *AE* curve and the size of the multiplier, while a lower marginal propensity to import does the opposite—it depends on the relative sizes of the two effects. (556–557)
9 F Increase in price level lowers *AE* through wealth effect, etc. (560)
10 U Depends on whether short run or long run, and on slope of *SAS* if short run. (561–563)

Multiple-Choice

1 b Definition. (546)
2 c The level of consumption when disposable income is zero. (544)
3 b $MPC = \Delta C/\Delta YD = (165 - 100)/(100 - 0) = 0.65$. (546)

4 **d** Only here is $YD > C$. (544–545)
5 **e** **a** and **b** are movements along the curve, **c** and **d** shift it downwards. (547–548)
6 **b** Definition. (550)
ⓒ 7 **d** Increase in inventories means $AE <$ real GDP and decreases in firms' sales, so they decrease production in response. (552–553)
ⓒ 8 **b** $Y = 200$ implies $AE = 50 + 0.6(200) = 170$. Unplanned inventories = $Y - AE = +30$. (552–523)
9 **c** Definition. (551)
10 **c** MPC = slope of consumption function = $\Delta C/\Delta Y = 90/100 = 0.9$. (546)
11 **c** Intercept of AE function. (551)
12 **c** Induced = aggregate – autonomous = 375 – 150 = 225. (551–553)
ⓒ 13 **d** Marginal propensity to import = MPC – slope of AE curve = 0.9 – 0.6 = 0.3, where the slope of AE curve = $\Delta AE/\Delta Y$ = 225/375 = 0.6. (551–553)
14 **d** Multiplier = 1/(1 – slope of AE function) = 1/(1 – 0.6) = 1/0.4 = 2.5. (556)
15 **b** Increase in expected future income leads to more consumption spending, less saving, and an increase in autonomous expenditure. (547–554)
16 **e** All of the choices discuss secondary, induced effects. (554–555)
ⓒ 17 **d** This change raises MPC and multiplier. Others lower multiplier. (556–557)
18 **d** Increase in price level leads to decrease in aggregate expenditure due to the three effects, leading to new equilibrium at lower real GDP = equilibrium expenditure. (560)
19 **a** Decrease in price level leads to increase in aggregate expenditure due to three effects, leading to movement along AD curve. (560)
20 **a** Multiplier effect raises AE and Y by 2 times original Δ autonomous expenditure, which leads to shift rightward by same amount in AD curve. (560–561)
21 **e** Multiplier effect of Question **20** is reduced by increase in price level due to positively sloped SAS curve. (560–562)
ⓒ 22 **c** Intercept = 200, slope = $\Delta C/\Delta YD$, and from $YD = 0$ to $YD = 800$, slope = +600/+800 = 0.75. (566–567)
23 **d** $C = YD - S = YD - (-25 + 0.4YD) = 25 + 0.6YD$. (566–567)
24 **e** $AE = 10 + 0.8Y + 6 + 10 + 10 - 0.1Y = 36 + 0.7Y$. (566–567)
25 **b** Solve $Y^* = 36 + 0.7Y^*$, which leads to $Y^*(1 - 0.7) = 36$, and therefore $Y^* = 36/0.3 = 120$. (566–567)

Short Answer Problems

1 The circular flow shows us that firms produce goods and services, sell them on the market to consumers, investors, governments, and the rest of the world, and use the money earned to pay factors of production, who in turn buy goods and services. The circular flow thus shows us the secondary, induced effects of the multiplier process in action. An initial increase in autonomous expenditure means more sales for firms, which means more household income, which means more consumption expenditure, etc.

2 If aggregate planned expenditure is greater than real GDP, inventories will decrease more than planned, and firms will increase output to replenish those depleted inventories. As a result, real GDP increases. This procedure continues as long as real GDP is less than aggregate planned expenditure. Thus it will stop only when equilibrium is attained—when real GDP equals aggregate planned expenditure.

3 Autonomous expenditure is the part of aggregate expenditure that does not vary with real GDP, but varies as a result of changes in other variables such as the real interest rate. Induced expenditure is the part of aggregate expenditure that does vary with real GDP. The multiplier process starts out with a change in autonomous expenditure that changes aggregate expenditure, which in turn changes real GDP. This change in real GDP creates secondary effects by changing induced expenditure in the same direction, which in turn changes aggregate expenditure and real GDP, leading to a total effect that is a multiple of the initial change in autonomous expenditure.

4 Any initial stimulus to autonomous expenditure will generate a direct increase in real GDP. The basic idea of the multiplier is that this initial increase in real GDP will generate further increases in real GDP as increases in consumption expenditure are induced. At each round of the multiplier process, the increase in spending, and thus the further increase in real GDP, are partially determined by the marginal propensity to consume. Since a larger marginal propensity to consume means a larger increase in real GDP at each round, the total increase in real GDP will also be greater. Thus the multiplier will be larger if the marginal propensity to consume is larger.

5 The aggregate demand curve illustrates the relationship between the price level and aggregate expenditures. The aggregate expenditure diagram shows the level of equilibrium expenditure holding the price level constant. If the price level changes, the *AE* curve will shift and a new level of equilibrium expenditure will result. Thus for each price level, there is a different level of equilibrium expenditure. These combinations of price level and corresponding aggregate expenditure are points on the aggregate demand curve. For example, if the price level increases, autonomous expenditure will decline, and the *AE* curve will shift downward. This shift will lead to a decrease in equilibrium expenditure. Since an increase in the price level is associated with a reduction in equilibrium expenditure, the *AD* curve is negatively sloped.

6 The answers to **a** are shown in Table 25.2 Solution, where saving = *YD* – *C*.

TABLE **25.2** SOLUTION

Disposable Income (1992 $)	Consumption Expenditure (1992 $)	Saving (1992 $)
0	3,000	–3,000
3,000	5,250	–2,250
6,000	7,500	–1,500
9,000	9,750	–750
12,000	12,000	0
15,000	14,250	+750

b The *MPC* = change in consumption/change in disposable income. Using the first two entries in the table, we can see that change in consumption is 2,250, and the change in disposable income is 3,000, so that the *MPC* = 0.75 = 2,250/3,000. The *MPS* = change in saving/change in disposable income. Using the first two entries in the table, we can see that change in saving is +750, and the change in disposable income is 3,000, so that the *MPS* = 0.25 = 750/3,000. Using any other two adjacent entries in the table will yield the same result.

c The consumption function is shown in Fig. 25.6, and the saving function is illustrated in Fig. 25.7.

FIGURE **25.6**

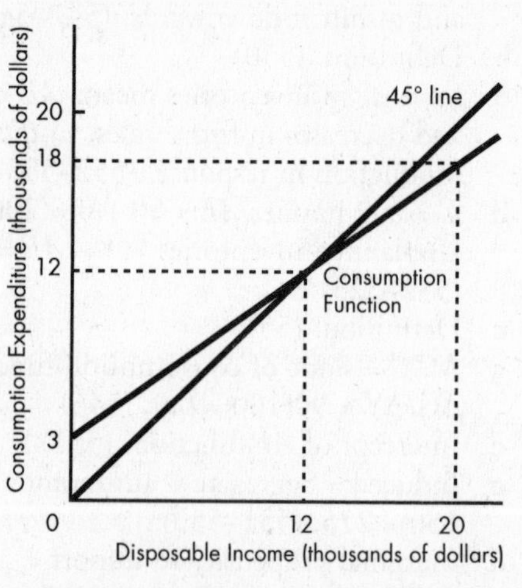

FIGURE **25.7**

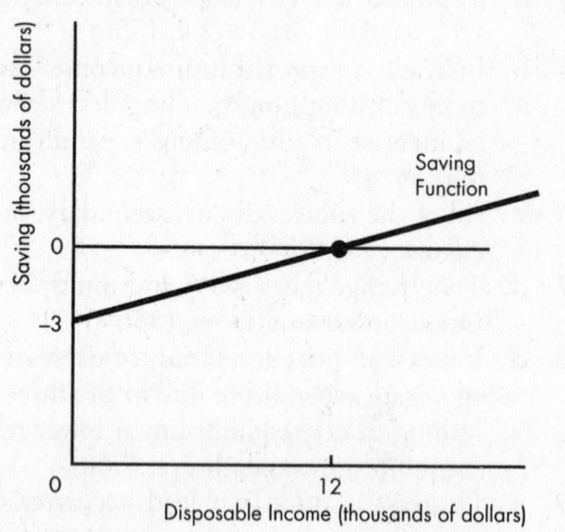

d The equation of the consumption function is based on an intercept of 3,000 and the slope (*MPC*) of 0.75. $C = 3{,}000 + 0.75YD$. Similarly, for the saving function, $S = -3{,}000 + 0.25YD$.

7 **a** From the consumption function equation we know this value is $0.8 = \Delta C/\Delta Y$.

b Substitute the various equations into $AE = C + I + G + X - M$: $AE = 20 + 0.8Y + 30 + 8 + 4 - 2 - 0.2Y = 60 + 0.6Y$.

c The slope of the *AE* function comes from the equation and equals $\Delta AE/\Delta Y = 0.6$.

d The answer is presented in Table 25.3 Solution below. The table is constructed by substituting the various values of *Y* into the equations. Note that equilibrium occurs when *AE* = *Y* at a value of 150.

TABLE **25.3** SOLUTION

Y	*C*	*I*	*G*	*X*	*M*	*AE*
0	20	30	8	4	2	60
30	44	30	8	4	8	78
60	68	30	8	4	14	96
90	92	30	8	4	20	114
120	116	30	8	4	26	132
150	140	30	8	4	32	150
180	164	30	8	4	38	168

e Equilibrium occurs when

$$Y = AE, \text{ or}$$
$$Y^* = 60 + 0.6Y^*, \text{ or}$$
$$Y^*(1 - 0.6) = Y^*(0.4) = 60, \text{ or}$$
$$Y^* = 60/0.4 = 150$$

f The multiplier = 1/(1 – slope of *AE* function) = 1/(1 – 0.6) = 1/0.4 = 2.5.

8 a Autonomous expenditure is the sum of the autonomous part of consumption expenditure, investment, government expenditure on goods and services, and exports. This sum is $60 billion.

b The equation is of the form $AE = A + eY$, where A is autonomous expenditure and e is the slope of the *AE* function. In this case, the equation is $AE = 60 + 0.5Y$, where units are billions of dollars.

c See the curve labelled AE_0 in Fig. 25.8. The curve was drawn by noting that the amount of autonomous expenditure ($60 billion) gives the vertical intercept and that the slope of the *AE* function is 0.5.

FIGURE **25.8**

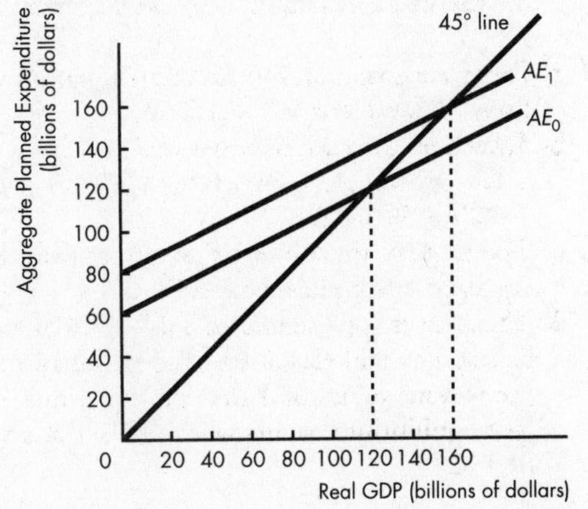

d Equilibrium expenditure can be solved one of two ways. Equilibrium expenditure occurs at the intersection of the AE_0 curve and the 45° line. Equilibrium expenditure is $120 billion. Secondly, it can be calculated by solving the $AE = Y$ equation:

$$Y^* = 60 + 0.5Y^*, \text{ or}$$
$$Y^*(1 - 0.5) = 60, \text{ or}$$
$$Y^* = 60/0.5 = 120$$

e Induced expenditure = total expenditure – autonomous expenditure = 120 – 60 = 60 in this case.

9 a See the curve labelled AE_1 in Fig. 25.8. The new curve reflects the fact that autonomous expenditure increases by $20 billion but the slope of the *AE* function remains unchanged.

b The new equilibrium expenditure is $160 billion. This answer is given by the intersection of the AE_1 curve with the 45° line, or by solving the new equilibrium condition:

$$Y^* = 80 + 0.5Y^*, \text{ or}$$
$$Y^*(1 - 0.5) = 80, \text{ or}$$
$$Y^* = 80/0.5 = 160$$

c Since a $20 billion increase in autonomous expenditure generated a $40 billion increase in equilibrium expenditure, the multiplier is 2. This value can be obtained by using the formula that the multiplier = $1/(1 - e)$ where e is the slope of the *AE* function.

d The total change in real GDP is $40 billion. First, we can note that the change in autonomous expenditure is just the increase in government expenditures of $20 billion, and we can further note:

$$\Delta \text{ total expenditure} = \Delta \text{ autonomous expenditure} + \Delta \text{ induced expenditure}$$

or

$$+\$40 \text{ billion} = +\$20 \text{ billion} + \$20 \text{ billion}$$

so that the change in induced expenditure is also $20 billion.

Second, since real GDP has increased, this will have increased both consumption and imports, since they are part of induced expenditure. However, investment is autonomous, and is therefore not affected by the change in real GDP.

10 An increase in expected future income leads to less saving (so that the saving function shifts downward at each level of disposable income) and more consumption out of current disposable income (so that the consumption function shifts upward). This change is an increase in autonomous consumption, and is therefore an increase in aggregate expenditure, and leads to a shift upward in the aggregate expenditure function. This shift creates multiplier effects and a shift rightward in the aggregate demand curve at the current price level.

Chapter **26**

Fiscal Policy

KEY CONCEPTS

Government Budgets

The **federal budget** is annual statement of revenue and outlays of government of Canada (**provincial budget** is for provincial governments).

- Budgets finance government activities and achieve macroeconomic policy objectives (**fiscal policy**).
- Fiscal policy is made by government and Parliament, in consultation with bureaucrats, provinces, business and consumer groups.
- Budgetary revenues—personal income taxes, corporate income taxes, indirect taxes (GST), investment income.
- Budgetary outlays—transfer payments, expenditures on goods and services, debt interest payments.
- Budget balance = revenues – outlays.
  - **Budget surplus** when revenues > outlays.
  - **Budget deficit** when revenues < outlays.
  - **Balanced budget** when revenues = outlays.
- Federal budget slid into deficit in 1974, deficit grew in early 1980s, remained high until eliminated in 1998.
  - Total outlays increase and decrease with business cycle, but also increase over this period as interest payments increase steadily.
- **Government debt** = total borrowing by governments = sum of past deficits – sum of past surpluses.
  - Persistent deficits of the 1980s increased borrowing, which increased interest payments and increased deficit, etc.
  - Balanced budget of 1998 stopped this cycle—government debt is falling.
- Provincial government outlays are almost as large as federal, focused on hospitals, schools, and colleges/universities.
  - Fluctuate with federal outlays.
  - Less fiscal policy at provincial level.
- Canada's budget situation is similar to that of other industrial nations.

Fiscal Policy Multipliers

Fiscal policy actions can either be **discretionary** (initiated by act of Parliament, involves Δ government outlays and Δ taxes), or **automatic** (triggered by state of economy).

- Initially, assume a model economy with only **autonomous taxes** (do *not* vary with real GDP), and no exports or imports.
- Discretionary fiscal policy changes expenditures, taxes, and transfers to attempt to smooth business cycle fluctuations.
- **Government expenditures multiplier** = (Δ real GDP)/(Δ government expenditures) = $1/(1 - MPC) > 1$.
  - Initial increase in government expenditures increases real GDP, leading to secondary, induced effects.
- **Autonomous tax multiplier** = (Δ real GDP)/(Δ taxes) < 0.
  - Increase in taxes decreases disposable income, decreases consumption, and therefore decreases aggregate expenditure and real GDP, creating secondary, induced effects.
  - Since some of tax change affects saving, initial Δ consumption = $MPC \times$ Δ taxes, so that the autonomous tax multiplier = $-MPC/(1 - MPC)$.

- Autonomous transfers multiplier = $MPC/(1 - MPC)$ since transfers are negative taxes.

Induced taxes, transfer payments and imports are **automatic stabilizers**—mechanisms that reduce fluctuations in real GDP automatically.

- **Induced taxes** and induced transfer payments vary with real GDP and reduce multiplier effects.
  - The larger the marginal tax rate, the smaller the multipliers.
- Higher marginal propensity to import reduces multiplier effects.

Budget deficits fluctuate with business cycle due to cyclical fluctuations in net taxes.

- **Structural surplus or deficit** is budget balance when real GDP = potential.
- **Cyclical surplus or deficit** = actual deficit – structural balance.
- Cyclical deficit is due only to fact that real GDP ≠ potential.

Fiscal Policy Multipliers and the Price Level

Price level adjustments change outcome of fiscal policy.

- **Expansionary fiscal policy** (increased *G* or decreased *NT*) leads to rightward shift *AD* curve by amount = multiplier × policy change.
- **Contractionary fiscal policy** (decreased *G* or increased *NT*) leads to leftward shift *AD* curve.
- In short run, expansionary policy has positive but reduced effects because increase in *AD* increases price level, which decreases *AE*, creating movement along *AD*, partially offsetting initial effect.
- If real GDP at potential, expansionary policy increases *AD* and increases price level, which decreases *AE*, creating movement up along *AD*, fully offsetting initial effect.
- Even short-run fiscal policy is limited by:
  - Slowness of the legislative process.
  - Difficulties in telling if real GDP is above or below potential GDP.

Fiscal Policy and Aggregate Supply

Cutting tax rates might increase potential GDP and shift *LAS* rightward.

- Higher income taxes decrease incentives to work and save, which decreases labour supply and capital supply.
- Tax cut shifts *AD* curve rightward *and* shifts *SAS* rightward due to increased incentives.
- Size of rightward shift is controversial.

Mathematical Note to Chapter 26: The Algebra of Fiscal Multipliers

- Aggregate planned expenditure (*AE*) = $C + I + G + X - M$.
  - Net taxes = autonomous taxes – autonomous transfer payments + induced taxes: $NT = T_a - T_r + tY$
  - Consumption depends on disposable income: $C = a + b(Y - NT) = a - bT_a + bT_r + b(1 - t)Y$
  - Imports (*M*) = mY
- Substitute consumption equation and import equation into *AE* equation: $AE = a - bT_a + bT_r + b(1 - t)Y + I + G + X - mY$
  - Or: $AE = [a - bT_a + bT_r + I + G + X] + [b(1 - t) - m]Y$
  - Or: $AE = A + [b(1 - t) - m]Y$, where A = autonomous expenditure (= $[a - bT_a + bT_r + I + G + X]$) and $[b(1 - t) - m]$ is slope
- Equilibrium occurs when $Y = AE$:
  - $Y = A + [b(1 - t) - m]Y$, which can be solved:
  - $Y = \dfrac{A}{1 - [b(1 - t) + m]}$
- Δ government expenditures affects *A* directly ($\Delta A = \Delta G$):
  - $\Delta Y = \dfrac{1}{1 - [b(1 - t) + m]}\Delta G$, so that
  - government expenditures multiplier $= \dfrac{\Delta Y}{\Delta G} = \dfrac{1}{1 - [b(1 - t) + m]}$
- Δ autonomous taxes affects *A* indirectly ($\Delta A = -b\,\Delta T_a$):
  - $\Delta Y = \dfrac{-b}{1 - [b(1 - t) + m]}\Delta T_a$, so that
  - autonomous tax multiplier $= \dfrac{\Delta Y}{\Delta T_a} = \dfrac{-b}{1 - [b(1 - t) + m]}$
- Similarly, autonomous transfer payments multiplier can be solved for

$$\frac{\Delta Y}{\Delta T_r} = \frac{b}{1 - [b(1 - t) + m]}$$

HELPFUL HINTS

1 It is crucial to distinguish between two types of autonomous shocks. One type adds to the instability of the economy; it includes changes in autonomous consumption, investment, and exports. The other is planned to (hopefully) reduce the instability of the economy; it includes fiscal policy—changes in government expenditures and taxes. Because both shocks work through the same multiplier process, the same process that creates instability can also help to reduce instability.

2 In this chapter, as in Chapter 25, we first derive fiscal policy multipliers for a case where there are no induced taxes, and no foreign sector. In this case, the size of the *MPC* is crucial in determining the size of the multiplier.

We then add the more realistic case of induced taxes, and an import sector where the level of imports rises if real GDP rises. The multiplier is smaller than in the first case, and the higher the marginal tax rate or the higher the marginal propensity to import, the smaller the multiplier. Figure 26.1 below shows why. A crucial part of the multiplier process is the changes in induced expenditure in the second round of the multiplier. With induced taxes and imports, these induced expenditures are reduced as income is siphoned off to pay for taxes and buy imported goods!

FIGURE **26.1**

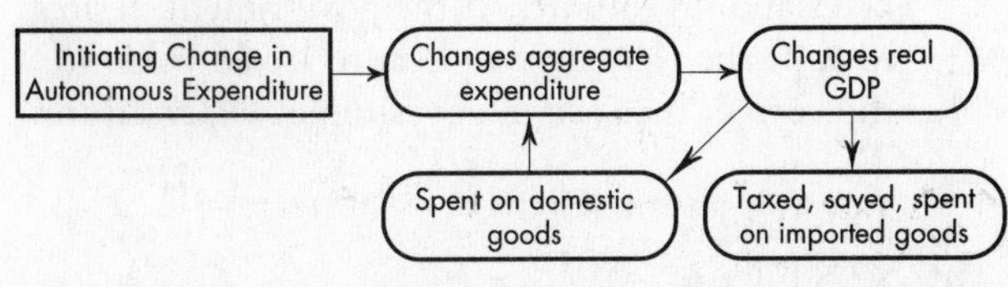

3 Helpful Hint 4 in Chapter 22 emphasized the difference between government expenditure on goods and services and government transfer payments. The difference is crucial once again in understanding why the government expenditures multiplier (= $1/(1 - MPC)$) is larger than the autonomous transfer payments multiplier (= $MPC/(1 - MPC)$).

A $1 increase in government expenditures on goods and services directly raises autonomous expenditure by $1 in the first round of the multiplier. However, a $1 increase in spending on autonomous transfer payments raises consumers' disposable income by $1, and some of this extra income is saved, so that only $1 × *MPC* is consumed, and autonomous expenditure increases by $*MPC* < $1 in the first round of the multiplier.

SELF-TEST

True/False/Uncertain and Explain

1 The federal deficit is the total amount of borrowing that the federal government has undertaken.

2 Only government expenditures on goods and services, not transfer payments, are crucial in analysing the federal deficit.

3 A government starts out with a balanced budget. In the next year, the percentage growth in outlays is higher than the percentage growth in revenues. It will now have a deficit.

4 An increase in autonomous transfer payments matched by an increase in autonomous taxes will lead to an increase in real GDP.

5 Taxes and transfer payments that vary with income act as automatic stabilizers in the economy.

6 The autonomous transfer payments multiplier is smaller than the government expenditures multiplier.

7 If the price level is variable, an increase in government expenditures will never lead to an increase in real GDP.

8 A cut in autonomous taxes of $1 million will increase equilibrium real GDP by more than $1 million.

9 An increase in government expenditures will shift the *AE* curve upward and shift the *AD* curve to the right.

10 Cutting income taxes will shift the *AD* curve rightward, but shift the *SAS* curve leftward.

Multiple-Choice

Government Budgets

1 Provincial government outlays

a are small and irrelevant to the economy.
b are an important source of fiscal policy.
c are always equal to provincial government revenues.
d are focused on transfer payments to individuals, such as employment insurance.
e tend to fluctuate with federal outlays.

2 Which of the following would *not* increase the budget deficit?

a an increase in interest on the government debt
b an increase in government expenditures on goods and services
c an increase in government transfer payments
d an increase in indirect business taxes
e a decrease in government investment income

3 The budget deficit grew as a percentage of GDP after 1974 because

a government expenditures on goods and services rose, while tax revenues remained constant.
b government expenditures on goods and services remained constant, while tax revenues fell.
c debt interest payments rose, while tax revenues remained constant.
d debt interest payments rose, while tax revenues fell.
e none of the above.

4 Federal fiscal policy is influenced by

a government bureaucrats.
b provincial governments.
c Parliament.
d business and consumer groups.
e all of the above.

5 Which of the following is a budgetary outlay?

a personal income taxes
b government investment income
c debt interest payments
d indirect taxes
e all of the above

Fiscal Policy Multipliers

6 Which of the following happens *automatically* if the economy goes into a recession?

a Only government outlays increase.
b Only net taxes increase.
c The deficit increases.
d The deficit decreases.
e Both government outlays and net taxes increase, and the deficit stays the same.

7 During an expansion, tax revenue

a and government outlays decline.
b declines and government outlays increase.
c increases and government outlays decline.
d and government outlays increase.
e stays constant and government outlays increase.

8 Consider the economy of NoTax, where the *MPC* is 0.6, and where there are no induced taxes and no imports. If the government desires to shift the *AD* curve rightward by $5 billion, the correct increase in government expenditures is

a $2 billion.
b $2.5 billion.
c $3 billion.
d $7.5 billion.
e $8.33 billion.

9 How does an increase in the marginal tax rate affect the size of the multiplier?

a It has no impact.
b It makes the multiplier larger.
c It makes the multiplier smaller.
d It makes the multiplier smaller, but only if the new tax rate is larger than the *MPC*.
e It makes the multiplier smaller, but only if the new tax rate is smaller than the *MPC*.

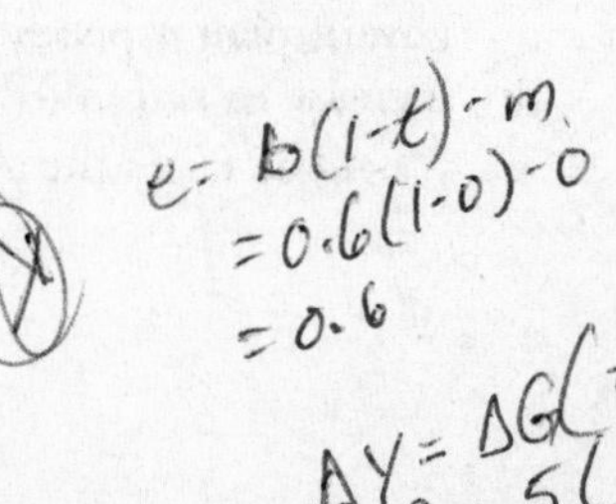

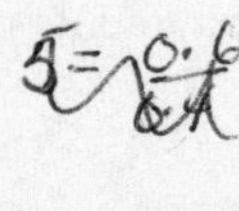

10 The cyclical deficit or surplus
- a is present only if real GDP is greater than potential.
- b would exist even if real GDP equals potential.
- c equals the actual deficit minus the structural deficit.
- d destabilizes the economy.
- e is none of the above.

11 Currently the country of Ricardia has a budget plan with constant government outlays equal to \$100 billion and taxes related positively to real GDP by the equation: Taxes = \$25 billion + $0.1Y$. If the structural deficit is \$10 billion, what is potential GDP in this economy?
- a \$65 billion
- b \$75 billion
- c \$650 billion
- d \$750 billion
- e \$850 billion

12 If the *MPC* is 0.75, and there are no induced taxes or imports, what is the government expenditures multiplier?
- a 0
- b 0.57
- c 1.33
- d 3
- e 4

13 If the *MPC* is 0.75, and there are no induced taxes or imports, what is the autonomous tax multiplier?
- a –4
- b –3
- c –0.43
- d 3
- e 4

14 If the *MPC* is 0.75, and there are no induced taxes or imports, what is the change in *Y* if *both* government expenditures and autonomous taxes increase by \$200?
- a 0
- b 200
- c 600
- d 800
- e not calculable with the information given.

15 If the *MPC* is 0.75, and there are no induced taxes or imports, what is the autonomous transfer payments multiplier?
- a –4
- b –3
- c 0.43
- d 3
- e 4

Fiscal Policy Multipliers and the Price Level

16 An *expansionary* fiscal policy leads to a(n)
- a rightward shift in the *AD* curve equal to the multiplier times the policy change.
- b leftward shift in the *AD* curve equal to the multiplier times the policy change.
- c leftward shift in the *SAS* curve.
- d increase in *Y* equal to the multiplier times the policy change, in the short run.
- e increase in *Y* equal to the multiplier times the policy change, in the long run.

17 Short-run fiscal policy is limited by the fact that
- a the *LAS* curve is vertical.
- b the legislative process is slow.
- c real GDP is typically not equal to potential GDP.
- d the policy might shift the *SAS* curve to the right.
- e the policy might shift the *SAS* curve to the left.

18 Which of the following is an example of an *expansionary* fiscal policy?
- a increasing debt interest payments
- b increasing taxes
- c decreasing transfer payments
- d increasing transfer payments
- e decreasing government expenditures on goods and services

Fiscal Policy and Aggregate Supply

19 Which of the following quotations correctly refers to the effects of fiscal policy in the *long run*?
- a "The increase in taxes will increase real GDP."
- b "The increase in taxes will raise prices only."
- c "A change in the budget has no impact on real GDP unless it changes aggregate supply."
- d "A change in the budget has no impact on real GDP."
- e All of the above.

20 Which of the following statements about expansionary fiscal policy is *false*?
- a It may have no long-run impact on real GDP.
- b It can offset fluctuations in aggregate expenditure and aggregate demand.
- c The *AD* curve shifts rightward by an amount = multiplier × policy change.
- d It never has an impact on aggregate supply.
- e It usually raises the price level.

21 If a tax cut increases potential GDP, the long-run autonomous tax multiplier must be
a larger than 1.0.
b between 0 and 1.0.
c larger than 0.
d 0.
e negative.

Mathematical Note to Chapter 26: The Algebra of Fiscal Multipliers

22 The formula for the tax function is
a $G = G_a + gY$.
b $M = mY$.
c $NT = T_a - T_r + tY$.
d $NT = 1/(1 - [b(1 - t) + m])$.
e none of the above.

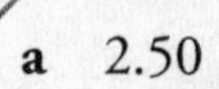

23 Consider an economy where the marginal propensity to consume is 0.875, the marginal tax rate is 20 percent, and the marginal propensity to import out of real GDP is 0.10. What is the autonomous transfer payments multiplier?
a 2.50
b –2.50
c 2.1875
d –2.1875
e 0.3125

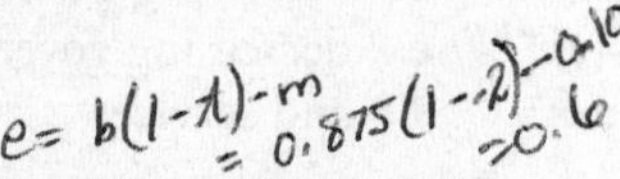

FACT **26.1**

The economy of New Estevan has the following consumption and tax functions:

Consumption: $C = a + 0.5(Y - NT)$

Net taxes: $NT = T_a - T_r + 0.5Y$

This economy has no exports or imports.

24 Consider Fact 26.1. The government expenditures multiplier for this economy is
a 0.25.
b 0.5.
c 1.33.
d 2.0.
e not calculable with the given information.

25 Consider Fact 26.1. The autonomous tax multiplier for this economy is
a –0.667.
b –1.0.
c –1.33.
d –2.0.
e 0.667.

Short Answer Problems

1 What changes in the components of the federal government budget after 1974 were the principal causes of continuing large government deficits?

2 During the summer of 1995, Saskatchewan had a provincial election. A central plank of the Saskatchewan Liberal Party's election strategy was a promise to cut taxes dramatically, stating that these cuts would create 50,000 new jobs (about 10 percent of the labour force) over the next 5 years. Critics claimed that this policy would have only a small effect in Saskatchewan, that most of the new jobs from the tax cuts would show up in other provinces.
a What economic concept underlies the Liberals' promise?
b What economic concept underlies the critics' argument?
c The Liberals lost the election, so we do not get to see if the tax cuts would have had the promised effect, but what do you think would have happened?

3 Suppose you are visiting the town of Elbow, Saskatchewan, which is suffering a depressed economy due to low wheat prices. You spend \$100 on accommodation and another \$100 golfing and dining at the excellent local golf club.
a What factors will influence how much extra real GDP will be generated within Elbow by your \$200 of expenditure? (Treat Elbow as if it were a separate economy.)
b What does your answer imply for the argument made by the Elbow town council that the Saskatchewan government should shift a government department to the town in order to stimulate the town's economy?

4 Explain why the multiplier of an expansionary fiscal policy is smaller once we consider the aggregate supply curve. What happens if there are incentive effects on *AS*?

5 Explain whether or not the following events will shift the *AE* curve and/or the *AD* curve and briefly explain why. (For each case, assume that the other variables are not changing.)
a an increase in the price level
b an increase in expected future profits for businesses
c a cut in autonomous taxes
d an increase in government expenditures

ⓔ **6** Some politicians and economists argue tax cuts are beneficial for the economy in the short run *and* the long run. Explain their arguments, and evaluate them briefly.

7 You may wish to review the mathematical notes to Chapters 25 and 26 before doing this problem. Consider the expenditure functions for the following economy:

Consumption:	$C = 4{,}000 + 0.7(Y - NT) - 20P$
Investment:	$I = 2{,}000$
Government:	$G = 5{,}000$
Exports:	$X = 400$
Imports:	$M = 0.1Y$
Taxes:	$NT = 2{,}000$

where P is the price level.

a What is the equation of the aggregate expenditure function? What is autonomous expenditure in this economy? What is the slope of the *AE* function?

b Assume that the price level is equal to 100. Calculate equilibrium real GDP, consumption, and imports.

c If the price level is now equal to 200, what is the new equilibrium real GDP?

d Using your information from **b** and **c**, sketch the *AD* curve for this economy.

e Calculate the government expenditures multiplier, the autonomous tax multiplier, and the autonomous transfer payments multiplier for this economy.

f Suppose that the price level is equal to 100, and that government expenditures increase by 2,000. What is the resulting change in real GDP demanded, holding constant the price level? Suppose that the change in real GDP demanded raises the price level by 100. What is the overall change in real GDP from the two effects? What is the multiplier after the two effects have worked through the economy? Why is your answer different from **e**?

8 As finance minister for the government of Adanac, your crack team of economists has estimated the economy's *MPC* to be 0.75, price level held constant. (There are no induced taxes or imports.) You are confident that this estimate is correct, since you threatened to exile the economists to the North Pole should they err. You have decided that in order to get reelected next year, you need to raise real GDP by $200 billion.

a If you decide to change only government expenditures, how much change is required to accomplish your goal?

b If you decide to change only autonomous taxes, how much change is required to accomplish your goal?

c Having selected method **a**, you find that the increase in real GDP is less than $200 billion, jeopardizing your chance for reelection. Before you exile the poor economists to the North Pole, is there any excuse for their mistake? (In other words, what went wrong?)

9 Suppose that the economy is in equilibrium at the point where the *AD* curve crosses the *SAS* curve. (Assume that the economy stays in the short run for the rest of this question, and ignore any incentive effects.) Suppose that the government raises autonomous taxes dramatically.

a Initially, assume the price level is held constant. Carefully explain what happens to aggregate expenditure, aggregate demand, and real GDP as a result of this autonomous shock. Draw a two-part graph as part of your answer, showing aggregate expenditure and the 45° line on the top, and the *AD-SAS* curves on the bottom.

ⓔ **b** What happens to the levels of the components of aggregate expenditure after this shock?

c Next, show on the graph from **a** what happens when the price level changes. Explain the overall effect on aggregate expenditure, aggregate demand, short-run aggregate supply, the price level, and real GDP from the combined effects of the shock and the resulting change in the price level.

10 In the economy of Paridisio, government outlays are related to the level of real GDP by the formula: Outlays = $500 - 0.6Y$, while tax revenues are related to the level of real GDP by the formula: Taxes = $100 + 0.2Y$.

a Complete Table 26.1.

TABLE **26.1**

Real GDP	Outlays	Revenues	Budget Balance
0			
100			
200			
300			
400			
500			
600			

b If potential GDP is 300, what is the structural balance for Paridisio?

c If real GDP is currently 200, what are the values of the cyclical deficit, the structural deficit, and the actual deficit?

d Is the tax structure in this economy acting as an automatic stabilizer?

ANSWERS

True/False/Uncertain and Explain

1 F Deficit is when outlays > revenues in current year. (573)

2 F Government expenditures on goods, transfer and interest payments are all part of outlays. (573)

3 T If outlays grow faster than taxes, then outlays > taxes next year and therefore there is a deficit. (573)

4 F They exactly offset each other (Δ net taxes = 0), so Δ real GDP = 0. (580–581)

5 T If income decreases, this leads to decrease in taxes + increase in transfers, and so an increase in disposable income, which increases aggregate expenditure, leading to increase in income, offsetting initial decrease. (581–582)

6 T Since *MPC* < 1, government multiplier $[1/(1 - MPC)]$ > transfer multiplier $[MPC/(1 - MPC)]$. (579–581)

7 F In short run, increase in *G* leads to rightward shift in *AD*, and increase in real GDP. (585–587)

8 U Depends on whether short run or long run, on size of *MPC*, and on slope of *SAS* if short run. (581–587)

9 T Increase in government expenditures = increase in autonomous expenditure, so *AE* curve shifts upward, leading to higher level of *AD*, same price level. (584–585)

10 F Income tax cut raises *YD* and shifts *AD* rightward, and it raises incentives to work and save, shifting *SAS* curve *rightward.* (587–589)

Multiple-Choice

1 e They may have a deficit, they are not really used for fiscal policy, they are almost as large as the federal government outlays, and *federal* government does employment insurance. (576–577)

2 d This effect is increase in revenue. (572–573)

3 c See text discussion. (573–574)

4 e See text discussion. (572)

5 c Others are sources of revenue. (572–573)

6 c In recession, decrease in *Y* leads to decrease in taxes and increase in spending on employment insurance, etc., which leads to increase in deficit. (581–582)

7 c Increase in real GDP leads to increase in tax revenue. Decrease in unemployment leads to decrease in transfer payments. (581–582)

ct **8 a** Government expenditures multiplier $= 1/(1 - MPC) = 1/(1 - 0.6) = 2.5$. Invert ΔY = multiplier $\times \Delta G$: $\Delta G = \Delta Y/$multiplier $= 5/2.5 = 2$. (579)

9 c It decreases *YD* at each stage of the multiplier process, reducing the amount of extra consumption spending. (582)

10 c Definition. (583)

ct **11 c** \$10 billion = $G - NT$ = \$100 billion – \$25 billion – 0.1 (potential GDP), therefore potential GDP = (100 – 25 – 10)/0.1 = \$650 billion. (583)

12 e Multiplier $= 1/(1 - MPC) = 1/(1 - 0.75) = 4$. (579)

13 b Autonomous tax multiplier $= -MPC/(1 - MPC) = -0.75/(1 - 0.75) = -3$. (580)

14 b Impact of government expenditures multiplier is $4 \times 200 = 800$, impact of autonomous tax multiplier is $-3 \times 200 = -600$, total impact $= 800 - 600 = 200$. (579–580)

15 d Autonomous transfer payments multiplier $= MPC/(1 - MPC) = 0.75/(1 - 0.75) = 3$. (580)

16 a Increase in government expenditures or tax cut would shift *AD* curve rightward by this amount. The *SAS* curve would shift *rightward* if there are incentive effects; and the ΔY is smaller than this amount due to the increase in the price level. (584–589)

17 b Others are irrelevant or not limitations. (587)

18 d Definition. (585)

19 c In long run, changes in fiscal policy have an impact only if they change potential GDP (aggregate supply). (587–589)

20 d If tax rates affect incentives, policy could affect *AS*. (587–589)

21 c Rightward shift *LAS* leads to increase in real GDP, so multiplier is greater than zero, but cannot say by how much. (587–589)

22 c Definition. (592–593)

23 c $[b(1 - t) + m] = 0.875(1 - 0.2) - 0.1 = 0.6$. Autonomous transfers multiplier $= MPC/(1 - [b(1 - t) + m]) = 0.875/(1 - 0.6) = 2.1875$. (592–593)

24 c Multiplier $= 1/(1 - [b(1 - t) + m])$, where $[b(1 - t) + m] = 1/(1 - [0.5(1 - 0.5)]) = 1.33$. (592–593)

25 **a** Autonomous multiplier = $-MPC/(1 - [b(1 - t) + m]) = -0.5/(1 - 0.25) = -0.667$. (592–593)

Short Answer Problems

1 The deficit increased because the level of government outlays as a percentage of GDP increased, while taxes as a percentage of GDP fell during the late 1970s and then slowly increased. The components of spending that showed the most consistent growth were transfer payments and interest payments on government debt.

2 **a** The Liberals are counting on the autonomous tax multiplier to boost aggregate expenditure and create new jobs.

b The critics are arguing that most of the new expenditure would be on products from outside the province—they are arguing that the marginal propensity to import for a province is very high, so that the multipliers are very low.

c It is likely that fiscal policy multipliers are low for individual provinces due to high marginal propensities to import. For your information, in Saskatchewan imports were about 62 percent (= 15.14 billion/24.28 billion) of provincial real GDP in 1995.[1]

3 **a** Your \$200 will trigger a multiplier process—the owners of the factors of production at the golf course will spend their extra income, for example. This spending induces second-round increases in consumption expenditure, leading to a final change in real GDP in Elbow that is a multiple of \$200. The size of the multiplier effect will be determined by two things. First, the larger the marginal propensity to consume in Elbow and the smaller the marginal propensity to import (from outside Elbow), the larger the multiplier will be. In a small town, the marginal propensity to import from outside the town is likely to be quite high, making the multiplier much smaller. Second, the effect is smaller if the aggregate supply curve is steeper—the increase in aggregate demand gets reduced by an increase in the price level.

b Clearly, such a shift could stimulate the town's economy, since the annual increase in government expenditures will create multiplier effects. The usefulness of this endeavour is limited by the factors mentioned that might reduce the size of the multiplier. (This policy was actual government policy in Saskatchewan until the Conservatives were defeated in 1991, at least partially because of this policy.)

4 The multiplier tells us the size of the change in real GDP (the shift in the *AD* curve) relative to the size of an initial change in government expenditure or autonomous taxes, holding constant the price level. Once we consider the *AS* curve, we know the price level will increase as aggregate demand increases—the increase in the price level being higher, the steeper the *AS* curve. This increase in the price level lowers aggregate expenditure, shown by the movement up the *AD* curve, leading to a smaller increase in real GDP.

Incentive effects would potentially shift the *AS* curve rightward, increasing the value of the multiplier.

5 Any change that does not initiate as a change in real GDP will shift the *AE* curve. Therefore all four changes will shift the *AE* curve. Any change in autonomous expenditure that is not caused by a change in the price level will shift the *AD* curve. Therefore **a** involves a movement along an *AD* curve, while **b–d** involve shifts in the *AD* curve.

6 A cut in taxes will increase disposable income, and shift the *AD* curve rightward in the normal multiplier manner. However, supply-side economists argue that tax cuts will also increase the after-tax returns to work and saving, which in turn will lead to an increase in labour supply and saving, shifting the *AS* curves rightward.

An evaluation is still somewhat premature. As the text points out, it is still a matter of opinion whether the *AS* effects are small or large. So far, there is no hard empirical evidence one way or the other.

7 **a** The equation can be found by totalling the components of aggregate expenditure:

$$AE = 4{,}000 + 0.7(Y - 2{,}000) - 20P + 2{,}000 + 5{,}000 + 400 - 0.1Y, \text{ or}$$
$$AE = 10{,}000 - 20P + 0.6Y$$

Autonomous expenditure, which does not depend on real GDP, is 10,000 + 20*P*. The slope is 0.6.

b Substitute $P = 100$ into the *AE* function, and solve for $Y^* = AE$:

[1] *Source:* Statistics Canada, *CANSIM* matrices D21425 and D31874.

$Y^* = 10{,}000 - 20(100) + 0.6Y^*$, or

$Y^*(1 - 0.6) = 8{,}000$, or

$Y^* = 8{,}000/0.4 = 20{,}000$

Equilibrium consumption equals 4,000 + 0.7(20,000 – 2,000) – 20(100) = 14,600. Imports = 0.1(20,000) = 2000.

c Substitute $P = 200$ into the *AE* function from **a:**

$Y^* = 10{,}000 - 20(200) + 0.6Y^*$, or

$Y^*(0.4) = 6{,}000$, or

$Y^* = 6{,}000/0.4 = 15{,}000$

d One point on the curve is $P = 100$, $Y = 20{,}000$ and another point is $P = 200$, $Y = 15{,}000$. These points are illustrated in Fig. 26.2.

FIGURE **26.2**

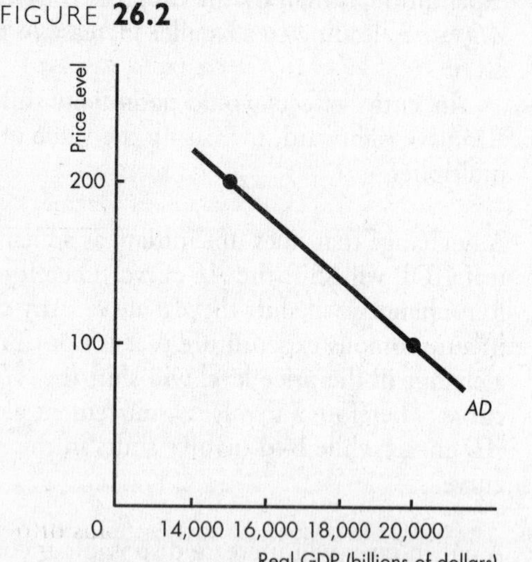

e The government expenditures multiplier = 1/(1 – slope of the *AE* function) = 1/(1 – 0.6) = 2.5.
The autonomous tax multiplier = –*MPC*/(1– slope of the *AE* function) = –0.7/(1 – 0.6) = –1.75.
The transfer payments multiplier = *MPC*/(1– slope of the *AE* function) = 0.7/(1 – 0.6) = 1.75.

f The change in real GDP demanded equals the change in government expenditures times the government expenditures multiplier, or 2,000 × 2.5 = 5,000. If the price level increases by 100, then autonomous expenditure decreases by 5,000, as we saw in **d**. This decrease completely offsets the increase in real GDP due to the increase in government expenditures on 2,000. Therefore the overall change in real GDP is equal to zero, and the multiplier is equal to zero. The answer is different here compared with part **e**, because the price level is allowed to adjust which leads to the offsetting effects.

8 a The government expenditures multiplier equals 1/(1 – *MPC*) = 1/(1 – 0.75) = 4 in this case, so in order to raise real GDP by $200 billion you need to increase government expenditures by $50 billion = $200/4 billion.

b The autonomous tax multiplier equals –*MPC*/(1 – *MPC*) = –0.75/(1 – 0.75) = –3 in this case, so in order to raise real GDP by $200 billion you need to lower taxes by $66.6 billion = $200/3 billion.

c The multiplier effects we have been analysing are based on the assumption that the price level is constant. In the real world, the stimulation of aggregate demand that you have carried out would raise the price level, which would lower aggregate expenditure, and partially (or completely) offset the increase in real GDP from your policy.

9 a Figure 26.3 shows what happens to aggregate expenditure (top of the graph) and to aggregate demand and supply (bottom). As taxes increase, disposable income decreases, and household consumption decreases, leading to a decrease in autonomous expenditure, shown by the shift downward in aggregate expenditure from AE_0 to AE_b. This decrease leads to a decrease in real GDP (holding constant the price level) from Y_0 to Y_b, with the new equilibrium at the point *b*, which is shown in the bottom graph as the shift leftward in the *AD* curve from AD_0 to AD_1.

FIGURE 26.3

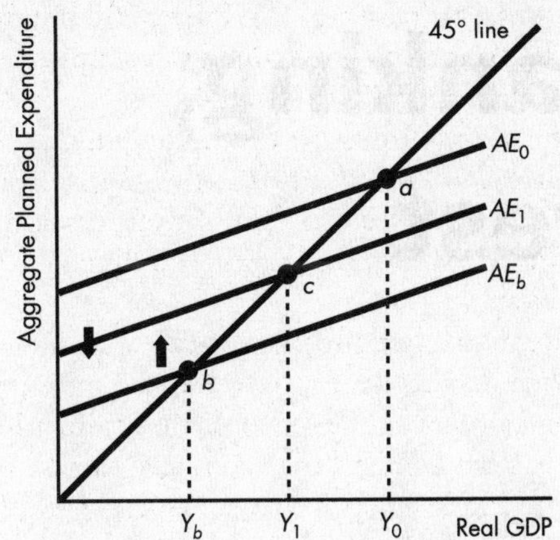

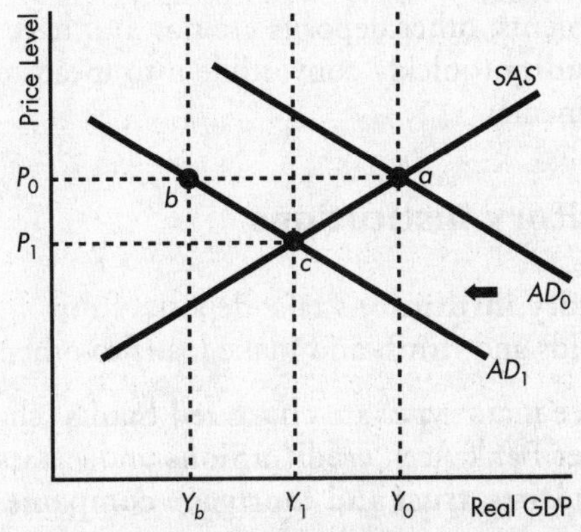

b Since the decrease in real GDP equals the decrease in aggregate expenditure, we know that the five components of aggregate expenditure have decreased in value. Since government expenditures, investment, and exports are autonomous, they are unchanged. Consumption will have decreased for two reasons—the decrease in autonomous expenditure that initiated the changes, plus a decrease in induced consumption due to the decrease in real GDP. Imports will have decreased due to the decrease in real GDP.

c At the original price level P_0, there is excess supply. This surplus leads to firms cutting their prices, leading to a decrease in the price level. This decrease gets rid of the excess supply, leading to a new equilibrium at the point *c*. The decrease in the price level raises aggregate expenditure back upward to the level AE_1, which also shows up as the movement along the curve AD_1 from *b* to *c*. The decrease in the price level leads to a movement along the *SAS* curve from point *a* to point *c*. At the new equilibrium, the overall effect of the shock is a lower level of aggregate expenditure, a lower level of aggregate demand, a lower level of aggregate supply, a lower price level, and a lower level of real GDP.

10 a Table 26.1 is completed as Table 26.1 Solution below, using the two formulas plus the fact that the budget balance = revenues – outlays.

TABLE **26.1**

Real GDP	Outlays	Revenues	Budget Balance
0	500	100	–400
100	440	140	–300
200	380	180	–200
300	320	220	–100
400	260	260	0
500	200	300	100
600	140	340	200

b The structural balance is the surplus or deficit that would exist with the existing budget structure at potential GDP, and is equal to a deficit of 100.

c The structural deficit is still 100, the actual deficit is 200 at real GDP of 200, and the cyclical deficit = actual – structural = 100.

d Yes it is, since as real GDP decreases, tax revenues decrease and outlays increase, creating upward pressure on aggregate expenditure.

Chapter 27

Money, Banking, and Interest Rates

KEY CONCEPTS

What Is Money?

Money is something acceptable as a **means of payment** (method of settling a debt).
Money has three functions—medium of exchange, unit of account, store of value.

- Medium of exchange—accepted in exchange for goods and services.
  - Better than **barter** (direct exchange of goods for goods)—guarantees double coincidence of wants.
  - Smoothes exchanges.
- Unit of account—agreed measure for prices.
  - Simpler to keep track of prices in terms of one good (money).
- Store of value—exchangeable at a later date.
  - Underpins medium-of-exchange function.
  - Weakened by inflation.

Money today is currency + deposits, with two measures:

- **Currency** is coins + Bank of Canada notes.
- Deposits are money because can be converted into currency and used to pay debts, but cheques are only an instruction to bank.
- Debit cards are like cheques, while credit cards are ID cards for loans—neither is money.
- There are two official measures of money:
  - **M1**—currency outside banks + private demand deposits at banks
  - **M2+**—M1 + personal savings deposits at banks + nonpersonal notice deposits at banks + all deposits at other financial institutions
- Currency plus some deposits are means of payments: other deposits are not, but have **liquidity** (quickly convertible into means of payments).

Depository Institutions

Depository institutions take deposits from households and firms, and make loans to others.

- Three main types are **chartered banks** (chartered under Bank Act), **credit unions** and caisses populaires, **trust and mortgage companies**.
- Bank's balance sheet shows liabilities + net worth = assets.
- Banks maximize net worth by lending out deposits.
  - Must be prudent about risk to avoid crises.
  - Banks keep **reserves** (cash + deposits at Bank of Canada) to meet cash withdrawals.
  - Banks divide other assets into very short-term liquid assets, longer-term investment securities, and loans.
- Depository institutions make money by paying depositors low interest rates and lending at high rates. In return they provide four main economic services:
  - Create liquid assets.
  - Minimize cost of borrowing funds.
  - Minimize cost of monitoring borrowers.
  - Pool and therefore reduce risks.

How Banks Create Money

Depository institutions create money (deposits) by making loans.

- Banks create money when they lend out excess reserves.

- **Reserve ratio** = reserves/total deposits.
- **Desired reserve ratio** = ratio banks wish to hold.
- **Excess reserves** = actual reserves – desired reserves.

◆ If a bank gets new deposit, this creates excess reserves.

- Bank loans out excess reserves.
- Borrower spends loan, recipient of money deposits it at new bank.
- New bank has excess reserves, leading to further steps in deposit multiplier process.

◆ Total Δ deposits = deposit multiplier × initial Δ reserves, which implies **deposit multiplier** = Δ deposits/Δ reserves = 1/desired reserve ratio > 1.

◆ Actual deposit multiplier smaller because some loan money held back as cash.

The Demand for Money

People chose an inventory of money on the basis of four factors—price level, interest rate, real GDP, financial innovation.

◆ People hold money for its buying power.

- Select amount of nominal money to achieve desired real money = nominal/price level.
- Increase in price level causes equal increase in nominal money demanded, so no change in real money demanded.

◆ Interest rate = opportunity cost of holding money.

- Higher interest rate decreases quantity of real money demanded.
- **Demand for money curve** (*MD*) is relationship between quantity of real money demanded and interest rate, other things remaining the same.

◆ Increase in real GDP leads to rightward shift *MD* curve.

◆ Recent financial innovations (development of new financial products) decrease demand for M1 and increase demand for M2+.

Interest Rate Determination

People divide their wealth between bonds and money.

◆ **Interest rate** is amount paid by borrower to lender = percentage of loan.

◆ Bond prices are inversely related to interest rates:

$$\text{Interest rate} = \frac{\$\ \text{payment/year}}{\text{Bond price}} \times 100$$

◆ Interest rates are determined where quantity of real money demanded = quantity of real money supplied—the interest rate adjusts to create money market equilibrium.

Changes in real money supply (*MS*) lead to Δ interest rates and Δ prices of financial assets.

◆ Increase in *MS* creates excess money holdings, so people buy financial assets, which increases price of financial assets, and decreases interest rates.

◆ Decrease in *MS* creates shortage of money, so people sell financial assets, which decreases price of financial assets, and increases interest rates.

◆ Monetary policy also influences the exchange rate (price at which Canadian dollar exchanges for another currency).

- Increase in *MS* decreases interest rate, decreasing demand for Canadian dollar, decreasing exchange rate.
- Decrease in *MS* increases interest rate, increasing demand for Canadian dollar, increasing exchange rate.

The Interest Rate and Expenditure Plans

People's spending decisions are affected by real interest rate.

◆ **Nominal interest rate** is percentage return on an asset in terms of money.

◆ **Real interest rate** is percentage return in terms of what money will buy = nominal rate – inflation rate.

◆ Nominal interest rate is opportunity cost of holding money, real rate is opportunity cost of spending.

◆ The lower real interest rate, the greater autonomous consumption expenditure and investment.

◆ The lower real interest rate, the lower Canadian dollar's exchange rate.

- Lower Canadian dollar, lower imports and higher exports.
- Therefore, if real interest rate decreases, net exports increase.

◆ Increase in real money supply decreases nominal interest rate (and therefore real interest rate) and increases interest-sensitive expenditure.

HELPFUL HINTS

1 What is money? In one sense, whatever meets the functions of money is money. For example, cigarettes fulfilled the functions of money in prisoner-of-war camps and similar situations. However, you should be able to answer this question on several levels. First, at the level of general definition: money is a medium of exchange. Second, at the level of classification: chequable deposits are money but savings deposits are not. Third, at the level of specific definitions: M1 and M2+ are official definitions of money.

Finally, note that we often refer to our income earnings as the "money we make working." However, in economics, money means the *stock* of money we are holding in currency plus deposits (M1 or M2+). It does *not* mean the *flow* of income earnings—be careful of this distinction.

2 As we work through the text, notice the important role of changes in interest rates and the exchange rate in creating shifts in aggregate demand, and therefore business cycle shocks. Chapters 27 and 28 begin the process of learning what affects the values of the interest and exchange rates, showing that the money market plays a crucial role. Chapter 27 explains the demand for money, and part of the supply of money. Supply is determined by the actions of the Bank of Canada (Chapter 28) and the deposit creation process. An important concept in this chapter is the deposit multiplier process by which banks create money. Become thoroughly familiar with this process.

There are two fundamental facts that allow banks to create money. First, banks create money by creating new chequable deposits. Second, banks hold fractional reserves. Fractional reserves mean that when a bank receives a deposit, it only holds part of it as reserves and lends the rest. Note that the bank is not indulging in a scam—it is still maintaining assets (reserves plus loans) to match its liabilities (deposits). When that loan is spent, at least part of the proceeds will likely be deposited in another bank, creating a new deposit (money).

The deposit multiplier process follows from this last fact: banks make loans when they receive new deposits; these loans are spent and then return to another bank, creating another new deposit. The process then repeats itself, adding more deposits (but in progressively smaller amounts) in each round. Practise going through examples until the process becomes second nature.

3 To reinforce how the deposit multiplier process works, turn to Text Fig. 27.3. We will examine the balance sheets (also known as T-accounts) for the first two banks in the multiplier process. In your analysis, note that at every step the change in liabilities must be matched by an equivalent change in assets. All figures are in thousands.

The initial deposit by Art of $100 at Art's Bank creates the changes in its T-account shown in Table 27.1(a). This deposit leaves the bank with $100 extra reserves, but they desire only $25 extra reserves (= 25 percent of the new deposits of $100). Art's Bank therefore lends the excess reserves to Amy, crediting her account with an extra $75, shown in part (b) of Table 27.1. Amy spends her money buying a copy-shop franchise from Barb, leading to the withdrawal of $75 shown in part (c) of Table 27.1. (Barb deposits this money at Barb's Bank, discussed below.) The final (net) position of Art's Bank is shown in part (d) of Table 27.1. Note that the initial deposit has led to $100 in new deposits for Art's Bank, $25 in new reserves, and $75 in new loans.

The entire process starts anew with the deposit by Barb of the $75 she got from Amy for the franchise. This deposit in Barb's Bank is shown in part (a) of Table 27.2. Barb's Bank now has $75 in actual reserves, but only desires to hold $18.25 in reserves (= 25 percent of the $75 in new deposits), leaving Barb's Bank with $56.25 in excess reserves. These excess reserves are lent to Bob. His account is credited with the $56.25, as shown in part (b) of Table 27.2. In turn, Bob uses his money to pay off a loan from Carl, leading to the withdrawal shown in part (c) of Table 27.2. (Carl will deposit this money, leading to the further expansions shown in Text Fig. 27.2, but we will examine only these two banks.) The final position of Barb's Bank is shown in part (d) of Table 27.2. Note that they have $75 in new deposits, $18.25 in new reserves, and $56.25 in new loans.

TABLE **27.1** ART'S BANK

(a) Initial New Deposit of $100

Assets		**Liabilities**	
Reserves	+$100	Deposits	+$100

(b) Loan Creation of $75

Assets		**Liabilities**	
Loans	+$75	Deposits	+$75

(c) Withdrawal of Loan Money

Assets		**Liabilities**	
Reserves	–$75	Deposits	–$75

(d) Final Position

Assets		**Liabilities**	
Reserves	+$25	Deposits	+$100
Loans	+$75		
	+$100		

TABLE **27.2** BARB'S BANK

(a) Initial New Deposit of $75

Assets		**Liabilities**	
Reserves	+$75.00	Deposits	+$75.00

(b) Loan Creation of $56.25

Assets		**Liabilities**	
Loans	+$56.25	Deposits	+$56.25

(c) Withdrawal of Loan Money

Assets		**Liabilities**	
Reserves	–$56.25	Deposits	–$56.25

(d) Final Position

Assets		**Liabilities**	
Reserves	+$18.75	Deposits	+$75.00
Loans	+$56.25		
	+$75.00		

The crucial point that drives this multiplier process is the desire of the banks to make profits, by turning reserves, which earn no revenues, into loans, which earn revenues.

SELF-TEST

True/False/Uncertain and Explain

1 Money is anything that is generally acceptable as a medium of exchange.

2 A notice deposit at a chartered bank is an example of money.

3 Individual households are generally better at pooling risk than are depository institutions.

4 Bank reserves consist of cash in the bank's vault plus its deposits at the Bank of Canada.

5 If a depositor withdraws currency from a bank, that bank's actual reserve ratio declines.

6 The deposit multiplier is equal to 1 divided by the desired reserve ratio.

7 If the price level increases, there will be an increase in the quantity of real money people will want to hold.

8 If interest rates increase, the quantity of real money demanded decreases.

9 If households or firms have more money than they want to hold, they will buy financial assets, causing asset prices to increase and the interest rate to decrease.

10 The opportunity cost of holding money is the real interest rate.

Multiple-Choice

What Is Money?

1 Which of the following is a function of money?

a medium of exchange
b measure of liquidity
c pooling risk
d store of exchange
e reducing transactions costs

2 Which of the following is a component of M2+ but *not* of M1?

a currency in circulation
b personal demand deposits at chartered banks
c personal savings deposits at chartered banks
d currency in bank vaults
e Canada Savings Bonds

3 Which of the following is *most* liquid?

a demand deposits
b real estate
c government bonds
d savings deposits
e cheques

4 Which of the following is *not* a store of value?

a credit cards
b demand deposits
c term deposits
d other chequable deposits
e savings deposits

Depository Institutions

5 Which of the following statements about depository institutions is *false*?

a They maximize net worth, ignoring all else.
b They keep reserves to meet cash withdrawals.
c A credit union is an example of a depository institution.
d They pool and therefore reduce risk.
e They borrow at low interest rates and lend high.

6 Which of the following is a liability of a depository institution?

a vault cash
b loans
c securities
d demand deposits
e its deposits at the Bank of Canada

7 Which of the following is an economic service provided by a depository institution?

a borrowing low and lending high
b keeping cash reserves
c pooling liquidity
d minimizing the cost of borrowing funds
e creating liquid liabilities

How Banks Create Money

8 Consider Fact 27.1. Based on the Bank of Speedy Creek's initial balance sheet, what is their desired reserve ratio?

a 4 percent
b 8 percent
c 12.5 percent
d 25 percent
e 40 percent

FACT **27.1**

The Bank of Speedy Creek is one of many banks in the economy, and has chosen the following initial balance sheet:

Assets		Liabilities	
Reserves	$40	Deposits	$500
Loans	$460		
	$500		

9 Consider Fact 27.1. Frodo Baggins comes along and deposits $10. After Frodo's deposit, but before any other actions have occurred, the total amount of money in the economy has

a stayed the same, with its components unchanged.
b stayed the same, with currency falling and deposits rising.
c decreased, with currency falling and deposits staying the same.
d increased, with currency unchanged and deposits rising.
e decreased, with currency falling and deposits unchanged.

10 Consider Fact 27.1. Frodo Baggins comes along and deposits $10. After Frodo's deposit, but before any other actions have occurred, the Bank of Speedy Creek will have excess reserves of

a zero.
b $9.00.
c $9.20.
d $10.00.
e $40.00.

11 Consider Fact 27.1. Frodo Baggins comes along and deposits $10. After Frodo's deposit, given that the bank is profit-seeking, how much will its new lending be?

a zero
b $9.00.
c $9.20
d $10.00
e $40.00

12 Consider Fact 27.1. Frodo Baggins comes along and deposits $10. After Frodo's deposit, and after the bank has lent the amount it wishes to lend, the total amount of reserves in the Bank of Speedy Creek will be $________, the total amount of loans will be $________, and the total amount of deposits will be $________

a 40.80; 469.20; 510.00
b 40.00; 460.00; 500.00
c 50.00; 470.00; 520.00
d 41.00; 469.00; 510.00
e 42.50; 467.50; 510.00

13 Consider Fact 27.1. Frodo Baggins comes along and deposits $10. If all the banks in the banking system had the same desired reserve ratio as the Bank of Speedy Creek, what would be the total change in deposits within the system resulting from Frodo's initial deposit?

a $125.00
b $100.00
c $80.00
d $40.00
e $12.50

14 If all banks hold 100 percent reserves, what is the deposit multiplier?

a 0
b 1
c 10
d 100
e infinite

The Demand for Money

15 Consider Fig. 27.1. Which of the following best describes the response of this household to an *increase* in their annual income?

a movement from *a* to *f*
b movement from *a* to *c*
c movement from *e* to *a*
d movement from *b* to *a*
e movement from *a* to *e*

FIGURE **27.1** THE DEMAND FOR REAL MONEY BALANCES BY AN INDIVIDUAL HOUSEHOLD

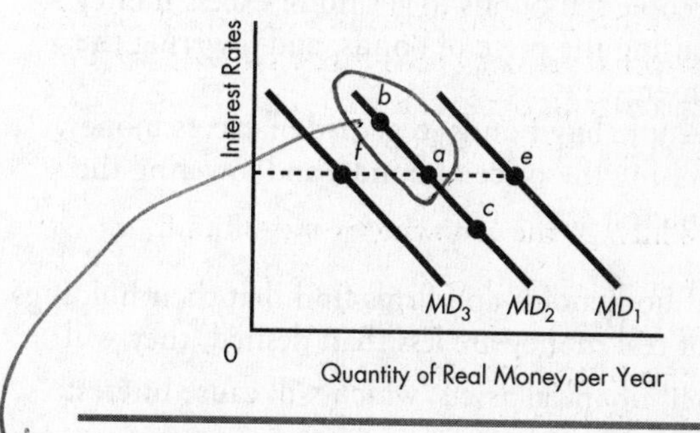

16 Consider Fig. 27.1. Which of the following best describes the response of this household to a *decrease* in the market price of bonds?

a movement from *a* to *b*
b movement from *a* to *c*
c movement from *a* to *f*
d movement from *a* to *e*
e movement from *e* to *a*

17 Which of the following will cause the demand curve for real money to shift to the left?

a an increase in real GDP
b a decrease in interest rates
c the expanded use of credit cards
d an increase in the quantity of money supplied
e an increase in the price level

18 Real money is equal to nominal money

a divided by real GDP.
b minus real GDP.
c divided by the price level.
d minus the price level.
e divided by velocity.

Interest Rate Determination

19 If the interest rate is above the equilibrium rate, how is equilibrium achieved in the money market?

- **a** People buy goods to get rid of excess money, lowering the price of goods, and lowering the interest rate.
- **b** People sell goods to get rid of excess money, lowering the price of goods, and lowering the interest rate.
- **c** People sell bonds to get rid of excess money, lowering the price of bonds, and lowering the interest rate.
- **d** People sell bonds to get rid of excess money, raising the price of bonds, and lowering the interest rate.
- **e** People buy bonds to get rid of excess money, raising the price of bonds, and lowering the interest rate.

20 If households and firms find that their holdings of real money are less than desired, they will

- **a** sell financial assets, which will cause interest rates to increase.
- **b** sell financial assets, which will cause interest rates to decrease.
- **c** buy financial assets, which will cause interest rates to increase.
- **d** buy financial assets, which will cause interest rates to decrease.
- **e** buy goods, which will cause the price level to increase.

21 Money market equilibrium occurs

- **a** when interest rates are constant.
- **b** when the level of real GDP is constant.
- **c** when quantity of real money supplied equals real money demanded.
- **d** only under a fixed exchange rate.
- **e** when bond prices are constant.

22 An increase in the quantity of real money supplied will

- **a** increase interest rates and decrease the exchange rate.
- **b** have no impact on interest rates, but increase the exchange rate.
- **c** have no impact on interest rates nor on the exchange rate.
- **d** decrease interest rates and increase the exchange rate.
- **e** decrease interest rates and the exchange rate.

The Interest Rate and Expenditure Plans

23 If the inflation rate increases by 3 percent and the nominal interest rate increases by 2 percent, then the

- **a** real interest rate increases.
- **b** opportunity cost of holding money increases.
- **c** opportunity cost of holding money decreases.
- **d** opportunity cost of spending increases.
- **e** autonomous consumption expenditure decreases.

24 An increase in the real interest rate will

- **a** decrease consumption expenditure.
- **b** increase investment.
- **c** decrease the exchange rate.
- **d** increase net exports.
- **e** decrease the nominal interest rate.

higher cost of borrowing decreases borrowing + spending

25 A decrease in the quantity of real money supplied will

- **a** decrease the real interest rate, the inflation rate held constant.
- **b** decrease nominal interest rates.
- **c** decrease aggregate expenditure.
- **d** increase aggregate expenditure.
- **e** not change the nominal interest rate.

less $ means ↑ interest rate & ↓AE

Short Answer Problems

1 Banks can no longer issue their own paper money, but can create money by creating deposit money by crediting people's deposits. Since there is no paper money deposited to back up this creation, is this created money real? Is it acceptable in society? Why or why not?

2 Carefully explain how and why banks create new money during the deposit multiplier process (in a multibank system).

3 Why do people care about the quantity of real money they hold rather than the quantity of nominal money?

4 Suppose an individual sells $1,000 worth of government securities to the Bank of Canada and deposits the proceeds ($1,000) in bank 1. Note that this new deposit initially increases the quantity of money by $1,000. (In the next chapter we will see how such a new deposit arises.) Assume that the desired reserve ratio for all banks in the multibank system is 20 percent (0.2). There is no currency drain. Table 27.3 gives information for the first round of the money expansion process that will be generated by this new deposit.

a Follow the first six rounds of the money creation process by completing Table 27.3.

TABLE **27.3** MONEY CREATION PROCESS—NO CURRENCY DRAIN

Bank Number	New Deposits	New Loans	New Reserves	Increase in Deposits	Cumulative Increase in Deposits
1	1,000	800	200	1,000	1,000
2					
3					
4					
5					
6					

b What is the total increase in the quantity of money after six rounds?
c What is the deposit multiplier?
d After all rounds have been completed, what will be the total increase in deposits?

5 For the first two banks in Short Answer Problem 4, show their balance sheets for each stage of the process (initial deposit, loan creation, borrower's withdrawal, final position).

ⓒⓣ **6** For the entire banking system in Short Answer Problem 4, what do the final balance sheet changes look like? (Assume that banks have only reserves, loans, and deposits.)

7 Assume that the changes in the banking system in Short Answer Problems 4–6 are economically significant. Explain what they will do to
a the quantity of real money supplied.
b the nominal interest rate.
c the real interest rate, the inflation rate held constant.
d aggregate expenditure.

8 There is only one chartered bank in Gondor, and it has the following assets and liabilities (none is missing from the list except as indicated):

Currency reserves	$20 million
Reserves held at the Bank of Gondor	$10 million
Loans	?
Securities	$25 million
Demand deposits	$150 million
Notice deposits	$600 million

a Construct the balance sheet for this bank. What is the amount of loans?
b Assuming that the bank has freely chosen its reserves, what is its desired reserve ratio? What is the deposit multiplier?
c If the amount of currency in circulation is $50 million, what is M1? M2+?

9 Consider a perpetuity with an annual payment of $100. What is the interest rate on this financial asset, if its price is
a $1,000?
b $900?
c $1,100?

10 Show on a graph and briefly explain what each of the following will do (in sequence) to the demand for real money (defined as M1) and therefore the equilibrium interest rate. Assume that the real money supply remains constant.
a The price level rises.
b There is a financial innovation (the widespread adoption of electronic funds transfers) that reduces the need to use chequing accounts.
c Real GDP falls during a recession.

ANSWERS

True/False/Uncertain and Explain

1 T Basic function of money. (598–600)
ⓒⓣ **2 U** Depends on definition of money—notice accounts not part of M1, but part of M2+. (598–600)
3 F Large size allows banks to pool risk. (601–603)
4 T Definition. (601–603)
ⓒⓣ **5 T** Withdrawal leads to decrease in reserves = decrease in deposits, which leads to decrease in reserve/deposit ratio—do a balance sheet. (603–606)
6 T Definition. (603–606)
7 F Real money demand independent of price level. (607–610)
8 T Increase in interest rate leads to increase in opportunity cost of holding money, leading to decrease in quantity money demanded. (607–610)
9 T Agents substitute towards bonds, leading to increase in bond demand, leading to increase in bond price, which implies decrease in bond interest rate. (610–612)
10 F Nominal interest rate—see text discussion. (613–614)

Multiple-Choice

1 a See text discussion. (598–600)
2 c Definition. (598–600)
3 a Most readily changed into currency. (598–600)
4 a Credit cards cannot necessarily be used for purchases in the future, the credit card company could refuse to honour your card. (598–600)
5 a Must be prudent about risk too. (601–603)
6 d Others are all assets = claims on someone else. (601–603)
7 d See text discussion. (601–603)
8 b Desired reserve ratio = chosen reserves/deposits = 40/500 = 0.08. (603–606)
9 b Decrease in currency as deposit made = increase in deposits. (603–606)
10 c Excess = actual ($50) – desired ($40.80 = 0.08 × $510). (603–606)
11 c Banks will lend the amount of excess reserves. (603–606)
ⓒⓣ 12 a Work through balance sheet changes as shown in Helpful Hint 3. (603–606)
ⓒⓣ 13 a Δ deposits = (1/(desired reserve ratio)) × Δ reserves = (1/0.08) × $10 = $125. (603–606)
14 b Multiplier = 1/(desired reserve ratio) = 1/1 = 1. (603–606)
15 e *a* to *f*, *e* to *a* are decreases in income, others are Δ interest rates. (607–610)
16 a Decrease in price of bonds leads to increase in interest rates. *a* to *f*, *a* to *e*, *e* to *a*, are income changes, *a* to *c* is decrease in interest rates. (607–610)
17 c Financial innovation means people use less money. (607–610)
18 c Definition. (607–610)
ⓒⓣ 19 e If interest rate > equilibrium, this implies too much money, which implies buying bonds, leading to increase in price of bonds and therefore decrease in interest rates. (610–612)
20 a They substitute money for bonds, extra sales leads to decrease in price of bonds and increase in interest rates. (610–612)
21 c Definition. (610–612)
22 e Increase in money supply leads to excess supply of money, creating excess demand for financial assets, which leads to increase in price of financial assets and decrease in interest rates, which leads to decrease in demand for Canadian dollar and therefore decrease in exchange rate. (610–612)
ⓒⓣ 23 b Nominal interest rate increases, opportunity cost of money increases. Real interest rate decreases since increase in inflation rate > increase in nominal interest rate, so opportunity cost of spending decreases and spending increases. (613–615)
24 a Higher cost of borrowing decreases borrowing and spending. (613–615)
25 c Less money means increased interest rates and therefore decreased consumption, investment and net exports. (613–615)

Short Answer Problems

1 This created money is real because it is backed by the assets of the bank, which consist of the bank's reserves, loans, and holdings of securities. Deposit money is generally accepted in society (you can buy goods, pay debts, etc., with it) because people know that the banks will provide currency upon demand.

2 Banks create money by making new loans. When banks get a new deposit, this deposit leaves them with excess reserves. Their desire to make profits (maximize net worth) leads banks to lend out the excess reserves, creating a matching deposit, which is new money. When the proceeds of these loans are spent, the person receiving the money will deposit much of it in a bank deposit, which is also new money.

3 Nominal money is simply the number of dollars, while real money is a measure of what money will buy. Real money will decrease if the price level rises, and if the number of dollars is constant. What matters to people is the quantity of goods and services that money will buy, not the number of dollars. If the price level rises by 10 percent, people will want to hold 10 percent more dollars (given a constant real income and interest rates) in order to retain the same purchasing power.

4 a Table 27.3 is completed here as Table 27.3 Solution. Note that 80 percent of each new deposit will be lent and 20 percent will be held as reserves. When a new loan is deposited in the next bank, it becomes a new deposit.

TABLE **27.3** SOLUTION

Bank Number	New Deposits	New Loans	New Reserves	Increase in Deposits	Cumulative Increase in Deposits
1	1,000	800	200	1,000	1,000
2	800	640	160	800	1,800
3	640	512	128	640	2,440
4	512	410	102	512	2,952
5	410	328	82	410	3,362
6	328	262	66	328	3,690

b After six rounds, the total (cumulative) increase in the quantity of money is $3,690 (the last number of Table 27.3 Solution).
c The deposit multiplier in this case is equal to 1/(desired reserve ratio). Since the desired reserve ratio is 0.2, the deposit multiplier is 5.
d The total increase in money will be $5,000 after all rounds are completed. This value is obtained by multiplying the initial increase in deposits ($1,000) by the deposit multiplier (5).

5 Bank 1's balance sheets are shown in Table 27.4, and Bank 2's are shown in Table 27.5.

TABLE **27.4** BANK 1

(a) Initial New Deposit of $1,000

Assets		Liabilities	
Reserves	+$1,000	Deposits	+$1,000

(b) Loan Creation of $800

Assets		Liabilities	
Loans	+$800	Deposits	+$800

(c) Withdrawal of Loan Money

Assets		Liabilities	
Reserves	–$800	Deposits	–$800

(d) Final Position

Assets		Liabilities	
Reserves	+$200	Deposits	+$1,000
Loans	+$800		
	+$1,000		

TABLE **27.5** BANK 2

(a) Initial New Deposit of $800

Assets		Liabilities	
Reserves	+$800	Deposits	+$800

(b) Loan Creation of $640

Assets		Liabilities	
Loans	+$640	Deposits	+$640

(c) Withdrawal of Loan Money

Assets		Liabilities	
Reserves	–$640	Deposits	–$640

(d) Final Position

Assets		Liabilities	
Reserves	+$160	Deposits	+$800
Loans	+$640		
	+$800		

ⓔ **6** The total change in reserves in the system must be equal to the initial new reserves of +$1,000. Total new deposits have been calculated as +$5,000. For the balance sheet to balance therefore, loans must be +$4,000, and the balance sheet is as shown in Table 27.6.

TABLE **27.6**

Assets		Liabilities	
Reserves	+$1,000	Deposits	+$5,000
Loans	+$4,000		
	+$5,000		

7 a The increase in deposits increases the quantity of real money supplied.
b This increase will lead to an excess supply of money, so that people buy bonds, bidding up bond prices and lowering the nominal interest rate.
c If the inflation rate is held constant, the real interest rate = nominal rate – inflation rate will decrease as the nominal rate decreases.
d The lower real interest rate will decrease the opportunity cost of spending, so aggregate expenditure will increase.

8 a The balance sheet is shown in Table 27.7 (all values are in millions). Since assets must equal liabilities in the balance sheet, loans = \$750 – \$30 – \$25 = \$695.

TABLE **27.7**

Assets		**Liabilities**	
Reserves	+\$30	Demand Deposits	+\$150
Securities	+\$25	Notice Deposits	+\$600
Loans	+\$695		+\$750
	+\$750		

b The desired reserve ratio = desired reserves/deposits = 30/750 = 0.04. The deposit multiplier = 1/(desired reserve ratio) = 1/0.04 = 25.

c M1 = currency in circulation + demand deposits = \$200 million. M2+ = M1 + notice deposits = \$800 million.

9 The interest rate on a perpetuity is obtained using the formula

$$r = \frac{\text{fixed dollar payment}}{\text{price}} \times 100:$$

a $r = \frac{100}{1{,}000} \times 100 = 10$ percent

b $r = \frac{100}{900} \times 100 = 11.11$ percent

c $r = \frac{100}{1{,}100} \times 100 = 9.09$ percent

10 a A change in the price level will have no impact on real money demand, and therefore no impact on the equilibrium interest rate (r). In Fig. 27.2, demand for real money remains at MD_0, and the interest rate remains at r_0.

FIGURE **27.2**

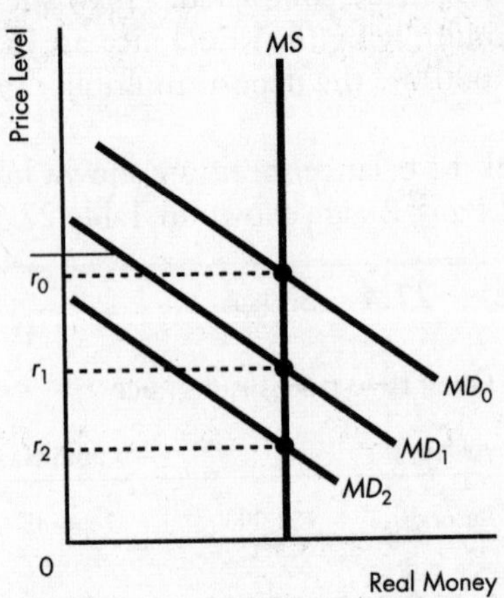

b This financial innovation would reduce the need to use chequing accounts, which are part of M1. Therefore the demand for real money falls to MD_1, and the equilibrium interest rate falls to r_1 in Fig. 27.2.

c The decrease in real GDP lowers the demand for real money to MD_2, and the equilibrium interest rate falls to r_2 in Fig. 27.

Chapter 28 Monetary Policy

KEY CONCEPTS

The Bank of Canada

The **Bank of Canada** is Canada's **central bank**. It supervises financial institutions and conducts monetary policy.

- **Monetary policy** attempts to control inflation and business cycle by Δ money supply and by adjusting interest rates and the exchange rate.
- Canada's central bank is somewhat subordinate to the federal government.
  - An independent central bank determines monetary policy with no government interference. Possible advantage—central bank can better stand up to short-term pressures.
  - A subordinate central bank must follow government directions, but can still have significant power.
- Bank of Canada balance sheet shows
  - liabilities = Bank of Canada notes + deposits (reserves) of chartered banks + government deposits
  - assets = government securities + loans to banks
  - **monetary base** = Bank of Canada notes outside bank + chartered bank deposits + coins in circulation
- Monetary policy is difficult because current tools create delayed, future effects, so Bank must try to predict economy's future course.
- **Monetary policy indicators** are current features of economy that help predict future course.
- Main indicator is **overnight loans rate** (interest rate on loans banks make to each other).

Bank of Canada attempts to Δ bank reserves, which leads to Δ overnight rate, which leads to Δ quantity of money, etc. by manipulating four main policy tools:

- Δ required reserve ratio will Δ minimum reserves banks must hold (currently = 0).
- Δ **bank rate**—the rate it lends to chartered banks.
  - Increase in bank rate increases costs of borrowing reserves, which increases reserves held by banks, who decrease loans to public.
  - Increase in banker's deposit rate (= rate earned by banks' deposits at Bank of Canada = bank rate – 0.5%) increases overnight loans rate.
- **Open market operations**—buying/selling government bonds, which Δ monetary base with further effects.

Government deposit shifting—transferring government funds between Bank of Canada and chartered bank deposits. If shift deposits out of Bank of Canada into chartered banks, then chartered banks get more deposits and more reserves, so more loans and money created.

Controlling the Money Supply

The major policy tool of the Bank is an open market operation.

- Bank of Canada carries out open market operations with banks or public (same essential outcome).
- Bank of Canada buying government bonds increases chartered bank reserves = increase in excess reserves, which increases lending. When loans are used to make payments, these payments increase new deposits elsewhere and increase currency held by public.

- The new deposits lead to increase in chartered bank reserves (= increase in desired reserves + increase in excess reserves).
- The excess reserves are used to make new loans, leading to further second-round or multiplier effects.
- Overall result is increase in currency held by households (**currency drain**) and increase in deposits = increase in money supply.
- *Bank of Canada buying government bonds increases the money supply.*

◆ Bank of Canada selling government bonds decreases chartered bank reserves, which leads to loans called in, which decreases deposits, leading to further second-round effects, and a decrease in money supply.

- *Bank of Canada selling government bonds decreases the money supply.*

◆ **Money multiplier** = amount Δ monetary base (*MB*) is multiplied by to get resulting Δ in quantity of money = $\Delta M/\Delta MB$.

◆ Size of Δ money supply depends on size of second-round effects, which are larger if

- currency drain is smaller.
- desired reserve ratio is smaller.

Ripple Effects of Monetary Policy

The quantity of money affects aggregate demand (*AD*) and therefore real GDP and price level through several channels.

◆ Open market operations of buying bonds increases money supply (*MS*), which decreases interest rate (*r*) which

- decreases exchange rate, increasing net exports and *AD*.
- increases consumption and investment, increasing *AD*.

◆ With unemployment, increased *MS* increases *AD*, which increases real GDP and price level, leading to a faster convergence to full employment.

◆ If real GDP > potential (inflationary pressure), decrease in *MS* decreases *AD*, which lowers pressure.

◆ Monetary policy is sometimes wrong due to time lags before policy takes effect, and changes in economic factors.

◆ Historical evidence shows that actual Canadian interest rates move inversely with ΔMB, but in a manner not completely predictable.

The Bank of Canada targets the interest rate rather than the *MS* due to worries about fluctuations in money demand (*MD*).

◆ If the Bank targeted *MS*, ΔMD would create Δr that affects economy.

◆ By trying to keep *r* at target level, the Bank keeps *MS* at an average level—to raise target *r*, lower average *MS*.

The exchange rate responds to changes in Canadian interest rate relative to world rates.

◆ Historical evidence shows increase in interest rate gap between Canada and United States leads to upward pressure on exchange rate.

Historical evidence shows that when the Bank stimulates *AD* (lowers short-term interest rates), real GDP growth speeds up, but with a lag.

The Bank of Canada in Action

Strong downward pressure on money growth rates in early 1980s sharply increased *r*, which created recession, slowed inflation.

◆ Similar policy in late 1980s decreased inflation some more, but contributed to 1990–91 recession.

◆ Since then, lower interest rates have helped stimulate growth.

HELPFUL HINTS

1 Open market operations are the most important policy tool of the Bank of Canada, and it is important to understand how they affect the quantity of money. To understand the effect of open market operations on the monetary base and thus the quantity of money, remember that one liability of the Bank of Canada is banks' deposits at the Bank of Canada that serve as bank reserves. These deposits, combined with currency in circulation (the other major liability of the Bank of Canada), constitute the monetary base. The largest class of assets of the Bank of Canada is its holdings of government securities. Finally, recall that if total assets increase, due to the conventions of double-entry bookkeeping, total liabilities must increase by the same amount.

An open market purchase of government securities is an increase in the assets of the Bank of Canada (government securities) paid for by an increase in its liabilities, principally an increase in the deposits of banks at the Bank of Canada. This increase in liabilities of the Bank of Canada is an increase in the monetary base, which will have a multiplied effect on the quantity of money.

2 Here are some further notes on open market operations:

a To remember whether an open market purchase will lead to a decrease or an increase in money, think of open market operations as an exchange of government securities for cash. For example, think of an open market purchase as the Bank of Canada acquiring government securities by giving cash to the public. The purchase increases the money supply.

Be careful to avoid making a very common error when working through open market operations. When the Bank of Canada buys or sells securities, chartered bank reserves at the Bank of Canada change. Many students automatically place the changed bank reserves at the Bank of Canada under assets in the Bank's balance sheet, because they are an asset on the chartered bank balance sheet. However, this placement is an error—the reserves are a deposit at the Bank of Canada, and therefore a *liability* to the Bank of Canada.

b Remember that government securities are assets to the Bank of Canada just as they are to members of the public who hold them. They are liabilities of the government of Canada.

c Government securities are traded in two markets: the primary market in which the Treasury sells newly issued government securities, and the secondary market in which government securities previously purchased in the primary market are bought and sold. This secondary market is the open market in which *open market* operations take place.

d To understand how an open market operation changes interest rates, consider the changes in the banking sector. For example, an open market purchase of government securities (which will increase the money supply) leaves the banking sector with excess reserves. Profit-seeking banks attempt to lend these excess reserves. At the original interest rate, loan demand (borrowing) equaled loan supply. To convince economic agents to borrow more money, banks must decrease interest rates. The result is that as the money supply increases, interest rates decrease. Therefore we can see intuitively how an open market purchase leads directly to decreased interest rates.

e The text does not work through an open market sale, so for the extra practice let's try one. Suppose that the Bank of Canada wishes to decrease the money supply and decides to decrease the monetary base by $100 million. It decides to do so by selling $100 million worth of securities to the Royal Bank. The Royal Bank pays for the securities out of its reserves held at the Bank of Canada. Table 28.1 shows the changes in the two balance sheets. The Royal Bank now has a decrease in its reserves, and if desired reserves are too low, must call in some loans to increase reserves. This action will trigger a decrease in deposits and the overall money supply, as desired by the Bank of Canada.

TABLE **28.1**

Bank of Canada

Assets		Liabilities	
Securities	−100	Deposits (reserves) of Royal Bank	−100

Royal Bank

Assets		Liabilities
Reserves	−100	
Securities	+100	
	0	

SELF-TEST

True/False/Uncertain and Explain

7/10

1 Increasing the bank rate will increase the amount of lending by chartered banks.

F

2 Chartered bank deposits at the Bank of Canada are an asset of the Bank of Canada and a liability of the chartered bank.

F

3 If the Bank of Canada sells government securities in the open market, chartered bank reserves increase.

F they decrease

X **4** The higher the banks' desired reserve ratio, the larger the money multiplier.

T F

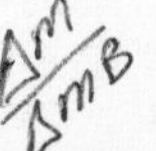

5 The presence of a currency drain increases the size of the money multiplier.

6 If real GDP is increasing and the real money supply is increasing, interest rates will also be increasing.

7 An increase in the quantity of money shifts the aggregate demand curve rightward.

8 A increase in the money supply decreases the exchange rate.

9 If the Bank of Canada wants to decrease interest rates, it should sell government securities in the open market.

10 Historical evidence for Canada shows that lowering the money supply growth rate lowers inflation.

Multiple-Choice

The Bank of Canada

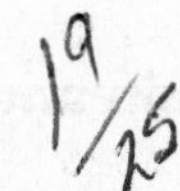

1 Which of the following is a main policy tool of the Bank of Canada?

- a prime rate
- b exchange rate
- c currency ratio
- d bankers' deposit rate
- e none of the above

2 The bank rate is the interest rate

- a banks charge their very best loan customers.
- b banks pay on term deposits.
- c the Bank of Canada pays on reserves held by banks.
- d the Bank of Canada charges when it lends reserves to banks.
- e received for holding Government of Canada Treasury bills.

3 The bank rate is an effective signal of monetary policy because it is

- a a measure of the return on keeping reserves.
- b useful for predicting monetary policy.
- c equal to the prime rate.
- d a rough approximation of the value of the money multiplier.
- e changed only during open market operations.

4 Which of the Bank of Canada's policy tools is the most important?

- a choosing exchange rate regimes
- b setting reserve requirements
- c changing the bank rate
- d paying for the government's deficit
- e open market operations

5 The Bank of Canada

- a is totally controlled by the federal government.
- b is totally independent of the federal government.
- c has always been subordinate to the federal government.
- d was originally independent of the federal government, but after 1967 became subordinate.
- e was originally subordinate to the federal government, but after 1967 became independent.

Controlling the Money Supply

6 Which of the balance sheets in Table 28.2 shows the initial impact on the banking sector of an open market purchase by the Bank of Canada of $100 worth of government securities from the banking sector?

- a (a)
- b (b)
- c (c)
- d (d)
- e none of the above

TABLE **28.2** CHARTERED BANKS' BALANCE SHEETS

(a)

Assets	**Liabilities**
Reserves +100	
Securities –100	

(b)

Assets	**Liabilities**
Reserves –100	
Securities +100	

(c)

Assets	**Liabilities**
Reserves +100	Deposits +100

(d)

Assets	**Liabilities**
	Deposits +100
	Securities –100

7 Which of the balance sheets in Table 28.2 shows the initial impact on the banking sector of an open market purchase by the Bank of Canada of $100 worth of government securities from a private individual?

a (a)
b (b)
c (c)
d (d)
e none of the above

8 Which of the balance sheets in Table 28.2 shows the initial impact on the banking sector of an open market sale by the Bank of Canada of $100 worth of government securities to a private individual?

a (a)
b (b)
c (c)
d (d)
e none of the above

9 Which of the balance sheets in Table 28.2 shows the initial impact on the banking sector of an open market sale by the Bank of Canada of $100 worth of government securities to a bank?

a (a)
b (b)
c (c)
d (d)
e none of the above

10 Which of the following would *not* affect the size of the monetary base?

a A bank exchanges government securities for a deposit at the Bank of Canada.
b A bank exchanges vault cash for a deposit at the Bank of Canada.
c The Bank of Canada buys government securities from a bank.
d The Bank of Canada buys government securities from someone other than a bank.
e The Bank of Canada sells government securities to a bank.

11 The monetary expansion process continues until

a required reserves are eliminated.
b the Bank of Canada eliminates required reserves.
c the discount rate is lower than the prime rate.
d the prime rate is lower than the discount rate.
e excess reserves are eliminated.

12 In an expansionary open market operation, the Bank of Canada

a sells government bonds, decreasing bank reserves, decreasing lending, decreasing the money supply.
b sells government bonds, decreasing bank reserves, decreasing lending, increasing the money supply.
c sells government bonds, decreasing bank reserves, increasing lending, increasing the money supply.
d buys government bonds, increasing bank reserves, increasing lending, decreasing the money supply.
e buys government bonds, increasing bank reserves, increasing lending, increasing the money supply.

13 Suppose there is an increase in the tendency for loans to return to banks in the form of new deposits and reserves; in other words, there is a *decrease* in the currency drain. Select the best statement.

a The deposit multiplier will decrease.
b The deposit multiplier will increase.
c The money multiplier will decrease.
d The money multiplier will stay constant.
e The money multiplier will increase.

14 The money multiplier will increase if either the fraction of deposits that households and firms want to hold as currency

a increases or the desired reserve ratio increases.
b decreases or the desired reserve ratio decreases.
c decreases or the desired reserve ratio increases.
d increases or the desired reserve ratio decreases.
e none of the above.

Ripple Effects of Monetary Policy

15 Why is the exchange rate a key monetary variable?

a It is one of the four main policy tools.
b It is a key policy objective.
c It is a barometer of monetary policy.
d It shows how much the monetary base must be multiplied in order to measure the resulting increase in the money supply.
e It is part of the channel by which a change in money supply affects aggregate demand.

16 The following headline: "The Bank of Canada Has Cut the Bank Rate" suggests that the Bank of Canada is trying to

- **a** lower inflationary pressures.
- **b** increase the overnight loans rate.
- **c** stimulate aggregate expenditure.
- **d** raise the value of the Canadian dollar.
- **e** help banks make profits.

17 In a situation of unemployment, an increase in the money supply will lead to a(n)

- **a** increase in real GDP and the price level.
- **b** increase in real GDP, but a decrease in the price level.
- **c** increase in real GDP, but no change in the price level.
- **d** increase in the price level, but no change in real GDP.
- **e** decrease in the price level and real GDP.

18 Consider Fig 28.1. Which graph represents an anti-inflationary monetary policy?

- **a** (a)
- **b** (b)
- **c** (c)
- **d** (d)
- **e** none of the above

FIGURE **28.1**

(a)

P, LAS, SAS, AD_1, AD_0, Y

(b)

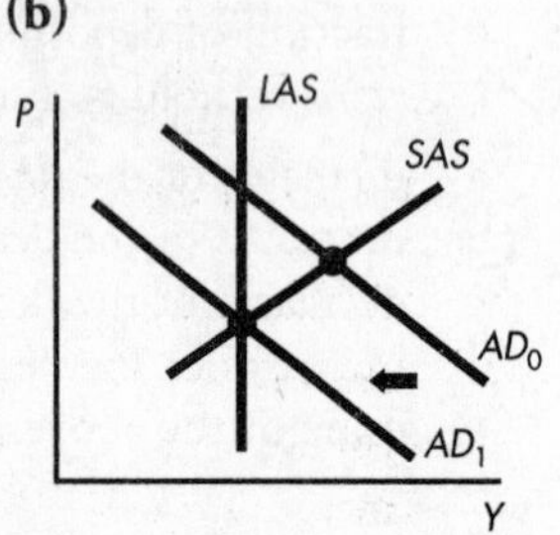

(c)

P, LAS, SAS, AD_1, AD_0, Y

(d)

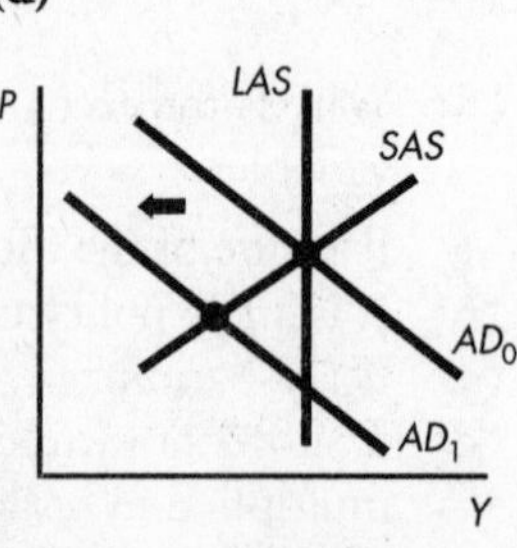

19 Consider Fig 28.1. Which graph shows an example of an attempt to lower unemployment with monetary policy?

- **a** (a)
- **b** (b)
- **c** (c)
- **d** (d)
- **e** none of the above

20 An expansionary monetary policy will

- **a** increase interest rates and decrease the exchange rate.
- **b** have no impact on interest rates, but increase the exchange rate.
- **c** have no impact on interest rates nor on the exchange rate.
- **d** decrease interest rates and increase the exchange rate.
- **e** decrease interest rates and the exchange rate.

21 If the Bank of Canada buys government securities in the open market, the supply curve of real money will shift

- **a** leftward, and the interest rate will increase.
- **b** leftward, and the interest rate will decrease.
- **c** rightward, and the interest rate will increase.
- **d** rightward, and the interest rate will remain constant as money demand will shift rightward as well.
- **e** none of the above.

22 If the Bank of Canada targets the level of the money supply,

- **a** the interest rate will be constant.
- **b** real GDP will be constant.
- **c** there will be no inflation.
- **d** the interest rate will fluctuate.
- **e** the money supply will fluctuate.

23 If the Bank of Canada wishes to raise the exchange rate, they should

- **a** target the money supply.
- **b** buy government bonds.
- **c** lower Canadian interest rates.
- **d** sell government bonds.
- **e** target the interest rate.

24 Which of the following statements about historical evidence on monetary policy is *true*?

- **a** Canadian interest rates move positively with the monetary base.
- **b** Canadian interest rates are not related to the monetary base.
- **c** When the Bank of Canada lowers short-term interest rates, real GDP rises immediately.
- **d** When the gap between Canadian and U.S. interest rates increases, the exchange rate tends to decrease in value.
- **e** When the gap between Canadian and U.S. interest rates increases, the exchange rate tends to increase in value.

The Bank of Canada in Action

25 The Bank of Canada's anti-inflationary policy of the early 1980s resulted in

- **a** an increase in the real money supply.
- **b** lower interest rates as the policy was carried out.
- **c** higher chartered bank reserves.
- **d** a strong increase in aggregate demand.
- **e** a recession.

Short Answer Problems

1 The Bank of Canada often uses monetary policy to increase interest rates, in order to offset downward pressure on the exchange rate. Explain briefly how this policy works.

2 How does an open market purchase of government securities lead to an increase in the monetary base? What are the ripple effects of this policy on the different components of aggregate expenditure?

3 How does the currency drain affect the size of the money multiplier?

4 Figure 28.2 illustrates the current equilibrium in the money market where *MD* is the demand curve for real money and *MS* is the supply curve for real money.

- **a** Suppose that the Bank of Canada wants to stimulate aggregate expenditure by decreasing the interest rate to 6 percent. By how much must the Bank of Canada increase the nominal money supply if the price level is 2?

FIGURE **28.2**

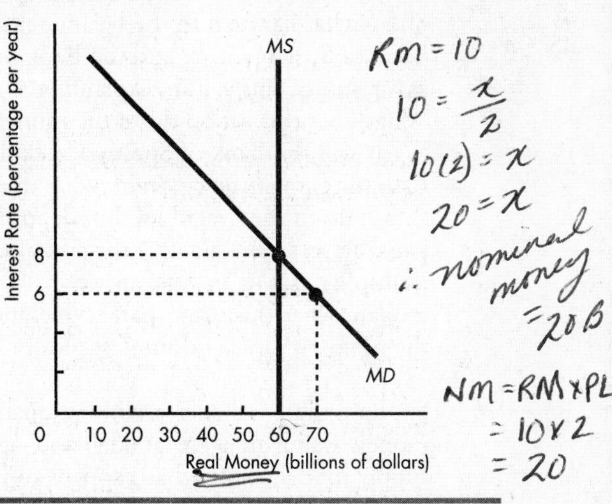

- **b** Having determined the amount by which the Bank of Canada must increase the nominal supply of money, we now want to determine the open market operation that will be necessary if the money multiplier is 4. Will the Bank of Canada need to buy or sell government securities in the open market and in what amount? (Assume the Bank of Canada deals directly with chartered banks.)

5 Consider the following balance sheets for the Bank of Canada and the Bank of Speedy Creek:

TABLE **28.3**

Bank of Speedy Creek

Assets		Liabilities	
Reserves	60	Deposits	1,000
Securities	100		
Loans	840		
	1,000		

Bank of Canada

Assets		Liabilities	
Government securities	9,000	Bank of Canada notes	10,000
Loans to banks	500	Ch. banks' deposits	1,000
Other net assets	2,000	Government deposits	500
	11,500		11,500

- **a** The Bank of Speedy Creek has chosen this balance sheet position—what is their desired reserve ratio? Explain.

b Suppose that the Bank of Canada buys all \$100 of securities from the Bank of Speedy Creek. Show what happens to the balance sheets of the Bank of Speedy Creek and the Bank of Canada as a result of this action, explaining as you go. What does this action do to the monetary base?

c What will the Bank of Speedy Creek do next? Assuming no currency drain, what does this action do to the overall level of deposits in the banking sector? (Calculate the size of the deposit multiplier as part of your answer.)

d Explain what this open market operation does to the money supply and interest rates.

6 Suppose there is a decrease in the quantity of money. Using an aggregate demand–aggregate supply model, show what happens to the price level and the level of real GDP in the short run and in the long run.

7 Given the following data from the Canadian economy, graph the money market, showing the initial equilibrium in 1988 and the new equilibrium in 1989. Briefly explain why you decided *MD* and *MS* would be placed where you placed them in the graph.

Interest rate (1988) = 10.8%
Interest rate (1989) = 13.4%
Inflation rate (1988–89) = 5.0%
Nominal money growth (1988–89) = 4.6%
Real GDP growth (1988–89) = 2.3%

ⓒ **8** In Short Answer Problem 7, if the Bank of Canada was using money-supply targeting in 1988–89, do you think they were successful in achieving their policy goal?

9 Consider the following data, from the imaginary country of Sarconia:

Current inflation rate	8% per year
Current growth rate of real GDP	3% per year
Current unemployment rate	5%
Estimate of natural unemployment rate	7%
Current growth rate of nominal money supply	12% per year

a Is Sarconia suffering from an inflationary gap, is it suffering from a recessionary gap, or is it right at potential GDP? How do you know?

b In part **a**, if you thought Sarconia was suffering from a problem, explain the correct monetary policy to deal with this problem.

10 Briefly explain the argument for using interest-rate targeting over money-supply targeting.

ANSWERS

True/False/Uncertain and Explain

1 F Higher bank rate increases cost of borrowing reserves, so chartered banks wish to hold more reserves, so they *decrease* loans. (625)

2 F Asset of chartered bank (part of reserves) and liability of Bank of Canada (deposit at Bank). (623)

3 F If securities are sold, people buy them with their deposits, leading to decrease in reserves. (627–629)

4 F Higher desired reserve ratio means more deposits kept back, less lent out, at each stage of money multiplier process. (627–631)

5 F Makes it smaller due to more withdrawals of cash at each round of the multiplier process. (629–630)

ⓒ **6 U** Increase in real GDP shifts *MD* rightward. Since *MS* shifting rightward too, impact on *r* uncertain. (634–635)

7 T Increase in *MS* decreases *r*, which decreases exchange rate, which increases *NX, C, I,* which together shift *AD* rightward. (631–632)

8 T Increase in *MS* decreases *r*, which decreases demand for Canadian dollar and exchange rate. (635–636)

9 F Selling government bonds decreases reserves, which decreases loans and deposits, so *MS* decreases, creating *increase* in interest rates. (631–632)

10 T See text discussion. (637)

Multiple-Choice

1 d Definition. (625)

2 d Definition. (625)

3 b Because bank rate is barometer of open market operations. (625)

4 e See text discussion. (625)

5 d See text discussion. (622)

6 a Bank of Canada credits banking sector's reserves at central bank and in return gets securities from banking sector. (627–628)

7 c Individual gets bank draft from Bank of Canada, which is deposited in his/her bank, so Bank of Canada credits the reserves of his/her bank. (627–628)

8 e Open market sale would look like (c), except both values would be –100. (627–628)

9 b Bank gets \$100 worth of securities, and pays for it with debit of its reserves held at Bank of Canada. (627–628)

10 b Others are all examples of open market operations. (627–628)

11 e Until this event occurs, banks will keep lending out excess reserves. (627–628)

12 e Buying bonds increases reserves to pay for them, which creates excess reserves, leading to increase in lending to make profits, leading to increase in spending and in deposits, which increases money supply. (627–628)

ⓔ **13 e** Deposit multiplier does not depend on currency drain. Decrease in currency drain will result in more loan creation and more deposit (= money) creation at each stage of the multiplier. (629–631)

14 b Both decreases mean there is more reserves to create new loans at each stage of the multiplier process. (629–631)

15 e ΔMS leads to Δr, which Δ demand for Canadian dollar and exchange rate, which ΔNX and AD. (631–632)

16 c Lowering the bank rate lowers costs of borrowing to replenish reserves, so chartered banks will maintain lower reserves, and lend out more money, lowering interest rates (which lowers exchange rate) and stimulating *AE*. (631–632)

17 a Increase in money supply shifts *AD* rightward, increasing real GDP and price level if initial equilibrium is left of full employment (draw a graph). (631–632)

18 b Here, output is above natural rate (inflationary gap), and policy is attempting to reduce *AD* to reduce the gap. (632–633)

19 c Here, output is below the natural rate (recessionary gap) and policy is attempting to increase *AD* to reduce the gap. (631–632)

20 e Increase in money supply leads to excess supply of money, which decreases interest rates, which decreases demand for Canadian dollar and therefore exchange rate. (635–636)

21 e Buying bonds increases reserves, leading to increase in deposits and money supply, creating excess supply of money, which leads to excess demand for financial assets, creating increased price of financial assets and therefore decreased interest rates. (634–635)

22 d Due to fluctuations in *MD*. (634–635)

23 d This action will lower the money supply and raise interest rates and the demand for the Canadian dollar. (631–635)

24 e See text discussion. (635–636)

25 e See text discussion. (637)

Short Answer Problems

1 Increasing interest rates will increase the interest rate gap between Canada and other countries, increasing the demand for the Canadian dollar. This increase in turn will tend to increase the exchange rate, offsetting the initial downward pressure.

2 An open market purchase of government securities by the Bank of Canada increases the monetary base by increasing one of its components—banks' deposits at the Bank of Canada. The process depends on whether the securities are purchased from banks or from the nonbank public.

If the purchase is from banks, the process is direct—the Bank of Canada pays for the securities by crediting the bank's deposit at the Bank of Canada, which directly increases the monetary base. If the purchase is from the nonbank public, the Bank of Canada pays by writing cheques on itself which the sellers of the securities deposit in their banks. The banks, in turn, present the cheques to the Bank of Canada, which credits the banks' deposits at the Bank of Canada. Thus in either case, the monetary base increases by the amount of the open market purchase.

With the extra reserves, banks now have excess reserves. They will seek to lend out these reserves, creating an increase in the money supply via the money multiplier process. The extra money pushes down interest rates, which increases consumption and investment spending. The lower interest rates lower the demand for the Canadian dollar, which lowers the value of the exchange rate, and increases net exports.

3 During each round of the money multiplier process new loans are used for payments. Some of these payments are redeposited (triggering further loan and deposit expansion), and some are held back as currency. The higher the currency drain, the higher the amount held back, the smaller the amount redeposited, the smaller the amount available for further loan and deposit expansion, the smaller the overall deposit expansion, and the smaller the multiplier.

4 a The current equilibrium interest rate is 8 percent and the Bank of Canada would like to increase the money supply sufficiently to decrease the interest rate to 6 percent. Since the quantity of real money demanded at an interest rate of 6 percent is $70 billion, the Bank of Canada will want to increase the supply of real money by \$10 billion: from \$60 billion to \$70 billion.

Real money is nominal money divided by the price level and the Bank of Canada only controls the supply of *nominal* money. Since the price level is 2, the supply of *nominal* money must increase by \$20 billion in order to increase the supply of real money by \$10 billion. Therefore the Bank of Canada will need to increase the *nominal* money supply by \$20 billion.

b To increase the supply of money, the Bank of Canada will need to buy government securities in the open market, which will increase bank reserves and the monetary base. Given the money multiplier is 4, if we want a total increase in money of \$20 billion, we need a \$5 billion increase in the monetary base. This increase would require an open market purchase of \$5 billion in government securities.

5 Desired reserve ratio = chosen reserves/deposits = 60/1,000 = 0.06 or 6 percent.

TABLE **28.4**

(a) Changes in Balance Sheets

Bank of Speedy Creek

Assets		**Liabilities**	
Reserves	+100	Deposits	0
Securities	−100		
Loans	0		
	0		

Bank of Canada

Assets		**Liabilities**	
Government securities	+100	Bank of Canada notes	0
Loans to banks	0	Ch. banks' deposits	+100
Other net assets	0	Government deposits	0
	+100		+100

(b) Positions After the Open Market Operation

Bank of Speedy Creek

Assets		**Liabilities**	
Reserves	160	Deposits	1,000
Securities	0		
Loans	840		
	1,000		

Bank of Canada

Assets		**Liabilities**	
Government securities	9,100	Bank of Canada notes	10,000
Loans to banks	500	Ch. banks' deposits	1,100
Other net assets	2,000	Government deposits	500
	11,600		11,600

b The Bank of Canada increases its securities by 100, and pays for it by increasing the Bank of Speedy Creek's deposits by 100, which is an increase in this bank's reserves by 100 (matching the decrease in security holdings). The balance sheets in Table 28.4 show the changes, and then the new positions.

The increase in chartered banks' deposits of 100 will also increase the monetary base (= notes in circulation + chartered banks' deposits) by 100.

c The Bank of Speedy Creek now has excess reserves of 100, since deposits are unchanged by the operation. They will lend out these excess reserves, creating a multiplier process that will result in an increase in loans and deposits throughout the entire system. The deposit multiplier is 1/(desired reserve ratio) = 1/0.06 = 16.67, so that the total increase in deposits is 1,667.

d Clearly there is an increase in the money supply, which creates an excess supply of money at the original interest rate. People spend their excess supply of money on bonds, driving up the price of bonds, and therefore decreasing interest rates.

6 The consequences of a decrease in the quantity of money are illustrated in Fig 28.3. The economy is initially in long-run equilibrium at point *a*, the intersection of AD_0 and SAS_0 (and *LAS*). The price level is P_0 and GDP is at potential, Y^*. A decrease in the quantity of money will shift the *AD* curve leftward, from AD_0 to AD_1. The new short-run equilibrium is at point *b*. The price level decreases to P_1 and real GDP decreases to Y_1. In the long run, however, input prices will also decrease, which will shift the *SAS* curve rightward, from SAS_0 to SAS_1. A new long-run equilibrium is achieved at point *c*. Thus in the long run, the price level decreases further to P_2, while real GDP returns to potential, Y^*.

FIGURE **28.3**

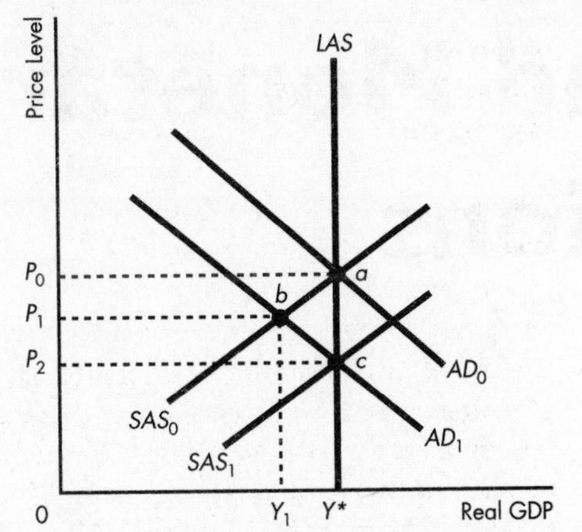

7 The initial 1988 equilibrium is indicated in Fig 28.4 at the intersection of MD_{1988} and MS_{1988}, with an interest rate of 10.8 percent. The increase in real GDP from 1988 to 1989, *ceteris paribus,* will mean an increase in real money demanded, shown by the shift rightward from MD_{1988} to MD_{1989}. The inflation rate is higher than the growth rate of the nominal money supply, so that the real money supply shrinks by a small amount from 1988 to 1989, shown by the shift leftward from MS_{1988} to MS_{1989}. The net result of these two changes is an increase in the interest rate from 1988 to 1989.

FIGURE **28.4**

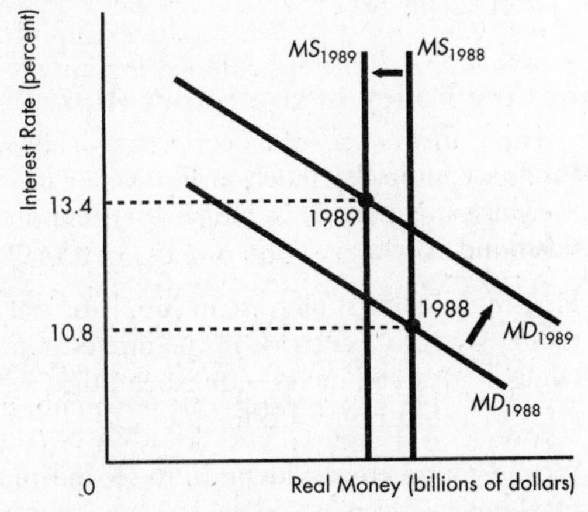

ⓔ **8** Their policy goal was probably to manipulate the money supply in order to affect interest rates and therefore inflation or real GDP growth. However, since the rate of interest rose dramatically, due partially to the affect on money demand of the increase in real GDP growth, it is likely that the rise in the rate of interest was more than the Bank desired, so that their policy was overly contractionary.

9 a Since unemployment is below the natural rate, real GDP is above potential GDP and there is an inflationary gap.

b The problem is that inflation is likely to start rising, so the correct policy is to shrink the money supply to lower aggregate demand, and relieve the inflationary pressure.

10 If a central bank pursues monetary targeting, they keep the money supply constant at a level that they hope will affect the economy appropriately. However, if the demand for money fluctuates, then the rate of interest will fluctuate and therefore affect the economy undesirably. On the other hand, if the central bank picks an interest rate target that is aimed at an average money supply level (where the interest rate target crosses the average demand for money curve), there will not be undesirable fluctuations in the rate of interest.

Chapter 29
Fiscal and Monetary Interactions

KEY CONCEPTS

Macroeconomic Equilibrium

Real GDP and the price level are determined by the interaction of *AD* and *SAS*.

- Demand for real money (*MD*) and supply of real money (*MS*) determine interest rate (*r*).
- This chapter explores how real GDP and interest rate are simultaneously determined.
- *AD-SAS* equilibrium is where *AD* = *SAS*.
  - *AD* is a function of *I*, *C*, *G*, and *NX*.
  - Crucial is interest-sensitive expenditure (*IE*) curve—relationship between *C* + *I* + *NX* and *r*.
  - Higher *r* creates lower expenditure, and lower level of *AD*, lower *Y* and *P*.
  - *AD* depends on *r*.
- Money market equilibrium is where *MD* = *MS*.
  - *MD* is a function of *Y*, *MS* is a function of *P*.
  - Higher *AD* creates higher *Y* (and higher *MD*) and higher *P* (lower *MS*), and therefore higher *r*.
  - *r* depends on *AD*.
- There is only one value of *Y* and one value of *r* that give simultaneous or joint money market equilibrium and *AD-SAS* equilibrium.

Fiscal Policy in the Short Run

Expansionary fiscal policy is an increase in government expenditures, increase in transfer payments, or decrease in taxes which increases *AD*, and has first- and second-round effects.

- First-round effects: increase in government expenditure creates multiplier effects and increases quantity of real GDP demanded.
- Second-round effects: increase in real GDP demanded increases real GDP and price level.
  - Increase in *Y* shifts *MD* rightward, which increases *r* and decreases *IE*, shifting *AD* curve leftward somewhat.
  - Increase in *P* shifts *MS* leftward, which increases *r* and decreases *IE* and quantity of real GDP demanded (movement along *AD* curve).
- Tendency for expansionary fiscal policy to increase *r* and decrease *I* is called **crowding out**.
  - Expansionary fiscal policy may increase *I* (**crowding in**) if it increases expected future profits or increases profitability of current capital or decreases taxes.
  - Increase in *r* may cause **international crowding out** by increasing exchange rate, which leads to decrease in *NX*.

Monetary Policy in the Short Run

Expansionary monetary policy is an increase in money supply which increases *AD*, and has first-round and second-round effects.

- First-round effects: increase in supply of real money leads to a decrease in the interest rate, which leads to an increase in expenditure, which leads to a shift rightward in *AD*.
- Second-round effects: identical to second-round fiscal policy effects.
- There is an exchange rate effect that augments the monetary policy—the overall decrease in the interest rate leads to a decrease in demand for the Canadian dollar, which leads to a decrease in exchange rate, which leads to an increase in net exports.

Relative Effectiveness of Policies

- Fiscal policy is more powerful if less crowding out, which occurs if
  - money demand *responsive* to interest rates (ΔMD leads to small Δr).
  - interest-sensitive expenditure *unresponsive* to interest rates (given Δr leads to small Δ expenditure).
- Monetary policy is more powerful if
  - money demand *unresponsive* to interest rates (ΔMS leads to large Δr).
  - interest-sensitive expenditure *responsive* to interest rates (given Δr leads to large Δ expenditure).
- The Keynesian-monetarist controversy of the 1950s centred around whether fiscal policy or monetary policy was more effective:
  - **Keynesians** believed economy was inherently unstable, fiscal policy more effective, due to little crowding out.
  - **Monetarists** believed economy was inherently stable, monetary policy more effective, due to lots of crowding out.
  - Empirical evidence showed both policies were effective.

Policy Actions at Full Employment

Results of fiscal and monetary policy are different if the economy starts at full employment.

- Expansionary fiscal policy shifts *AD* rightward, and creates above full-employment equilibrium (inflationary gap).
  - Labour shortage puts upward pressure on money wages.
  - This pressure creates third-round effects—increasing wages shift *SAS* leftward.
  - As *SAS* shifts leftward, *Y* decreases and *P* increases as economy moves to long-run equilibrium.
  - Result is complete crowding out—*IE* decreases by amount *G* increases.
- An expansionary monetary policy at full employment creates third-round effects identical to fiscal policy third-round effects.
  - These effects create the **long-run neutrality proposition**—in the long run, a change in the quantity of money changes the price level only, and leaves all real variables unchanged.

Policy Coordination and Conflict

Government and Bank of Canada can work together to achieve common goals (**policy coordination**), or pursue conflicting goals (**policy conflict**).

- Monetary and fiscal policy both alter *AD*, but have opposite effects on interest and exchange rates.
  - Expansionary fiscal policy increases *r* and increases exchange rate, leading to decrease in *C, I, NX*.
  - Expansionary monetary policy decreases *r* and decreases exchange rate, leading to increase in *C, I, NX*.
  - Coordination allows an increase in *AD* with desired Δr by correctly mixing monetary and fiscal policy.
  - Conflicts arise when government and Bank of Canada disagree on policy.
- One crucial conflict is about financing deficit.
  - If government borrows from Bank of Canada, it avoids interest costs, but resulting increase in *MS* leads to inflationary pressures.
  - In Canada, only small part of deficits are financed by Bank of Canada.

HELPFUL HINTS

1 Chapters 25 and 26 examined the goods and services markets in isolation using the *AD-SAS* model and assuming that the interest rate was given. When the interest rate changed, aggregate demand changed, resulting in a new equilibrium level of real GDP.

Similarly, Chapter 28 examined the money market in isolation by using the money supply and money demand model and assuming that the level of real GDP was given. When the level of real GDP changed, the demand for real money changed, resulting in a new equilibrium. The equilibrium value of real GDP was determined assuming a value for the interest rate and the equilibrium interest rate was determined assuming a value for real GDP.

This chapter puts the two models of these markets together and simultaneously determines equilibrium real GDP and the equilibrium interest rate. Examining the simultaneous equilibrium reveals important *second round* effects of fiscal and monetary policy that did not appear in the partial analysis of earlier chapters. One example of these second-round effects is crowding out. Because of crowding out, the fiscal policy multipliers in the full model are smaller than the multipliers examined in the partial model of Chapter 26.

2 The major focus of this chapter is on channels of monetary or fiscal policy—how an initial change in monetary or fiscal policy is transmitted through the economy to its eventual effect on aggregate demand. The graphical analysis in the text is valuable in studying these channels.

The economy initially starts out in equilibrium, then a change in either monetary or fiscal policy throws a market out of equilibrium. As this market changes and moves towards a new equilibrium, changes are triggered in other markets. Eventually a new, simultaneous equilibrium is achieved in all markets.

It is helpful to augment the graphical analysis with simple "arrow diagrams" that show the *sequence* of changes as the economy adjusts to an initial policy change. For example, the interest rate transmission channel of monetary policy is represented by the following arrow diagram:

(i) First round:

$$\uparrow M \rightarrow \uparrow MS$$
$$\uparrow MS \rightarrow \downarrow r \text{ (link 1)}$$
$$\downarrow r \rightarrow \uparrow IE \text{ (link 2)}$$
$$\uparrow IE \rightarrow \uparrow AD$$
$$\uparrow AD \rightarrow \uparrow \text{real GDP}, \uparrow P$$

Second round:

$$\uparrow \text{real GDP} \rightarrow \uparrow MD$$
$$\uparrow P \rightarrow \downarrow MS$$
$$\downarrow MS, \uparrow MD \rightarrow \uparrow r$$
$$\uparrow r \rightarrow \downarrow IE$$
$$\downarrow IE \rightarrow \downarrow AD$$
$$\downarrow AD \rightarrow \downarrow \text{real GDP}, \downarrow P$$

This diagram indicates that an expansionary monetary policy (an open market purchase of government securities by the Bank of Canada) will cause the quantity of money to increase (↑ *M*), which leads to an increase in the real supply of money (↑ *MS*). This increase in turn will result in a decrease in the interest rate (↓ *r*) that will increase expenditure (↑ *IE*), which is a part of aggregate demand (↑ *AD*). This increase will cause real GDP and the price level to begin increasing (↑ real GDP, ↑ *P*), the end of the first round effects.

However, the increase in real GDP and the price level cause second round effects—the higher real GDP leads to a rightward shift in the demand for real money (↑ *MD*), the higher price level shifts the supply of real money leftward (↓ *MS*). The increase in the demand for real money and the decrease in the supply of real money will cause the interest rate to increase (↑ *r*) and thus expenditure (↓ *IE*) and aggregate expenditure (↓ *AD*) will decrease, which will lead to a decrease in real GDP and the price level (↓ real GDP, ↓ *P*). This crowding-out effect offsets somewhat the initial changes, but the economy still eventually converges to a new equilibrium. (Ignore link 1 and link 2 in the arrow diagram for the moment.)

An arrow diagram can be a convenient way of summarizing the more detailed graphical analysis. Arrow diagrams can also be useful to reveal effects that can weaken or strengthen the ability of policy to change aggregate demand.

3 The transmission channel of fiscal policy (for example, an increase in government expenditures on goods and services), is represented by the following arrow diagram:

(ii) First round:

$$\uparrow G \rightarrow \uparrow AD$$
$$\uparrow AD \rightarrow \uparrow \text{real GDP}, \uparrow P$$

Second round:

$$\uparrow \text{real GDP} \rightarrow \uparrow MD$$
$$\uparrow P \rightarrow \downarrow MS$$
$$\downarrow MS, \uparrow MD \rightarrow \uparrow r \text{ (link 1)}$$
$$\uparrow r \rightarrow \downarrow IE \text{ (link 2)}$$
$$\downarrow IE \rightarrow \downarrow AD$$
$$\downarrow AD \rightarrow \downarrow \text{real GDP}, \downarrow P$$

The amount of government expenditures on goods and services is represented by *G*. Otherwise the notation is the same as used above. (Once again, ignore link 1 and link 2.)

4 The text indicates that the strength of the effect of a change in the money supply on aggregate demand depends on the responsiveness of the demand for real money to changes in the interest rate and the responsiveness of expenditure to changes in the interest rate.

The arrow diagram given by (i) illustrates how these factors affect the strength of monetary policy. The link between the increase in the supply of real money and the subsequent decrease in the interest rate is indicated as link 1. If the demand for real money is very sensitive to interest rate changes (the *MD* curve is very flat or interest-elastic), then this link is quite weak—a given increase in the supply of real money will have only a small effect on the interest rate. This small effect in turn means a relatively small effect on expenditure. Link 2 captures the effect of a change in the interest rate on expenditure. If expenditure is very sensitive to interest rate changes (the interest-sensitive expenditure curve is very flat or interest-elastic), then this link is quite strong—a given decrease in the interest rate will have a very large effect on expenditure.

We can also examine the factors that determine the strength of the effect of fiscal policy on aggregate demand. Links 1 and 2 of (ii) are the relevant links; indeed they are the same as links 1 and 2 for monetary policy. If the demand for real money is very sensitive to interest rate changes (the *MD* curve is very flat), then link 1 is quite weak, the amount of crowding out is small, and fiscal policy is strong. Similarly, if expenditure is very sensitive to interest rate changes (the interest-sensitive expenditure curve is very flat), then link 2 is quite strong, the amount of crowding out is large, and fiscal policy is weak.

Links 1 and 2 are critical in the transmission process and the focus of the Keynesian-monetarist controversy. It is interesting to think about the extreme Keynesian and monetarist positions in terms of these links. The existence of a liquidity trap (horizontal *MD* curve assumed by an extreme Keynesian) makes monetary policy ineffective because it completely breaks link 1—an increase in the supply of real money will have no effect on the interest rate. It also makes fiscal policy very strong, because there is no crowding out (an increase in real GDP has no impact on interest rates and expenditure).

The existence of a vertical interest-sensitive expenditure curve (assumed by an extreme Keynesian) makes monetary policy ineffective because it completely breaks link 2. Similarly, the existence of a horizontal interest-sensitive expenditure curve or a vertical *MD* curve (assumed by an extreme monetarist) implies complete crowding out and therefore ineffective fiscal policy.

Note that the same effects that create a strong fiscal policy create a weak monetary policy, and vice versa.

5 The effect of changes in monetary policy or fiscal policy on the exchange rate are very important in economies with large foreign sectors such as Canada. Changes in interest rates change the demand for the Canadian dollar in the same direction. This change in turn causes an appreciation in the Canadian dollar if the interest rate increases, and a depreciation in the exchange rate if the interest rate decreases. However, there is a crucial difference between fiscal and monetary policy for this effect, because of the fact the two policies have opposite effects on interest rates.

An expansionary fiscal policy will *increase* interest rates, *increasing* the exchange rate, *decreasing* net exports, thus *offsetting* the expansionary policy. However, an expansionary monetary policy *decreases* interest rates, *decreasing* the exchange rate, *decreasing* net exports, thus *augmenting* the expansionary policy.

SELF-TEST

True/False/Uncertain and Explain

1 An increase in the interest rate will cause the interest-sensitive expenditure curve to shift leftward.

2 Crowding in is more powerful than crowding out.

3 If aggregate demand is increased by an increase in government expenditures on goods and services, interest rates decrease and investment increases.

4 If aggregate demand is increased by an increase in the supply of real money, interest rates decrease and investment increases.

5 An increase in the money supply will cause the interest rate to increase.

6 An increase in the money supply will cause the exchange rate to increase.

7 Other things equal, a change in the money supply will have a larger effect on aggregate planned expenditure the more responsive expenditure is to the interest rate.

8 Crowding out will be greater if the interest-sensitive expenditure curve is very steep.

9 In the *AD-AS* model, an expansionary monetary policy leads only to an increase in price, not an increase in real GDP.

10 Coordination of monetary and fiscal policy means that an expansionary policy can be carried out without any crowding out.

Multiple-Choice

Macroeconomic Equilibrium

1 Which of the following best describes how the level of aggregate demand affects the interest rate?

a An increase in the level of aggregate demand increases the price level, which in turn increases money demand and therefore increases the interest rate.
b An increase in the level of aggregate demand decreases the price level, which in turn increases the supply of money and therefore increases the interest rate.
c A decrease in the level of aggregate demand decreases the price level, which in turn increases money demand and therefore increases the interest rate.
d An increase in the level of aggregate demand increases real GDP, which in turn increases money demand and therefore increases the interest rate.
e An increase in the level of aggregate demand increases real GDP, which in turn decreases the supply of real money and therefore increases the interest rate.

2 Which of the following best describes how the interest rate affects aggregate demand?

a A lower interest rate increases investment demand, which in turn increases aggregate demand.
b A higher interest rate increases investment demand, which in turn increases aggregate demand.
c A higher interest rate decreases investment demand, which in turn increases aggregate demand.
d A higher interest rate increases consumption, which in turn increases aggregate demand.
e A higher interest rate increases net exports, which in turn increases aggregate demand.

3 Consider Fig. 29.1. Why is the situation depicted *not* a consistent equilibrium?

a The level of aggregate demand is inconsistent with the interest rate.
b The money market and the *AD-AS* graph are not individually in equilibrium.
c The *AD-AS* equilibrium occurs at a different level of real GDP than the level of real GDP assumed when the demand curve is drawn for real money.
d The level of expenditure in part (b) is inconsistent with the level of expenditure in part (c).
e Aggregate demand is greater than aggregate supply.

FIGURE **29.1**

(a)

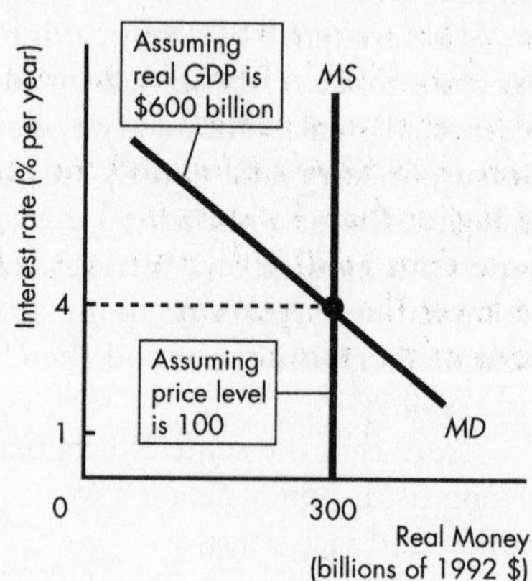

(b)

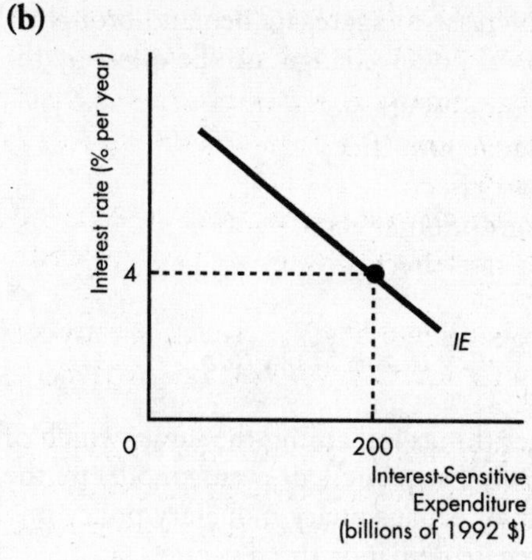

(c)

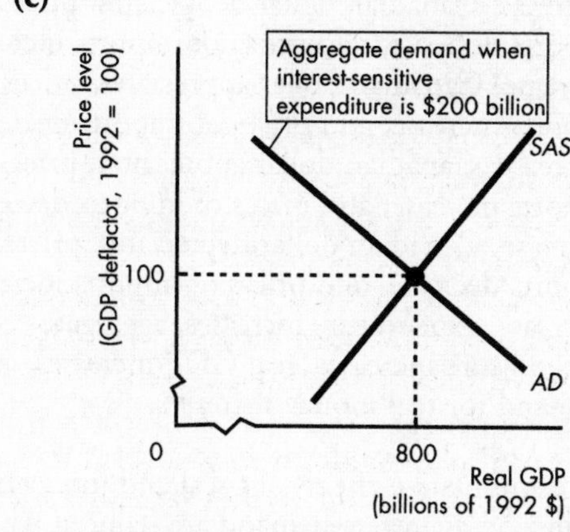

4 Suppose Fig. 29.1 depicts the actual current position of an economy. When this economy moves to equilibrium, real GDP will be

a less than $800 billion and the interest rate will be higher than 4 percent.
b less than $800 billion and the interest rate will be lower than 4 percent.
c more than $800 billion and the interest rate will be higher than 4 percent.
d more than $800 billion and the interest rate will be lower than 4 percent.
e none of the above.

5 A change in interest rates (price level held constant) will affect aggregate demand through which one of the following changes?

a a shift of the interest-sensitive expenditure curve and movement along the aggregate demand curve
b a shift of the demand for real money curve and the interest-sensitive expenditure curve
c a shift of both the interest-sensitive expenditure and the aggregate demand curves
d movements along both the interest-sensitive expenditure and the aggregate demand curves
e a movement along the interest-sensitive expenditure curve and a shift of the aggregate demand curve

Fiscal Policy in the Short Run

6 Which of the following best describes an expansionary fiscal policy? Government expenditures increase, therefore aggregate demand

a increases, leading to an increase in real GDP, leading to an increase in money demand, leading to a decrease in the interest rate, leading to a further increase in real GDP.
b increases, leading to an increase in the price level, leading to an increase in supply of real money, leading to a decrease in the interest rate, leading to a further increase in real GDP.
c decreases, leading to an increase in real GDP, leading to an increase in money demand, leading to a decrease in the interest rate, leading to a further increase in real GDP.
d increases, leading to a decrease in the price level, leading to an increase in money demand, leading to a decrease in the interest rate, leading to a partially offsetting increase in real GDP.
e increases, leading to an increase in real GDP, leading to an increase in money demand, leading to an increase in the interest rate, leading to a partially offsetting decrease in real GDP.

7 Crowding in refers to the tendency for an increase in government expenditures on goods and services to

a induce an increase in money demand, leading to an increase in interest rates and a decrease in investment.
b induce a decrease in money demand, leading to a decrease in interest rates and an increase in investment.
c induce an increase in the money supply.
d raise interest rates, which leads to an increase in the exchange rate, leading to a decrease in net exports.
e raise profit expectations in the private sector, leading to an increase in investment demand.

8 Crowding out is the effect of expansionary fiscal policy on

a the exchange rate and therefore the level of the supply of real money.
b the exchange rate and therefore the level of imports.
c the exchange rate and therefore investment demand.
d the interest rate and therefore investment demand.
e the interest rate and therefore money demand.

9 Counting the first and second round effects, the impact of a *contractionary* fiscal policy is to decrease real GDP,

a reduce the interest rate, and reduce investment.
b reduce the interest rate, and increase investment.
c increase the interest rate, and reduce investment.
d increase the interest rate, and increase investment.
e none of the above.

10 Overall, a tax cut will

a increase aggregate demand by causing consumption to increase.
b increase aggregate demand by causing the interest rate to decrease.
c decrease aggregate demand by causing consumption to decrease.
d decrease aggregate demand by causing the interest rate to increase.
e increase aggregate demand by causing investment to increase.

11 An increase in aggregate demand brought about by fiscal policy changes can be offset by the

a crowding-in effect.
b exchange rate effect.
c import effect.
d consumption effect.
e bond rate effect.

Monetary Policy in the Short Run

12 Other things remaining the same, which of the following sequences of events moderate the effect of expansionary monetary policy on aggregate demand? Interest rates

a decrease, Canadian dollar depreciates, prices of exports decrease, and prices of imports increase.
b increase, Canadian dollar appreciates, prices of exports increase, and prices of imports decrease.
c decrease, Canadian dollar appreciates, prices of exports increase, and prices of imports decrease.
d increase, Canadian dollar depreciates, prices of exports decrease, and prices of imports increase.
e decrease, expenditure increases, aggregate expenditure increases, real GDP increases, and demand for real money increases.

13 The stimulative effects of fiscal and monetary policy on aggregate demand are reduced when the resulting increase in the price level increases interest rates, that in turn decrease

a investment.
b net exports.
c consumption.
d all of the above.
e none of the above.

14 Consider the *AD-AS* model with unemployment. After an expansionary monetary policy has increased aggregate demand, the overall effect on real GDP is

a a decrease because of the increase in the price level.
b an increase even more than the initial aggregate demand effect because of the increase in the price level.
c zero due to the increase in the price level.
d zero due to the decrease in the price level.
e an increase, but by a smaller amount than the initial aggregate demand effect because of the increase in the price level.

15 Counting the first and second round effects, the total impact of a contractionary monetary policy is to decrease real GDP,

- **a** reduce the interest rate, and reduce investment.
- **b** reduce the interest rate, and increase investment.
- **c** increase the interest rate, and reduce investment.
- **d** increase the interest rate, and increase investment.
- **e** none of the above.

16 An increase in the money supply will eventually lead to an increase in real GDP, which will shift the demand curve for real money

- **a** leftward, causing the interest rate to decrease.
- **b** leftward, causing the interest rate to increase.
- **c** rightward, causing the interest rate to decrease.
- **d** rightward, causing the interest rate to increase.
- **e** rightward, causing the supply of real money to increase.

Relative Effectiveness of Policies

17 Monetary policy will have the *smallest* effect on aggregate demand when the sensitivity of the demand for real money to the interest rate is

- **a** large and the sensitivity of expenditure to the interest rate is large.
- **b** large and the sensitivity of expenditure to the interest rate is small.
- **c** small and the sensitivity of aggregate supply to the interest rate is large.
- **d** small and the sensitivity of expenditure to the interest rate is small.
- **e** small and the sensitivity of expenditure to the interest rate is large.

18 Consider an economy where the demand for real money is very sensitive to changes in the interest rate. The problem with monetary policy in this economy is that

- **a** there will be a high level of crowding out.
- **b** monetary policy will create changes in the exchange rate that offset the monetary policy.
- **c** a change in the interest rate creates only a small change in expenditure.
- **d** a change in the supply of real money creates too large a change in the interest rate.
- **e** a change in the supply of real money creates only a small change in the interest rate.

19 Statistical evidence from a variety of historical and national experiences suggests that

- **a** fiscal policy affects aggregate demand and monetary policy does not.
- **b** monetary policy affects aggregate demand and fiscal policy does not.
- **c** both fiscal policy and monetary policy affect aggregate demand.
- **d** neither fiscal policy nor monetary policy affect aggregate demand.
- **e** fiscal policy affected aggregate demand only during the Great Depression of the 1930s.

20 A Keynesian believes the economy is inherently

- **a** unstable, and fiscal policy is more important than monetary policy.
- **b** unstable, and monetary policy is more important than fiscal policy.
- **c** stable, and fiscal policy is more important than monetary policy.
- **d** stable, and monetary policy is more important than fiscal policy.
- **e** stable, and crowding out is strong.

Policy Actions at Full Employment

21 If the aggregate supply curve was vertical, expansionary fiscal policy would cause all of the following *except*

- **a** an increase in investment.
- **b** a decrease in the supply of real money.
- **c** an increase in interest rates.
- **d** an increase in the price level.
- **e** a decrease in investment.

22 Which of the following is the long-run neutrality proposition?

- **a** Changes in the money supply change the price level only, not real variables.
- **b** Changes in the money supply change real variables only, not the price level.
- **c** In the long run, fiscal policy is 100 percent crowded out.
- **d** In the long run, expenditure is completely unresponsive to changes in the interest rate, so monetary policy does not work.
- **e** In the long run, money demand is completely unresponsive to changes in the interest rate, so fiscal policy does not work.

23 If there is an expansionary fiscal policy at full employment, which of the following effects does *not* occur in the long run?
a Crowding out.
b Crowding in.
c International crowding out.
d Labour shortages increase the wage rate.
e Increases in money demand increase the interest rate.

Policy Coordination and Conflict

24 Coordinating fiscal and monetary policy is better for the economy because it
a allows cheap financing of the deficit.
b allows the desired change in interest rates by appropriately mixing monetary and fiscal policy.
c has the opposite effects on the interest rate and the exchange rate.
d can stop inflation.
e none of the above.

25 Aggregate demand can be increased by increasing the supply of real money (expansionary monetary policy) or by increasing government expenditures on goods and services (expansionary fiscal policy). Which of the following is a correct comparison?
a The interest rate will increase under the monetary policy and decrease under the fiscal policy, while consumption will increase under both.
b The interest rate will decrease under the monetary policy and increase under the fiscal policy, while consumption will increase under both.
c Consumption will increase under the monetary policy and decrease under the fiscal policy, while the interest rate will increase under both.
d Consumption will increase under the monetary policy and decrease under the fiscal policy, while the interest rate will decrease under both.
e Consumption will decrease under both the monetary policy and fiscal policy, while the interest rate will increase under both.

Short Answer Problems

1 Trace the main steps following an increase in the supply of real money.

2 Why does an increase in the supply of real money have a smaller effect on aggregate demand if the demand for real money is very sensitive to changes in the interest rate?

3 Explain how an increase in the supply of real money leads to an increase in aggregate demand through a change in the exchange rate.

4 How does crowding out take place?

ⓒⓣ 5 Consider an economy that has real GDP less than potential, and needs an expansionary policy. Evaluate an expansionary fiscal policy versus an expansionary monetary policy, on the basis of the following four considerations:
a the empirical evidence on the relative effectiveness of each policy
b the impacts of each on expenditure
c the impacts of each on potential GDP
d the impacts of each on the deficit

6 Figure 29.2 depicts an economy. Note that MD_0 corresponds to real GDP = $400 billion, MD_1 corresponds to real GDP = $500 billion, and MD_2 corresponds to real GDP = $600 billion. MS_0 corresponds to a price level of 110, and AD_0 corresponds to an expenditure level of 100.
a What are the equilibrium values for real GDP, the interest rate, and expenditure?
b Is this equilibrium a consistent equilibrium? Why or why not?

FIGURE **29.2**

(a)

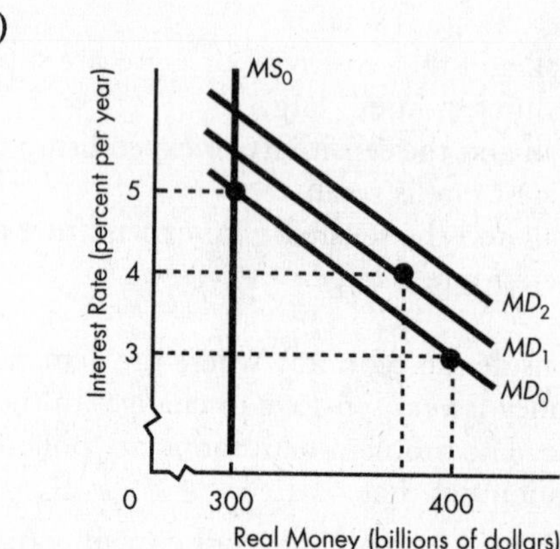

(b)

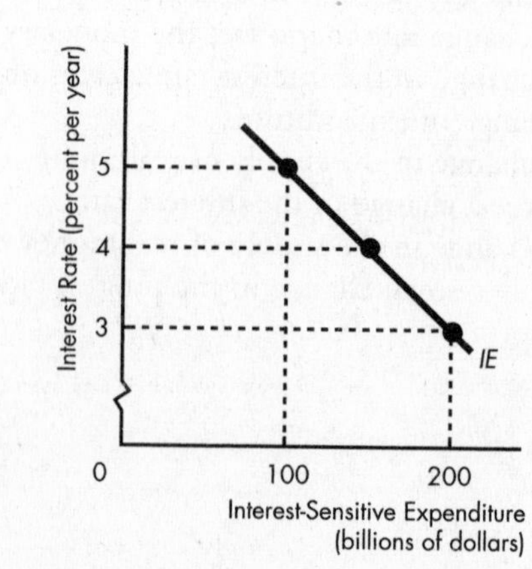

(c)

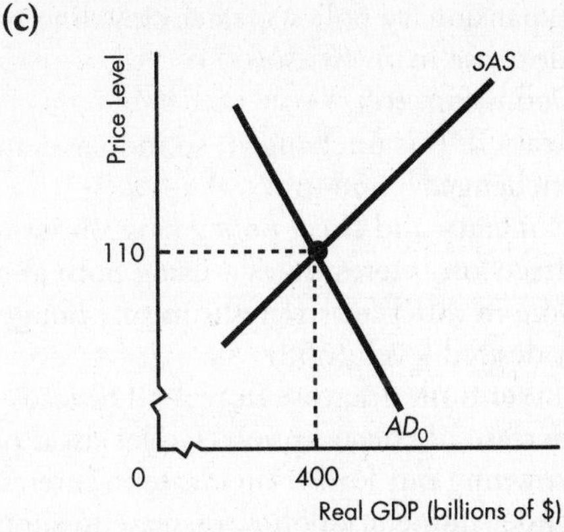

7 Consider again the economy depicted by Fig. 29.2. Suppose that the Bank of Canada increases the supply of real money from $300 billion to $400 billion.
  a What is the initial effect on the interest rate? Illustrate this effect on Fig. 29.2.
  b What effect will this change in the interest rate have on expenditure?
  c As a result of this change in expenditure, what happens to the quantity of real GDP demanded if the multiplier is 2? Illustrate this change on Fig. 29.2.
  d As best as you can (not worrying too much about exact numbers), show on Fig. 29.2 what the final equilibrium is after this change, explaining what has happened to the interest rate, expenditure, real GDP and the price level as a result of the increase in the money supply.

8 Suppose that as a result of the increase in real GDP in Short Answer Problem 7, firms' expectations of future profits increase.
  a What happens to expenditure as a result? What is this effect called?
  b What will be the first- and second-round results of this increase in firms' profit expectations? Specifically, what happens to *AD*, *IE*, *MD*, *r*, real GDP and the price level? (A written explanation is sufficient.)

9 Suppose the economy is Short Answer Problem 7 was initially at full employment. Describe what would happen in the *AD-SAS* equilibrium in the long run after the increase in the supply of real money.

10 Why will more crowding out take place if expenditure is very sensitive to interest rate changes?

ANSWERS

True/False/Uncertain and Explain

1 F Increase in *r* leads to movement along *IE* curve. (644–645)
2 U Depends on relative strength of each effect, which is unknown. (649)
3 F Increase in *G* leads to an increase in real GDP and *P*, which leads to an increase in *MD* and a decrease in *MS*, creating an increase in *r* and therefore a decrease in *I*. (646–649)
4 T Increase in *MS* leads to a decrease in *r*, which leads to increase in *I*, which shifts *AD* rightward. (650–653)
5 F Increase in *MS* creates an excess supply of money, which leads to a decrease in interest rates. (650)
6 F Increase in *MS* leads to a decrease in *r*, which leads to a decrease in demand for Canadian assets, leading to decrease in demand for Canadian dollar and therefore a decrease in the exchange rate. (653)
7 T ΔMS works by Δr to ΔIE and therefore to ΔAD, so if impact of *r* on *IE* is larger, impact of ΔMS on *AD* is larger. (654)
8 F Steep *IE* curve is not responsive to an increase in *r*. Crowding out happens due to expansionary fiscal policy creating an increase in *r*, and the smaller the impact of the increase in *r*, the smaller the crowding out. (655)
ⓒⓣ **9 U** Depends on whether originally unemployment or full-employment equilibrium. (657)
10 T By picking the appropriate mixture of fiscal policy (which tends to increase *r*) and monetary policy (which tends to decrease *r*), the authorities can have no change in *r*, and therefore no crowding out. (658)

Multiple-Choice

1 d Increases in aggregate demand increase the price level (and therefore lower the supply of real money and raise the interest rate). (644)
2 a See text description. (644)
ⓒⓣ **3 c** The higher equilibrium real GDP will shift money demand—therefore current money demand is inconsistent. (644–645)
ⓒⓣ **4 a** The current real GDP of $800 billion will raise money demand, which leads to increase in interest rate, and therefore a decrease in expenditure, which leads to decrease in aggregate demand and in equilibrium real GDP. (644–645)

5 e By definition of *IE* curve and components of *AD*. (644–645)
6 e An increase in *G* leads to an increase in *AD*, which creates an increase in real GDP, and therefore an increase in *MD*, which creates an increase in *r*, and therefore a decrease in *IE*, resulting in a decrease in *AD* and in real GDP. (646–649)
7 e Definition. (649)
8 d Definition. (649)
9 b Decrease in real GDP and *P* leads to decrease in money demand and increase in *MS*, which leads to decrease in interest rate and therefore increase in expenditure. (646–649)
10 a Decrease in taxes increases disposable income, leading to increase in consumption and aggregate demand. (649)
11 b Increase in real GDP leads to an increase in money demand, which leads to an increase in *r* and therefore the exchange rate, as well as a decrease in expenditure. (649)
12 e The increase in *AD* increases *MD*, which leads to an increase in *r* and a decrease in expenditure, a decrease in *AD*, which leads to a decrease in real GDP, moderating the increase in real GDP. (650–653)
13 d Increase in price level creates an increase in *r*, which leads to an increase in cost of borrowing, lowering *C* and *I*; increase in *r* leads to an increase in demand for Canadian dollar, which leads to increase in exchange rate and a decrease in *NX*. (651–653)
14 e Shift rightward in *AD* curve leads to an increase in price level leads, which leads to an increase in *r* and a decrease in aggregate demand. (651–653)
15 c Decrease in real GDP and *P* leads to decrease in money demand and increase in *MS*, which leads to decrease in interest rate (somewhat offsetting original increase), which leads to increase in expenditure but not enough to overcome initial decrease in expenditure. (651–653)
16 d Money demand depends positively on real GDP, so higher real GDP leads to increase in money demand and increase in interest rate. (651–653)
17 b Sensitive *MD* implies a ΔMS leads to small Δr, and insensitive *IE* implies Δr leads to small Δ expenditure. (654)
18 e Because with sensitive money demand, Δ interest rate needed to get money market in equilibrium after Δ supply of real money is small. (654)
19 c See text discussion. (655)
20 a See text discussion. (654)
21 a Expansionary policy creates crowding out (decrease in *I*). (656–657)
22 a Definition. (657)
ⓒⓣ **23** e Real GDP is unchanged, so money demand is unchanged. (656–657)
24 b Monetary and fiscal policy have opposite effects on interest rates—using both at same time in different strengths means can get Δr at desired level. (658)
ⓒⓣ **25** b Under both, increase in real GDP leads to increase in consumption. Under fiscal policy, crowding out leads to increase in interest rate. Under monetary policy, increase in supply of real money leads to decrease in interest rate. (658)

Short Answer Problems

ⓒⓣ **1** An increase in the supply of real money
- will shift the supply curve of real money rightward and decrease the interest rate.
- the lower interest rate will cause expenditure to increase.
- the increase in expenditure means that aggregate demand increases.
- the increase in aggregate demand increases real GDP and the price level.
- rising real GDP causes the demand curve for real money to shift rightward and the rising price level causes the supply of real money to shift leftward, causing the interest rate to increase.
- the higher interest rate will cause expenditure to decrease.
- the decrease in expenditure means that aggregate demand decreases somewhat, but the economy converges to a new equilibrium with higher real GDP.

2 If the demand for real money is very sensitive to changes in the interest rate, the demand curve for real money is very flat. Thus when the money supply increases and the supply curve for real money shifts rightward, the resulting change in the equilibrium interest rate will be small. *Ceteris paribus*, a small interest rate change will lead to a small change in expenditure and a small change in aggregate demand.

3 An increase in the supply of money will shift the supply curve of real money rightward and decrease the interest rate. The lower interest rate (relative to interest rates in other countries) will cause people to want to sell low-interest Canadian financial assets and buy relatively high-interest foreign financial assets. Therefore the demand for dollars decreases and the demand for foreign currencies increases, which results in a lower exchange rate relative to foreign currencies. This decrease in the exchange rate will cause net exports to increase as foreigners can now buy Canadian goods for less (in terms of their currencies) and Canadians must pay more (in dollars) for foreign goods. The increase in net exports creates an increase in aggregate demand.

4 Crowding out is the tendency for expansionary fiscal policy to cause the interest rate to increase and thus investment to decline. Expansionary fiscal policy "crowds out" investment. An increase in government expenditure on goods and services increases real GDP and the price level, causing the demand curve for real money to shift rightward, and the supply of real money to shift leftward. Thus the equilibrium interest rate will increase.

5 a The empirical evidence is that both policies work with a fair degree of strength, so you could pick either.

b An expansionary fiscal policy raises interest rates, and therefore will decrease investment, while an expansionary monetary policy decreases interest rates and will raise investment. On these grounds, you would tend to pick monetary policy.

c The fiscal policy decreases investment, which means in the long run less capital stock and less growth of potential GDP, while the monetary policy has the opposite effect. On these grounds, you would tend to pick monetary policy.

d Expansionary fiscal policy usually means some combination of more spending and lower taxes, which leads to a higher deficit. Expansionary monetary policy has no impact on the deficit, so you would tend to pick it.

6 a The equilibrium value for real GDP is at the intersection of the AD_0 and *SAS* curves—\$400 billion. The equilibrium value for the interest rate is 5 percent, since the relevant *MD* curve is MD_0 when real GDP is \$400 billion. At an interest rate of 5 percent, expenditure is \$100 billion (part (b)).

b This equilibrium is a consistent equilibrium because equilibrium real GDP is \$400 billion when the interest rate is 5 percent and the equilibrium interest rate is 5 percent when real GDP is \$400 billion. In other words, it is a consistent equilibrium because the values of real GDP and the interest rate that give money market equilibrium and *AD-SAS* equilibrium are the same.

7 a The initial effect of an increase in the supply of real money from \$300 billion to \$400 billion is to decrease the interest rate from 5 percent to 3 percent. This shift is illustrated in part (a) of Fig. 29.2 Solution as the shift from MS_0 to MS_1.

b The decrease in the interest rate from 5 percent to 3 percent will increase expenditure from \$100 billion to \$200 billion.

c If the multiplier is 2, the \$100 billion increase in expenditure translates into a rightward shift of the *AD* curve by \$200 billion (quantity of real GDP demanded rises by \$200 billion), as shown.

d The increase in the quantity of real GDP demanded will raise real GDP and the price level. The rise in real GDP will shift the *MD* curve rightward, and the rise in the price level will shift the *MS* curve leftward, as shown in Fig. 29.2 Solution. Your graph might have different numerical values, but the final value of the interest rate should be between 3 percent and 5 percent, etc. The result is a shift leftward in the *AD* curve to AD_2.

FIGURE **29.2** SOLUTION

(a)

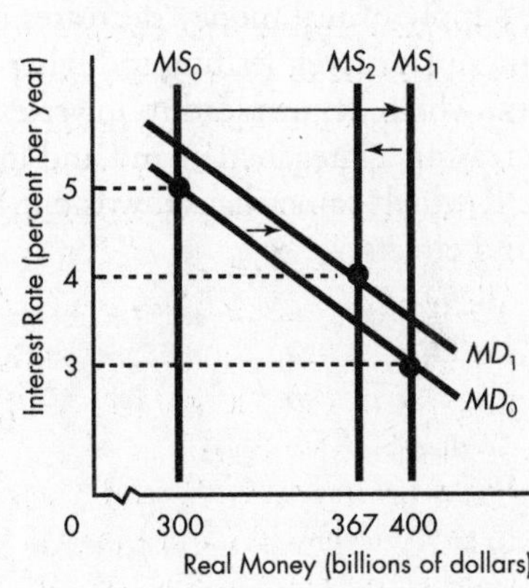

(b)

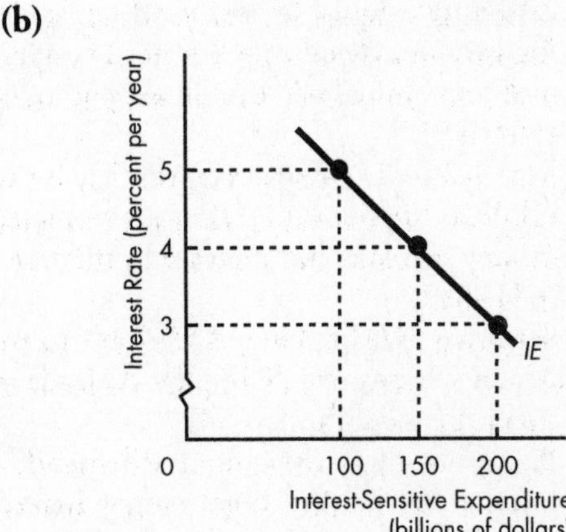

(c)

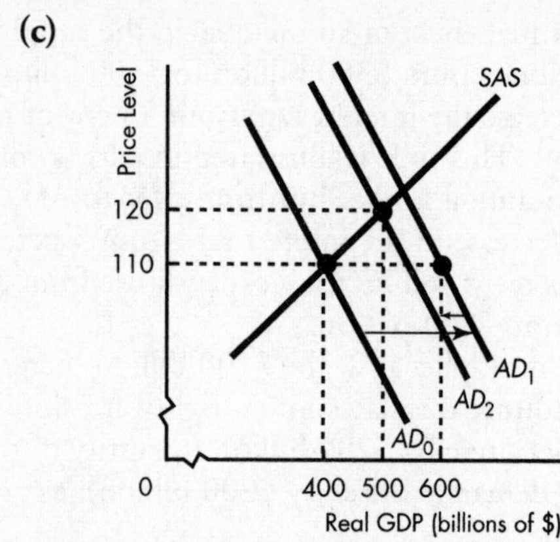

8 a The higher profit expectations leads firms to raise their investment demand, shifting the *IE* curve rightward. This effect is called crowding in.

b The higher investment demand leads to an increase in the quantity of real GDP demanded—the *AD* curve shifts rightward. The shift in the *AD* curve leads to higher real GDP and a higher price level, which leads to the second-round effects—real money demand increases as a result of the higher real GDP and the supply of real money decreases due to the higher price level, leading to higher interest rates, which in turn lead to lower expenditure, decreasing aggregate demand and lower real GDP, which somewhat crowds out the first-round effects.

9 If the economy was initially at full employment, after the move to the new equilibrium at the intersection of AD_2 and *SAS*, the economy is in an above-full-employment equilibrium. As a result, there will be a shortage of labour, which will lead to an increase in the wage rate. This increase in the wage rate increases the costs of production, and aggregate supply decreases—the *SAS* starts shifting leftward, until the economy goes back to full employment at the original level of real GDP, with a higher price level.

10 If expenditure is very sensitive to changes in the interest rate, the increase in the interest rate that initiates the crowding out effect will induce large decreases in expenditure, which means large crowding out.

Chapter **30**

Inflation

KEY CONCEPTS

Inflation and the Price Level

Inflation occurs when price level (*P*) is rising and money is losing value.

- It is average of prices, and an ongoing process, not just one-time change.
- Inflation rate = annual percentage change in price level = $\frac{P_1 - P_0}{P_0} \times 100$.

Demand-Pull Inflation

Demand-pull inflation arises from increasing aggregate demand.

- Main sources are increases in money supply or in government purchases or exports.
  - *AD* shifts rightward.
  - In short run, with no Δ potential GDP or money wage rate, result is increase in *P* (inflation), increase in *Y*, decrease in unemployment to below natural rate.
- Unemployment less than natural rate creates labour shortage, which leads to increase in wages and costs, so that *SAS* shifts leftward, and price level increases even more, but real GDP back to original level.
- If *AD* shifts rightward again, and wages increase again, a *price-wage spiral* may result.
- Persistent inflation requires persistent increases in money supply.

Cost-Push Inflation

Cost-push inflation arises from decreasing aggregate supply, due to increase in costs.

- Main sources are increase in money wage rates and in money prices of raw materials.
  - Firms decrease production, so that *SAS* shifts leftward creating **stagflation** (increase in price level, decrease in real GDP).
- If government or Bank of Canada shifts *AD* rightward in response, price level increases again, so that input owners raise input prices again, and a cost-push inflation spiral may result.
- If there is no government or Bank response—economy remains below full employment.

The Quantity Theory of Money

Quantity theory of money predicts increase in money supply leads to increase in price level by same percentage.

- Quantity theory starts with definition of **velocity of circulation** ($V = PY/M$), which leads to the **equation of exchange** ($MV = PY$).
  - Assumes velocity and potential GDP are unaffected by Δ money supply.
  - Then, in long run $\Delta P = (V/Y)\Delta M$, which implies $\Delta P/P = \Delta M/M$ and $\%\Delta P = \%\Delta M$.
- Historical evidence suggests money growth rate strongly influences inflation.

Effects of Inflation

Firms and households make economic decisions on the basis of forecasts of inflation.

Incorrect forecasts in labour markets lead to costly departures from full employment and income redistribution.

- If inflation > anticipated, then money wages set too low and employers gain, workers lose income, but firm has trouble keeping workers as a result.
- If inflation < anticipated, then money wages set too high, and employers lose, workers gain income, but firm lays off workers as a result.

◆ Incorrect forecasts in capital markets lead to incorrect borrowing/lending and income redistribution.

- If inflation > anticipated, then interest rates set too low, and borrowers gain at expense of lenders, but both wished to have made different decisions.
- If inflation < anticipated, then interest rates set too high, lenders gain at expense of borrowers, but both wished to have made different decisions.

People forecast inflation in different ways, including hiring specialists, who make best possible forecast on the basis of all relevant information (a **rational expectation**).

◆ If increase in *AD* correctly anticipated, then money wages adjust to keep up with anticipated inflation, and *SAS* shifts leftward as *AD* increases so that Δ price level only, no Δ real GDP or employment – actual inflation = expected inflation.

◆ If increase in *AD* more than expected, then increase in money wage only reflects expected part, so that *SAS* leftward by less than if fully expected.

- Result is new above full-employment equilibrium to right of potential GDP, which leads eventually to increase in money wages and *SAS* leftward again.

◆ If increase in *AD* less than expected, then increase in money wage to reflect expected change leads to *SAS* leftward by more than if correctly expected.

- Result is new below full-employment equilibrium to left of potential GDP, which eventually leads to decrease in money wages and *SAS* rightward.

Anticipated inflation decreases potential GDP and lowers economic growth due to higher transactions costs, tax effects, and increased uncertainty.

◆ It is more costly the higher the inflation.

Inflation and Unemployment: The Phillips Curve

Phillips curve shows relationship between inflation and unemployment.

◆ **Short-run Phillips curve** (*SRPC*) shows relationship between inflation and unemployment for a given expected inflation rate and a given natural rate of unemployment. It is negatively sloped.

◆ In short run, if actual inflation > expected, then *AD* curve shifts rightward further than expected, movement along *SAS*, real GDP > potential, unemployment < natural rate – movement up and leftward along *SRPC*.

Long-run Phillips curve (*LRPC*) shows relationship between inflation and unemployment when actual inflation = expected. It is vertical at the natural rate of unemployment.

◆ If actual inflation = expected, then *AD* curve shifts rightward as expected, real GDP = potential, unemployment = natural rate.

◆ A decrease in expected inflation rate shifts *SRPC* downward.

◆ An increase in natural unemployment rate shifts both *LRPC* and *SRPC* rightward.

Interest Rates and Inflation

A large part of changes in nominal rate of interest are due to changes in expected inflation.

◆ Real interest rate determined by global investment demand and saving supply plus national risk differences.

◆ Nominal interest rate determined by money demand and money supply.

◆ The two rates are linked because capital and money markets are interconnected.

◆ An increase in expected inflation leads to an increase in nominal interest rate by equivalent amount, keeping real rate of interest constant.

HELPFUL HINTS

1 An important concept introduced in this chapter is that of a *rational expectation*—the best possible forecast based on all relevant information. Text Fig. 30.7 applies this concept to forecasting the

price level. We know the *actual* price level is found in the short run at the intersection of the *AD* curve and the *SAS* curve, and in the long run at the intersection of the *AD* curve and the *LAS* curve. Thus in Fig. 30.7, when *AD* is expected to increase to AD_1, the best *forecast* of the new price level (the forecast most likely to be correct) is at the intersection of AD_1 and *LAS*, yielding a wage demand that in turn leads to SAS_1.

Note that the rational expectation of the price level will be at the intersection of the *expected* aggregate demand curve and the *expected short-run* aggregate supply curve in the short run, and the *expected long-run* aggregate supply curve in the long run. The *actual* equilibrium, which determines the *actual* price level, is at the intersection of the *actual* aggregate demand curve and the *actual short-run* aggregate supply curve.

2 An important implication of the assumption people forecast using rational expectations is that the consequences of any macroeconomic event (a monetary or fiscal policy) depend on expectations. The effect on the price level and real GDP of a given increase in the money supply will be different for different price level expectations. The position of the short-run aggregate supply curve depends on the expected price level, which in turn depends on the expected policy, and thus so does the macroeconomic equilibrium. Depending on whether the actual level of policy is anticipated or unanticipated, different outcomes will occur.

For example, a given increase in the money supply can result in an increase in real GDP, no change in real GDP, or even a reduction in real GDP depending solely on the expected policy. An increase in real GDP will result if the increase in aggregate demand is not anticipated (or underanticipated); no change in real GDP will result if the increase in aggregate demand is correctly anticipated; and reduction in real GDP will result if the increase in aggregate demand is less than anticipated (overanticipated).

3 An important equation in this chapter is the equation of exchange:

$$\begin{matrix}\text{Quantity} \\ \text{of money}\end{matrix} \times \begin{matrix}\text{Velocity of} \\ \text{circulation}\end{matrix} = \begin{matrix}\text{Price} \\ \text{level}\end{matrix} \times \begin{matrix}\text{Real} \\ \text{GDP}\end{matrix}$$

This equation simply says that the quantity of money times the average number of times each dollar is spent (equaling total expenditure) is equal to the dollar value of the goods and services on which it was spent. The equation is always true by definition—it is an identity. If we further assume that the velocity of circulation and potential GDP are independent of the quantity of money, we get the quantity theory of money. These assumptions imply that when the quantity of money increases by 10 percent, the price level must increase by 10 percent in order to maintain equality between the two sides of the equation.

4 Students (and politicians and commentators!) are often confused by the fact that sometimes a decrease in the growth rate of the money supply leads to an *increase* in the interest rate, and sometimes it leads to a *decrease* in the interest rate. The key to understanding this difference is to focus on the time frame—short- or long-run. Figure 30.1 illustrates the changes in the nominal rate of interest over time when the growth rate of the money supply is lowered. Initially, the rate of interest is r_0, and then there is an unanticipated decrease in the growth rate of the money supply at time T*, which leads to an unexpectedly low level of the supply of real money. As we saw in Chapter 29, in the short run this decrease in the supply of real money will lead to an increase in the rate of interest (to the level r_1), which in turn leads to a decrease in investment demand and aggregate demand. If this change is unexpected, it leads to lower inflation and lower real GDP. In the long run, once economic agents realize that the lower inflation is going to remain in place, they lower their forecast of inflation, which in turn lowers the nominal rate of interest to a level such as r_2.

FIGURE **30.1**

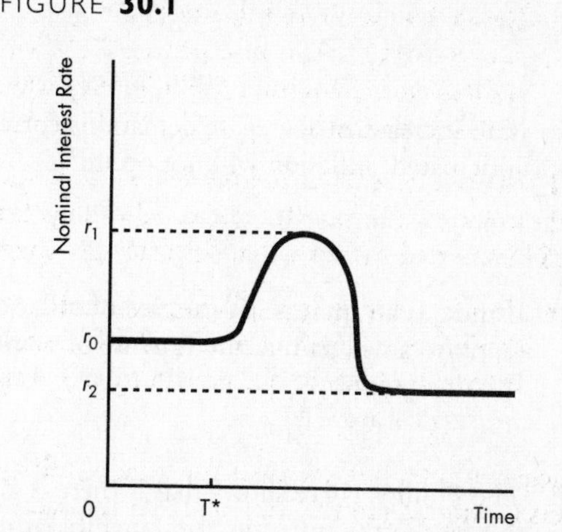

SELF-TEST

True/False/Uncertain and Explain

1 If the price level at the beginning of 2000 is 120 and the price level at the beginning of 2001 is 130, the rate of inflation is 8.3 percent.

2 The inflation resulting from expansionary monetary policy is an example of cost-push inflation.

3 Stagflation occurs when real GDP decreases and the price level increases.

4 If the quantity of money is $50 billion and nominal GDP is $200 billion, the velocity of circulation is 1/4.

5 When inflation is unanticipated there are no negative effects on the economy.

6 If people expect aggregate demand to increase but it does not, the price level will increase and real GDP will decrease.

7 If an increase in aggregate demand is correctly anticipated, inflation will not occur.

8 If there is an increase in the rate of inflation, employers will gain at the expense of workers.

9 The Phillips curve shows that if there is an increase in the inflation rate, unemployment will decrease.

10 The long-run Phillips curve shows a tradeoff between inflation and unemployment.

Multiple-Choice

Inflation and the Price Level

1 The current year's price level is 180, and the rate of inflation over the past year has been 20 percent. What was last year's price level?
a 100
b 144
c 150
d 160
e 216

Demand-Pull Inflation

2 Demand-pull inflation occurs when
a aggregate demand increases.
b aggregate supply decreases.
c input costs increase.
d people incorrectly forecast inflation.
e unemployment is above the natural rate.

3 Which of the following would cause the aggregate demand curve to keep shifting rightward year after year?
a a one-time tax cut
b a one-time increase in government purchases of goods and services
c inflation
d excess wage demands
e a positive rate of growth in the quantity of money

Cost-Push Inflation

4 An increase in the price level due to an increase in the price of oil
a will create a stagflation in the short run and *will* trigger a price-wage spiral.
b will create a stagflation in the short run and *may* trigger a price-wage spiral.
c will raise output above potential GDP.
d must lead to an increase in the wage rate.
e must lead to a decrease in the wage rate.

5 Figure 30.2 illustrates an economy initially in equilibrium at point *a*. What would cause the short-run aggregate supply curve to shift from SAS_0 to SAS_1?

a an increase in the price of oil
b an increase in the price level
c an increase in the marginal product of labour
d an increase in the demand for money
e a decrease in wages

FIGURE **30.2**

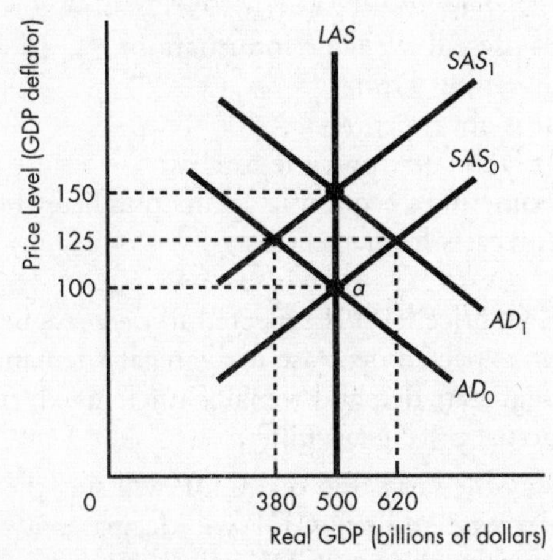

The Quantity Theory of Money

6 The quantity theory of money begins with the equation of exchange—$MV = PY$—and then adds the assumptions that

a velocity varies inversely with the rate of interest, and the price level is independent of the level of the money supply.
b velocity and the price level are independent of the level of the money supply.
c potential GDP and the money supply are independent of the price level.
d potential GDP and the price level are independent of the level of the money supply.
e velocity and potential GDP are independent of the level of the money supply.

7 According to the quantity theory of money,

a V/M is constant.
b Y/M is constant.
c Y/P is constant.
d M/P is constant.
e M/V is constant.

8 According to the quantity theory of money, an increase in the quantity of money will lead to an increase in the price level

a but have no effect on real GDP or the velocity of circulation.
b as well as increasing both real GDP and the velocity of circulation.
c as well as increasing real GDP but decreasing the velocity of circulation.
d as well as decreasing real GDP but increasing the velocity of circulation.
e but have no effect on real GDP while decreasing velocity.

Effects of Inflation

9 If the *AD* curve in Fig. 30.2 is correctly expected to shift from AD_0 to AD_1, what will be the new equilibrium real GDP and price level?

a \$380 billion and price level = 125
b \$500 billion and price level = 150
c \$500 billion and price level = 100
d \$620 billion and price level = 125
e \$500 billion and price level = 125

10 If the *AD* curve in Fig. 30.2 is expected to shift from AD_0 to AD_1 but, in fact, remains at AD_0, what will be the new equilibrium real GDP and price level?

a \$380 billion and price level = 100
b \$500 billion and price level = 150
c \$500 billion and price level = 100
d \$620 billion and price level = 125
e \$380 billion and price level = 125

11 If the *AD* curve in Fig. 30.2 is expected to remain at AD_0 but, in fact, shifts to AD_1, what will be the new equilibrium real GDP and price level?

a \$380 billion and price level = 125
b \$500 billion and price level = 150
c \$500 billion and price level = 100
d \$620 billion and price level = 125
e \$500 billion and price level = 125

12 Which of the following business quotes illustrates costs associated with an anticipated inflation?

a "The bank is losing money on its loans, given the current rate of interest."
b "Wage increases were low last year, but I am having trouble keeping workers."
c "I find I have to send invoices out to customers twice a month now, because of the higher inflation."
d "The low inflation rate means my borrowing costs are too high."
e None of the above.

13 If the rate of inflation is lower than anticipated,

a lenders will gain at the expense of borrowers, and workers will gain at the expense of employers.
b borrowers will gain at the expense of lenders, and workers will gain at the expense of employers.
c lenders will gain at the expense of borrowers, and employers will gain at the expense of workers.
d borrowers will gain at the expense of lenders, and employers will gain at the expense of workers.
e lenders will gain at the expense of borrowers, and whether employers or workers will gain is uncertain.

14 In an economy with the price level greater than expected and output above the natural rate, which of the following is a possible explanation, *ceteris paribus*?

a Potential real GDP has increased by more than expected.
b Potential real GDP has increased by less than expected.
c Aggregate demand has decreased by more than expected.
d Aggregate demand has increased by less than expected.
e Aggregate demand has increased by more than expected.

15 A fully anticipated increase in the rate of inflation

a is not costly because contracts can be adjusted.
b benefits both workers and employers.
c is costly because it increases the value of money.
d is costly because it encourages an increase in the frequency of transactions that people undertake.
e is costly because it redistributes from lender to borrower.

16 Which of the following is *not* true of a rational expectation forecast?

a It uses all available information.
b It can be wrong.
c It is always correct.
d It is the best possible forecast.
e Sometimes economic agents purchase their forecasts from specialists.

17 The price level is expected to decrease because of an expected decrease in aggregate demand. If aggregate demand remains unchanged, then the actual price level will

a stay the same and real GDP will stay the same.
b decrease and real GDP will decrease.
c increase and real GDP will increase.
d increase and real GDP will decrease.
e decrease and real GDP will increase.

Inflation and Unemployment: The Phillips Curve

18 The short-run Phillips curve shows the relationship between

a the price level and real GDP in the short run.
b the price level and unemployment in the short run.
c unemployment and real GDP in the short run.
d inflation and unemployment, when inflation expectations can change.
e inflation and unemployment, when inflation expectations do not change.

19 Figure 30.3 illustrates an economy's Phillips curves. What is the natural rate of unemployment?

- **a** 9 percent
- **b** 6 percent
- **c** 4 percent
- **d** depends on the actual inflation rate
- **e** cannot be determined without more information

FIGURE **30.3**

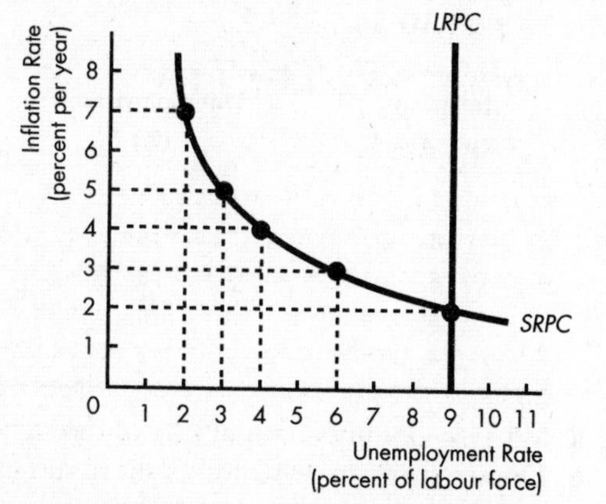

20 Figure 30.3 illustrates an economy's Phillips curves. What is the expected inflation rate?

- **a** 9 percent
- **b** 4 percent
- **c** 2 percent
- **d** depends on the actual inflation rate
- **e** cannot be determined without more information

21 Figure 30.3 illustrates an economy's Phillips curves. If the current inflation rate is 4 percent, what is the current unemployment rate?

- **a** 9 percent
- **b** 6 percent
- **c** 4 percent
- **d** 3 percent
- **e** cannot be determined without more information

22 If the inflation rate is lower than the expected inflation rate,

- **a** unemployment will be above the natural rate.
- **b** the natural rate of unemployment will increase.
- **c** the expected inflation rate will increase.
- **d** unemployment will be below the natural rate.
- **e** the economy must off the *SRPC*.

23 If there is an increase in the inflation rate that is fully anticipated, then

- **a** unemployment will be below the natural rate.
- **b** unemployment will be above the natural rate.
- **c** the natural rate of unemployment will increase.
- **d** the economy must be off the *LRPC*.
- **e** the economy must be on the *LRPC*.

Interest Rates and Inflation

24 Suppose that initially the nominal rate of interest is 8 percent and the expected rate of inflation is 5 percent. If the expected rate of inflation increases to 8 percent, what will the new nominal rate of interest be?

- **a** 3 percent
- **b** 8 percent
- **c** 11 percent
- **d** 13 percent
- **e** 16 percent

25 A correctly anticipated increase in the rate of growth of the money supply will cause nominal interest rates to

- **a** decrease and real interest rates to decrease.
- **b** decrease and leave real interest rates unchanged.
- **c** increase and real interest rates to increase.
- **d** increase and leave real interest rates unchanged.
- **e** increase and real interest rates to decrease.

Short Answer Problems

1 What will happen to the price level and real GDP if the government increases its purchases of goods and services and that increase is not anticipated (the price level is not expected to change)?

2 Explain how the events in Short Answer Problem **1** could lead to a price-wage spiral.

3 What is the relationship between the expected rate of inflation and nominal interest rates?

4 Explain carefully the difference between the short-run Phillips curve and the long-run Phillips curve.

Ⓒ **5** Sometimes politicians or other commentators make the following type of statement: "Unemployment is a more serious economic and social problem than inflation. Increasing inflation by a small amount in order to lower unemployment is therefore worthwhile." Briefly evaluate this statement.

6 Why does inflation start? Why does it persist?

7 Table 30.1 gives the initial actual aggregate demand and short-run aggregate supply schedules for an economy in which the expected price level is 80, and potential real GDP is 500.

a What is actual real GDP and the actual price level?

TABLE **30.1** AGGREGATE DEMAND AND SUPPLY

Price Level	Real GDP Demanded	Real GDP Supplied
60	600	400
80	500	500
100	400	600
120	300	700
140	200	700

b In year 1 the economy is in the equilibrium characterized in **a**. It is *expected* that in year 2, aggregate demand will be as given in Table 30.2. (Assume that the long-run aggregate supply curve is not expected to shift, and does not shift.) What is the *vertical* amount of the expected shift in the aggregate demand curve when real GDP is $500 billion?

TABLE **30.2** AGGREGATE DEMAND AND SUPPLY

Price Level	Real GDP Demanded	Real GDP Supplied
60	800	
80	700	
100	600	
120	500	
140	400	

ⓒ c What is the (long-run) rational expectation of the price level for year 2?

ⓒ d The expected shift in aggregate demand will cause the short-run aggregate supply (*SAS*) curve to shift. What will the new *SAS* curve be? For each price level, give the new values of real GDP supplied in the last column of Table 30.2.

8 According to the quantity theory of money, what is the effect of an increase in the quantity of money? What assumptions of the theory are crucial for this effect to occur? Why?

9 We observe an economy in which the price level is 1.5, real GDP is $240 billion, and the money supply is $60 billion.

a What is the velocity of circulation?

b According to the quantity theory of money, what will be the result of an increase in the quantity of money to $80 billion?

10 The country of Colditz has an expected inflation rate of 8 percent, and its recent inflation and unemployment history is summarized in Table 30.3. Originally both unemployment and inflation are each 8 percent.

TABLE **30.3**

Inflation (% per year)	Unemployment (%)
12	4
10	6
8	8
6	10
4	12

a What is Colditz's natural rate of unemployment?

b Draw a diagram of Colditz's short-run and long-run Phillips curves.

c If inflation unexpectedly increases to 12 percent per year, explain what happens to unemployment.

d Return to the original situation. If the expected inflation rate increases to 10 percent, and the actual inflation rate increases to 10 percent, explain and show on your graph what happens, *ceteris paribus*, to inflation and unemployment.

ANSWERS

True/False/Uncertain and Explain

1 T Inflation rate = $[(P_1 - P_0)/P_0] \times 100 = [(130 - 120)/120] \times 100 = 8.3$. (666)

2 F Cost-push inflation is due to increase in input costs. (667–671)

3 T Definition. (669–671)

4 F $V = PY/M = 200/50 = 4$. (672–673)

5 F It makes payments from long-term contracts unpredictable, hurting one side or other. (674–677)

ⓒ 6 T If expected increase in aggregate demand, then there is an increase in wage demands, which leads to leftward shift *SAS* curve, but no Δ *AD* curve, resulting in stagflation. (674–677)

7 F *AD* shifts rightward, *SAS* shifts leftward due to higher wage demands, so that price level increases. (674–677)

ⓔ **8 U** True if unanticipated, false if anticipated. (674–677)
9 U True if short run, false if long run. (678–681)
10 F It is vertical at the natural rate of unemployment. (678–681)

Multiple-Choice

ⓔ **1 c** Inflation rate = $[(P_1 - P_0)/P_0] \times 100$, or $20 = [(180 - P_0)/P_0] \times 100$—solve this for P_0. (666)
2 a Definition. (667–669)
3 e **a** and **b** have one-time effects, **c** is caused by ΔAD, and **d** is a supply-side effect. (667–669)
4 b Increase in price of oil leads to shift leftward in *SAS* curve, creating cost-push inflation (stagflation), which *may* trigger price-wage spiral if government raises aggregate demand. (669–671)
5 a Increase in price of crucial input leads to increase in costs of production, and shift leftward in *SAS*. (669–671)
6 e See text discussion. (672–673)
ⓔ **7 d** Because theory assumes Y/V (= M/P) is constant. (672–673)
8 a Due to assumption that neither is affected by Δ money supply. (672–673)
9 b Expected *P* found from intersection of $EAD = AD_1$, and actual new *SAS* is set here, and new equilibrium is where actual *AD* and new *SAS* cross. (674–677)
10 e Expected *P* found from intersection of $EAD = AD_1$, and actual new *SAS* is set here, and new equilibrium is where actual *AD* and new *SAS* cross. (674–677)
11 d Expected *P* found from intersection of $EAD = AD_0$, and actual new *SAS* is set here, and new equilibrium is where actual *AD* and new *SAS* cross. (674–677)
12 c Example of higher transactions costs, the others are unanticipated inflation costs. (674–677)
13 a Because interest rates and wage rates too high given actual inflation rate. (674–677)
ⓔ **14 e** Draw a graph. (674–677)
15 d Higher inflation decreases value of money, so people decrease money holdings, which leads to increase in transactions. (674–677)
16 c It is correct on *average*. (674–677)
17 e Decrease in expected price level leads to shift rightward *SAS*, so new equilibrium to the right of *LAS* along original *AD* curve. (674–677)
18 e Definition. (678–681)
19 a *LRPC* is at natural rate. (678–681)
20 c Expected inflation rate is where *SRPC* crosses *LRPC*. (678–681)
21 c Found by reading off the *SRPC*. (678–681)
22 a Draw a Phillips curve. (678–681)
23 e Economy just moves up the *LRPC*. (678–681)
24 c Initially, real rate = 8 – 5 = 3 percent. New nominal rate = real rate + expected inflation = 3 + 8 = 11 percent. (682–683)
25 d Increase in growth rate of money supply leads to increase in inflation rate, which leads to increase in nominal rate by same amount (since anticipated). No change in real rate, which is determined on world capital markets. (682–683)

Short Answer Problems

1 An increase in government purchases of goods and services will shift the aggregate demand curve rightward. If the price level is not expected to change, the short-run aggregate supply curve remains unchanged, and the increase in aggregate demand will cause the price level to increase and real GDP to increase.

2 The higher price level leads to demands for higher wages, which push up the costs of production and shift the *SAS* curve leftward, leading to a further increase in the price level and a decrease in real GDP. A price-wage spiral could result *if* the government once again raises the level of their purchases or if the government continues to run a deficit (financed by printing money), then *AD* will continue to shift rightward, triggering leftward shifts in *SAS*, leading to the price-wage spiral.

3 When the rate of inflation is expected to increase, the nominal interest rate will also increase to compensate for the increased rate at which the purchasing power of money is eroding. The essential point is that lenders and borrowers are interested in the quantity of goods and services that a unit of money will buy. Lenders will insist on the higher interest rate, to compensate for the loss of purchasing power of money, and borrowers will agree because they realize that the dollars they repay will buy fewer goods and services.

4 The short-run Phillips curve is constructed assuming that the expected inflation rate is constant, and is therefore downward-sloping. As a result, if there is an increase in the inflation rate (and therefore a decrease in real wages), there will be a decrease in unemployment to a rate below the natural rate. The long-run Phillips curve is constructed assuming that the expected inflation rate adjusts fully to reflect changes in the actual inflation rate, and is therefore vertical at the natural rate of unemployment. If there is an increase in the actual inflation rate, there is an equivalent increase in the expected inflation rate (so that the real wage rate stays constant), and the rate of unemployment stays constant at the natural rate.

5 Partially this statement is a value judgement, based on the tradeoff of a higher cost to society from the higher inflation versus the gain to society from a lower inflation rate. In this case, we would need to evaluate the costs of inflation vis-à-vis the costs of unemployment. However, there is also an objective (normative) problem with this statement. In the short run, such a tradeoff does exist, represented by the downward-sloping short-run Phillips curve. In the long run, there is no such tradeoff. As a result, a higher inflation rate will lead to a lower unemployment rate in the short run, but eventually inflation expectations will increase, represented by a shift upward in the short-run Phillips curve, and unemployment will return to the natural rate. Therefore in the long run, increasing inflation will have no impact on the unemployment rate, but will increase the costs to society that come from the higher inflation.

6 Inflation is an increase in the price level, and starts with either a shift rightward in the *AD* curve due to an increase in the money supply, government spending, or exports (demand-pull inflation), or with a shift leftward in the *SAS* curve due to an increase in wages or raw materials prices (cost-push inflation). However, the increase in the price level in either case can only persist if a price-wage spiral results from the initial shock. A price-wage spiral starts when increases in aggregate demand and shifts leftward in *SAS* chase each other up the long-run aggregate supply curve.

7 a Actual real GDP and the actual price level are determined by the intersection of the aggregate demand curve and the short-run aggregate supply curve. Real GDP is $500 billion and the price level is 80, because at a price level of 80, the quantity of real GDP demanded equals the quantity of real GDP supplied ($500 billion).

b The price level associated with $500 billion of real GDP demanded for the original aggregate demand curve (Table 30.1) is 80. The price level associated with $500 billion of real GDP demanded for the new expected aggregate demand curve (Table 30.2) is 120. Therefore the aggregate demand curve is expected to shift upward by 40.

c The rational expectation of the price level is given by the intersection of the expected aggregate demand curve (Table 30.2) and the expected long-run aggregate supply curve. Long-run aggregate supply is equal to $500 billion and is not expected to change. Since the price level associated with $500 billion of real GDP demanded is 120, the rational expectation of the price level is 120.

d The quantities of real GDP supplied for the new *SAS* curve are shown in completed Table 30.2 Solution. The original expected price level is 80. From part **b** we know that the new expected price level is 120, which implies that the *SAS* curve shifts up by 40. Thus at each quantity of real GDP supplied, the price level on the new *SAS* curve is 40 points higher than on the original *SAS* curve (Table 30.1).

For example, real GDP supplied of $500 billion now requires a price level of 120 rather than 80. Similarly, real GDP supplied of $400 billion now requires a price level of 100 rather than 60. (*Note*: The values in parentheses in this table are inferred by extrapolation rather than calculated from Table 30.1.)

TABLE **30.2** SOLUTION
AGGREGATE DEMAND AND SUPPLY

Price Level	Real GDP Demanded	Real GDP Supplied
60	800	(200)
80	700	(300)
100	600	400
120	500	500
140	400	600

8 According to the quantity theory of money, an increase in the quantity of money will cause the price level to increase by an equal percentage. The required assumptions are that velocity and potential GDP are independent of changes in the money supply, so that the change in the money supply affects only the price level.

9 a The velocity of circulation is defined by

$$\text{Velocity of circulation} = \frac{\text{Price level} \times \text{Real GDP}}{\text{Quantity of money}}$$

With the values for the price level, real GDP, and the quantity of money given in this problem, we have

$$\text{Velocity of circulation} = \frac{1.5 \times 240}{60} = 6$$

b The quantity theory of money predicts that an increase in the quantity of money will cause an equal percentage increase in the price level. An increase in money from $60 billion to $80 billion is a one-third (33 percent) increase. Thus the quantity theory of money predicts that the price level will increase by a third (33 percent). Since the initial price level is 1.5, the predicted price level will be 2.0. (This value can also be confirmed by using the equation of exchange.)

10 a The natural rate of unemployment is the rate of unemployment that occurs when the actual rate of inflation equals the expected rate of inflation—in this case, the natural rate of unemployment is 8 percent.

b See Fig. 30.4. The long-run Phillips curve is vertical at the natural rate of unemployment. The current short-run curve is $SRPC_0$ (ignore the other short-run curve for the moment).

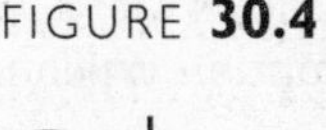
FIGURE **30.4**

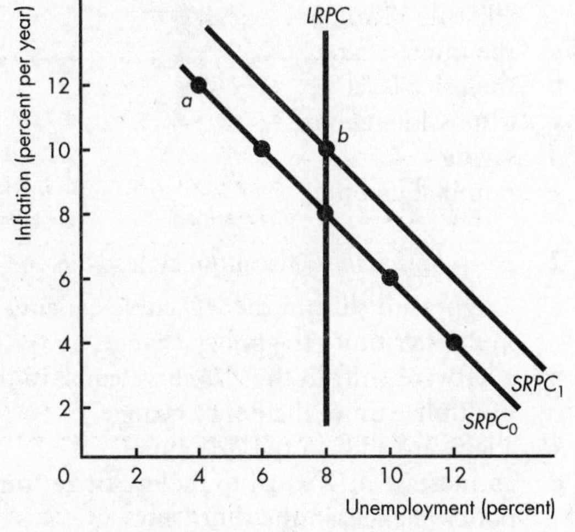

c In this case, the relevant short-run Phillips curve is $SRPC_0$, the curve for an expected inflation rate of 8 percent. From the curve (or Table 30.3), it can be seen that with inflation equal to 12 percent, unemployment is 4 percent at the point *a*.

d An increase in the expected inflation rate will shift the short-run Phillips curve to a new curve, with the new curve crossing the long-run Phillips curve at the new expected inflation rate of 10 percent. (The actual shape of the curve is not clear without further information, so it has been assumed that the new curve is parallel to the old curve.) If the actual inflation rate is 10 percent, the unemployment rate will be 8 percent, at the natural rate, at the point *b*.

Part 8 Overview

Chapters

25–30

Understanding Aggregate Demand and Inflation

PROBLEM

The Canadian economy is originally in a full-employment equilibrium. Suppose that the U.S. economy *unexpectedly* goes into recession.

a Holding constant the price level, carefully explain (and show on a graph) what these changes do to aggregate expenditure and aggregate demand. Explain what happens to each component of aggregate expenditure and real GDP.

b Next, show on your graph and explain what happens to aggregate expenditure and aggregate demand in the short run when the price level adjusts.

The Bank of Canada decides to redress the economy's problems by carrying out an expansionary monetary policy.

c Give an example of the type of open market operation the Bank of Canada would carry out in such a circumstance. Show what happens to the balance sheets of the Bank of Canada and the banking sector as a result of the initial impacts of the operation. What is the overall impact of such an operation on chartered bank reserves, loans, deposit, and the money supply?

d Explain what this policy will do to the real money supply, money demand, the interest rate, investment, net exports, and aggregate demand, holding constant the price level.

e Next, with the price level adjusting, explain what this policy does to the *AD-SAS* equilibrium in the short run.

f Does the quantity theory of money hold in this economy?

MIDTERM EXAMINATION

You should allocate 48 minutes for this examination (24 questions, 2 minutes per question). For each question, choose the best answer.

1 The consumption function shows the relationship between consumption expenditure and

a the interest rate.
b the price level.
c disposable income.
d saving.
e nominal income.

2 An *contractionary* fiscal policy leads to

a a rightward shift in the *AD* curve equal to the multiplier times the policy change.
b a leftward shift in the *AD* curve equal to the multiplier times the policy change.
c a leftward shift in the *SAS* curve.
d an increase in *Y* equal to the multiplier times the policy change, in the short run.
e an increase in *Y* equal to the multiplier times the policy change, in the long run.

3 The Bank of Canada and the government have a potential conflict about the government borrowing from the Bank of Canada because the borrowing will have an impact in the money market. It will

a increase money demand and increase interest rates, lowering investment too much.
b increase money demand and increase interest rates, which puts too much upward pressure on aggregate demand.
c lower the money supply and increase interest rates, lowering investment too much.
d increase the money supply, creating deflationary pressures.
e increase the money supply, creating inflationary pressures.

4 A rise in the natural rate of unemployment is shown as a

a rightward shift in the long-run Phillips curve only.
b leftward shift in the long-run Phillips curve only.
c rightward shift in the short-run Phillips curve only.
d leftward shift in both the short-run and long-run Phillips curves.
e rightward shift in both the short-run and long-run Phillips curves.

5 Which of the following quotations *correctly* describes the impact of monetary policy on the economy?

a "House sales are down a lot, due to the higher money growth."
b "The extra money pumped into the economy by the central bank is creating less exports."
c "The tightening of money growth is helping sell goods abroad."
d "Businesses are investing more, now that monetary policy has become less expansionary."
e "The extra money pumped into the economy by the central bank is creating more jobs."

6 International crowding out refers to the tendency for an increase in government expenditures on goods and services to induce a(n)

a decrease in interest rates, leading to a decrease in the exchange rate, leading to an increase in net exports.
b decrease in interest rates, leading to a withdrawal of foreign funds from Canada.
c increase in interest rates, leading to a decrease in the exchange rate, leading to an increase in net exports.
d increase in interest rates, leading to an increase in the exchange rate, leading to an increase in net exports.
e increase in interest rates, leading to an increase in the exchange rate, leading to a decrease in net exports.

7 If real GDP is less than aggregate planned expenditure,

a aggregate planned expenditure will increase.
b real GDP will decrease.
c the price level must decrease to restore equilibrium.
d imports must be too large.
e aggregate planned expenditure will decrease.

8 Which of the following is *not* a source of budgetary revenues?

a personal income taxes
b transfer payments
c corporate income taxes
d indirect taxes
e investment income

9 Suppose OPEC unexpectedly collapses, leading to a decrease in the price of oil. This is a positive aggregate supply shock. As a result, the price level will

a increase and real GDP will increase.
b increase and real GDP will decrease.
c decrease and real GDP will increase.
d decrease and real GDP will decrease.
e increase and real GDP will stay the same.

10 A chartered bank can create money by

a selling some of its investment securities.
b increasing its reserves.
c lending its excess reserves.
d printing more cheques.
e converting reserves into securities.

11 According to the quantity theory of money, a decrease in the quantity of money will cause

- **a** both the price level and real GDP to decline in the short run, but, in the long run, only the price level will decrease as real GDP returns to its initial level.
- **b** both the price level and real GDP to increase in the short run, but, in the long run, only the price level will increase as real GDP returns to its initial level.
- **c** the price level to decrease in the short run, but, in the long run, the price level will return to its initial level.
- **d** the price level to decrease and real GDP to increase in both the short run and the long run.
- **e** the price level to decrease and real GDP to decrease in both the short run and the long run.

12 The presence of induced taxes means

- **a** fiscal policy multipliers are made stronger.
- **b** discretionary fiscal policy is eliminated.
- **c** there is always a structural deficit.
- **d** there is always a cyclical deficit.
- **e** fluctuations in aggregate expenditure are reduced. b/a t act as an automatic stabilizer

13 An open market purchase of government securities by the Bank of Canada will

- **a** increase bank reserves and thus increase the monetary base.
- **b** decrease bank reserves and thus decrease the monetary base.
- **c** increase bank reserves and thus decrease the monetary base.
- **d** decrease bank reserves and thus increase the monetary base.
- **e** decrease bank reserves but increase the money supply if banks have excess reserves.

14 When is there complete crowding out of an expansionary fiscal policy?

- **a** if the economy was originally in an under full-employment equilibrium
- **b** if the economy was originally in a full-employment equilibrium
- **c** when there is policy conflict with the Bank of Canada
- **d** when there is policy coordination to ensure the resulting change in the interest rate is zero
- **e** if there is a liquidity trap in the money market

15 An expansionary monetary policy will lead to a decrease in interest rates, which will lead to a(n)

- **a** increase in the demand for the dollar, leading to an increase in the exchange rate, which leads to a decrease in net exports.
- **b** increase in the demand for the dollar, leading to an increase in the exchange rate, which leads to an increase in net exports.
- **c** increase in the demand for the dollar, leading to a decrease in the exchange rate, which leads to an increase in net exports.
- **d** decrease in the demand for the dollar, leading to a decrease in the exchange rate, which leads to an increase in net exports.
- **e** decrease in the demand for the dollar, leading to a decrease in the exchange rate, which leads to a decrease in net exports.

16 Suppose that investment increases by $10 billion. Which of the following would *reduce* the effect of this increase in autonomous expenditure on equilibrium real GDP?

- **a** an increase in the marginal propensity to consume
- **b** a decrease in the marginal propensity to import
- **c** a decrease in the marginal tax rate
- **d** a steeper aggregate supply curve
- **e** a flatter aggregate supply curve

17 An increase in expected inflation raises the nominal interest rate because

- **a** borrowers require compensation for the inflation eroding the value of money.
- **b** lenders require compensation for the inflation eroding the value of money.
- **c** the inflation creates higher transactions costs.
- **d** the real rate of interest rises by an amount equal to the increase in expected inflation.
- **e** none of the above.

18 In a recent study, the University of Underfunded argued that it created four times as many jobs as people it hired directly. This argument illustrates the idea of

- **a** the marginal propensity to consume.
- **b** the multiplier.
- **c** government spending.
- **d** the tax multiplier.
- **e** universities wasting taxpayers' dollars.

19 If the *MPC* is 0.6, what is the autonomous tax multiplier?
- **a** –1.50
- **b** –1.67
- **c** –2.50
- **d** 2.50
- **e** impossible to calculate without further information

20 Consider the following data on the economy of Adanac:

Currency reserves of private banks	$5 billion
Currency in circulation	15 billion
Demand deposits of banks	40 billion
Demand deposits of other financial institutions	50 billion
Personal savings deposits at other financial institutions	125 billion
Nonpersonal notice deposits at banks	200 billion

What is the value of M1 and the value of M2+ in this economy in billions of dollars?
- **a** 105; 230
- **b** 110; 235
- **c** 55; 430
- **d** 55; 230
- **e** 60; 430

21 Which of the following statements about depository institutions is *false*?
- **a** They aim to maximize net worth without other considerations.
- **b** They take deposits from households and firms, and lend to other households and firms.
- **c** They minimize the cost of borrowing.
- **d** They pool and reduce risk.
- **e** They hold a variety of assets, not just loans.

22 An attempt to stimulate the economy by using the bank rate would work by
- **a** lowering the bank rate, resulting in more excess reserves, resulting in more loans, resulting in more deposits and money.
- **b** raising the bank rate, resulting in more excess reserves, resulting in more loans, resulting in more deposits and money.
- **c** raising the bank rate, resulting in less excess reserves, resulting in less loans, resulting in less deposits and money.
- **d** lowering the bank rate, resulting in less excess reserves, resulting in less loans, resulting in less deposits and money.
- **e** lowering the bank rate, resulting in more excess reserves, resulting in more loans, resulting in less deposits and money.

23 There will be no crowding out if
- **a** the demand for real money is totally unresponsive to changes in the price level.
- **b** the supply of real money is totally unresponsive to changes in the interest rate.
- **c** investment is very responsive to changes in the interest rate.
- **d** investment is totally unresponsive to changes in real GDP.
- **e** the demand for real money is totally unresponsive to changes in real GDP.

24 The amount of real money people want to hold will increase if either real income increases or the
- **a** price level increases.
- **b** price level decreases.
- **c** interest rate increases.
- **d** interest rate decreases.
- **e** price of bonds decreases.

ANSWERS

Problem

a The U.S. recession leads to a decrease in their imports of Canadian goods, which means a decrease in our exports. This decrease in exports leads to a decrease in aggregate planned expenditure, represented by a shift downward in the *AE* curve to AE_b in Fig. P8.1. The decrease in aggregate expenditure leads to an increase in inventories, which leads to firms lowering production, leading to a decrease in real GDP that is a multiple of the initial decrease in aggregate expenditure—the new equilibrium is at *b*, compared with the original equilibrium at *a*. The shift down in aggregate expenditure is also shown as a shift leftward in aggregate demand in part (b) of the graph.

Consumption is lower because of the decrease in real GDP. Investment is unchanged. Government purchases are unchanged. Exports are lower because of the shock, and imports are also lower because of the decrease in real GDP.

FIGURE **P8.1**

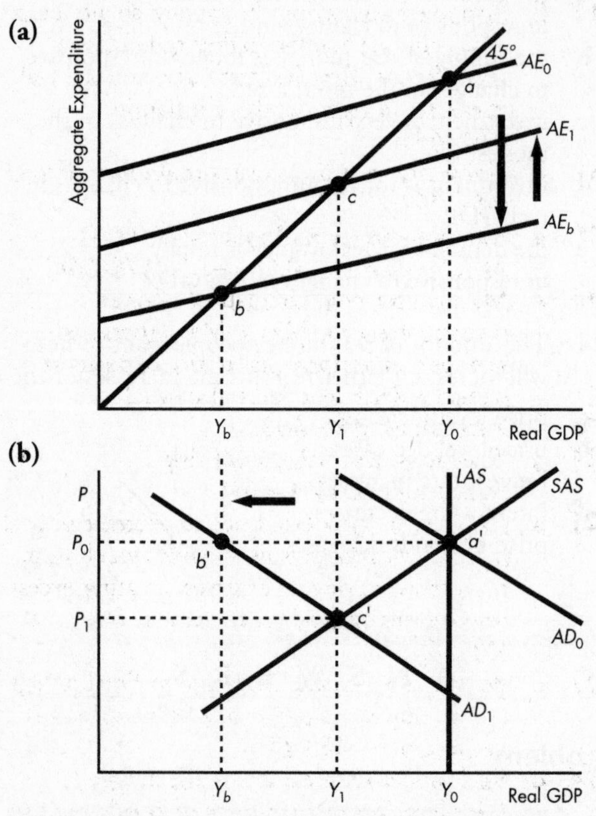

b After the shock, at the original price level aggregate demand is less than aggregate supply ($Y_b < Y_0$). This surplus leads to a decrease in the price level. *Since the decrease in AD was unexpected, so is the decrease in the price level—there is no shift in the SAS curve.* This decrease in the price level in turn leads to a decrease in the real quantity supplied in the short run (the movement from a' to c'), as well as an increase in the real money supply, which leads to a decrease in the interest rate, an increase in investment and aggregate expenditure (from AE_b to AE_1), and a movement along the aggregate demand curve from b' to c'.

c The Bank of Canada wants to increase the money supply, and will do so by purchasing government securities. If, for example, they buy these securities directly from the chartered banks, they will pay for them by crediting the chartered banks' deposits at the Bank of Canada (which are reserves). The result of such a purchase is shown in Table P8.1.

TABLE **P8.1**

Bank of Canada		Chartered Banks	
Assets	**Liabilities**	**Assets**	**Liabilities**
Government securities (+)	Bank deposits (+)	Reserves (+)	
		Government securities (–)	

This operation will lead to a deposit multiplier effect, leading to more reserves, more loans, more deposits, and a higher money supply.

d The higher nominal money supply will lead to a higher real money supply, price level held constant. This in turn creates a surplus of money, which leads to an increase in the demand for financial assets, which leads to an increase in the price of these assets, which leads to a decrease in the interest rate. The lower interest rate leads to an increase in investment demand and aggregate demand, as well as a decrease in the demand for Canadian dollars and therefore a decrease in the value of the Canadian dollar and an increase in net exports and aggregate demand.

e The higher aggregate demand translates into a shift rightward in the aggregate demand curve, which leads to an increase in the price level, which triggers a movement along the short-run aggregate supply curve, leading to an increase in real GDP.

f No, it does not because one of the crucial assumptions of the quantity theory does not hold—since the economy is in the short run, real GDP is not independent of changes in the money supply.

Midterm Examination

1 c Definition. (544–549)

2 b Multiplier calculation holds constant the price level. (584–587)

3 e If government borrows from Bank of Canada, the Bank prints money to give to government, which leads to increase in money supply, which leads to increase in *AD*, creating inflation. (658–659)

4 e *LRPC* is vertical at new higher natural rate, and *SRPC* shifts with it since it crosses *LRPC* at natural rate. (678–681)

5 e Increase in *MS* leads to decrease in *r*, which leads to increase in *C* (so **a** wrong), increase in *I* (so **d** wrong), increase in *NX* (so **b** and **c** wrong), and they all lead to increase in *AD*, which creates more jobs. (631–636)

6 e Definition. (646–649)

7 a Firms' sales > production leads to decrease in inventories, which leads to increase in production. New equilibrium has higher real GDP = higher *AE*. (549–553)

8 b Outlay. (572–577)

9 c This will lead to a fall in the cost of production and a rightward shift in *SAS*. (669–671)

10 c Lending its reserves is done by crediting borrowers' deposits, creating more deposits = more money. (603–606)

11 a In long run, real GDP is independent of Δ money supply. (672–673)

12 e Induced taxes act as automatic stabilizer. Multipliers are weaker, can still do discretionary policy, and there may or may not be a cyclical/structural deficit depending on other factors. (578–584)

13 a Bank of Canada pays for securities by crediting banks' reserves, which are part of monetary base. (627–631)

14 b At full employment, shift in *SAS* offsets shift in *AD*. (655–659)

15 d Decrease in interest rates leads to Canadian assets being less desirable, which leads to decrease in demand for these assets and for Canadian dollars, which leads to decrease in exchange rate, etc. (631–636)

16 d This effect leads to more ΔP, less ΔY. All others make effect larger. (559–563)

17 b Borrowers are paying the money, so are happy if its value erodes, the higher transactions costs do not affect interest rates, and the real rate is set independently of inflation. (682–683)

18 b University spending creates multiplier effects. (554–559)

19 a Autonomous tax multiplier = $-MPC/(1 - MPC) = -0.6/(1 - 0.6) = -1.5$. (578–584)

20 c M1 = currency in circulation + banks' demand deposits, M2+ = M1 + (personal savings and nonpersonal notice deposits at banks) + deposits at other financial institutions. (598–600)

21 a They must also balance off risk considerations. (601–603)

22 a Decrease in bank rate leads to decrease in cost of borrowing from central bank, which leads to decrease in desired reserves, creating excess reserves, which leads to increase in loans, etc. (622–626)

23 e Because then Δ real GDP due to fiscal policy has no impact on real money demand or on interest rates. (653–655)

24 d Real money demand is not affected by Δ price level, decrease in price of bonds leads to increase in interest rate, which lowers quantity of real money demanded. (607–610)

Chapter **31**

The Economy at Full Employment

KEY CONCEPTS

Real GDP and Employment

To increase real GDP in the short run, we must increase quantity of labour employed.

- The **production possibility frontier** (*PPF*) is the boundary between combinations of goods that can be produced and those that cannot.
  - We can show such a relationship between real GDP and leisure.
  - More real GDP requires less leisure and more time spent working.
- We can use the *PPF* to derive the **production function** (*PF*)—relationship between real GDP and quantity of labour employed, all other influences constant.
  - Increase in quantity of labour employed creates movement along *PF*.

Labour productivity is real GDP per hour of labour, which is influenced by three factors:

- More physical capital increases labour productivity.
- More **human capital** (people's knowledge and skills) increases labour productivity. Human capital can increase from **learning-by-doing** (on-the-job education from experience).
- Technological advances can also increase labour productivity.
- An increase in labour productivity shifts *PF* upward.

The Labour Market and Aggregate Supply

The labour market determines the quantity of labour hours employed and real GDP supplied.

- **Quantity of labour demanded** = number of labour hours hired by all firms.
- **Demand for labour** (*LD*)—quantity of labour demanded at each real wage rate.
- **Real wage rate** is wage per hour in constant dollars = **money wage rate** (in current dollars)/price level.
- **Marginal product of labour** = Δ real GDP per hour additional labour.
  - Decrease in marginal product as increase in labour used (diminishing marginal product of labour) because of constant capital stock and given technology.
- Firms hire labour as long as the marginal product of labour > real wage rate. Since marginal product of labour decreases as labour hired increases, *LD* slopes downward.
- Δ in real wage can be due to Δ money wage or Δ price level.
- Demand for labour curve shifts rightward if marginal product of labour increases.

Quantity of labour supplied = number of hours labour services households plan to work.

- **Supply of labour** (*LS*)—quantity of labour supplied at each real wage rate.
- Increase in real wage rate will increase quantity labour supplied because
  - hours per person increase if effect of increasing opportunity cost of leisure (= real wage rate) outweighs effect of desire for more leisure due to higher income.
  - labour force participation rate increases as new higher real wage exceeds value of activities outside labour force.

Labour market equilibrium occurs when *LD* = *LS*—the real wage rate adjusts to create this full-employment equilibrium.

- The level of real GDP at full employment is potential GDP.
- Long-run aggregate supply curve is relationship between quantity of real GDP supplied and price level when real GDP = potential GDP.
  - Vertical *LAS* curve graphs this relationship.
  - When *P* changes, money wage rate also changes to keep real wage rate at the level that makes *LD* = *LS*, so that employment is unchanged and therefore *LAS* curve is vertical at potential GDP.
- **Short-run aggregate supply curve** is relationship between quantity of real GDP supplied and *P*, money wage and all other influences constant.
  - Upward-sloping *SAS* curve graphs this relationship.
  - Along *SAS*, if *P* increases the money wage stays constant, so real wage falls and therefore quantity of labour demanded increases and real GDP increases.
  - Along *SAS*, if real GDP ≠ potential GDP, production is on *PPF*, *but* not at an efficient point from households' viewpoint.

Changes in Potential GDP

Real GDP increases if economy recovers from recession or potential GDP increases.

- Potential GDP increases if population or labour productivity increase.
- Increasing population increases the supply of labour.
  - As a result, real wage rate decreases, which increases hiring and potential GDP.
  - Due to diminishing returns, potential GDP per hour of work decreases.
- An increase in labour productivity increases demand for labour.
  - As a result, real wage rate increases, so more labour supplied, and potential GDP increases.
  - Potential GDP per hour of work also increases.

Unemployment at Full Employment

The unemployment rate at full employment is the **natural rate of unemployment**.

- Two broad reasons for unemployment—job search and job rationing.
- **Job search** unemployment occurs when people take time to find jobs while unemployed.
  - Constant change in labour market implies there is always job search.
  - When real wage rate at equilibrium value, normal job search generates the natural rate of unemployment.
  - If real wage rate > equilibrium, job search high.
  - Job search increases if proportion of working-age population increases, if unemployment compensation increases, or if technological change increases structural change.
- **Job rationing** is paying a wage that creates an excess supply of labour and frictional unemployment. Two reasons:
  - Firms pay **efficiency wages**—higher wages designed to maximize profits by increasing work effort, decreasing labour turnover rate (therefore lowering recruiting costs), and increasing quality of labour.
  - **Minimum wage** legally keeps wages above equilibrium value for covered workers.
- Job rationing creates a surplus of labour that adds extra job search.

Appendix: Deriving the Aggregate Supply Curves

LAS curve is vertical at potential GDP.

- When price level changes, money wage rate also changes to keep real wage rate at the level that makes *LD* = *LS*, so that employment and real GDP produced is unchanged.
- *LAS* shifts rightward if increase in labour productivity or in labour supply.

SAS curve is derived holding money wage constant.

- With fixed money wage in short run, real wage rate changes as *P* changes, so that *LD* changes.
- It is assumed employment is set by firms choosing how much to hire given real wage—*LD* may not equal *LS*.
- As a result, in short run, increase in *P* leads to decrease in real wage rate, so that labour demand increases and so does employment, leading to increase in real GDP produced—the *SAS* is upward-sloping.
- *SAS* shifts rightward with *LAS*.
  - *SAS* shifts rightward by itself if decrease in money wages.
  - If Δ*AD*, in short run this leads to movement along *SAS* curve, Δ price level and real GDP.

HELPFUL HINTS

1 The purpose of this chapter is to deepen our understanding of aggregate supply: the relationship between the price level and the quantity of real GDP supplied. Chapter 24 introduced the basic *AD-AS* model, and showed some of its usefulness in exploring the economy. The next part of the text examined aggregate demand in detail (Chapters 25–30), while Chapters 31 and 32 examine aggregate supply in detail in order to explore its composition, and the variables that affect it. As we will see in Chapters 33 and 34, aggregate supply is a crucial variable in understanding macroeconomic problems and policy.

2 Our work at understanding aggregate supply is broken down into two constituent issues—the production function and the labour market.

The first issue is: How is the quantity of real GDP supplied determined in general? When the capital stock and the state of technology are given, the maximum amount of real GDP that can be produced depends on the quantity of labour employed. This relationship between employment and the quantity of real GDP supplied is captured by the production function.

To understand the determination of the quantity of real GDP supplied, it is necessary to pursue the second issue: How is the level of employment determined? The answer is in the labour market. The demand for labour is determined by firms, and the supply of labour is determined by households. If money wages continuously adjust to clear the labour market, the level of employment will always be the equilibrium level with full employment. If, on the other hand, money wages are fixed in the short run, the level of employment can deviate from its equilibrium level.

Since our interest is in aggregate supply, we want to know how the quantity of real GDP varies as the price level varies. This desire brings us to a third issue: How do changes in the price level affect employment and real GDP? It turns out that if money wages continuously adjust, the level of employment, and thus the quantity of real GDP supplied, is independent of the price level. Whatever the price level, the wage rate will adjust so that the unique equilibrium level of employment is achieved. This adjustment implies a long-run aggregate supply curve that is vertical at potential GDP.

On the other hand, if wages are constant, the level of employment, and thus the quantity of real GDP supplied, depends on the actual value of the price level relative to the expected value of the price level. If the price level turns out to be equal to its expected value, the equilibrium level of employment (full employment) results. If the price level is higher than expected, the level of employment turns out to be higher than the equilibrium value and thus real GDP supplied will be larger than potential GDP. If the price level is lower than expected, employment will be less than equilibrium and real GDP supplied will be less than potential GDP. This result implies a positively sloped short-run aggregate supply curve.

3 As Chapter 23 explained, there are four different *types* of unemployment—frictional, structural, seasonal, and cyclical. The first three of these make up the natural rate of unemployment.

Defining the types of unemployment does not *explain* them. This chapter advances two basic explanations of unemployment to help us to see the origin of the three types of natural unemployment.

Frictional unemployment comes from job search (there is always job search in the economy because of changes in the fortunes of individual firms, people searching for good matches), and from job rationing leading to a wage above the equilibrium wage, with queuing for jobs as a result. It is often the result of a downturn in one firm.

Structural unemployment comes from excessive job search in times of structural change due to technological change. It is due to a downturn in a specific industry or region.

Seasonal unemployment is due to job search in specific seasons when certain types of jobs do not exist.

SELF-TEST

True/False/Uncertain and Explain

1 The production possibilities frontier is the relationship between real GDP and the quantity of labour employed.

2 More human capital creates a movement along the production function.

3 If the real wage rate decreases, the opportunity cost effect implies that households will increase the time spent working.

4 The diminishing marginal product of labour implies that the demand for labour curve is negatively sloped.

5 As the real wage rate increases, the quantity of labour demanded decreases, other things remaining constant.

6 If the marginal product of each unit of labour increases, the demand for labour curve shifts rightward.

7 Increasing population decreases the real wage rate and potential GDP.

8 Job rationing keeps real wages too high and creates cyclical unemployment.

9 Equilibrium in the labour market is when labour demand equals labour supply and unemployment is zero.

10 A decrease in the price level will lead to an increase in unemployment.

Multiple-Choice

Real GDP and Employment

1 The production function shows

a how much real GDP changes as the capital stock changes, all else remaining the same.
b how much real GDP changes as the price level changes, all else remaining the same.
c how much labour demand changes as the real wage rate changes, all else remaining the same.
d how much labour demand changes as the money wage rate changes, all else remaining the same.
e none of the above.

2 Which of the following would shift the production function upward?

a a decrease in the stock of capital
b a decrease in the real wage rate
c an increase in labour employed
d an increase in the price level
e a technological advance

3 An increase in an economy's stock of human capital would lead to

a a shift outward in the production possibilities frontier and a movement along the production function.
b a movement along the production possibilities frontier and a shift upward in the production function.
c a shift outward in the production possibilities frontier and a shift upward in the production function.
d a movement along the production possibilities frontier and a movement along the production function.
e no change in the production possibilities frontier and a movement along the production function.

4 An increase in the quantity of labour supplied (driven by a fall in leisure consumed) would lead to

a a shift outward in the production possibilities frontier and a movement along the production function.
b a movement along the production possibilities frontier and a shift upward in the production function.
c a shift outward in the production possibilities frontier and a shift upward in the production function.
d a movement along the production possibilities frontier and a movement along the production function.
e no change in the production possibilities frontier and a movement along the production function.

The Labour Market and Aggregate Supply

5 Which one of the following quotations describes a rightward shift in the labour demand curve?

a "Recent higher wage rates have led to more leisure being consumed."
b "The recent lower price level has induced people to work more hours."
c "The recent higher real wage rate has induced people to work more hours."
d "The recent high investment in capital equipment has raised hiring by firms."
e "Adding extra workers leads to lower productivity of each additional worker."

6 If tacos sell for $2 each at the Burning Belly Taco Stand, and the wage rate of a taco maker is $60 per day, the real wage rate faced by the Burning Belly manager is equivalent to:

a 2 tacos per day.
b $60 per day.
c 120 tacos per day.
d $2 per day.
e 30 tacos per day.

7 Initially, tacos sell for $2.00 each at the Burning Belly Taco Stand, and the wage rate of a taco maker is $60.00 per day. Suppose that the price of a taco increases to $2.50 after a *National Inquisitor* story linking tacos to baldness cures. The profit-maximizing Burning Belly manager will

a employ more taco makers because the real wage rate has increased to $2.50 per day.
b employ fewer taco makers because the real wage rate has increased to $2.50 per day.
c employ the same number of taco makers because the wage rate is unchanged.
d employ more taco makers because the real wage rate has decreased to 24 tacos per day.
e start advertising "I'm the owner, but I'm a customer too."

8 The labour demand curve is

a positively sloped and shifts when there is a change in the capital stock.
b positively sloped and shifts when there is a change in the quantity of labour employed.
c negatively sloped and shifts when there is a change in the capital stock.
d negatively sloped and shifts when there is a change in the quantity of labour employed.
e negatively sloped and shifts when there is a change in the real wage rate.

9 The demand for labour curve shows that, as the

a price level increases, the quantity of labour demanded decreases.
b real wage rate increases, the quantity of labour demanded increases.
c money wage rate increases, the quantity of labour demanded decreases.
d money wage rate increases, the quantity of labour demanded increases.
e real wage rate increases, the quantity of labour demanded decreases.

10 In the short run, if the price level decreases, the real wage rate will be

a lower than the equilibrium real wage rate, and employment will decrease.
b lower than the equilibrium real wage rate, and employment will increase.
c higher than the equilibrium real wage rate, and employment will decrease.
d higher than the equilibrium real wage rate, and employment will increase.
e equal to the equilibrium real wage rate, and employment will stay constant.

11 In the long run, if the price level decreases, the real wage rate will be

a less than the equilibrium real wage rate, and employment will decrease.
b less than the equilibrium real wage rate, and employment will increase.
c higher than the equilibrium real wage rate, and employment will decrease.
d higher than the equilibrium real wage rate, and employment will increase.
e equal to the equilibrium real wage rate, and employment will stay constant.

12 If the money wage rate is $12 per hour and the GDP deflator is 150, what is the real wage rate per hour?

a $18
b $15
c $12
d $8
e $6

13 A profit-maximizing firm will hire additional units of labour up to the point at which

a workers are no longer willing to work.
b the marginal product of labour is zero.
c the marginal product of labour is a maximum.
d the marginal product of labour is equal to the real wage.
e the marginal product of labour is equal to the money wage.

Changes in Potential GDP

14 The demand for labour and the supply of labour are both increasing over time, but the demand for labour is increasing at a faster rate. Over time we expect to see the

a real wage rate rising and employment decreasing.
b real wage rate and employment increasing.
c real wage rate decreasing and employment increasing.
d real wage rate and employment decreasing.
e long-run aggregate supply curve shifting leftward.

15 An increase in potential GDP would be shown as

a a shift outward in the production possibilities frontier and a movement along the production function.
b a movement along the production possibilities frontier and a shift upward in the production function.
c a shift outward in the production possibilities frontier and a shift upward in the production function.
d a movement along the production possibilities frontier and a movement along the production function.
e either a shift in the production possibilities frontier and the production function, or a movement along each curve, depending on the source of the change.

16 *Ceteris paribus*, an increase in labour productivity results in

a a higher real wage rate and higher potential GDP per hour of work.
b a lower real wage rate and higher potential GDP per hour of work.
c a higher real wage rate and lower potential GDP per hour of work.
d a lower real wage rate and lower potential GDP per hour of work.
e a constant real wage rate in the long run.

17 *Ceteris paribus*, an increase in the population results in

a a higher level of labour employed and higher potential GDP per hour of work.
b a lower level of labour employed and higher potential GDP per hour of work.
c a higher level of labour employed and lower potential GDP per hour of work.
d a lower level of labour employed and lower potential GDP per hour of work.
e a constant level of labour employed and constant potential GDP per hour of work.

Unemployment at Full Employment

18 Which of the following is *not* a possible explanation for unemployment?

a job search
b efficiency wages
c minimum wages
d job market turnover
e part-time searches

19 Job search unemployment increases if
- **a** the proportion of working-age population increases.
- **b** unemployment compensation becomes more generous.
- **c** technological change speeds up.
- **d** all of the above.
- **e** none of the above.

20 An efficiency wage refers to wages
- **a** paid below the equilibrium wage rate in order to increase the firm's efficiency.
- **b** set to generate the efficient level of employment.
- **c** paid above the equilibrium wage rate in order to increase worker productivity.
- **d** being too high because of minimum wage laws.
- **e** off of the production possibilities frontier.

21 Which of the following government policies would *lower* the unemployment rate?
- **a** increasing unemployment benefits
- **b** raising the minimum wage
- **c** closing down employment agencies
- **d** reducing unemployment benefits
- **e** decreasing aggregate demand

Appendix: Deriving the Aggregate Supply Curves

22 Which one of the following quotations describes a movement along a long-run aggregate supply curve?
- **a** "The recent higher price levels have lowered production in the country."
- **b** "The recent higher price levels have raised production in the country."
- **c** "The recent higher price levels have led to compensating increases in wages, with no changes in labour hired or production."
- **d** "The recent lower price levels have led to lower production in the country."
- **e** None of the above.

23 Which one of the following quotations describes a shift rightward in a short-run aggregate supply curve?
- **a** "The recent higher price levels have lowered production in the country."
- **b** "The recent higher price levels have raised production in the country."
- **c** "The recent higher price levels have led to compensating increases in wages, with no changes in labour hired or production."
- **d** "The recent lower price levels have led to lower production in the country."
- **e** None of the above.

24 Figure 31.1 depicts the labour market. The price level, measured by the GDP deflator, is 150. What is the money wage rate in equilibrium?
- **a** \$8
- **b** \$12
- **c** \$15
- **d** \$18
- **e** \$24

FIGURE **31.1**

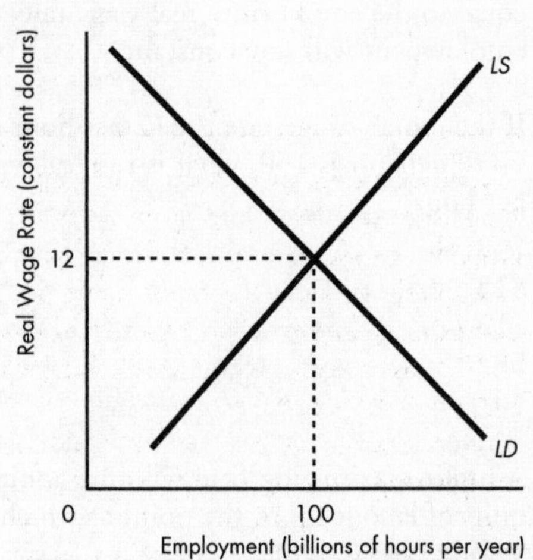

25 Refer to Fig. 31.1 and assume that when the money wage was set, the GDP deflator was expected to remain constant at 150. If the GDP deflator actually turns out to be 200 in the short run, the real wage rate will be
- **a** \$9, and employment will be less than 100 billion hours per year.
- **b** \$9, and employment will be more than 100 billion hours per year.
- **c** \$24, and employment will be less than 100 billion hours per year.
- **d** \$24, and employment will be more than 100 billion hours per year.
- **e** \$6, and employment will be more than 100 billion hours per year.

Short Answer Problems

1 Explain why the labour force participation rate increases as the real wage rate increases. Why does this factor help explain the positive slope of the labour supply curve?

2 What determines the demand for labour?

3 Table 31.1 gives information about the production function for the country of Orania, where L = units of labour per day (measured in the millions) and Y = units of output per day (real GDP, millions of constant dollars per day).

TABLE **31.1** PRODUCTION FUNCTION

L	Y	MP_L
0	0	
1	8	
2	15	
3	21	
4	26	
5	30	
6	33	

a There are a total of 6 units of labour available for leisure or labour supply in Arcadia. Graph Arcadia's production possibilities frontier.

b Complete the last column of Table 31.1 by computing the marginal product of labour (MP_L). Remember to place the marginal product halfway between the two rows.

c How much labour will be demanded if the money wage rate is $6 and the GDP deflator is 150?

d Draw a graph of the demand for labour.

4 Table 31.2 gives the supply of labour schedule for Orania.

TABLE **31.2** SUPPLY OF LABOUR

Real Wage Rate	Quantity of Labour Supplied
8	7.5
7	6.5
6	5.5
5	4.5
4	3.5
3	2.5

a On the graph from Short Answer Problem **3d**, draw the supply of labour curve.

b What is the equilibrium real wage rate?

c What is the equilibrium level of employment?

d What is the level of output at this level of employment?

ⓔ **e** If the natural rate of unemployment in Orania is 10 percent, calculate the labour force and the units of labour unemployed in equilibrium.

ⓔ **5** Suppose Orania is operating on its long-run aggregate supply curve.

a If the GDP deflator is 100, what is the equilibrium money wage rate, the level of employment, and the level of output?

b If the GDP deflator is 80, what is the equilibrium money wage rate, the level of employment, and the level of output?

c If the GDP deflator is 120, what is the equilibrium money wage rate, the level of employment, and the level of output?

d Draw Orania's long-run aggregate supply curve.

ⓔ **6** Now suppose Orania has a fixed money wage, set at $4.50. Assuming Orania is in the short run, answer the following questions.

a If the actual value of the GDP deflator is 100, what is the real wage rate, the level of employment, and the level of output?

b If the actual value of the GDP deflator is 82, what is the real wage rate, the level of employment, and the level of output?

c If the actual value of the GDP deflator is 128, what is the real wage rate, the level of employment, and the level of output?

d On the graph from Short Answer Problem **5d**, indicate three points on the short-run aggregate supply curve for Orania. Draw part of that curve by connecting the points.

7 Now suppose that a technological advance gives Orania a new production function summarized in Table 31.3.

TABLE **30.3** NEW PRODUCTION FUNCTION

L	Y	MP_L
0	0	
1	10	
2	19	
3	27	
4	34	
5	40	
6	45	

a On your *PPF* graph from Short Answer Problem **3a**, graph Orania's new *PPF*.

b Complete the last column of Table 31.3 by computing the marginal product of labour. Remember to place the marginal product halfway between the two rows.

c On the graph from Short Answer Problems **3c** and **4a**, draw the new demand for labour curve.

d In the long run, what will be the new equilibrium real wage rate, level of employment, and level of output? (The supply of labour curve is unchanged.)

e What happened to the *SAS* and *LAS* curves?

8 "The theory of job rationing tells us firms keep real wages too high and therefore create extra unemployment. Real wages should be forced downward to create more employment." Discuss this statement in light of efficiency wages.

9 Consider the following statement. "A major source of unemployment is job search due to employment insurance. It would be better for the economy if we eliminated employment insurance." What would eliminating employment insurance do to job search and unemployment levels? Is it clearly better for the economy if we eliminate employment insurance? Explain briefly.

10 Is the natural rate of unemployment constant? Briefly explain what factors can change the natural rate of unemployment.

ANSWERS

True/False/Uncertain and Explain

1 F Definition given is for production function. (696)

2 F Creates shift in *PF*. (697–698)

3 F Decrease in real wage rate leads to decrease in opportunity cost of leisure, which leads to increase in leisure. (702)

4 T If hire more labour, diminishing marginal product leads to decrease in marginal product. Therefore firms will hire more labour only if decrease in real wage rate. (701)

5 T Definition of labour demand curve. (699–700)

6 T Increase in marginal product leads to increase in output per worker and therefore increase in number desired at a constant real wage rate. (699–701)

7 F Increasing population increases labour supply, and decreases real wage, but more labour is hired so potential GDP increases. (704–705)

8 F It creates frictional unemployment, since it is independent of the cycle. (710)

9 F Even in equilibrium there is natural unemployment. (709)

10 U It depends on whether money wages constant. (719)

Multiple-Choice

1 e Definition: how much real GDP changes as the labour hired changes. (696–698)

2 e Technological advance leads to increase in productivity of labour. (696–698)

3 c The change increases labour productivity, which shifts both curves. (696–698)

4 d Decreasing leisure creates move along *PPF* (more real GDP, less leisure), and the increase in labour supply creates move along *PF*. (696–698)

5 d This change leads to higher productivity and more labour demand. **a**, **b**, and **c** are *LS* effect, **e** movement along curve. (699–700)

6 e Real wage rate = money wage rate/price of good = \$60/\$2 = 30. (699)

7 d Real wage = \$60.00/\$2.50 = 24 < 30 leads to hire more labour since cheaper. (699–700)

8 c Negatively sloped due to diminishing marginal product. **d** and **e** imply movements along the curve. (699–701)

9 e Demand for labour depends inversely on real wage rate. (699–701)

10 c Lower actual price level leads to higher real wage (since money wage constant), so labour demanded decreases. (703–704)

11 e Money wage adjust to any price level changes, so real wage constant, and therefore no change in labour hired. (703–704)

12 d Real wage = money wage/price level × 100. (699)

13 d Here profits maximized. (699–701)

14 b Draw a graph. (708)

15 e If labour productivity is the original change, then there is a shift in the curves. If the change is due to a change in labour force participation rates, then there is a movement along the curves. If it is due to a population change, then there is a shift in the *PPF* and a movement along the *PF*. (704–708)

16 a Productivity increase creates an increase in labour demand, which raises real wage rate. Potential GDP per hour of work = productivity, so it must have increased. (706–707)

17 c Labour supply shifts right, real wage falls, more people are hired, but due to diminishing marginal productivity potential GDP per hour of work falls. (704–705)

18 e These workers are employed while searching. (709–711)

19 d See text discussion. (709–711)

20 c Definition. (709–711)

21 d This change will reduce length of job search. (709–711)

22 c No Δ employment leads to no Δ production leads to vertical *LAS*. (714–719)

23 e **a** is nonsense, **b**, **c**, and **d** are movements along curves. (714–719)

24 d Real wage set where *LD* = *LS* at $12, money wage = real wage × price level/100. (714–719)

25 b Actual real wage = money wage/price level × 100, and lower real wage leads to more labour demanded. (714–719)

Short Answer Problems

1 Individuals compare the value of working (the real wage) to the value of activities outside the labour force (for example, education, taking care of children). If the real wage rate is too low, an individual will not even enter the labour force. As the real wage rate increases, it will exceed the value of alternative activities of an increasingly larger group of people; thus the labour force increases relative to the size of the working age population; the labour force participation rate increases.

As this rate increases, more individuals offer to supply labour; thus the quantity of labour supplied increases. Because the original impetus was an increasing real wage rate, the real wage rate and the quantity of labour supplied are positively related.

2 The demand for labour is set where the real wage rate equals the marginal product of labour. The marginal product of labour is affected by the physical and human capital stock, and the technology. Therefore in the short run the demand for labour is affected by the real wage rate, physical and human capital stock, and level of technology.

3 a The *PPF* graph is labelled as PPF_0 in Fig. 31.2 below.

FIGURE **31.2** ACADIA'S *PPF*

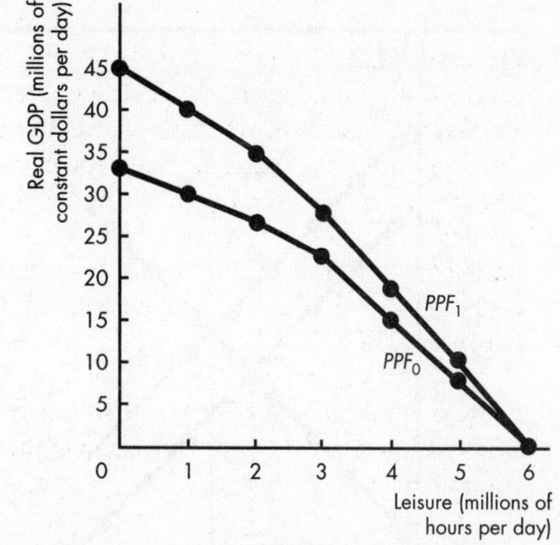

b Completed Table 31.1 is shown here as Table 31.1 Solution. The marginal product of labour is the additional output produced by an additional unit of labour.

TABLE **31.1** SOLUTION

L	*Y*	MP_L
0	0	
		8
1	8	
		7
2	15	
		6
3	21	
		5
4	26	
		4
5	30	
		3
6	33	

c The real wage rate is computed as follows: real wage rate = money wage rate × 100/GDP deflator.

In this case, the money wage rate is $6 per unit and the GDP deflator is 150. Therefore the real wage is $4. Since a profit-maximizing firm will hire labour until the marginal product of labour is equal to the real wage rate, we can see that the quantity of labour demanded at a real wage rate of $4 is 4.5 units.

d The graph of the demand curve for labour (labelled LD_0) is given in Fig. 31.3. The demand curve for labour is the same as the marginal product of labour curve (see Table 31.1 Solution).

FIGURE **31.3**

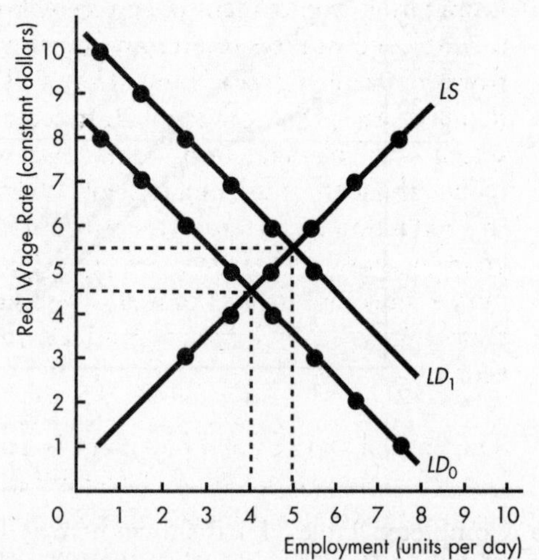

4 a Figure 31.3 illustrates the supply curve of labour (labelled *LS*) on the same graph with the LD_1 curve from Short Answer Problem **3**.

b The equilibrium real wage rate is $4.50 since the quantity of labour demanded and supplied are both equal to 4 units per day. This result can be seen from the graph or the tables.

c The equilibrium level of employment is 4 units.

d From the production function in Table 31.1, we can see that 4 units of labour will yield 26 units of output per day.

ⓒⓣ **e** If the unemployment rate is 10 percent, then
- 0.10 = (labour force – employed)/labour force, or
- labour force × 0.10 = labour force – 4, or
- labour force × 0.9 = 4, or
- labour force = 4/0.9 = 4.44

Therefore there are 0.44 units unemployed.

ⓔ **5** Regardless of the value of the GDP deflator, in the long run, the equilibrium real wage rate is $4.50, the level of employment is 4 units per day, and the level of output is 26 units per day. If we know the real wage rate and the GDP deflator, the money wage rate can be found as follows:

Money wage rate = Real wage rate × GDP deflator/100.

a If the GDP deflator is 100, a real wage rate of $4.50 implies a money wage rate of $4.50.

b If the GDP deflator is 80, a real wage rate of $4.50 suggests a money wage rate of $3.60.

c If the GDP deflator is 120, a real wage rate of $4.50 suggests a money wage rate of $5.40.

d The long-run aggregate supply curve (labelled *LAS*) is given in Fig. 31.4. Parts **a**, **b**, and **c** indicate that at every price level output is 26 units per day.

FIGURE **31.4**

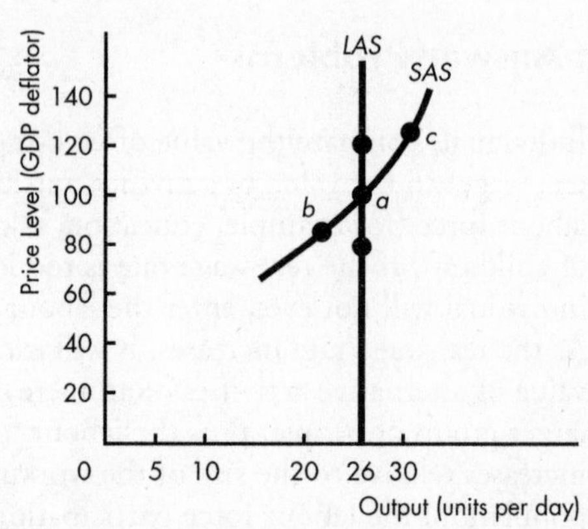

ⓔ **6 a** If the actual value of the GDP deflator is 100, since the money wage rate is fixed at $4.50, the real wage rate is $4.50. This real wage rate implies that employment is 4 units and output is 26 units.

b If the actual value of the GDP deflator is 82, since the money wage rate is fixed at $4.50, the real wage rate is $5.50 (4.5/82 × 100 = 5.5). Employment is determined by the demand for labour which, at a real wage of $5.50, is 3 units per day. This employment level means that (from Table 31.1) output is 21 units per day.

c If the actual value of the GDP deflator is 128, since the money wage rate is fixed at $4.50, the real wage rate is $3.50. Employment is determined by the demand for labour and is 5 units per day. From Table 31.1, this employment level implies a daily output of 30 units.

d Figure 31.3 indicates three points on the short-run aggregate supply curve in the sticky-wage economy: point *a* corresponds to output = 26, GDP deflator = 100; point *b* corresponds to output = 21, GDP deflator = 82; point *c* corresponds to output = 30, GDP deflator = 128. The points are connected to give a portion of the short-run aggregate supply curve (labelled *SAS*).

7 a The new production possibilities graph is graphed in Fig. 31.2 as PPF_1.

b Completed Table 31.3 is shown here as Table 31.3 Solution. Note that the marginal product of each unit of labour has increased as a result of the technological advance.

TABLE **31.3** SOLUTION

L	Y	MP_L
0	0	
		10
1	10	
		9
2	19	
		8
3	27	
		7
4	34	
		6
5	40	
		5
6	45	

c Figure 31.3 gives the graph. Notice that the new labour demand curve, LD_1 (which comes from the new MP_L relationship), lies rightward of LD_0.

d It can be seen from Fig. 31.3 or Tables 31.2 and 31.3 that the quantity of labour demanded equals the quantity of labour supplied at a real wage rate of \$5.50. The level of employment is now 5 units of labour per day, which implies an output of 40 units per day (from Table 31.3).

e The *LAS* shifts rightward from 26 to 40, and the *SAS* curve moves with it.

8 Yes, firms keep real wages too high, but the result is higher productivity. Forcing real wages down might create more employment, but it would also create lower productivity and lower potential GDP. It is not clear that this change is desirable.

9 Eliminating employment insurance will mean unemployed workers receive no government payments while job searching. They will therefore accept job offers much faster, and search less. This reduction in searching will reduce the level of unemployment. However, this reduction in unemployment is not clearly good, because workers may settle for poor job matches because they cannot afford to keep searching, which will reduce productivity in the economy.

10 The natural rate of unemployment is determined by the amount of job search and job rationing. Job search is affected by the proportion of working-age population, by unemployment compensation, and by technological change. Job rationing is affected by the use of efficiency wages and the level of the minimum wage. Changes in any of these underlying factors will change the level of the natural rate of unemployment.

Chapter 32

Economic Growth

KEY CONCEPTS

Long-Term Growth Trends

We study long-term growth to understand what creates rising incomes per person.

- Canada's growth rate high in earlier part of century, decreased between World Wars, increased until 1973, slower since then.
- Internationally, between 1960 and 1990, Canada caught up to the United States, but Japan and other Asian countries have been catching up to both countries.
- Since 1990 Canada has fallen behind somewhat.

The Causes of Economic Growth: A First Look

Growth requires essential preconditions—most basic is an appropriate *incentive* system.

- Three institutions are crucial:
  - Markets—prices send signals that create incentives, and enable people to specialize, trade, save, and invest
  - Property rights—if clearly established and enforced, give people assurance their income and savings will not be confiscated
  - Monetary exchange—facilitates transactions
- Incentive system allows people to specialize and trade, which leads to more goods/services for same labour, which increases real GDP per person.

This source of growth eventually runs its course—for further growth to continue we need

- saving and investment in new capital, which increases capital per worker, which increases productivity
- investment in human capital (by learning and repetitively doing tasks), which increases productivity
- discovery of new technologies

Growth Accounting

Growth accounting calculates how much of economic growth is due to growth of labour and capital or to technological change.

- Real GDP supplied (Y) depends on quantity of labour (N), quantity of capital (K), and state of technology (T)—summarized in **aggregate production function** $Y = F(N, K, T)$.
- **Labour productivity** (real GDP per hour of work = Y/N) determines how much income an hour of labour can earn.

Productivity growth comes from growth in capital per hour of labour and technological change (which includes human capital).

- **Productivity function** (*PF*) is relationship between real GDP per hour of labour and capital per hour of labour, holding constant technology.
  - Increase in capital per hour of labour increases real GDP per hour of labour (movement along *PF* function).
  - Technological change increases real GDP per hour of labour (upward shift of *PF* function).
  - Increase in one input, other inputs held constant, increases output at a diminishing rate—**law of diminishing returns**.
- *One-third rule* says, on average, one percent increase in capital per hour of labour (with no change in technology) leads to 1/3 of 1 percent increase in output per hour of labour.

- Can use one-third rule to calculate contribution of capital growth to real GDP growth, and to study reasons for changes in productivity growth:
  - 1965–73—high productivity growth due to high technological change and strong capital accumulation.
  - 1973–98—lower productivity growth due to slowdown in technological change and lower capital accumulation.
- Productivity slowdown after 1973 due to energy price shocks and environmental concerns diverting research efforts and capital accumulation.

Faster growth comes from increase in capital per hour of work or increase in technological advances.

- Main suggestions for increasing economic growth rates:
  - Stimulate saving by tax incentives.
  - Subsidize research and development by direct public funding.
  - Target high-technology industries for public research funds.
  - Encourage international trade to take advantage of gains from specialization and exchange.
  - Improve education quality by funding basic education.

Growth Theories

Causes of economic growth complex because of interaction of the factors that contribute to growth. There are three theories of economic growth.

Classical growth theory comes from late eighteenth century, a time of high population growth, and argues population growth is determined by level of income per person.

- Advances in technology increase demand for labour and real wage rate, which increases quantity of labour supplied.
- Since real wage rate > **subsistence real wage rate** (minimum needed to maintain life), population grows, which increases labour supply, which pushes real wage rate back to subsistence rate, which means workers' incomes have not increased.

Neoclassical growth theory says real GDP per person grows due to technological changing inducing growth in capital per person.

- Population growth rate is not determined by economic growth.
  - As real wage rate increases, this increases opportunity cost of women's time and of children, which decreases birth rate.
  - Technological advances also lower death rate.
  - Net result: population growth is roughly independent of economic growth.
- Driving force of economic growth is technological change.
  - Key variable is growth rate of capital stock, which is set by demand for and supply of capital.
  - Demand for capital from investment decision, supply of capital from saving decision.
  - Ongoing *exogenous* technological advances increase productivity of capital, increasing demand for capital, so that investment demand increases, which increases capital per person and real interest rate.
  - Increase in real interest rate means real interest rate > target real interest rate savers wish to achieve, which increases saving and supply of capital (which increases capital per person, which increases real GDP per person), which leads to decrease in real interest rate until = target rate, and growth stops (until technological change occurs again).
- Neoclassical growth theory predicts growth rates and income levels per person in different countries should converge, but this convergence doesn't happen empirically.

New growth theory attempts to overcome this shortcoming by explaining technological changes as a profit-maximizing choice.

- New discoveries are sought for (temporary) profits, but once made, discoveries are copied and benefits dispersed through economy, *without* diminishing returns.
- Knowledge is a special kind of capital not subject to diminishing returns—demand for knowledge capital curve is flat.
- Inventions increase rate of return to knowledge capital until > target saving rate, resulting in increased capital per person and real GDP growth.
- Rate of return > target rate, which increases saving and capital per person and real GDP growth with *no automatic slowdown* because return to capital does not diminish.

HELPFUL HINTS

1 Economic growth is a powerful force in raising living standards. Countries become rich by achieving high rates of growth in per person

GDP and maintaining them over a long period of time. The role of compounding of income can create startling effects in this regard. We can see this effect by examining the post-1973 productivity slowdown. Growth between 1947 and 1973 was 3.2 percent per year, but after 1973 only 1.8 percent per year. This slowdown means that between 1973 and 1995, real GDP per person rose by about 48 percent (= $[(1.018)^{22} - 1] \times 100$). However, if economic growth had continued at the pre-1973 rate of 3.2 percent, real GDP per person would have increased by about 100 percent (= $[(1.032)^{22} - 1] \times 100$). Even the worst recession over this time period only lowered real GDP per person by about 5 percent. Curing the productivity slowdown would clearly have a big payoff!

2 The key to understanding the different theories of growth is understanding the role of "the law of diminishing returns" in each theory. This law states that adding more of one input, other inputs held constant, eventually leads to a situation of diminishing returns to adding extra inputs.

In neoclassical theory, the discovery of a new technology increases the return on capital, the demand for capital, and the amount of capital used. In turn, the fact that the return for capital is above the target rate for savers increases saving, the supply of capital, and further increases the amount of capital used. However, the increase in capital eventually leads to diminishing returns. As an example, we might think of the introduction of new and more powerful computers. As the number of computers increases, holding constant the number of workers, the extra output of the *n*th computer will not be as high as the productivity of the first computer. Eventually, the productivity of the extra capital must decrease (the capital demand curve is downward-sloping), and economic growth automatically slows down.

New growth theory has a different idea of technology and capital, with no diminishing returns, and no slowdown in economic growth. New growth theory examines "knowledge capital," a concept of technology that is not embodied so much in capital, but in ideas. These ideas might include new management techniques, or new processes of production (such as the assembly line) that can be copied from business to business without encountering diminishing returns. As an example, consider the introduction of new and better software (such as the first word processing package). As more copies of the software are introduced into different businesses around the country, we do not run into diminishing returns, at least not until the entire country has access to the new knowledge. Even then, new software will be continually developed and introduced without diminishing returns (the knowledge capital demand curve is flat), and economic growth need not automatically slow down.

SELF-TEST

True/False/Uncertain and Explain

1 Canada's recent growth slowdown is quite unusual in Canadian history.

2 Other countries are catching up with Canada's real GDP per person.

3 Specialization is the crucial source of current growth.

4 When a country adopts a better technology, its productivity function will shift upward.

5 Rapid changes in technology create growth without need for new capital.

6 High economic growth has typically been accompanied by high saving rates.

7 The slowdown in productivity growth after 1973 was due to a slowdown in the growth of capital per hour of labour, with a constant rate of technological change.

8 Growth theory argues economic growth will eventually slow down because the return to capital begins to diminish as the amount of capital increases.

9 Classical growth theory argues that economic growth leads to a smaller population growth rate.

10 Neoclassical growth theory requires ongoing technological change to get ongoing economic growth.

Multiple-Choice

Long-Term Growth Trends

1 Canada's economic growth rates were highest in which of the following decades?

a the 1930s
b the 1950s and 1960s
c the 1970s
d the 1980s
e the 1990s

2 Compared to the growth in other countries, between 1960 and 1990 Canada

a fell behind most other countries.
b dramatically caught up to and passed other countries.
c worsened versus the United States, but did better versus other countries.
d did as well or better than most countries except certain Asian countries.
e none of the above.

3 Which of the following statements about Canada's long-term growth trends is *false*?

a Economic growth has tended to be steady, except for the business cycle.
b Economic growth shows periods of slow and high growth.
c Economic growth has been slow since 1973.
d Economic growth has been generally faster in Japan than in Canada.
e African countries have fallen further behind Canada in recent years.

The Causes of Economic Growth: A First Look

4 Which of the following is *not* a source of economic growth?

a increasing stock market prices
b better educated workers
c growing stock of capital equipment
d an appropriate incentive system
e advances in technology

5 Markets are an essential precondition to growth because

a they suffer from diminishing returns.
b they allow countries to benefit from high saving rates.
c prices send signals that create incentives.
d people have an assurance that their income and savings will not be confiscated.
e all of the above.

6 The basic sources of economic growth include

a saving and investment in new capital.
b investment in human capital.
c discoveries of new techniques.
d discoveries of new management processes.
e all of the above.

7 A good incentive system

a leads to specialization and exchange, with higher GDP per person.
b is all that is needed to have continuous growth.
c solves the problem of diminishing returns.
d has no role for government.
e can have the real interest rate above the target rate of savers for an extended period of time.

Growth Accounting

8 Suppose that productivity increased 24 percent last year. Capital per hour of work increased by 12 percent as well. The increase in capital was responsible for

a all of the increase in productivity.
b 5/6 of the increase in productivity.
c 1/2 of the increase in productivity.
d 1/3 of the increase in productivity.
e 1/6 of the increase in productivity.

9 Suppose that productivity increased 24 percent last year. Capital per hour of work increased by 12 percent as well. An increase in technology was responsible for

- **a** all of the increase in productivity.
- **b** 5/6 of the increase in productivity.
- **c** 1/2 of the increase in productivity.
- **d** 1/3 of the increase in productivity.
- **e** 1/6 of the increase in productivity.

10 Which of the following was a cause of Canada's post-1973 growth slowdown?

- **a** higher population pressures
- **b** lower amounts of saving
- **c** diminishing returns
- **d** slowdowns in technological change
- **e** too-rapid increases in technological change

11 If there were significant technological advances last year, and the capital stock per hour of work grew by 9 percent,

- **a** the real rate of interest must have decreased.
- **b** economic growth would have been significantly less than 3 percent.
- **c** economic growth would have been significantly more than 3 percent.
- **d** economic growth would have been about 3 percent.
- **e** the target rate of savers must have fallen.

12 Which of the following is a suggestion for increasing Canadian economic growth rates?

- **a** Stimulate saving by taxing consumption.
- **b** Reduce the time period for patents to increase replication.
- **c** Put less public research funds into universities.
- **d** Protect our industries from foreign competition.
- **e** Tax education.

13 One of the reasons technological change slowed down after 1973 was the

- **a** energy-inefficiency of the new capital stock.
- **b** lack of new capital stock.
- **c** one-third rule.
- **d** law of diminishing returns.
- **e** introduction of new environmental protection laws and regulations.

14 The law of diminishing returns

- **a** holds only for knowledge capital.
- **b** states that if capital increases by 1 percent, real GDP increases by about 1/3 of a percent.
- **c** states that if capital increases by 1 percent, real GDP increases by about 3 percent.
- **d** holds for both physical and knowledge capital.
- **e** does not hold for knowledge capital.

15 It is argued that governments must subsidize research and development

- **a** because there is too little private saving.
- **b** it is too expensive for small firms.
- **c** there are external benefits to research and development that firms ignore.
- **d** in order to take advantage of the gains from specialization and exchange.
- **e** in order to overcome diminishing returns.

Growth Theories

16 In neoclassical growth theory, if the real interest rate exceeds the target rate of savers, then

- **a** the real interest rate will eventually decline.
- **b** capital per hour of work will increase.
- **c** real GDP per hour of work will increase.
- **d** all of the above.
- **e** only **b** and **c**.

17 In new growth theory, if the real interest rate exceeds the target rate of savers, then

- **a** the real interest rate will eventually decline.
- **b** capital per hour of work will increase.
- **c** real GDP per hour of work will increase.
- **d** all of the above.
- **e** only **b** and **c**.

18 Which theory of economic growth argues that growth always slows down unless there are new technological inventions?

- **a** classical theory
- **b** neoclassical theory
- **c** new growth theory
- **d** all of the theories
- **e** none of the theories

19 Which theory of economic growth concludes that technological advances increase the demand for capital?

- **a** classical theory
- **b** neoclassical theory
- **c** new theory
- **d** all of the theories
- **e** none of the theories

20 A technological advance leads to

a only a movement along the productivity function, and an increase in real GDP per person.
b only a movement along the productivity function, and a decrease in real GDP per person.
c a decrease in the real rate of interest, and an increase in real GDP per person.
d a shift upward in the productivity function, and a movement along the productivity function.
e an increase in capital per hour of labour, and only a movement along the productivity function.

21 Incentives are important in the new growth theory because they

a imply there are no diminishing returns.
b lead to higher rates of saving.
c imply that economic growth does not lead to population growth.
d create specialization and exchange.
e lead to profit-seeking searches for new discoveries.

22 In the classical growth theory, economic growth eventually stops after a technological advance because of

a diminishing returns.
b knowledge capital being easily replicated.
c the real rate of interest decreasing back down to the target rate of savers.
d the real wage rate becoming too high.
e high population growth resulting from the increase in real wages.

23 Knowledge capital is different from ordinary capital because

a it can be replicated without diminishing returns.
b its demand curve is flat.
c it does not lead to an automatic slowdown in growth.
d all of the above.
e none of the above.

24 The capital demand curve is flat in new growth theory because

a the productivity of capital diminishes as more capital is employed per hour of labour.
b technological advances occur frequently due to profit-seeking activities.
c discoveries can be replicated without diminishing their marginal productivity.
d the target rate of savers is constant.
e population growth in response to high wages lowers the real wage rate.

25 The key difference between neoclassical growth theory and new growth theory is that

a capital is not subject to diminishing returns under new growth theory.
b capital is subject to diminishing returns under new growth theory.
c increases in technology increase population which drives workers' incomes back down to the subsistence level in neoclassical theory.
d technological advances are exogenous in new growth theory.
e the one-third rule only holds in new growth theory.

Short Answer Problems

1 Why is an appropriate incentive system a precondition to growth?

2 Why does this source of growth eventually run its course?

3 Explain what happens in classical growth theory when advances in technology increase the real wage rate.

4 Some economists speculate that the Asian miracle economies have achieved such fast growth at least partially due to their adeptness at replicating new technology from other countries. Explain how and why this replicating is such a good source of growth.

5 Paul Krugman and others have argued that in fact the Asian miracle economies' extra-high economic growth is mostly due to the mobilization of capital and labour resources that were previously underutilized, and that therefore North American worries that these countries will catch up to and surpass Canada and the United States are unfounded. Assuming his argument is true, explain why this argument implies that these worries are unfounded.

6 Use the concept of a productivity function to explain why an increase in the amount of capital per worker will lead to economic growth.

ⓔ **7** You are given the data in Table 32.1 on the economy of Erehwon where the one-third rule holds, and the labour supply and population is unchanging over these three years. Do the calculations needed to show the contributions of changes in capital per worker (as a fraction of the total change) and technological change to productivity, and fill in the rest of the table.

TABLE **32.1**

Year	1998	1999	2000
Capital per hour of work ($)	125	150	200
Productivity ($)	35	40	44.4
Contribution of capital	—	?	?
Contribution of technological change	—	?	?

8 On a graph, sketch the productivity functions from Short Answer Problem 7 for the three years, showing the production points for each of the three years.

9 Consider the following productivity function:

TABLE **32.2**

Capital per Hour of Work	Real GDP per Hour of Work
100	60
120	64
156	70

The economy is originally producing 60 units of real GDP per hour of work in year 1.

a Does this productivity function roughly meet the one-third rule?

b Graph this function, and the current point of production. Suppose that there is a technological advance that increases real GDP per hour of work by 20 percent, holding constant the capital per hour of work. Show the impact of this change on your graph.

c In year 2, real GDP per hour of work is now 84 units. Show this point on your graph. How much (if any) of the increase in real GDP was due to the technological advance, and how much (if any) was due to an increase in the capital per hour of work?

ⓒⓣ **10** Some commentators have argued that Japan has had a higher growth rate than countries like Canada or the United States because the Japanese care more about the future and less about present consumption, reflected in a lower target interest rate for savers. Explain within the context of growth theory whether or not this argument seems likely to be true.

ANSWERS

True/False/Uncertain and Explain

1 F Growth also slowed down between World Wars. (724)
2 U Some countries are (Asian), some are not (African and Central and South American). (725–726)
3 F It is the initial source of growth, but once specialization is high, growth slows down. (727)
4 T Technological advance increases productivity, capital per worker unchanged. (730)
5 F Rapid technological change is embodied in new human and physical capital. (730)
6 T See discussion of East Asian economies. (732)
7 F Due to slowdown in both—see text discussion. (731–732)
8 U Depends on which theory—T if neoclassical, F if new growth. (733–739)
9 F Economic growth increases real wage rate, which increases population growth. (733–734)
10 T A technological advance increases demand for capital, which increases capital per person, which increases economic growth. Real rate of interest > target rate, which increases supply of capital, which leads to more economic growth, but real rate of interest down due to diminishing returns, which means growth eventually stops, unless there is more technological change. (735–737)

Multiple-Choice

1 b See text discussion. (724)
2 d See text discussion. (725)
3 a Growth rates have fluctuated. (724–725)
4 a This factor has no impact on productivity, others increase it. (727–728)
5 c Incentives to specialize, trade, save, and invest. (727)
6 e See text discussion. (727–728)
7 a It eventually no longer contributes to growth, does not solve diminishing returns, government is needed to allocate property rights, and has little to do with real rate of interest. (727)
ⓒⓣ **8 e** By one-third rule, capital increase of 12 percent leads to real GDP per hour of work increase in 4 percent, or 1/6 of increase in productivity. (730–731)
ⓒⓣ **9 b** From 8, 5/6 is left over for technology to explain. (730–731)

10 d See text discussion. (731)

11 c One-third rule says capital growth leads to real GDP per hour of labour of about 3 percent, but technological growth will add to this amount. (730–731)

12 a **b** would lower return to and number of inventions, **c** would lower research and number of inventions, and trade and education should be encouraged. (732)

13 e See text discussion. (732)

14 e Holds for ordinary capital, but not for knowledge capital. (730)

15 c See text discussion. (732)

16 d If real rate of interest > target rate, saving increases supply of capital, which leads to more capital per hour of work (and more real GDP per hour of work), decreasing real rate of interest since capital demand curve downward-sloping (draw a graph). (735–736)

ⓒⓣ **17 e** If real rate of interest > target rate, saving increases supply of capital, leading to increase in capital per hour of work (and in real GDP per hour of work), but no change in real rate of interest since capital demand curve flat (draw a graph). (737–739)

18 b Due to diminishing returns to capital (downward-sloping capital demand curve). (735–736)

19 d All conclude technological advances lead to increase in productivity of capital. (733–739)

20 d Technological advance shifts *PF* upward, and increases productivity of capital, which increases demand for capital, creating movement along *PF.* (735–736)

21 e This assumption makes technological change endogenous, and continuous. (737–739)

22 e This growth leads to decrease in real wages. (733–734)

23 d **a** due to its nature, which implies **b**, which in turn implies **c**—see text discussion. (737–739)

24 c Therefore as increase in capital stock, real rate of interest does not diminish. (737–739)

25 a Due to the different nature of knowledge capital. (735–739)

Short Answer Problems

1 The incentive system includes

- markets to send signals and enable people to specialize, exchange, save, and invest (all of which increase growth)
- property rights to ensure income and savings are not confiscated and hence encourage people to work and save
- monetary exchange to facilitate transactions and encourage trade

2 This source creates growth by increasing specialization. Eventually the level of specialization is so high, there is little left to be gained from further specialization.

3 Technology advances imply increases in the demand for labour, and the real wage rate. As the real wage rate goes up, the rate of population growth increases, increasing the supply of labour, decreasing the real wage rate back down to the subsistence wage rate, so workers are no better off than at the beginning.

4 Knowledge capital can be replicated without running into diminishing returns, so that the real rate of interest increases after the replication, which in turn brings more saving, and more supply of capital, and therefore capital per hour of work can increase without limit, implying that growth can increase without limit.

5 If the growth is due to increasing the amounts of capital and labour, then eventually these countries will run into diminishing returns to each of these inputs, which means that the increases in productivity will slow down, meaning that economic growth will also slow down.

6 The productivity function illustrates how per person output increases as the per person stock of capital increases, given the state of technology. If the amount of capital per worker increases, then the productivity of workers is increasing more rapidly, which means that per person output is increasing more rapidly—that is, there is faster economic growth. This effect is illustrated graphically by more rapid movements up along the graph of the productivity function.

ⓒⓣ **7** Table 32.1 is reproduced below as Table 32.1 Solution, with the calculations in place.

TABLE **32.1** SOLUTION

Year	1998	1999	2000
Capital per hour of work ($)	125	150	200
Productivity ($)	35	40	44.4
Contribution of capital	—	46.6%	100%
Contribution of technological change	—	53.4%	0

The percentage change in capital from 1998 to 1999 was 20 percent ((25/125) × 100), implying a resulting percentage change in productivity of 6.67 percent. The total change in productivity was 14.3 percent ((5/35) × 100), leaving 7.63 percent due to technological change. Capital's contribution was (6.67/14.3) × 100 = 46.6 percent, and technology's contribution was 53.4 percent.

The percentage change in capital from 1999 to 2000 was 33 percent ((50/150) × 100), implying a resulting percentage change in productivity of 11 percent. The total change in productivity was 11 percent ((4.4/40) × 100), leaving no contribution due to technological change. Capital's contribution was 100 percent.

8 The graphs are shown in Fig. 32.1. Note that from Table 32.1 the three yearly points must be where shown, and given our result about technological change in 1999 and 2000, the shift in 1999 and no shift in 2000 must be so.

FIGURE **32.1**

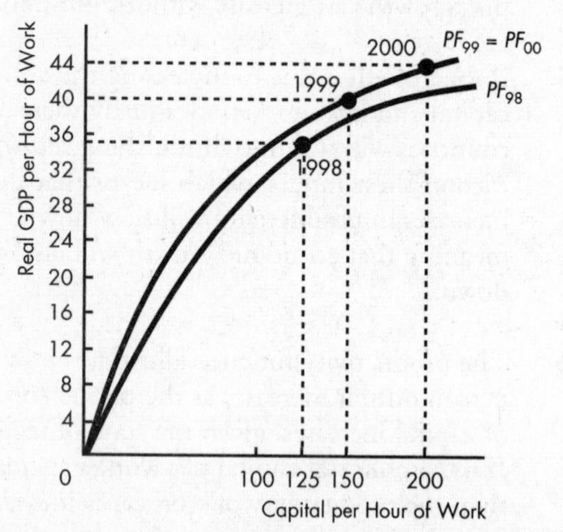

9 a Between 100 and 120, the percentage change in capital per hour is (20/100) × 100 = 20 percent, while the percentage change in real GDP per hour is (4/60) × 100 = 6.67 percent. One-third of 20 percent is 6.67 percent. Between 120 and 156, the percentage change in capital per hour is (36/120) × 100 = 30 percent, while the percentage change in real GDP per hour is (6/64) × 100 = 9.4 percent. One-third of 30 percent is 10 percent, a little bit higher than 9.4 percent. The one-third rule roughly holds.

b Figure 32.2 shows the original productivity function as PF_0, with the three points from the table graphed on it, with the current production point marked as year 1. A 20 percent increase in productivity would lead to a shift upwards in the productivity function to PF_1, shown in Table 32.3, and graphed as PF_1, with the new production point marked as year 2.

TABLE **32.3**

Capital per Hour of Work	Real GDP per Hour of Work
100	72
120	76.8
156	84

FIGURE **32.2**

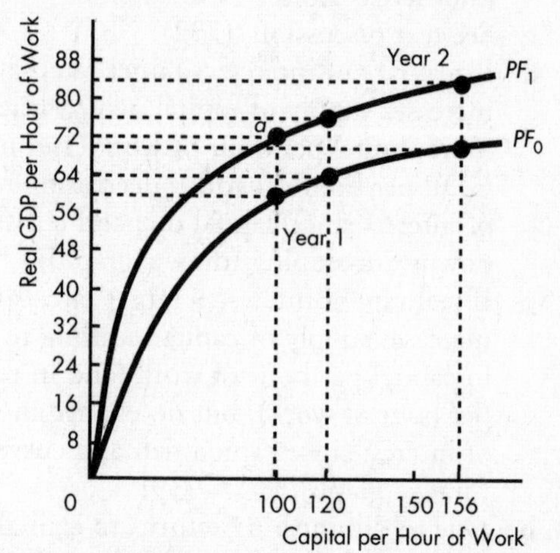

c The point is labelled as year 2 on the graph. We can see that the increase in real GDP per hour of work from 60 to 84 units is broken down into two components. The technological change is shown as the movement from the point Year 1 to the point *a*, a total change of 12 units or 50 percent (= (12/24) × 100) of the total change. The increase in capital per hour must be from 100 to 156 units to get production up to 84 units, and is shown as the movement from the point *a* to the point Year 2. This change is a total of 12 units or 50 percent (= (12/24) × 100) of the total change.

ⓒⓣ **10** The lower the target interest rate for savers, the more willing a person or country is to forgo current consumption and save for the future. Since Japan has a lower target rate, in any given situation Japan's saving rate will be higher. This higher saving in turn means the increase in the supply of capital in Japan is higher in any situation. Therefore, in general, Japan will have a higher capital stock per person than Canada, and it will generally be increasing each year at a higher rate, which in turn leads to a higher growth rate of real GDP per person in Japan than in Canada. Thus this argument seems to be true.

Chapter **33**

The Business Cycle

KEY CONCEPTS

Cycle Patterns, Impulses, and Mechanisms

There are different theories of the business cycle, emphasizing different outside initiating *impulses*, and different cycle mechanisms—but all theories emphasize the role of investment.

- In an expansion, investment is high and capital stock increases quickly, so there is an increase in capital per hour of labour, creating diminishing returns to capital and decreasing profit rate, leading to decreased investment, and eventually recession begins.
- In a recession, investment low and capital stock increases slowly or not at all, so that capital per hour of labour decreases, leading to increased marginal product of capital and profit rate, increasing investment and eventually recession ends.

Aggregate Demand Theories of the Business Cycle

Three *AD* theories of the business cycle.

- **Keynesian theory of the business cycle** regards volatile expectations as main cycle source.
- Keynesian impulse is Δ expected future sales/profits, which leads to Δ demand for capital and investment.
- Expectations are volatile because crucial events are unknown, impossible to forecast, and have large effects when they change.
- Keynesian cycle mechanism has two aspects:
  - Initial change in investment has a multiplier effect, which creates strong shifts in *AD* curve.
  - Due to sticky money wages, *SAS* curve is assumed nearly horizontal to left of potential GDP—therefore decrease in *AD* leads to unemployment equilibrium with no natural restoration to full employment until increase in expectations.
  - Above full employment, wages very flexible and *LAS* curve vertical—prices adjust quickly, economy stays near full employment.

Monetarist theory of the business cycle regards Δ money stock as main source of the cycle.

- Monetarist impulse is Δ growth rate of the money supply by the Bank of Canada.
- Monetarist cycle mechanism is:
  - Decrease in money growth increases interest rates (and exchange rate), so that investment demand and exports decrease, and multiplier effects shift *AD* leftward.
  - *SAS* curve upward-sloping, so decrease in *AD* decreases both real GDP and price level.
  - Money wage only temporarily sticky, so that unemployment equilibrium decreases money wage rate, and *SAS* adjusts rightward, with decreased price level, increase in real GDP towards full-employment equilibrium.

Rational expectations theories of cycle claim money wages set by **rational expectation** of price level (forecast based on all available information).

- **New classical theory of the business cycle** regards unanticipated fluctuations in *AD* as main source of cycle.
  - Unanticipated decrease in *AD* decreases price level, so real wage increases (since money wage constant), increasing unemployment.
  - Money wages adjust quickly because of unemployment, *SAS* shifts rightward, economy moves back to full employment.

- Anticipated change *AD* fully built into flexible money wages so *SAS* adjusts instantly—no change employment or real GDP, just in price level.
- Since economy adjusts quickly towards full employment on its own, there is little need for government policy.

◆ **New Keynesian theory of the business cycle** regards unanticipated *and* anticipated fluctuations in *AD* as sources of the cycle.

- Initial effects of decrease in *AD* the same as in new classical, but money wages are assumed sticky because of long-term nature of most wage contracts, so money wages adjust slowly in face of the shock, *SAS* curve adjusts slowly.
- If anticipated change in *AD*, because current wages built on past expectations due to long-term contracts, money wages cannot adjust to anticipated change, so anticipated change affects both real GDP and employment.
- Economy adjusts slowly towards full employment, implying need for government policy.

Real Business Cycle Theory

Real business cycle (RBC) theory regards random fluctuations in productivity as main source of the cycle.

◆ RBC impulse is Δ pace of technological change leading to Δ growth rate of productivity.

◆ Key assumption of strong *intertemporal substitution effect*—when current real wage or current real interest rate temporarily high, people increase labour supply strongly, and vice versa.

◆ Assumes money wage rate adjusts freely, so unemployment always at natural rate (only *LAS* matters).

◆ RBC recession starts with technological change that makes existing capital obsolete—temporary decrease in productivity.

- Fall in productivity decreases demand for labour and capital (which decreases real rate of interest).
- Decreasing real rate of interest decreases labour supply, leading to small decrease in real wage rate, large decrease in employment.
- Decrease in investment demand decreases *AD*, and decrease in employment decreases *LAS*, resulting in decreased real GDP, Δ price level can be up or down.

◆ Δ *AD* affects price level only, not real variables.

Critics of RBC theory argue:

◆ Money wages are sticky.

◆ Intertemporal substitution is too weak to account for big Δ employment.

◆ Technological shocks are *caused by AD* fluctuations.

Defenders of RBC theory argue that:

◆ It is consistent with facts (explains both growth *and* cycles) and microeconomic theory.

◆ Technological change does Δ *AD*, not reverse.

Recessions During the 1990s

Three causes of the 1990–91 Canadian recession:

◆ Bank of Canada's price stability policy decreases money growth, increases real interest rates.

◆ U.S. recession decreased exports.

◆ Canada–United States Free Trade Agreement increased uncertainty, decreased investment.

◆ The first two causes shifted *AD* leftward, while the third shifted both *AD* and *SAS* leftward—increased price level, decreased real GDP.

◆ In labour market, slowdown in inflation not anticipated, so real wages increased and employment decreased.

The Japanese recession of the 1990s started with a collapse in overvalued asset prices in 1990, creating a negative wealth effect that lowered consumption, investment, and therefore *AD* and potential GDP growth.

◆ Japan's fiscal policy was strongly expansionary (except for in 1996–97), while monetary policy had little impact.

◆ Some of the Japanese problem is due to delayed structural change slowing productivity growth.

The Great Depression

Great Depression had decrease in real GDP of 30 percent, increase in unemployment from 2.9 percent to 20 percent.

◆ Primary cause of Great Depression was increased uncertainty and pessimism creating decreased investment and consumer spending and stock market crash, which creates worsening uncertainty and pessimism.

◆ These unexpected shocks shift *AD* more than *SAS*, resulting in decreased real GDP and price level.

- Depression prolonged by further unexpected shifts leftward in *AD*, driven by collapse of the financial system and the money supply in the United States, and by an international tariff war.
- One view argues collapse in spending due mostly to pessimism and uncertainty, other view argues collapse of money supply was crucial.
- Great Depression unlikely to occur again due to the presence of Bank of Canada acting as a lender of last resort, deposit insurance, a higher government presence, and multi-income families.

To help you remember and understand these theories, use Table 33.1. It highlights the similarities and differences between the theories, and it helps to highlight how radically different real business cycle theory is.

Theories differ based on two primary factors: the source of the cycle (*AD* versus *AS*), and the responsiveness of the labour market (sticky versus flexible wages). Be sure you can catalogue and understand these theories.

Remember, these are theories, ***not*** statements of facts, and their explanations could be incorrect. Only proper empirical investigation over time will cast light on their validity.

HELPFUL HINTS

1 This chapter should be very rewarding to those who have worked hard to understand the previous chapters. It introduces no new analytical structure, but instead demonstrates the power of the fully developed aggregate demand and aggregate supply model by analysing some interesting macroeconomic episodes, including the Great Depression. You should be pleased that you have mastered this powerful analytical tool.

2 As you examine various macroeconomic episodes, focus on these key factors: Are changes primarily in aggregate demand, aggregate supply, or both? As you follow the changes, be sure you understand what is going on in the labour market that underlies the goods and services market. The labour market will tell you what is happening to the key variables of employment and unemployment.

3 This chapter contains competing theories that explain real-world events. There is no dispute over the facts such as the level of prices or real GDP. The dispute centres around what changes in the economy created the facts, and touches on what government policies might affect the economy.

SELF-TEST

True/False/Uncertain and Explain

1 During the early stages of a recession, interest rates tend to decrease but later they typically increase.

2 Unanticipated decreases in aggregate demand cause recessions only in new Keynesian theory, not in new classical theory.

3 A decrease in aggregate demand will cause a recession.

4 Monetarists and real business cycle theorists tend to believe that wages are flexible and adjust quickly.

TABLE **33.1**

Labour Market Structure		Theory	Primary Source of the Cycle
Wages are sticky	U above natural rate for long time periods	Keynesian and New Keynesian	AD Shocks
Wages are flexible	U above natural rate for short time periods	New classical and Monetarist	
	U = natural rate always	Real business cycle	AS Shocks

5 Most fluctuations in real GDP are the best possible responses of the economy to the uneven pace of technological change.

6 In order for the RBC theory to explain the behaviour of the labour market (real wages and employment), it must assume that the natural rate of unemployment increases in a recession.

7 The reduction in the growth rate of the money supply by the Bank of Canada in 1988 and 1989 was generally anticipated by households and firms.

8 The unemployment of the 1990–91 Canadian recession could have been avoided by an expansionary monetary or fiscal policy.

9 A recession today is likely to be less severe than during the 1930s because the government sector is larger today.

10 The stock market crash of 1929 was the cause of the Great Depression.

Multiple-Choice

Cycle Patterns, Impulses, and Mechanisms

1 Recessions tend to begin when

- **a** consumption expenditure decreases.
- **b** investment decreases.
- **c** investment increases.
- **d** government purchases decrease.
- **e** net exports decrease.

2 Typically in a recession, investment

- **a** is low at the start, but eventually increases as the recession ends.
- **b** is high at the start, but eventually decreases as the recession ends.
- **c** has the same pattern as in an expansion.
- **d** is constant.
- **e** moves around, but with no distinct pattern.

Aggregate Demand Theories of the Business Cycle

3 If the Bank of Canada unexpectedly decreases the money supply during a recession,

- **a** nothing will happen since the recession is already occurring.
- **b** the recession will deepen, as higher interest rates discourage investment.
- **c** the recession will deepen, because the value of the Canadian dollar will decrease.
- **d** the recession will end, as higher interest rates encourage more saving.
- **e** interest rates will decrease, since the change in the money supply was unexpected.

4 Which of the following news quotes *best* describes a *Keynesian* view of a recession?

- **a** "Rapid computerization is creating obsolete workers and higher unemployment."
- **b** "The unexpectedly tight fiscal policy is lowering spending and creating unemployment."
- **c** "The promised anti-inflationary policy of the Bank of Canada is lowering spending as promised."
- **d** "The promised cuts in government spending have helped lower consumer spending and created unemployment."
- **e** "Businesses are very worried about future sales and have lowered their purchases of capital equipment."

5 Which of the following news quotes *best* describes a *new classical* view of a recession?

- **a** "Rapid computerization is creating obsolete workers and higher unemployment."
- **b** "The unexpectedly tight fiscal policy is lowering spending and creating unemployment."
- **c** "The promised anti-inflationary policy of the Bank of Canada is lowering spending as promised."
- **d** "The promised cuts in government spending have helped lower consumer spending and created unemployment."
- **e** "Businesses are very worried about future sales and have lowered their purchases of capital equipment."

6 What is the key impulse in the *Keynesian* theory of the business cycle?

- **a** changes in expected future sales and profits
- **b** changes in the money supply
- **c** unanticipated changes in aggregate demand
- **d** anticipated changes in aggregate demand
- **e** changes in the pace of technological change

7 Consider Fig. 33.1. Which graph(s) represent(s) an economy that is recovering from a recession without any government involvement?

a (a)
b (b)
c (c)
d (d)
e (b) and (d)

FIGURE 33.1

(a)

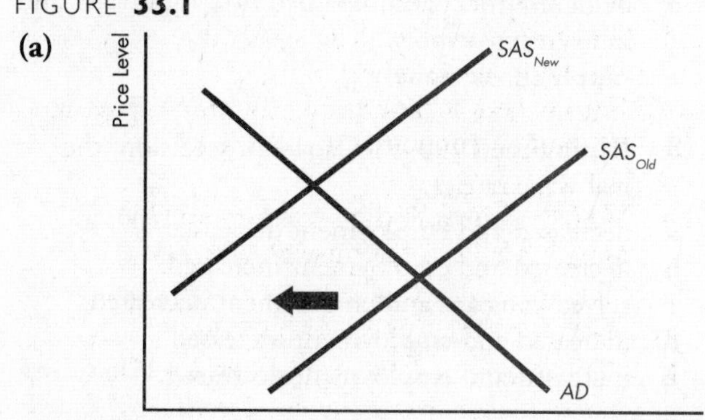

(b)

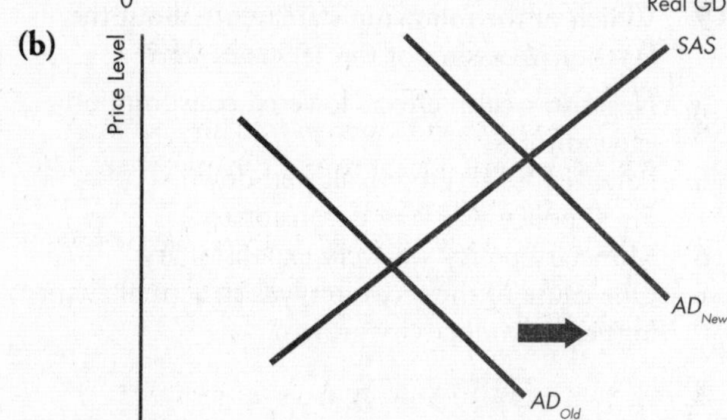

(c)

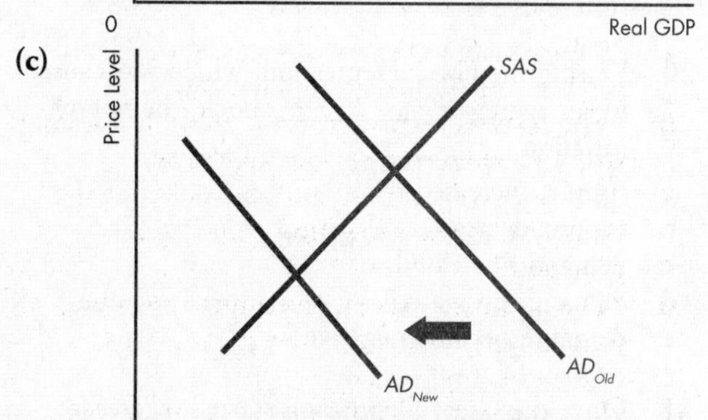

(d)

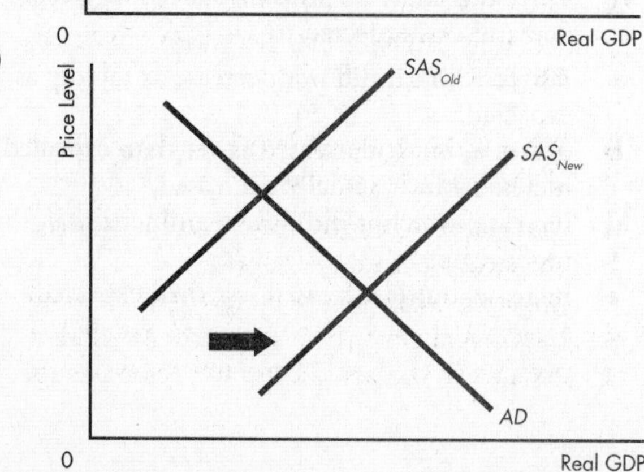

8 In Fig. 33.1, which graph(s) represent(s) an economy where the government is helping it recover from a recession?

a (a)
b (b)
c (c)
d (b) and (a)
e none of the graphs

9 In Fig. 33.1, which graph(s) represent(s) an economy entering a recession due to worsening consumer and investor expectations?

a (a)
b (b)
c (c)
d (b) and (d)
e none of the graphs

Real Business Cycle Theory

10 In Fig. 33.1, which graph(s) represent(s) an economy entering a recession due to a negative productivity shock?

a (a)
b (b)
c (c)
d (b) and (d)
e none of the graphs

11 An increase in aggregate demand causes GDP to increase by the least amount in the

a Keynesian theory.
b monetarist theory.
c new Keynesian theory.
d new classical theory.
e real business cycle theory.

12 In which theory of the business cycle is government policy likely to be most effective?

a Keynesian
b monetarist
c new classical
d new Keynesian
e real business cycle

13 If the intertemporal substitution effect is weak, then the RBC theory of the business cycle would have problems explaining

a a large decrease in employment in a recession.
b how a recession begins.
c why aggregate demand decreases in a recession.
d the automatic adjustment to full employment.
e what creates technological change.

14 The intertemporal substitution effect states that

- **a** in a recession, investment is low and the capital stock increases slowly, leading to a rising marginal product of capital.
- **b** money wages are based on a rational expectation of the price level.
- **c** a decrease in productivity leads to a decrease in the demand for capital, and a decrease in the real interest rate.
- **d** when current real wages and real interest rates are high, people decrease their labour supply strongly.
- **e** when current real wages and real interest rates are high, people increase their labour supply strongly.

15 According to the real business cycle theorists, the increase in the unemployment rate during a recession is due to an increase in the

- **a** deviation of the unemployment rate from the natural rate of unemployment resulting from a real wage rate that is too high to clear the labour market.
- **b** deviation of the unemployment rate from the natural rate of unemployment resulting from an increase in job market turnover.
- **c** natural rate of unemployment resulting from a real wage that is too high to clear the labour market.
- **d** natural rate of unemployment resulting from an increase in job market turnover.
- **e** rate of new entries into the labour market.

16 Which of the following news quotes *best* describes a *real business cycle* view of a recession?

- **a** "Rapid computerization is creating obsolete workers and higher unemployment."
- **b** "The unexpectedly tight fiscal policy is lowering spending and creating unemployment."
- **c** "The promised anti-inflationary policy of the Bank of Canada is lowering spending as promised."
- **d** "The promised cuts in government spending have helped lower consumer spending and created unemployment."
- **e** "Businesses are very worried about future sales and have lowered their purchases of capital equipment."

Recessions During the 1990s

17 The cause of the 1990–91 Canadian recession was an aggregate

- **a** supply shock, accompanied by a rightward shift in aggregate demand.
- **b** demand shock, accompanied by a leftward shift in aggregate supply.
- **c** demand shock alone.
- **d** demand shock, accompanied by a rightward shift in aggregate supply.
- **e** supply shock alone.

18 During the 1990–91 Canadian recession, the real wage rate

- **a** decreased and employment decreased.
- **b** decreased and employment increased.
- **c** stayed constant and employment decreased.
- **d** increased and employment increased.
- **e** increased and employment decreased.

19 Which of the following statements about the Japanese recession of the 1990s is *false*?

- **a** Negative wealth effects lowered consumption expenditures.
- **b** Potential GDP growth slowed down.
- **c** Fiscal policy was very expansionary.
- **d** Monetary policy was very expansionary.
- **e** One cause of the recession was structural change lowering productivity growth.

The Great Depression

20 During the Great Depression, which was caused by an aggregate _________ shock, the rate of inflation _________.

- **a** supply; increased
- **b** supply; decreased
- **c** demand; increased
- **d** demand; decreased
- **e** demand; became negative

21 Once the Great Depression started, aggregate demand was expected to

- **a** decrease, but it did not decrease as rapidly as expected.
- **b** decrease, but it decreased faster than expected.
- **c** increase, but it actually decreased.
- **d** increase, which it did due to an increase in the money supply.
- **e** increase, but it increased less than expected.

22 The Great Depression was prolonged by
- **a** a massive decrease in confidence following the stock market crash.
- **b** extended bank failures in the United States leading to a large decrease in the money supply.
- **c** structural reorganizing of the economy.
- **d** governments increasing their spending and cutting taxes.
- **e** a and b.

23 According to Friedman and Schwartz, the Great Depression was caused by
- **a** the stock market crash of 1929.
- **b** a decrease in the real money supply leading to higher interest rates and lower investment.
- **c** an increase in the real money supply leading to higher inflation.
- **d** decreases in business and consumer confidence.
- **e** imports decreasing.

24 The initial cause of the Great Depression was
- **a** a dramatic increase in the prices of raw materials during 1929.
- **b** a decrease in the money supply during 1929.
- **c** a decrease in investment and consumer spending because of uncertainty about the future.
- **d** the stock market crash of 1929.
- **e** none of the above.

25 Multi-income families reduce the probability of another Great Depression by
- **a** reducing the probability of everyone in the family being simultaneously unemployed.
- **b** investing more in the economy.
- **c** paying more taxes.
- **d** increasing fluctuations in consumption.
- **e** none of the above.

Short Answer Problems

1 What was the cause of the 1990–91 Canadian recession? What was the cause of the Great Depression?

2 What is the basic controversy among economists about the behaviour of the labour market during recession? Why is the controversy important for designing an appropriate anti-recessionary economic policy?

3 List the four important features of the Canadian economy that make severe depression less likely today.

4 How do government transfer payments in Canada help to reduce the severity of a recession?

ⓔ **5** Suppose that you have been selected to be the economic advisor to the prime minister, on the basis of your sterling performance in macroeconomics. You have been asked to evaluate the new Keynesian theory of the business cycle, and the real business cycle theory of the business cycle, and to explain what each theory argues should be the optimal government policy for a recession.
- **a** What does each theory argue is the likely cause of a recession, and why?
- **b** What does each theory argue is the best response to a recession? Why do the two theories differ? That is, what crucial differences in their approach to the economy leads to the different policy conclusions?
- **c** The prime minister wants to know which theory you think is better, and why. What would you tell him/her?

ⓔ **6** **a** If an individual was politically conservative and tended to distrust the government, which theory or theories of the business cycle do you think they would support?
- **b** If an individual was politically leftist and tended to trust the government, which theory or theories of the business cycle do you think they would support?

ⓔ **7** Table 33.2 gives data for a hypothetical economy in years 1 and 2.

TABLE **33.2**

	Year 1	Year 2
Real GDP (billions of dollars)	500	450
Price level (GDP deflator)	100	105

- **a** If the real business cycle theory is true, what happened to aggregate demand and aggregate supply in this economy?
- **b** If the new Keynesian theory is true, what happened to aggregate demand and aggregate supply in this economy?

ⓔ **8** Consider the labour market in the economy from Short Answer Problem 7.
- **a** If the real business cycle theory is true, what happened in the labour market? Is the unemployment natural or not?

b If the new Keynesian theory is true, what happened in the labour market? Is the unemployment natural or not?

ⓒ **9** Consider the economy from Short Answer Problem 7 again.

a Suppose instead that you knew that the expected price level in year 1 was 100 and that in year 2 it was 110. Would this information allow you to decide which theory was correct?

b Suppose instead that you knew that the expected price level in year 1 was 100 and that in year 2 it was 105. Would this information allow you to decide which theory was correct?

ⓒ **10** Some economists argue that real business cycle theory is false because it is unable to explain the events of the Great Depression, especially the events in the labour market. Briefly evaluate this argument.

ANSWERS

True/False/Uncertain and Explain

1 F Reverse occurs. (746)
2 F In both theories, unanticipated decrease means wages set too high, creating unemployment and recession. (750)
3 U F if RBC theory correct, T if others correct. (747–757)
4 T See text discussion. (747–757)
5 U Depends on whether RBC theory is correct. (750–757)
6 T All unemployment natural in RBC theory. (750–757)
7 F It was unanticipated, so unexpectedly low inflation led to recession. (757–758)
8 U Depends if sticky wage or flexible wage theories true. (757–758)
9 T Larger government sector leads to larger automatic stabilizers. (764–765)
10 F It was a symptom of uncertainty about future that was initial cause. (764)

Multiple-Choice

1 b See text discussion. (746)
2 a See text discussion. (746)
ⓒ **3 b** Decrease in real money supply increases interest rates, which decreases investment demand and aggregate demand. (748–749)
4 e Key impulse in Keynesian theory is Δ expected sales/profits. (747–748)
5 b Key impulse in new classical theory is unexpected change in *AD*. (750–752)
6 a See text discussion. (748–749)
7 d Recession leads to unemployment, which decreases real wages and shifts *SAS* rightward. (748–752)
8 b Expansionary policy shifts *AD* rightward. (748–752)
9 c Decrease in expectations decreases consumption and investment and shift leftward in *AD*. (748–752)
10 e In RBC theory, negative productivity shock shifts *LAS*, there is no *SAS*. (753–757)
11 e Vertical *AS* curve. (748–757)
12 a Flat *SAS* curve implies biggest swings in *Y* for a given Δ *AD*. (748–757)
13 a Intertemporal substitution means Δ current real wage or real interest rate leads to big Δ labour supply. (754–755)
14 e Definition. (754–755)
15 d All unemployment is natural, and real wage rate is always correct. (754–755)
16 a Key impulse is Δ pace of technological change. (753)
17 b Decrease in consumer and investor confidence shifts *AD* leftward, and increase in wages plus restructuring shifts *SAS* leftward. (757–759)
18 e See text discussion. (757–759)
19 d See text discussion. (760–761)
20 e Decrease in consumer and investor confidence shifts *AD* leftward so much it decreases price level. (762–765)
21 b See text discussion. (762–765)
22 e See text discussion. (762–765)
23 b They argue that monetary forces are most important. (762–765)
24 c See text discussion. (762–765)
25 a This arrangement leads to smaller decrease in consumer confidence when one member becomes unemployed. (762–765)

Short Answer Problems

1 The cause of the 1990–91 Canadian recession was an unanticipated reduction in the rate of growth of aggregate demand. This reduction resulted from the Bank of Canada's decision to reduce the rate of growth of the money supply, the U.S. recession lowering exports, and uncertainty lowering investment. Thus the aggregate demand curve did not shift rightward by as much as expected—it actually shifted leftward.

The major cause of the Great Depression was an unanticipated decrease in aggregate demand, which was the result of reduced investment and reduced consumer expenditure (especially on durable goods) due to uncertainty and pessimism. For several years (1930–32), aggregate demand decreased by more than expected. This change caused real GDP to decrease and the rate of inflation to decrease.

2 Economists disagree about the speed with which money wage rates adjust to clear the labour market. Some economists (Keynesians and new Keynesians) believe that money wages are sticky and adjust only slowly. As a consequence, when a recession occurs, the real wage does not decrease sufficiently to clear the labour market in the short run and there is an excess supply of labour (unemployment). Other economists (monetarists, new classical theorists, and real business cycle theorists) believe that wages are flexible. According to monetarists and new classical theorists, any recession is temporary in nature, because wages adjust downward quickly and the *SAS* shifts rightward, moving the economy towards full employment. According to RBC theorists, when a recession occurs, real wages adjust instantly. Any increase in unemployment is thus interpreted as an increase in natural unemployment.

These issues have significant implications for the design of an appropriate policy as a response to recession. If the Keynesians and new Keynesians are correct, then it may be useful to consider expansionary monetary or fiscal policies to counteract recession. If the others are correct, since the short-run aggregate supply adjusts quickly, or only the vertical *LAS* is relevant, expansionary monetary or fiscal policy will simply increase the rate of inflation and have no effect on real GDP or unemployment.

3 The four important features of the Canadian economy that make severe depression less likely today are: (1) bank deposits are insured; (2) the Bank of Canada is prepared to be the "lender of last resort"; (3) taxes and government spending play a stabilizing role; and (4) multi-income families are more economically secure.

4 When a recession arises, unemployment increases and disposable income declines. This decline in disposable income leads to a decline in consumption expenditure, which has a multiplied negative effect on real GDP. Transfer payments, however, reduce these secondary effects of a recession by moderating the decline in disposable income. As incomes decrease and unemployment increases, government transfer payments increase in the form of higher unemployment benefits or other welfare payments. As a result, the decline in consumption is less.

ⓒⓣ **5 a** The new Keynesian theory argues the likely source of a recession is a negative shock to aggregate demand, most likely due to unanticipated, and possibly anticipated, changes in one or more of the underlying variables. The RBC theory argues that the key impulse is a change in the pace of technological change, leading to a negative shock to the *LAS*.

b The new Keynesian theory also argues that money wages are sticky, so that the labour market and the *SAS* adjust slowly—the economy is in the recession for some time unless the government increases *AD*. The RBC theory argues that the labour market has already adjusted instantly, and output is at potential GDP. Any government policy will affect *AD*, but have no impact on real variables, so no policy should be carried out.

The crucial difference is due to the impulse variable that starts the recession—in one case it is an *AD* variable and can be counteracted by increasing *AD*, and in the other case it is a *LAS* variable, and increasing *AD* has no beneficial effect.

c This choice is personal, but should be based on an argument as to which impulse variable seems most likely to be correct to you.

ⓒⓣ **6 a** The monetarist, new classical, and RBC theories all argue government intervention to offset the business cycle is unneeded—a conservative person is most likely to support one of these.

b The Keynesian and new Keynesian theories all argue that government intervention can offset the business cycle, so a leftist is more likely to support one of these.

ⓒⓣ **7 a** Since real GDP has decreased, the *LAS* curve must have shifted leftward, since the only *AS* curve is a vertical *LAS* in a RBC world. For the price level to have increased, it must be the case that either the *AD* curve increased, or decreased so little that in combination with the *LAS* curve shift the price level has increased.

b In order to get both the price level rising, and real GDP decreasing, it must be the case that the *SAS* curve shifted leftward by more than the shift rightward in the *AD* curve (if there was one), indicating that people anticipated an increase in *AD* (leading to an increase in wages and a shift leftward in the *SAS*), but the actual increase was less than anticipated.

ⓒ **8 a** A real business cycle recession starts with a temporary decrease in productivity, which leads to a decrease in the marginal product of capital, and a decrease in the demand for capital (and therefore a decrease in the real interest rate), a decrease in the demand for investment, and a shift leftward in the *AD* curve. In addition, there is a decrease in the demand for labour because of the decrease in productivity, and a shift leftward in the supply of labour because of the lower real interest rate. These two shifts lead to a decrease in employment and a shift leftward in the *LAS* curve. All the unemployment is natural.

b In the new Keynesian labour market, money wages are based on wrong expectations, so that real wages are too high since the increase in money wages is more than the increase in the price level. Labour supply is greater than labour demand, creating the unemployment. All the extra unemployment is cyclical, not natural.

ⓒ **9 a** Since the actual price level was lower than the expected price level, the decrease in real GDP must have been due to an increase in aggregate demand that was less than expected. Therefore actual real GDP must be less than potential GDP—the new Keynesian theory is most likely to be correct.

b Since the actual price level is equal to the expected price level, then actual real GDP must equal potential GDP—the RBC theory is most likely to be correct.

ⓒ **10** In the Great Depression, the real wage rate stayed roughly constant, but the level of unemployment increased from about 3 percent to about 20 percent. If the RBC theory is correct, all of this unemployment is natural. This argument would require either an enormous negative productivity shock, or a huge intertemporal substitution effect in response to a large decrease in the real rate of interest. The real interest rate actually increased during the Great Depression, due to the large decrease in the money supply. It would seem unlikely that the RBC theory can explain the behaviour of the labour market in the Great Depression.

Chapter **34**

Macroeconomic Policy Challenges

KEY CONCEPTS

Policy Goals

Four main domestic macroeconomic goals:

- *Achieving highest sustainable rate of potential GDP growth* can dramatically improve real GDP per person.
- *Smoothing out avoidable business fluctuations* can reduce lost output and bottleneck costs.
- *Maintaining low unemployment* at the natural rate reduces losses from high unemployment and low unemployment (bottleneck costs), but difficult to estimate natural rate.
- *Maintaining low inflation* avoids transactions costs and costs of unpredictable inflation.

The goals of increasing real GDP growth, smoothing business cycle, and keeping unemployment at natural rate are complementary.

- Concentrating on real GDP growth is one core policy target, and inflation is the other.
- Real GDP growth goal conflicts with the inflation goal in the short run.

Policy Tools and Performance

Federal government uses **fiscal policy** (Δ tax rates, benefit rates, government expenditures), and Bank of Canada uses **monetary policy** (Δ money supply, interest rates) to achieve macroeconomic policy goals.

- Fiscal policy expansionary under Trudeau and contractionary under Mulroney—followed a cycle similar to business cycle.
- Monetary policy expansionary in late 1970s and anti-inflationary in early 1980s, and again in 1988–89.

Long-Term Growth Policy

Long-term growth comes from accumulation of physical and human capital, and new technology—government policy can affect these somewhat.

- National saving = private saving + government saving.
  - Private saving has increased since 1970, but rising government dissaving has meant national saving fluctuated around 20 percent until the early 1990s, when reduction in deficits raised national saving.
  - Decrease in government deficits leads to decrease in government dissaving, which leads to increase in national saving.
  - Decrease in specific taxes, decrease in inflation rate creates increase in private saving.
- Social returns to human capital > private returns—government wishes to increase investment in human capital by subsidizing schooling and health care.
- Investments in new technologies increase growth strongly due to lack of diminishing returns, spillovers—governments fund and provide tax incentives for research and development.

Business Cycle and Unemployment Policy

Three alternative policies to stabilize business cycle, and minimize cyclical unemployment:

- **Fixed-rule policy** is independent of state of the economy, such as always balancing budget.

- **Feedback-rule policy** specifies responses to changes in state of economy, such as cutting tax rates in a recession.
- **Discretionary policy** responds to state of economy in unique manner—learning from past mistakes in similar situations.

Fixed and feedback rules react differently to aggregate demand shocks.

- Suppose decrease in *AD* creates recession.
    - **Monetarists** advocate fixed rule of doing nothing—recession eventually ends when *AD* increases again (temporary shock), or *SAS* shifts rightward as wages decrease (permanent shock).
    - **Keynesian activists** advocate feedback rule of expansionary fiscal and monetary policy to try to counter swings in *AD*—returns economy to full employment quickly.
    - Economy stays in recession longer under fixed rule.
- In theory, feedback rules seem superior, but some economists argue that in practice they are flawed because they
    - require greater knowledge of potential GDP than currently available.
    - operate with time lags, making precise decisions difficult.
    - introduce unpredictability into long-term contracting.

Fourth argument against feedback rules is that they fail in face of aggregate supply shocks, such as productivity slowdowns emphasized by RBC theory.

- Feedback rule raises *AD*, leading to further increases in the price level, output unchanged.
- Fixed rule does nothing, leading to no further increases in price level, output unchanged.
- In reaction to these criticisms, **nominal GDP targeting** (keeping nominal GDP growth steady) is suggested—avoids excessive swings in inflation and real GDP.

Governments can also try to reduce natural rate of unemployment, by decreasing unemployment compensation and minimum wage.

Inflation Policy

Cost-push inflation arises from increase in resource prices shifting *SAS* leftward.

- Feedback rule raises *AD*, which further increases price level, output back to full employment. This rule *accommodates* inflation, encouraging further increases in resource prices.
- Fixed rule does nothing, no further increases in price level, eventually resource prices and *SAS* return to original levels.

In theory, inflation can be tamed by reducing the growth of aggregate demand in a credible and predictable manner, which reduces expectations and wage demands without creating recession.

- In practice, anti-inflationary policy leads to recession.
- Economic agents do not always believe an announced anti-inflationary policy (because past announced policies have been abandoned), so they do not revise expectations downward, and a recession results when actual *AD* less than expected.

HELPFUL HINTS

1 This chapter introduces only a few new concepts, and uses the model developed in previous chapters to analyse the effects of policy. This is the payoff for all your effort mastering that model.

However, this chapter asks the most important macroeconomic question: Can the government and the Bank of Canada carry out successful fiscal and monetary policies to reduce the problems of the business cycle?

2 Many complications arise in real-world use of the aggregate demand and aggregate supply models to make policy decisions. In previous chapters these complications were set aside. Here, we present a more realistic perspective of problems that confront a policy maker. Among the most important problems is the inability to predict the *magnitude* or the *timing* of factors that affect aggregate demand or aggregate supply.

a Our macroeconomic model is a good guide to the *qualitative* effects of changes in factors that affect aggregate demand and aggregate supply. For example, we know that an increase in the money supply will shift the aggregate demand curve rightward. When conducting policy, however, qualitative knowledge is not sufficient. We must also have *quantitative* knowledge. We must know *how much* a given increase in the money supply will increase aggregate demand.

While we may have an understanding of the direction of the effect, knowledge of the magnitude of the effect is much more difficult to obtain and much more limited. This problem reduces the potential to use policy to "fine-tune" the economy.

b In addition to direction and magnitude, we must also know *timing*. The full effect on aggregate demand of policy changes made today will not be immediate. Much, if not most, of that effect will occur only with considerable time lags. Thus it is important that policy makers be able to predict these time lags in order to be confident that the future effect of a policy change made today will be appropriate when the effect actually occurs.

Unfortunately, that is extremely difficult. Lags are often long, vary in length, and are unpredictable. As a result, policy makers may initiate a policy today which, when it has its effect sometime in the future, turns out to shift aggregate demand in the "wrong" direction because circumstances have changed. In such a case, policy will actually turn out to be destabilizing and therefore worse than doing nothing at all.

Consider the analogy of driving a car from your house to the house of a friend. The policy goal is to get the car from here to there. Suppose there is a single policy tool: the steering wheel. If you want the car to turn rightward, you turn the steering wheel clockwise. To turn leftward, you turn the steering wheel counterclockwise. Note that the direction in which the steering wheel turns is important, but so is the magnitude of the turn in order that the car can change direction without accident. Most of us can steer a car rather well because there is essentially no lag between the time we turn the steering wheel and the turning of the front wheels of the car. Now, consider how the task would be complicated if there is a time lag of one minute. In this case, a much better prediction of where the car will be one minute hence is required. Consider how the task would be complicated further if there is not only a time lag but the length of that time lag is variable, and thus unpredictable.

In the real world, cars do not operate with this type of lag, but policy makers do.

3 This chapter presents two opposing views of the usefulness of countercyclical policy. These views come partially from differing assumptions about one crucial factor—the speed with which the private sector reacts to macroeconomic shocks relative to the speed with which the government sector reacts.

The advocates of fixed rules (real business cycle theorists, monetarists, new classical theorists) believe on the whole that the private sector reacts quickly—people have rational expectations, process new information quickly because there are economic incentives to do so, sign flexible wage contracts that allow wages to react quickly to changes in the price level. They also believe that the government sector reacts slowly because of lags in recognizing problems, implementing policy, and carrying out policy. Fixed-rule advocates therefore arrive logically at the conclusion that feedback rules are doomed at best to impotence, and at worst can harm the economy.

The advocates of feedback rules (Keynesians, new Keynesian theorists) believe that the private sector reacts slowly—people sign long-term contracts that prevent wages from reacting quickly to changes in the price level. They also believe that the government sector can react more quickly than the private sector and, therefore arrive logically at the conclusion that feedback rules can make the economy better off by speeding up the recovery from recession.

As of yet, no clear-cut empirical evidence favours either viewpoint.

4 Many students (and policy makers!) fall into the trap of thinking that feedback rules must obviously be better than fixed rules, since theoretically feedback rules seem to be able to do everything fixed rules can, plus more. Do not fall into this trap! There are many problems with the actual implementation of feedback rules in the real world: they require very good knowledge of the economy (for example, the level of full employment); they introduce unpredictability into the economy; they can generate *bigger* fluctuations in aggregate demand, due to the lags mentioned previously; they do not work for aggregate supply shocks. These reasons make it far from obvious that feedback rules are better than fixed rules.

SELF-TEST

True/False/Uncertain and Explain

1 One of the goals of economic policy is to reduce the unemployment rate below its natural rate.

2 In Canada, fiscal policy is implemented by the federal government.

3 Increasing private saving and the government deficit will increase the economic growth rate.

4 The government may subsidize education because the social return to human capital is less than the private return.

5 Aggregate supply shocks are more frequent than aggregate demand shocks.

6 The use of feedback rules cannot make the business cycle worse.

7 A feedback policy rule is superior to a fixed rule.

8 The use of a feedback rule rather than a fixed rule increases the likelihood of cost-push inflation.

9 Recent Canadian monetary experience suggests that anti-inflationary monetary policy does not work.

10 Cost-push inflation cannot persist unless it is accommodated by the central bank.

Multiple-Choice

Policy Goals

1 Which of the following is a core macroeconomic policy target?

a unemployment constant at 6 percent
b steady growth in real GDP
c steady growth in nominal GDP
d a flexible exchange rate
e inflation at the natural rate

2 Which of the following is *not* a policy goal?

a achieving the highest sustainable growth rate of potential GDP
b smoothing out avoidable business fluctuations
c maintaining unemployment at the natural rate
d maintaining low inflation
e accommodating inflation

Policy Tools and Performance

3 Over the entire 1980s in Canada, fiscal policy featured

a constantly rising deficits.
b constantly decreasing deficits.
c an expansionary policy.
d a somewhat contractionary policy.
e small surpluses.

4 Over the entire 1980s in Canada, monetary policy featured

a rising growth of M2+.
b decreasing growth of M2+.
c rising inflation.
d zero inflation.
e a cycle in the growth of M2+ that tended to counter fiscal policy.

Long-Term Growth Policy

5 If the marginal tax rate ________, the returns to saving ________.

a increases; are unchanged
b decreases; decrease
c decreases; increase
d decreases; are unchanged
e increases; increase

6 Which of the following is *not* a determinant of long-term growth?

a national saving
b investment in human capital
c investment in consumer durables
d investment in new technologies
e government deficits

7 From 1970 to 1995, national saving averaged

a 10 percent.
b 15 percent.
c 20 percent.
d 25 percent.
e 30 percent.

8 Government deficits tend to lower economic growth because they
- **a** lower aggregate demand.
- **b** increase private investment and lower private saving.
- **c** are typically used to increase education spending.
- **d** lower expenditure on research and development.
- **e** crowd out national saving by using up some of private saving.

Business Cycle and Unemployment Policy

9 Which of the following is *true*? Monetary policy affects the economy
- **a** immediately, and fiscal policy affects it immediately.
- **b** immediately, and fiscal policy does not affect it at all.
- **c** immediately, and fiscal policy affects it after a lag.
- **d** after a lag, and fiscal policy affects it immediately.
- **e** after a lag, and fiscal policy affects it after a lag.

10 Nominal GDP targeting
- **a** is an example of a fixed rule.
- **b** is an example of a feedback rule.
- **c** is an example of a discretionary rule.
- **d** involves carrying out expansionary policy when inflation is high.
- **e** involves carrying out expansionary policy when unemployment is low.

11 An economy is initially in full-employment equilibrium when consumer confidence decreases. This is an example of an aggregate __________ shock and a __________ rule will raise real GDP back to its original value.
- **a** demand; fixed
- **b** demand; feedback
- **c** supply; monetary
- **d** demand; fiscal
- **e** supply; fixed

12 Which of the following is an example of a fixed policy rule?
- **a** Wear your boots if it snows.
- **b** Leave your boots home if it does not snow.
- **c** Wear your boots every day.
- **d** Take your boots off in the house if they are wet.
- **e** Listen to the weather forecast and then decide whether to wear your boots.

13 Which of the following is an argument *for* a feedback rule?
- **a** Feedback rules require greater knowledge of the natural rate than we have.
- **b** Feedback rules introduce unpredictability.
- **c** Aggregate supply shocks cause most economic fluctuations.
- **d** Aggregate demand shocks cause most economic fluctuations.
- **e** Feedback rules generate bigger fluctuations in aggregate demand.

14 Economists who favour fixed rules over feedback rules argue that policy lags are
- **a** shorter than the forecast horizon and that potential GDP is known reasonably well.
- **b** shorter than the forecast horizon and that potential GDP is not known.
- **c** longer than the forecast horizon and that potential GDP is known reasonably well.
- **d** longer than the forecast horizon and that potential GDP is not known.
- **e** equal to the forecast horizon and that full-employment real GDP is constant.

15 According to real business cycle theories,
- **a** any decline in real GDP is a decline in long-run real GDP.
- **b** wages are flexible but labour market equilibrium does not necessarily imply full employment.
- **c** fluctuations in aggregate demand change long-run real GDP.
- **d** fluctuations in aggregate demand cannot affect the price level.
- **e** feedback rules are best.

16 Which of the following would *lower* the natural rate of unemployment?
- **a** a feedback rule
- **b** a fixed rule
- **c** more unemployment compensation
- **d** reducing the minimum wage
- **e** accommodating inflation

17 Your desired inflation target is 1%. The correct nominal GDP target is nominal GDP growth of
- **a** 1 percent.
- **b** one percent plus the average rate of real GDP growth.
- **c** the average rate of real GDP growth.
- **d** the average rate of real GDP growth –1 percent.
- **e** –1 percent.

Inflation Policy

18 Cost-push inflation is best met by a(n)
- **a** fixed rule.
- **b** feedback rule.
- **c** discretionary policy.
- **d** political business cycle.
- **e** socialist approach.

19 Taming inflation is difficult because
- **a** the Bank of Canada is too independent.
- **b** the Phillips curve shows that unemployment always increases in the long run when inflation decreases.
- **c** the natural rate of inflation is equal to 6 percent.
- **d** surprise anti-inflationary policies work well.
- **e** central banks have credibility problems.

20 In practice, inflation reduction in Canada
- **a** worked in 1982 without any additional unemployment.
- **b** worked in 1990 without any additional unemployment.
- **c** never works.
- **d** works well due to its surprise nature.
- **e** none of the above.

21 Fighting inflation by using contractionary policy is
- **a** generally endorsed by politicians in election years.
- **b** generally unpopular with politicians in election years.
- **c** a zero-cost way to reduce inflation.
- **d** easily accepted by workers.
- **e** an example of a fixed rule.

22 Fixed-rule monetary policies are intended to
- **a** bring long-run inflationary pressures under control.
- **b** counteract temporary increases in aggregate demand.
- **c** counteract temporary decreases in real output.
- **d** offset supply shocks.
- **e** keep real GDP growth high.

23 If the Bank of Canada announces its intention to reduce the rate of growth of the money supply, but it lacks credibility, the short-run Phillips curve will
- **a** shift leftward.
- **b** shift rightward.
- **c** not move.
- **d** become vertical.
- **e** become flatter.

24 If the Bank of Canada announces its intention to slow the rate of growth of the money supply, and has full credibility, the short-run Phillips curve will
- **a** quickly shift leftward.
- **b** quickly shift rightward.
- **c** not shift.
- **d** become horizontal.
- **e** become vertical.

25 A fixed rule for monetary policy
- **a** requires considerable knowledge of how changes in the money supply affect the economy.
- **b** would be impossible for the Bank of Canada to achieve.
- **c** generates bigger fluctuations in aggregate demand.
- **d** would result in constant real GDP.
- **e** lowers the threat of cost-push inflation.

Short Answer Problems

1 The Bank of Adanac is attempting to lower inflation in Adanac from 8 percent, but the policy is leading to higher real interest rates and real wage rates.
- **a** What do the high real interest rates and real wage rates indicate about expectations and this policy?
- **b** Some business observers are objecting to this policy, arguing that the high real interest rates are choking off investment and future growth. Comment on the validity of this argument.

ⓒ **2** The prime minister of Adanac has made the following statement: "We are reducing government expenditure to reduce the deficit and create more jobs." How can this statement be true? Won't reducing government expenditure reduce aggregate demand and create unemployment?

3 In 1994, the personal saving rate by households was 7.5 percent of disposable income, but by 1998 it had fallen to 1.2 percent.[1]
- **a** Explain how this fall in the personal saving rate might hurt the economy.
- **b** What other factors might offset the damage created by this fall in the personal saving rate. (*Hint:* focus on the national saving rate.)

---

[1] *Source:* Statistics Canada's *The Daily*, March 1, 1999 and previous issues.

4 One purpose of policy is to stabilize aggregate demand. How can feedback rules result in even greater variability in aggregate demand?

ⓒ **5** If the Bank of Canada announced its intention to reduce the rate of inflation by reducing the rate of growth of the money supply, in theory expected inflation would decline accordingly, and thus a reduction in the actual rate of inflation could be achieved without a recession. Why doesn't this result seem to occur in practice?

6 Assume that the Bank of Canada knows exactly how much and when the aggregate demand curve will shift, both in the absence of monetary policy and when the Bank of Canada changes the money supply.

In this environment, compare the effects on real GDP and the price level of a temporary decline in aggregate demand that returns gradually to its previous level over several periods under fixed and feedback policy rules. Assume the economy is initially at long-run real GDP and that long-run real GDP is constant. Illustrate each of the following rules on a separate graph.

a First, assume that the Bank of Canada follows the fixed rule: Hold the money supply constant.

b Now, assume that the Bank of Canada follows the feedback rule: Increase the money supply whenever aggregate demand decreases and decrease the money supply whenever aggregate demand increases.

7 Consider an economy that experiences a temporary increase in aggregate demand. The Bank of Canada follows a feedback rule similar to the one given in Short Answer Problem **6b**, but now we assume that the Bank of Canada does not have perfect knowledge of how much and when aggregate demand will shift.

In year 1, the economy is in macroeconomic equilibrium at long-run real GDP, but, as the year ends, there is a burst of optimism about the future, which initiates a (temporary) increase in aggregate demand. As a result, in year 2, real GDP increases and the rate of unemployment decreases below its natural rate. Given its feedback rule, the Bank of Canada reduces the money supply "to keep the economy from overheating." The effect on aggregate demand, however, takes place only after a time lag of one year. In year 3, this burst of optimism returns to its previous level and thus so does aggregate demand. In addition, the monetary policy implemented in year 2 finally has its effect on aggregate demand in year 3. Analyse the behaviour of real GDP and the price level using three graphs: one each for years 1, 2, and 3. Assume that all changes in aggregate demand are unanticipated and that long-run real GDP is constant. Did a feedback monetary policy rule stabilize aggregate demand?

8 Assume that real business cycle theories are correct. There is a decrease in long-run real GDP due to droughts on the Prairies. First, graph the effect on real GDP and the price level if the Bank of Canada follows the fixed rule: Hold the money supply constant. Then, on the same graph, illustrate the effect on real GDP and the price level if the Bank of Canada follows the feedback rule: Increase the money supply whenever real GDP decreases and decrease the money supply whenever real GDP increases.

ⓒ **9** Consider a central bank that decides to start an anti-inflationary policy. Fig. 34.1 shows the initial state of the economy (point *a*) and the expected state next period (point *b*). The bank decides to carry out a gradual policy of inflation reduction. In year 1, it will reduce the growth in *AD* to 5 percent; in year 2 it will reduce the growth in *AD* to 2.5 percent. If the policy is unexpected initially, show on the graph what will occur over the next few years.

FIGURE **34.1**

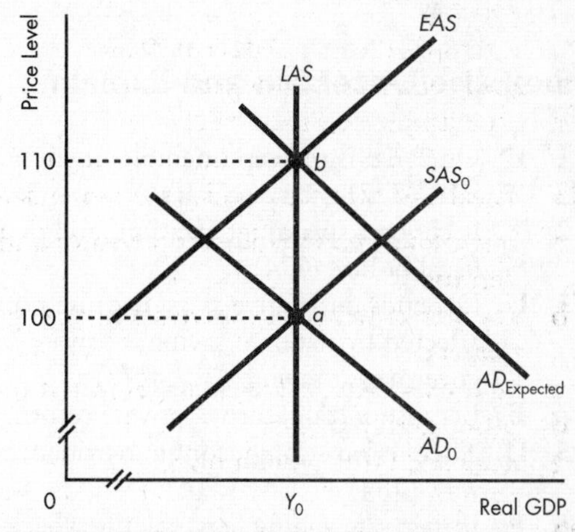

10 You are an economic advisor to the governor of the Bank of Adanac. Recently the economy has slid into a recession—unemployment has increased from 7 percent to 11 percent, the price level has increased from 125 to 135, and real GDP has decreased from 200 billion 1992 dollars to 180 billion 1992 dollars. Two other advisors are attempting to persuade the governor of the validity of their arguments. Ms. F. Ixed argues that there is an *LAS* shock, with full-employment real GDP decreasing and the natural rate of unemployment rising. Therefore, she insists, the optimal policy is to do nothing. Mr. F. E. Edback argues that this recession is due to an unexpectedly low *AD*, and that the optimal policy is to carry out an expansionary monetary policy.

a The governor, Jane Raven, has asked you to draw an *AS-AD* graph for each argument, to test its veracity. No explanation is necessary other than to indicate where the original and new equilibriums are. Are both arguments theoretically possible?

b Ms. Ixed also argues that even if it is an *AD* shock that has caused the current recession, using a feedback policy will just make the economy worse. She argues that timing lags in the implementation of monetary policy mean that the stimulation to aggregate demand will come too late to do any good and will just do harm. Explain and illustrate her argument on the graph you have drawn for Mr. Edback's explanation of the recession.

ⓒⓣ **c** Governor Raven wants your advice. Should she order an expansionary monetary policy? Why or why not?

ANSWERS

True/False/Uncertain and Explain

1 F One goal is to keep unemployment at natural rate. (772)

2 T It chooses spending, taxation, and deficit—fiscal policy. (774)

3 U Depends on relative sizes, because growth is affected by national saving = private saving + government saving. (776–778)

4 F Because social return > private return. (778)

5 U There is no strong economic evidence either way. (784)

6 F If there are timing lags, then feedback policy can arrive too late, which makes cycle worse. (782–784)

7 U It depends on which theory you think is best. (779–785)

8 T Feedback rules accommodate wage increases. (786–787)

9 F Inflation was lowered both in 1982–85 and in 1990–92, at the cost of increase in unemployment. (789)

10 T If not accommodated increase in unemployment leads to decrease in resource prices, which shifts *SAS* rightward, so price level returns to original level. (786–787)

Multiple-Choice

1 b See text discussion. (773)

2 e See text discussion. (772–773)

3 d See text discussion. (774–775)

4 e See text discussion. (775–776)

5 c Lower marginal tax rate leads to more after-tax earnings from saving. (777)

6 c See text discussion. (776–778)

7 c See text discussion. (776)

8 e Since national saving = private saving + government saving. (776–777)

9 e Due to policy lags and a short forecast horizon. (782–783)

10 b It depends on state of economy (**a** wrong), but not uniquely (**c** wrong). **d** and **e** should be contractionary. (785)

ⓒⓣ **11 b** Decrease in consumer confidence leads to decrease in consumption, so *AD* shifts leftward. A feedback rule will raise *AD* and counter shock. (780–781)

12 c Same choice regardless of circumstances. (780–781)

13 d Others are reasons *against* feedback rules. (782–783)

14 d Therefore policy arrives too late, and is often incorrect. (782–783)

15 a Because aggregate supply curves are all vertical at long-run real GDP. (784)

16 d See text discussion. (785)

17 b Nominal target = real GDP growth average + inflation target. (785)

18 a Keeping *AD* constant does not accommodate inflation and reduces chances of future cost-push inflation. (786–787)

19 e Time inconsistency means actual anti-inflationary policies are not always carried out, so it is hard to promise credibly to reduce inflation—expectations do not decrease easily, so that unemployment results when anti-inflationary policy is carried out. (787–789)

20 e In both 1982 and 1990, unemployment resulted due to credibility problems, but inflation was reduced. (784)

21 b Because it generally means unemployment, which voters weigh as being more important than inflation fighting. (789)

22 a They ignore short-run pressures. (786–789)

ⓒⓣ **23 c** Expectations will not change. (787–789)

ⓔ **24** a As inflation expectations are reduced. (787–789)

25 e Because it would not accommodate cost-push inflation, reducing likelihood of future cost-push inflation. (786–787)

Short Answer Problems

1 a The fact that real interest rates and real wage rates have shot up indicates that this policy is an unexpected policy—if it was expected and working, the rates would be constant.

b The higher real interest rates will indeed lower investment, meaning a lower capital stock and less growth of potential GDP in the long run. However, the lower inflation will also raise growth, as we saw in Chapter 30. The net effect is probably less growth in the short run, and more growth in the long run, once real interest rates come back down.

ⓔ **2** Indeed, in the short run, reducing government expenditures will reduce aggregate demand and create unemployment. However, in the long run, the lower government deficit will raise national saving, raise economic growth, and presumably create more jobs.

3 a A fall in the personal saving rate, *ceteris paribus*, will lead to a fall in the national saving rate. This fall will reduce capital accumulation, and therefore potentially reduce long-term economic growth.

b The national saving rate = private saving + government saving. Private saving includes personal saving by households and saving by firms. Therefore the fall in personal saving might be offset by higher firm saving, or higher government saving. In Canada over this time period, the overall government deficit fell from about 6 percent of real GDP to near 0 percent. This sharp rise in government saving completely offsets the fall in personal saving.

4 Policy actions, for example, an open market operation, will affect aggregate demand only after a time lag. Therefore a policy action taken today will have its intended effect sometime in the future. Therefore it is necessary to forecast the state of the economy for a year or two to be confident that the effect of today's policy action will be appropriate when the effect occurs. It is very difficult to do so, since the lags are long (one to two years) and unpredictable. As a result, there is a very good chance that today's policy action will have a future effect opposite to what originally seemed appropriate; in other words, policy could destabilize rather than stabilize aggregate demand.

ⓔ **5** The problem is that expected inflation may not decline as a result of the announcement by the Bank of Canada. There may be a credibility problem because expectations are much more strongly affected by the Bank's record of actions than by its announcement to take action. If people do not believe the Bank of Canada, they will not adjust expectations. Then if the Bank of Canada carries out the policy, a recession will result in spite of the fact that an announcement was made. In addition, sticky wages could slow down the adjustment of the labour market.

6 a The behaviour of real GDP and the price level under the fixed rule is illustrated in Fig. 34.2(a). The economy is initially at point *a* on the aggregate demand curve AD_0: the price level is P_0, and real GDP is at its long-run value denoted Y_0. The temporary decline in aggregate demand shifts the aggregate demand curve downward to AD_1.

Since the money supply is held constant under the fixed rule, the new equilibrium is at point *b*: the price level has decreased to P_1, and real GDP has decreased to Y_1. The economy is in recession. As the aggregate demand curve gradually returns to AD_0, the price level gradually increases to P_0 and real GDP gradually returns to Y_0.

FIGURE **34.2**

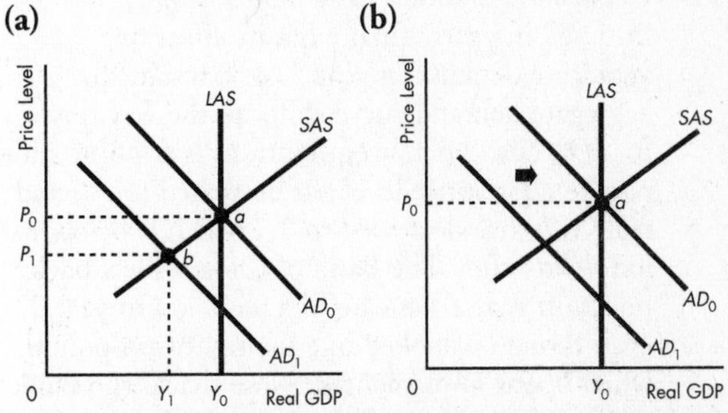

b The behaviour of real GDP and the price level under the feedback rule is illustrated in Fig. 34.2(b). Once again the economy is initially at point *a* on the aggregate demand curve AD_0. The temporary decline in aggregate demand temporarily shifts the aggregate demand curve to AD_1. Given the Bank of Canada's feedback rule, it will increase the money supply sufficiently to shift the AD_1 curve back to AD_0. Thus the Bank of Canada offsets the decline in aggregate demand and equilibrium remains at point *a*: the price level remains at P_0 and real GDP remains at Y_0.

As the temporary causes of the decline in aggregate demand dissipate, the aggregate demand curve will begin gradually shifting upward. The Bank of Canada will then decrease the money supply just enough to offset these shifts. As a result, the aggregate demand curve will remain at AD_0 and equilibrium will remain at point *a*. In these circumstances, the feedback rule is superior to the fixed rule—the recession is shorter in duration.

7 The state of the economy in years 1, 2, and 3 is illustrated in Fig. 34.3, parts (a), (b), and (c) respectively. The initial equilibrium (point *a*) in year 1 is illustrated in part (a). The economy is producing at long-run real GDP (Y_1) and the price level is P_1.

In year 2, the aggregate demand curve shifts to AD_2 in part (b) because of the burst of optimism. The Bank of Canada also reduces the money supply, but there is no immediate effect on aggregate demand. Therefore the equilibrium in year 2 occurs at the intersection of the AD_2 and *SAS* curves; at point *b* in part (b). Real GDP has increased to Y_2, which is above long-run real GDP, and the price level has increased to P_2.

In year 3, there are two effects on aggregate demand. First, the burst of optimism expires, pushing the aggregate demand curve back from AD_2 to AD_1. But, in addition, the Bank of Canada's reduction in the money supply initiated in year 2 finally has its effect on aggregate demand in year 3. As a result, the aggregate demand curve shifts all the way down to AD_3, and the new equilibrium is at point *c* in part (c). The price level has decreased to P_3, and real GDP has decreased to Y_3, which is below its long-run value. The Bank of Canada's feedback policy in year 2 has caused a recession in year 3 even though it looked like the rightward policy when it was implemented. Note that if the Bank of Canada had been following a fixed rule it would not have changed the money supply in year 2 and as a result, in year 3, the equilibrium would have been at point *a* and real GDP would have been at capacity. Because of imperfect knowledge on the part of the Bank of Canada and the delayed effect of policy changes, the feedback rule has resulted in destabilizing aggregate demand; policy has increased the *variability* of aggregate demand.

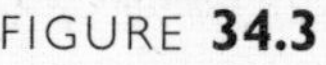
FIGURE **34.3**

(a)

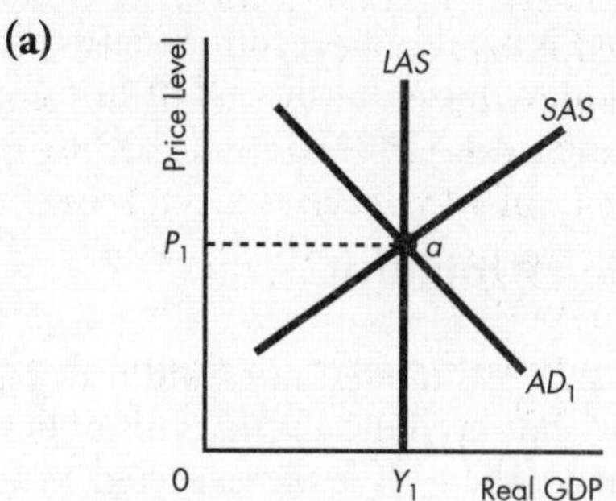

(b)

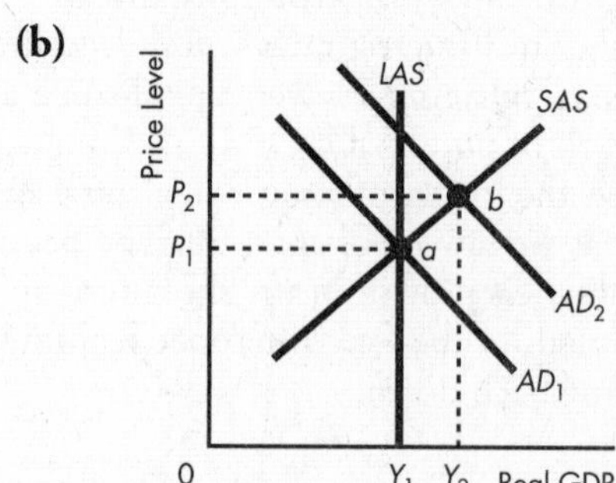

(c)

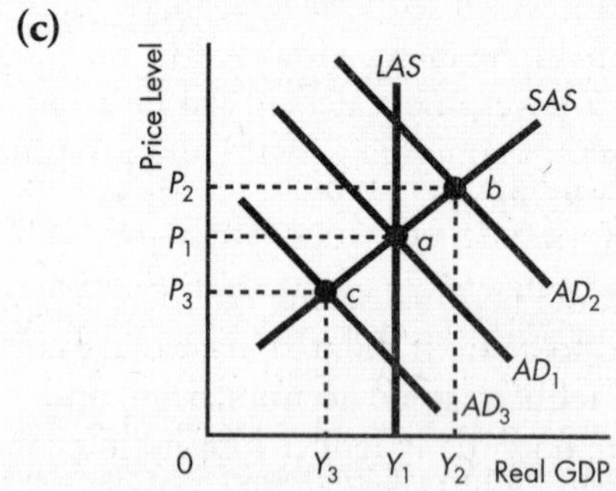

8 The effects on real GDP and the price level are illustrated in Fig. 34.4. Because we *assume* that real business cycle theories are correct, the only aggregate supply curve is the potential GDP curve. The economy is initially in equilibrium at the intersection of the AD_0 and LAS_0 curves, point *a*. Real GDP is Y_0, and the price level is P_0. Then long-run real GDP decreases, and the aggregate supply curve shifts leftward from LAS_0 to LAS_1.

If the Bank of Canada follows the fixed policy rule, it will hold the money supply constant, and the aggregate demand curve will remain at AD_0. Thus the new equilibrium is at point *b*: real GDP will decrease to Y_1 (the new capacity), and the price level will have increased to P_1. If, on the other hand, the Bank of Canada follows the feedback rule, the decrease in real GDP will lead the Bank of Canada to increase the money supply, which will shift the aggregate demand curve rightward from AD_0 to AD_1. Note that monetary policy will have no effect on long-run real GDP and thus no effect on the (long-run) aggregate supply curve. Therefore, under the feedback policy rule, the new equilibrium is at point *c*: real GDP has remained at Y_1, but the price level has increased to P_2. The consequence of a feedback rule is a larger increase in the price level (higher inflation) with no effect on real GDP.

FIGURE **34.4**

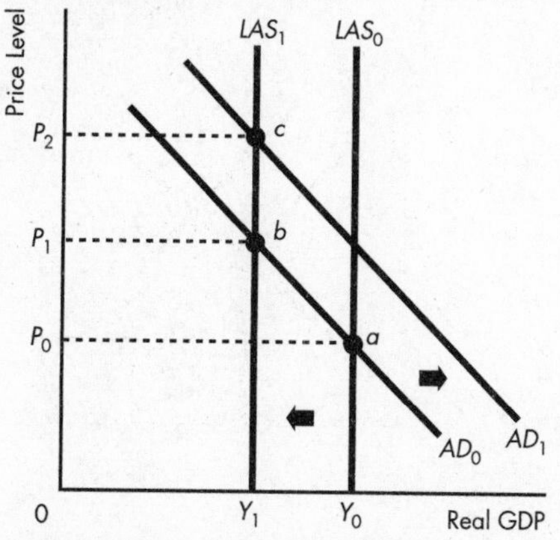

€t **9** The anti-inflationary policy is illustrated in Fig. 34.1 Solution. It will reduce the growth of aggregate demand to a (vertical) distance of 5 percent, at AD_1. However, the actual *SAS* will be based on the expected inflation rate of 10 percent, and therefore SAS_1 is the relevant curve, yielding an equilibrium in year 1 at the point *c*, with a decrease in real GDP, and an increase in inflation of (say) 7.5 percent, less than expected.

In year 2, the central bank allows aggregate demand to increase a further 2.5 percent, or a vertical increase to 107.625 (105 × 102.5), crossing the potential GDP curve at the point *d*, where AD_2 and *LAS* cross. The actual impact on the economy depends on how much adjustment of expectations occurs. If the policy is now credible, and if wages can adjust sufficiently, there will be a decrease in the short-run aggregate supply curve to SAS_2, and the equilibrium will be at the point *d*, with a very small inflation, and with real GDP back to the natural rate.

FIGURE **34.1** SOLUTION

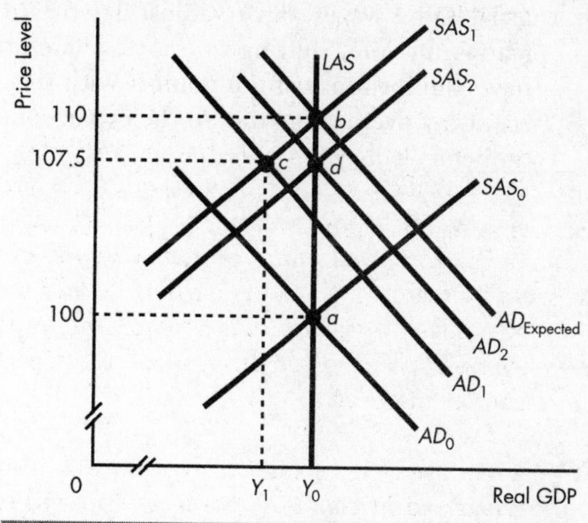

10 a Ms. Ixed's argument is shown in Fig. 34.5(a), and Mr. Edback's in Fig. 34.5(b). The original equilibrium is at point *a*, and the new equilibrium is at point *b*. As the graphs show, both arguments are theoretically possible.

FIGURE **34.5**

(a)

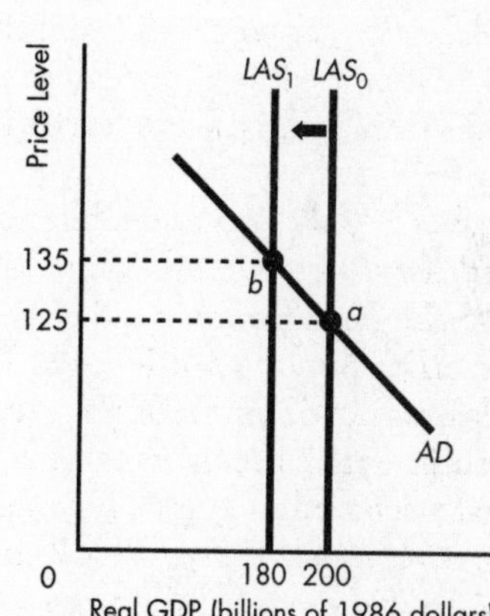

(b)

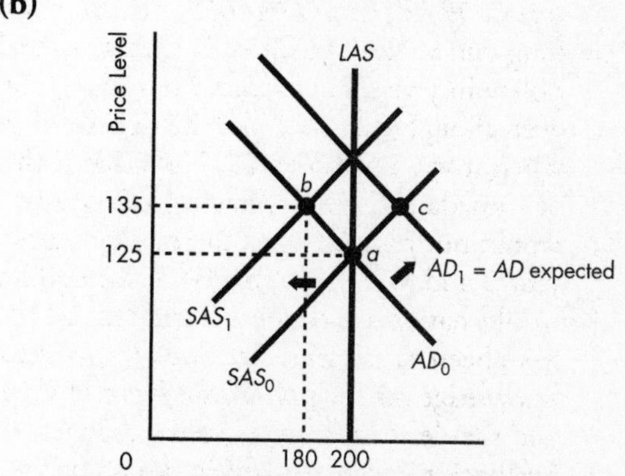

b She is arguing that the stimulation to aggregate demand (shown as the shift from AD_0 to AD_1) arrives after wages start to adjust downward (shown by SAS_1 shifting to SAS_0). Therefore the new equilibrium is at the point *c*, with the economy overheating due to the expansionary monetary policy.

c Which policy you pick is a matter of choice. However, your choice should be based on an economic argument. You would support a feedback rule if you thought (a) it was an *AD* shock, and (b) the central bank could successively and quickly implement the appropriate stimulation. You would pick a fixed rule of doing nothing if you thought (a) it was an *AS* shock, or (b) even if it was an *AD* shock, the Bank of Adanac reacts too slowly or incorrectly when carrying out the policy.

Part 9 Overview

Chapters 31–34

Understanding Aggregate Supply and Economic Growth

PROBLEM

You have been hired as an economic consultant for the premier of the country of Nova Calenia. The economy of Nova Calenia is experiencing a recession, reflected in the data in Table P9.1.

TABLE **P9.1**

	Year 1	Year 2
Price Level (GDP deflator)	125	130
Real GDP (billions of constant dollars)	200	190
Real wages (billions of constant dollars)	15.00	15.45
Employment (billions of hours)	100	90
Unemployment (%)	8	11

One set of advisors (new Keynesians) have told the premier that the recession has been caused by an unexpected decrease in aggregate demand (due to an unexpected decrease in exports), combined with sticky wages (inflation was expected to remain constant at 7 percent).

a Explain briefly to the premier what these advisors think is happening to the market for goods and services (draw an *AD-AS* graph as part of your answer), and in the labour market (just describe what is going on, do not draw a graph).

Another set of advisors (real business cycle theorists) have argued that the above events are due solely to an aggregate supply shock, driven by technological change.

b Explain briefly to the premier what these advisors think is happening to the market for goods and services (draw an *AD–AS* graph as part of your answer), and in the labour market (just describe what is going on, do not draw a graph of the labour market).

c After this explanation, and your sorry admission that there is no clear consensus on which view is correct, the premier wants to know what happens if

i he believes the new Keynesian argument, and follows the appropriate policy, *but* the real business cycle argument turns out to be correct, or if

ii he believes the real business cycle argument, and follows the appropriate policy, *but* the Keynesian argument turns out to be correct.

d The premier has decided to pick an expansionary policy, but cannot decide between raising government spending and cutting taxes. He wishes to know which policy is better if he is concerned about economic growth as well as the business cycle.

MIDTERM EXAMINATION

You should allocate 32 minutes for this examination (16 questions, 2 minutes per question). For each question, choose the one *best* answer.

1 Given that the use of all other factor inputs are held constant, a diminishing marginal product of labour might best be described as when the total number of hours worked in the economy

a increases and total output increases.
b increases and total output increases at a decreasing rate.
c increases and total output decreases.
d decreases and total output increases.
e increases and total output increases at an increasing rate.

2 New Keynesians would attribute the increase in unemployment during the 1990–91 Canadian recession to a(n)

a increase in the natural rate of unemployment.
b sharp decrease in real wages.
c increase in labour force participation.
d increase in real wages.
e increase in structural unemployment.

3 To _________ government saving, the government deficit must _________.

a decrease; decrease
b decrease; be zero
c increase; be zero
d increase; decrease
e increase; increase

4 Which one of the following quotations describes a shift rightward in an *LAS* curve?

a "The recent higher price levels have lowered production in the country."
b "The recent higher price levels have raised production in the country."
c "The recent higher price levels have led to compensating rises in wages, so that there have been no changes in labour hired or production."
d "The recent lower price levels have led to lower production in the country."
e None of the above.

5 Suppose that productivity has increased by 15 percent over last year. Capital per hour of work increased by 9 percent as well. The increase in capital was responsible for

a all of the increase in productivity.
b 4/5 of the increase in productivity.
c 1/3 of the increase in productivity.
d 3/5 of the increase in productivity.
e 1/5 of the increase in productivity.

6 Suppose that productivity has increased by 15 percent over last year. Capital per hour of work increased by 9 percent as well. An increase in technology was responsible for

a all of the increase in productivity.
b 4/5 of the increase in productivity.
c 1/3 of the increase in productivity.
d 3/5 of the increase in productivity.
e 1/5 of the increase in productivity.

7 How did monetary policy affect interest rates during the Great Depression?

a High real interest rates resulted from a decrease in the money supply.
b Low real interest rates resulted from a decrease in the money supply.
c High real interest rates resulted from an increase in the money supply.
d Low real interest rates resulted from an increase in the money supply.
e High real interest rates resulted from the positive inflation.

8 Which of the following supports the claim that feedback rules exaggerate fluctuations in aggregate demand? Policy makers

a use the wrong feedback rules to achieve their goals.
b must take actions today that will not have their effects until well into the future.
c do not really want to stabilize the economy.
d try to make their policies unpredictable.
e have enough knowledge of the economy.

9 Which theory of economic growth concludes that in the long run, people do not benefit from growth?

a classical theory
b neoclassical theory
c new growth theory
d all of the theories
e none of the theories

10 Which of the following quotations describes job rationing unemployment?

a "Wages are so good at the factory, they always have enough applicants to pick whomever they want for the job."
b "Professors with tenured jobs are taking pay cuts to help hire new professors."
c "Wages have failed to fall in the current economic downturn, creating extra unemployment."
d "People are taking too long to find jobs, because employment insurance is so generous."
e All of the above.

11 What is the key impulse in the RBC theory of the business cycle?

a changes in expected future sales and profits
b changes in the money supply
c unanticipated changes in aggregate demand
d anticipated changes in aggregate demand
e changes in the pace of technological change

12 Which of the following would tend to create the *worse* problems with persistent inflation?

a nominal GDP targeting
b fixed rules
c feedback rules
d credible policies
e promoting more saving

13 What is the key impulse in the new Keynesian theory of the business cycle?

a changes in expected future sales and profits
b changes in the money supply
c unanticipated changes in aggregate demand
d anticipated changes in aggregate demand
e changes in the pace of technological change

14 Which one of the following quotations describes a movement along the labour demand curve?

a "Recent higher wage rates have led to more leisure being consumed."
b "The recent lower price level has induced people to work more hours."
c "The recent higher real wage rate has induced people to work more hours."
d "The recent high investment in capital equipment has raised hiring by firms."
e None of the above.

15 The key difference between neoclassical growth theory and classical growth theory is that

a capital is not subject to diminishing returns under classical growth theory.
b capital is subject to diminishing returns under classical growth theory.
c increases in technology lead to increases in population that drive workers' incomes back down to the subsistence level in classical theory.
d technological advances are exogenous in classical growth theory.
e the one-third rule only holds in the neoclassical growth theory.

16 According to real business cycle theories, if the Bank of Canada increases the money supply when real GDP declines, real GDP

a will increase, but only temporarily.
b will increase permanently.
c and the price level will both be unaffected.
d will be unaffected, but the price level will increase.
e will decrease due to the inefficiencies introduced into production as a result.

ANSWERS

Problem

a The new Keynesian graph of the market for goods and services is shown in Fig. P9.1. Note the decrease in aggregate demand combined with the shift leftward in short-run aggregate supply (due to the rising wages).

The labour market has rising real wages, decreasing employment, and rising unemployment, implying that the real wage is too high (nominal wages were based on the expected inflation of 7 percent, but since *AD* was unexpectedly low, the actual inflation is only 4 percent, creating high real wages), creating (cyclical) unemployment above the natural rate.

FIGURE **P9.1**

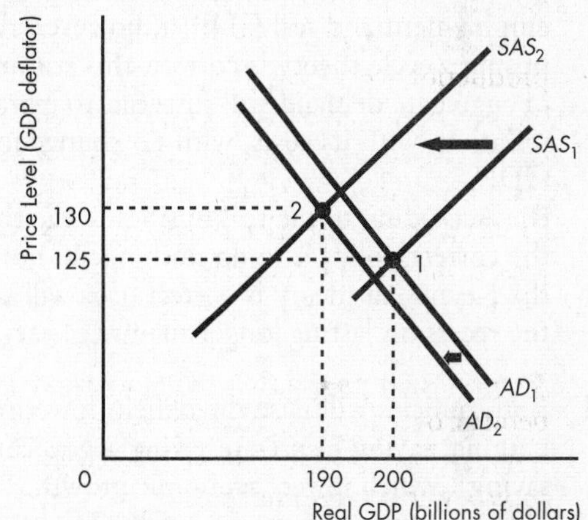

b The real business cycle graph of the market for goods and services is shown in Fig. P9.2. Note that aggregate demand is assumed constant, and that a shift leftward in long-run aggregate supply causes all the changes. This shift is due to a decrease in productivity, due to the technological change, which lowers the demand for labour and capital (lowering the real interest rate). There is also a decrease in the supply of labour, due to the lower real interest rate, creating a big decrease in labour hired, and therefore a shift leftward in the *LAS* curve. The extra unemployment is due to a rise in natural unemployment—the turnover rate has risen in the labour market.

FIGURE **P9.2**

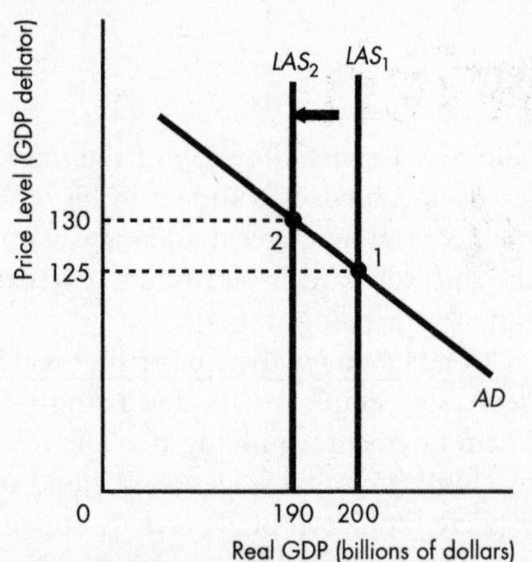

c **i** According to the new Keynesian theory, the right policy is to stimulate aggregate demand by an expansionary policy, attempting to raise the price level, lower real wages, and raise employment and real GDP. If, however, the real business cycle theory is correct, this stimulation of aggregate demand will just lead to extra inflation, with its costs, with no change in real GDP.

ii According to the real business cycle theory, the correct policy is to do nothing. If, however, the Keynesian theory is correct, this will result in the recession lasting longer than necessary.

d Both policies will raise the deficit, lowering national saving (= private saving + government saving), which lowers economic growth. However, cutting taxes on savings might raise private saving, and counter this effect.

Midterm Examination

1 b Definition. (700)

2 d Unexpectedly low inflation leads to unexpectedly high real wages and unemployment above the natural rate. (747–752)

3 d Because government saving = taxes – expenditures = – government deficit. (776)

4 e **a** is nonsense, **b**, **c**, and **d** are movements along curves. (714–719)

5 e By one-third rule, capital increase of 9 percent leads to increase in real GDP per hour of work of 3 percent, or 1/5 of increase in productivity. (730–731)

6 b Capital's effect was one-third of 9 percent or 3 percent, leaving 12 percent or 4/5 due to technology. (730–731)

7 a Banking failures led to a decrease in the real money supply, and even though nominal interest rates decreased, the negative inflation created higher real interest rates. (762–765)

8 b Therefore fluctuations in *AD* are exaggerated. (782–784)

9 a In long run, technological advances increase demand for labour and real wages, so population increases which lowers real wages. (733–739)

10 a This describes efficiency wages, a form of job rationing. (710)

11 e See text discussion. (753–757)

12 c Accommodates inflation. (786–787)

13 c Anticipated changes are not as important—see text discussion. (747–752)

14 e **a**, **b**, **c** are *LS* effect, **d** shift in *LD* curve. (699–701)

15 c In neoclassical theory, population growth is not driven by economic growth. In both theories, capital is subject to diminishing returns, technology is exogenous, and the one-third rule holds. (733–736)

16 d Because *LAS* is vertical. (784–785)

Chapter **35**

Trading with the World

KEY CONCEPTS

Patterns and Trends in International Trade

Imports are goods and services we buy from other countries, **exports** are what we sell to them.

- Canada's major exports and imports are motor vehicles and capital goods.
- Trade includes trade in services, such as tourism—an American vacationing in Banff is a Canadian export.
- Our major trading partner is the United States.
- **Balance of trade** = value of exports – value of imports.
  - Balance of trade > 0—we lend to foreigners.
  - Balance of trade < 0—we borrow from them.

Comparative Advantage and International Trade

International trade is generated by comparative advantage, based on divergent opportunity costs.

- Countries can produce anywhere on or inside production possibilities frontier (*PPF*).
- Slope of *PPF* = Δ *y*-axis variable/Δ *x*-axis variable = opportunity cost of one more *x*-axis variable.
- A country has **comparative advantage** in production of good for which it has lowest opportunity cost.

Gains from Trade

A country gains from trading by buying goods from other countries with lower opportunity costs and selling to other countries goods for which it has lowest opportunity cost.

- The post-trade price is between initial pre-trade opportunity costs of the two countries—buyer gains from price lower than their opportunity cost, seller gains from price higher than their opportunity cost.
- Countries pay for their imports with their exports—the value of exports = the value of imports (in the absence of international borrowing).

Both countries gain by specializing in production of goods in which they have a comparative advantage and trading for other goods—both can therefore *consume outside* their respective *PPF.*

- Since post-trade prices different than pre-trade opportunity costs, production levels adjust—countries produce more of their exported good, less of imported good.

Gains from Trade in Reality

Most trade can be explained by comparative advantage, but much trade is trade in similar goods, due to

- diversified tastes—demand for many (similar) products.
- economies of scale—cheapest way to make many products is specialization and trade.

Trade Restrictions

Governments restrict trade to protect domestic industries.

- Two methods of restriction—tariffs and nontariff barriers.
- Canada has always had tariffs, but they have decreased since 1930s, under **General Agreement on Tariffs and Trade**, an international agreement to limit government trade restriction.

- Its successor is World Trade Organization.
- North American Free Trade Agreement with the United States and Mexico further lowered barriers.

Tariffs are taxes on imported goods.

- Tariffs increase import price, which decreases imports and increases domestic production, which leads to net losses to importing country because opportunity cost of domestic production > original import price.
- Tariffs lower imports in home country, so exporters in foreign country sell fewer goods, which decreases their income and their imports = home country exports, so no change in balance of trade (if there is no international borrowing).

Nontariff barriers restrict supply of imports.

- **Quotas** set import quantity restriction, with quota licences distributed by home country.
- **Voluntary export restraints** (VERs) set export quantity restrictions, with foreign distributors having export licences.
- Quotas/VERs create decrease in import supply, which increases domestic price and domestic production.
  - Increase in import prices means owning quotas profitable.
  - Quotas and tariffs have similar effects on price and quantity, difference is who gains profit = selling price – import price.

The Case Against Protection

Trade restrictions are used despite losses of gains from trade for three somewhat credible reasons.

- Protecting strategic industries achieves national security—but hard to identify which industries are strategic and a subsidy would be more efficient.
- Protecting **infant industries** allows them to mature and allows learning-by-doing spillovers, but these seem unlikely in reality.
- Foreign companies may **dump** their products on world markets at prices less than cost in order to gain global monopoly.
  - But dumping is very hard to detect since costs are hard to determine.
  - Countervailing duties are tariffs imposed to discourage subsidized foreign companies.

A country may restrict trade for the following less credible reasons:

- To save jobs in import-competing industries—but free trade creates jobs elsewhere
- To compete with cheap foreign labour—but what counts is wages and productivity (comparative advantage)
- To bring diversity and stability (but economic size provides this)
- To penalize lax environmental standards—but trade and economic growth work better
- To protect a national culture—but protection just benefits producers
- To prevent rich countries from exploiting developing countries—but this ignores comparative advantage

The biggest problem with protection is that it invites retaliation.

Why Is International Trade Restricted?

There are two reasons for trade restrictions:

- Tariff revenue is an attractive tax base for governments in developing countries.
- To protect groups/industries that suffer disproportionately under freer trade.
  - Net gains from trade are positive, but there are losers in import-competing industries.
  - These losers have strong incentive to lobby and fight for protection (rent-seeking).
  - In Canada, employment insurance and interprovincial transfers provide some compensation for losses due to free trade.

The North American Free Trade Agreement

Despite protectionism pressures, Canada has free trade agreement with the United States and Mexico.

- This agreement involves
  - reducing common tariffs to zero in phases
  - reducing nontariff barriers
  - freer trade in energy and services
  - future negotiations on subsidies
  - a dispute-settling mechanism
- Total effects of the agreement are unknown at the moment, but they do include
  - large increase in total volume of trade
  - significant changes in some sectors leading to large adjustment costs

HELPFUL HINTS

1 This chapter applies the fundamental concepts of opportunity cost and comparative advantage discussed in Chapter 3 to the problem of trade between nations. The basic principles are the same for trade between individuals in the same country and between individuals in different countries.

Many people involved in debates about trade seem confused by the concept of comparative advantage, partially because they implicitly consider *absolute advantage* as the sole reason for trade. A country has an absolute advantage if it can produce all goods using less inputs than another country. However, such a country can still gain from trade. Consider California and Saskatchewan. California has a better climate and, with widespread irrigation, has an absolute advantage in the production of all agricultural products. Indeed, California frequently has more than one harvest a year! This absolute advantage would seem to imply that California has no need to trade with Saskatchewan. Saskatchewan, however, has a *comparative advantage* in the production of wheat. Therefore California will specialize in fruits and trade them for wheat. California could easily grow its own wheat, but the opportunity cost would be too high—the lost fruit crops. By specializing and trading, both California and Saskatchewan can gain.

2 One of the most crucial results of this chapter is that both countries can gain from trade. This gain occurs because the post-trade price is between the two countries' pre-trade opportunity costs. We can see this gain illustrated in Text Fig. 35.3, where the equilibrium price of a car is 3 tonnes of grain, between the pre-trade opportunity costs of 1 tonne and 9 tonnes.

Students are often puzzled by where to put the price when working through these types of examples. How did the authors come up with the value of 3? In a sense, it is an arbitrary value, one they just plucked out of a hat. Given the logic of voluntary trade, it must be between the two pre-trade values of 1 and 9. However, by redrawing the export supply and the import demand curves with different slopes, the authors might have arrived at a value of 6 tonnes. This result would have been equally logical, and equally valid.

In the real world, the strength of the demand for specific products by the consumers of each country will determine the slopes of the export supply and import demand curves, and determine just where the equilibrium price is set. In your examples, either you will be able to pick where you want the price to be (given that it must be between the two pre-trade opportunity costs) or you will be given some specific information telling you where the price is.

3 An important economic effect of trade restrictions is that a tariff and a quota have the same effect. A voluntary export restraint (VER) is also a quota, but it is a quota imposed by the exporting country rather than by the importing country.

All trade restrictions raise the domestic price of the imported goods and reduce the volume and value of imports. They also reduce the value of exports by the same amount as the reduction in the value of imports. The increase in price that results from each trade restriction produces a gap between the domestic price of the imported good and the foreign supply price of the good.

The difference between the alternative trade restrictions lies in which party captures this excess. In the case of a tariff, the government receives the tariff revenue. In the case of a quota imposed by the importing country, domestic importers who have been awarded a licence to import capture this excess through increased profit. When a VER is imposed, the excess is captured by foreign exporters who have been awarded licences to export by their government.

4 The major point of this chapter is that gains from free trade can be considerable. Why then do countries have such a strong tendency to impose trade restrictions? The key is that while free trade creates overall benefits to the economy as a whole, there are both winners and losers. The winners gain more in total than the losers lose, but the latter tend to be concentrated in a few industries.

Given this concentration, free trade will be resisted by some acting on the basis of rational self-interest. Even though only a small minority benefit while the overwhelming majority will be hurt, it is not surprising to see trade restrictions implemented. The cost of a given trade restriction to *each* of the majority will be individually quite small, while the benefit to *each* of the few will be individually large. Thus the minority will have a significant incentive to see that restriction takes place, while the majority will have little incentive to expend time and energy in resisting trade restriction.

5 To understand the source of pressures for trade restrictions, let us summarize those who win and lose from trade restrictions.

Under the three forms of restrictions (tariffs, quotas, and VERs) *consumers* lose, because the price of the imported good increases. *Domestic producers* of the imported good and their factors of production gain from all three, because the price of the imported good increases. *Foreign producers* and their factors of production lose under all three schemes, because their export sales decrease. Under quotas and VERs, the *holders of import licences* gain from buying low and selling high (they may be foreign or domestic). *Government* gains tariff revenue under tariffs and, potentially, votes under other schemes.

Given this list, it is hardly surprising that the main supporters of trade restrictions are domestic producers and their factors of production.

SELF-TEST

True/False/Uncertain and Explain

1 When a Canadian citizen stays in a hotel in France, Canada is exporting a service.

2 If a country can produce all goods cheaper than other countries, it will not benefit from trade.

3 Trading according to comparative advantage allows all trading countries to consume outside their *PPF.*

4 If Atlantis must give up 3 widgets to produce 1 watch and Beltran must give up 4 widgets to produce 1 watch, Atlantis has a comparative advantage in the production of watches.

5 Countries may exchange similar goods with each other due to economies of scale in the face of diversified tastes.

6 When governments impose tariffs, they are increasing their country's gain from trade.

7 A tariff on a good will raise its price and reduce the quantity traded.

8 A quota will cause the price of the imported good to decrease.

9 Elected governments are slow to reduce trade restrictions because there would be many fewer losers than gainers.

10 Japan is dumping steel if it sells steel in Japan at a lower price than it sells it in Canada.

Multiple-Choice

Patterns and Trends in International Trade

1 If we import more than we export,

- **a** we will be unable to buy as many foreign goods as we desire.
- **b** we will make loans to foreigners to enable them to buy our goods.
- **c** we will have to finance the difference by borrowing from foreigners.
- **d** our patterns of trade, including the direction of exports and imports, will be different than if exports equal imports.
- **e** none of the above.

2 Which of the following is a Canadian service export?

- **a** A Canadian buys dinner while travelling in Switzerland.
- **b** A Swiss buys a dinner while travelling in Canada.
- **c** A Canadian buys a clock made in Switzerland.
- **d** A Swiss buys a computer made in Canada.
- **e** A Canadian buys a Canadian computer in Switzerland.

Comparative Advantage and International Trade

3 In Atlantis, 1 unit of capital and 1 unit of labour are required to produce 1 watch, and 2 units of capital and 2 units of labour are required to produce 1 widget. What is the opportunity cost of producing one watch?

a the price of 1 unit of capital plus the price of 1 unit of labour
b 1 unit of capital and 1 unit of labour
c 2 units of capital and 2 units of labour
d 1/2 widget
e 2 widgets

4 Refer to Fig. 35.1. The opportunity cost of 1 beer in Partyland is ______, and the opportunity cost of 1 beer in Cowabunga is ______.

a dependent on where on the *PPF* we measure it; dependent on where on the *PPF* we measure it
b 100 pizzas; 25 pizzas
c 3 pizzas; 1 pizza
d 1 pizza; 1 pizza
e 1 pizza; 1/3 pizza

FIGURE **35.1** PARTYLAND AND COWABUNGA—*PPF* FOR BEER AND PIZZA

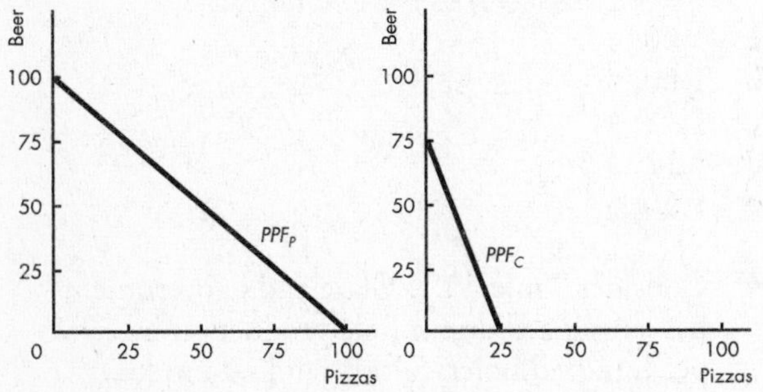

5 Refer to Fig. 35.1. The opportunity cost of 1 pizza in Partyland is ______, and the opportunity cost of 1 pizza in Cowabunga is ______.

a dependent on where on the *PPF* we measure it; dependent on where on the *PPF* we measure it
b 100 beers; 25 beers
c 3 beers; 1 beer
d 1 beer; 1 beer
e 1 beer; 3 beers

Gains from Trade

6 Refer to Fig. 35.1. If trade occurs between Partyland and Cowabunga,

a there will be a lot of drunk turtles.
b Partyland will supply both pizza and beer, because it has a comparative advantage in both.
c Cowabunga will supply both pizza and beer, because it has a comparative advantage in both.
d Partyland will supply pizza, and Cowabunga will supply beer.
e Partyland will supply beer, and Cowabunga will supply pizza.

7 Refer to Fig. 35.1. If trade occurs between Partyland and Cowabunga, the trade price for beer will be

a 1 beer for 1 pizza.
b 1 beer for 1/3 pizza.
c 1 beer for 3 pizzas.
d somewhere between 1 beer for 1 pizza and 1 beer for 3 pizzas.
e somewhere between 1 beer for 1 pizza and 1 beer for 1/3 pizza.

8 If Atlantis can produce everything cheaper than can any other country,

a no trade will take place because Atlantis will have a comparative advantage in everything.
b no trade will take place because no country will have a comparative advantage in anything.
c trade will probably take place, and all countries will gain.
d trade will probably take place, but Atlantis will not gain.
e trade will probably take place, but Atlantis will be the only one to gain.

9 International trade based on comparative advantage allows each country to consume

a more of the goods it exports, but less of the goods it imports than without trade.
b more of the goods it imports, but less of the goods it exports than without trade.
c more of the goods it exports and imports than without trade.
d less of the goods it exports and imports than without trade.
e more of either the good it exports or the good it imports, but not both.

Gains from Trade in Reality

10 We often observe countries trading virtually identical goods—for example, Canada exports cars to the United States and imports cars from them. This pattern of trade

- **a** indicates that the theory of comparative advantage is incorrect.
- **b** indicates most trade is due to absolute advantage.
- **c** reflects the presence of demand for only a few types of products.
- **d** reflects the presence of demand for a diversified set of products.
- **e** reflects the presence of diseconomies of scale.

Trade Restrictions

11 Consider Table 35.1. Under free trade, the international price of donut holes would be $____ per hundred donut holes, and _____ million holes would be exchanged.

- **a** 0.75; 6
- **b** 1.00; 3
- **c** 1.25; 4
- **d** 1.25; 5
- **e** 1.50; 4

TABLE **35.1** INTERNATIONAL TRADE IN DONUT HOLES

International Price (dollars per 100 holes)	Glazeland's Export Supply of Holes (millions)	Snorfleland's Import Demand for Holes (millions)
0.50	1	10
0.75	2	8
1.00	3	6
1.25	4	4
1.50	5	2
1.75	6	0

12 Consider Table 35.1. Snorfleland's donut hole producers manage to convince their government that there is a need to protect the domestic industry from Glazeland's cheap imports. (They argue that holes are a crucial food group.) In response, Snorfleland's government sets an import quota of 3 million donut holes. The resulting price of a donut hole in Snorfleland will be $_______ per hundred holes, and domestic production of donut holes will _______.

- **a** 0.75; decrease
- **b** 0.75; increase
- **c** 1.25; remain unchanged
- **d** 1.38; increase
- **e** 1.38; remain unchanged

13 Consider Table 35.1. Starting from the free-trade equilibrium, Glazeland's donut hole exporters convince their government that making donut holes is a way of life being threatened by the cruel vagaries of the international market and, therefore deserves to be subsidized. Glazeland's government responds by subsidizing donut hole production by $0.25 per hundred holes. The resulting *international price* will be approximately $_______ per hundred holes, and the quantity traded will be _______ million donut holes.

- **a** 1.00; 4
- **b** 1.00; 5
- **c** 1.12; 4
- **d** 1.12; 4.5
- **e** 1.50; 5

14 Consider Table 35.1. Glazeland's government has subsidized donut hole production by $0.25 per hundred holes. Snorfleland's domestic producers have responded by filing a suit with the government that domestic production has been hurt by the unfair subsidy. Snorfleland's government responds by charging a countervailing duty on Glazeland donut holes of $0.25 per hundred holes. The domestic price in Snorfleland after the net effects of the subsidy and the countervailing duty will be $______ per hundred holes, and Snorfleland will import ______ million holes.

- **a** 1.00; 4
- **b** 1.00; 5
- **c** 1.12; 4
- **d** 1.12; 5
- **e** 1.25; 4

15 Canada has an import quota of one million pairs of shoes per year, and is currently importing this many. An increase in the domestic demand for shoes will result in

- **a** no change in the domestic prices of shoes, but an increase in the quantity of shoes imported.
- **b** no change in the domestic prices of shoes or in the quantity of shoes imported.
- **c** an increase in the domestic prices of shoes and in the quantity of shoes imported.
- **d** an increase in the domestic prices of shoes and no change in the quantity of shoes imported.
- **e** an increase in the domestic prices of shoes and an uncertain change in the quantity of shoes imported, depending on whether the increase in demand is greater than one million pairs or not.

16 A tariff on watches which are imported by Atlantis will cause the

- **a** demand curve for watches in Atlantis to shift leftward.
- **b** demand curve for watches in Atlantis to shift rightward.
- **c** supply curve of watches in Atlantis to shift leftward.
- **d** supply curve of watches in Atlantis to shift rightward.
- **e** demand and the supply curve of watches in Atlantis to shift leftward.

17 When a *quota* is imposed, the gap between the domestic price and the export price is captured by

- **a** consumers in the importing country.
- **b** the domestic producers of the good.
- **c** the government of the importing country.
- **d** foreign exporters.
- **e** the person with the right to import the good.

18 When a *voluntary export restraint* agreement is reached, the gap between the domestic import price and the export price is captured by

- **a** consumers in the importing country.
- **b** the person with the right to import the good.
- **c** the government of the importing country.
- **d** foreign exporters.
- **e** the domestic producers of the good.

19 When a *tariff* is imposed, the gap between the domestic price and the export price is captured by

- **a** consumers in the importing country.
- **b** the person with the right to import the good.
- **c** the domestic producers of the good.
- **d** foreign exporters.
- **e** the government of the importing country.

20 Which of the following statements about international trade is *true*?

- **a** Tariffs will increase jobs in our export industries.
- **b** Quotas are better than tariffs because they do not raise prices.
- **c** Tariffs are needed to allow us to compete with cheap foreign labour.
- **d** No one gains from free trade between a poor and a rich country.
- **e** VERs raise prices as much as equivalent tariffs do.

21 Atlantis and Beltran are currently engaging in free trade. Atlantis imports watches from Beltran and exports widgets to Beltran. If Atlantis imposes a *quota* on watches, Atlantis' watch-producing industry will

- **a** expand, and its widget-producing industry will contract.
- **b** expand, and its widget-producing industry will expand.
- **c** contract, and its widget-producing industry will contract.
- **d** contract, and its widget-producing industry will expand.
- **e** expand, and its widget-producing industry will be unchanged.

The Case Against Protection

22 Which of the following is *not* an argument for protectionism?

- **a** to protect strategic industries
- **b** to save jobs in import-competing industries
- **c** to gain a comparative advantage
- **d** to allow infant industries to grow
- **e** to prevent rich nations from exploiting poor nations

23 Which of the following is a relatively *credible* argument for protectionism?

- **a** national security
- **b** helping infant industries grow up
- **c** to prevent exploitation of poor countries
- **d** to compete with cheap foreign labour
- **e** to save jobs in export industries

Why Is International Trade Restricted?

24 Why is international trade restricted?

- **a** because government revenue is costly to collect via tariffs
- **b** in order to get higher consumption possibilities
- **c** to realize the gains from trade
- **d** due to rent-seeking
- **e** because free trade creates economic losses on average

The North American Free Trade Agreement

25 Examining the implementation of the North American Free Trade Agreement has revealed that

- **a** Canada has been severely damaged by the agreement.
- **b** Canada has been helped enormously by the agreement.
- **c** free trade does not work.
- **d** all losers from free trade will be compensated.
- **e** there has been a large increase in trade, benefiting consumers, but at the cost of a high rate of job destruction in the late 1980s and early 1990s.

Short Answer Problems

1 Why can *both* parties involved in trade gain?

2 How does a tariff on a particular imported good affect the domestic price of the good, the export price, the quantity imported, and the quantity of the good produced domestically?

3 How does a tariff on imports affect the exports of the country?

4 It is often argued by union leaders that tariffs are needed to protect domestic jobs. In light of your answers to Short Answer Problems **2** and **3**, evaluate this argument.

5 Consider a simple world in which there are two countries, Atlantis and Beltran, each producing food and cloth. The *PPF* for each country is given in Table 35.2.

- **a** Assuming a constant opportunity cost in each country, complete the table.
- **b** What is the opportunity cost of food in Atlantis? of cloth?
- **c** What is the opportunity cost of food in Beltran? of cloth?
- **d** Draw the *PPFs* on separate graphs.

TABLE **35.2** ATLANTIS AND BELTRAN—*PPF* FOR FOOD AND CLOTH

Atlantis		Beltran	
Food (units)	**Cloth (units)**	**Food (units)**	**Cloth (units)**
0	500	0	800
200	400	100	600
400		200	
600		300	
800		400	
1,000		—	—

6 Suppose that Atlantis and Beltran engage in trade.

- **a** In which good will each country specialize?
- **b** If 1 unit of food trades for 1 unit of cloth, what will happen to the production of each good in each country?
- **c** If 1 unit of food trades for 1 unit of cloth, draw the consumption possibility frontiers for each country on the corresponding graph from Short Answer Problem **5**.
- **d** Before trade, if Atlantis consumed 600 units of food, the most cloth it could consume was 200 units. After trade, how many units of cloth can be consumed if 600 units of food are consumed?

7 Continue the analysis of Atlantis and Beltran trading at the rate of 1 unit of food for 1 unit of cloth.

- **a** If Atlantis consumes 600 units of food and 400 units of cloth, how much food and cloth will be consumed by Beltran?
- **b** Given the consumption quantities and the production quantities from Short Answer Problem **6b**, how much food and cloth will Atlantis and Beltran import and export?

8 Figure 35.2 gives the import demand curve for shirts for Atlantis, labelled *D*, and the export supply curve of shirts for Beltran, labelled *S*.

- **a** What is the price of a shirt under free trade?
- **b** How many shirts will be imported by Atlantis?

FIGURE **35.2**

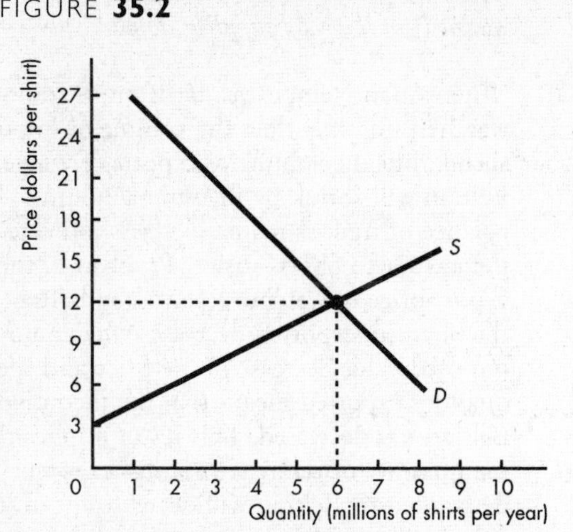

9 Suppose the shirtmakers in Atlantis of Short Answer Problem **8** are concerned about foreign competition and, as a result, the government of Atlantis imposes a tariff of $9 per shirt.

a What will happen to the price of a shirt in Atlantis?
b What is the price the exporter will actually receive?
c How many shirts will be imported by Atlantis?
d What is the revenue from the tariff? Who captures it?

10 Suppose that instead of a tariff, Atlantis imposes a quota of 4 million shirts per year.

a What will be the price of a shirt in Atlantis?
b What price will the exporter actually receive?
c How many shirts will be imported by Atlantis?
d What is the difference between the total amount paid by consumers and the total amount received by exporters—the "excess profit"? Who captures it?

ANSWERS

True/False/Uncertain and Explain

1 F Canada is importing (using) a service. (802)
2 U If comparative advantage exists, then gains from trade exist. (803–804)
3 T Countries will specialize and trade to consume outside *PPF.* (804–807)
4 T Atlantis has a lower opportunity cost (3 widgets < 4 widgets) = lost widgets per unit of gained watches. (804)
5 T Diversified tastes implies many products demanded. Economies of scale implies cheaper method of production, but requires specialization and trade. (808)
6 F Trade restrictions reduce gains from trade, which implies cost of purchasing export < current benefit – lost gains from trade. (809–812)
7 T Tariff shifts export supply curve leftward, which increases price and decreases quantity traded. (809–812)
8 F Quota decreases supply, which increases price. (809–812)
9 F They will be slow because losers' losses are individually much greater than winners' gains. (816–817)
10 F Dumping would be selling in Canada at lower price than in Japan. (813–816)

Multiple-Choice

1 c Necessary in order to get foreign exchange. General patterns of trade unchanged, once we have enough dollars. (802)
2 b **a** and **c** are imports, **d** and **e** are exports of a *good.* (802)
3 d Inputs required to make one watch could make 1/2 widget. (803–804)
4 e Opportunity cost of 1 more beer = lost pizza. For Partyland, going from 0 beer to 25 beers costs 25 pizzas (one for one). Do same calculation for Cowabunga. (803–804)
5 e Same type of calculation as in **4**. (803–804)
6 d Each specializes in where they have comparative advantage (lowest opportunity cost). (804–807)
7 e Trade price is between the opportunity costs in each country at the pre-trade equilibrium. (804–807)
8 c Even if Atlantis can produce everything cheaper, probably has comparative advantage in only some goods. (804–807)
9 c Consumption possibilities frontier is outside *PPF.* (804–807)
10 d See text discussion. (808)
11 c Equilibrium is where export supply = import demand. (809–812)
12 d Equilibrium is where quota = import demand increases price. Higher domestic price increases domestic production. (809–812)
13 d Subsidy increase in Glazeland's export supply by 1 million at each price leads to new equilibrium where new supply = old demand. (809–812)
14 e In addition to the change from 13, tariff decreases export supply by 1 million, exactly offsetting the subsidy. (809–812)

15 d Given quota, increase in demand leads only to increase in price. (809–812)
16 c Tariff increases domestic price = export price + tariff, or a shift leftward in supply curve. (809–812)
17 e Under quota, domestic government allocates the licence to import. (809–812)
18 d Because they have right to export. (809–812)
19 e They collect tariff revenue = import price – export price. (809–812)
20 e Tariffs decrease exports and jobs in export industries, quotas restrict supply and increase prices, cheap foreign labour doesn't necessarily hurt us, poor and rich countries can have comparative advantage and gain from trade. VERs restrict supply and raise prices just like tariffs. (809–812)
21 a Quota decreases imports, which increases domestic price of watches, which increases domestic production. Decrease in imports = decrease in Beltran's exports, which decreases its income and therefore its imports = decrease in Atlantis' exports, which decreases widget production in Atlantis. (809–812)
22 c See text discussion. (813–816)
23 a See text discussion. (813–816)
24 d See text discussion. (816–817)
25 e See text discussion. (818–819)

Short Answer Problems

1 For two potential trading partners to be willing to trade, they must have different comparative advantages; that is, different opportunity costs. Then they will trade and both parties will gain. If the parties do not trade, each will face its own opportunity costs. A price at which trade takes place must be somewhere between the opportunity costs of the two traders. This result means that the party with the lower opportunity cost of the good in question will gain because it will sell at a price above its opportunity cost. Similarly, the party with the higher opportunity cost will gain because it will buy at a price below its opportunity cost.

2 A tariff on an imported good will *raise its price to domestic consumers* as the export supply curve shifts leftward. The export price is determined by the original export supply curve. As the domestic price of the good increases, the quantity of the good demanded decreases, and thus the relevant point on the original export supply curve is at a lower quantity and a *lower export price.* This lower quantity means that the quantity imported decreases. The increase in the domestic price will also lead to an *increase in the quantity of the good supplied domestically.*

3 When Atlantis imposes a tariff on its imports of watches, not only does the volume of imports shrink, but the volume of exports of widgets to Beltran will shrink by the same amount. Thus a balance of trade is maintained. As indicated in the answer to Short Answer Problem **2**, the export price of watches received by Beltran and the quantity exported decreases when a tariff is imposed. This decrease in the price and the quantity exported means that the income of Beltran has decreased. This result implies that the quantity of widgets (Atlantis' export) demanded by Beltran will decrease and thus Atlantis' exports decline.

4 This argument has some truth to it. As Short Answer Problem **2** shows, the tariff will lead an increase in domestic production of the protected good, which will lead to an increase in jobs in that industry. However, as Short Answer Problem **3** shows, the same tariff will reduce foreign income, and reduce foreign purchases of our goods, reducing our exports and our export production, reducing jobs in the export industry. The net effect on jobs in unclear, but it is definitely not large.

5 a Completed Table 35.2 is shown here as Table 35.2 Solution. The values in the table are calculated using the opportunity cost of each good in each country. See **b** and **c** below.

TABLE **35.2** SOLUTION
ATLANTIS AND BELTRAN—PPF FOR FOOD AND CLOTH

Atlantis		Beltran	
Food (units)	**Cloth (units)**	**Food (units)**	**Cloth (units)**
0	500	0	800
200	400	100	600
400	300	200	400
600	200	300	200
800	100	400	0
1,000	0	—	—

b To increase the output (consumption) of food by 200 units, cloth production (consumption) decreases by 100 units in Atlantis. Thus the opportunity cost of a unit of food is 1/2 unit of cloth. This opportunity cost is constant as are all others in this problem, for simplicity. Similarly, the opportunity cost of cloth in Atlantis is 2 units of food.

c In Beltran a 100-unit increase in the production (consumption) of food requires a reduction in the output (consumption) of cloth of 200 units. Thus the opportunity cost of food is 2 units of cloth. Similarly the opportunity cost of cloth in Beltran is 1/2 units of food.

d Figure 35.3, parts (a) and (b) illustrate the production possibility frontiers for Atlantis and Beltran, respectively labelled PPF_A and PPF_B. The rest of the diagram is discussed in the solutions to Short Answer Problems **7** and **8**.

FIGURE **35.3**

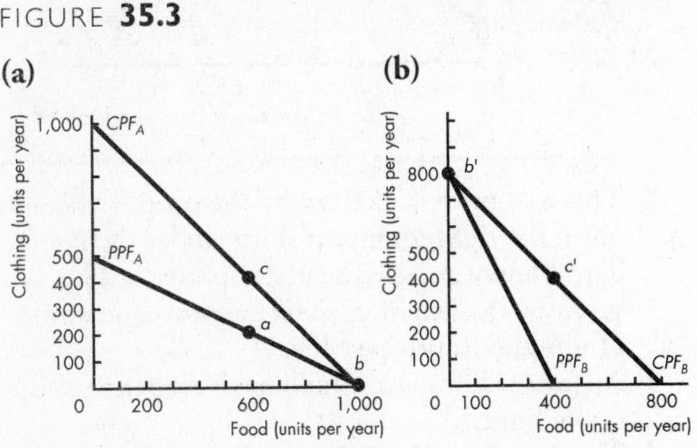

6 a We see from the solution to Short Answer Problems **5b** and **c** that Atlantis has a lower opportunity cost (1/2 unit of cloth) in the production of food. Therefore Atlantis will specialize in the production of food. Beltran, with the lower opportunity cost for cloth (1/2 unit of food), will specialize in cloth.

b Each country will want to produce every unit of the good in which they specialize as long as the amount they receive in trade exceeds their opportunity cost. For Atlantis, the opportunity cost of a unit of food is 1/2 unit of cloth, but it can obtain 1 unit of cloth in trade. Because the opportunity cost is constant, Atlantis will totally specialize by producing all of the food it can: 1,000 units per year, point *b* in Fig. 35.3(a). Similarly, in Beltran, the opportunity cost of a unit of cloth is 1/2 unit of food but a unit of cloth will trade for 1 unit of food. Since the opportunity cost is constant, Beltran will totally specialize in the production of cloth and will produce 800 units per year, point *b'* in Fig. 35.3(b).

c The consumption possibility frontiers for Atlantis and Beltran, labelled CPF_A and CPF_B, are illustrated in Fig. 35.3, parts (a) and (b) respectively. These frontiers are straight lines that indicate all the combinations of food and cloth that can be consumed with trade. The position and slope of the consumption possibility frontier for an economy depend on the terms of trade between the goods (one for one in this example) and the production point of the economy.

The consumption possibility frontier for Atlantis (CPF_A), for example, is obtained by starting at point *b* on PPF_A, the production point, and examining possible trades. For example, if Atlantis traded 400 units of the food it produces for 400 units of cloth, it would be able to consume 600 units of food (1,000 units produced minus 400 units traded) and 400 units of cloth, which is represented by point *c*.

d If Atlantis consumes 600 units of food, trade allows consumption of cloth to be 400 units, 200 units more than possible without trade. The maximum amount of cloth that can be consumed without trade is given by the production possibility frontier. If food consumption is 600 units, this outcome is indicated by point *a* on PPF_A. The maximum amount of cloth consumption for any level of food consumption with trade is given by the consumption possibility frontier. If food consumption is 600 units, this outcome is indicated by point *c* on CPF_A.

7 a Since Atlantis produces 1,000 units of food per year (point *b* on PPF_A), to consume 600 units of food and 400 units of cloth (point *c* on CPF_A) it must trade 400 units of food for 400 units of cloth. This outcome means that Beltran has traded 400 units of cloth for 400 units of food. Since Beltran produces 800 units of cloth, this result suggests that Beltran must consume 400 units of food and 400 units of cloth (point *c'* on CPF_B).

b Atlantis exports 400 units of food per year and imports 400 units of cloth. Beltran exports 400 units of cloth per year and imports 400 units of food.

8 a The price of a shirt under free trade will occur at the intersection of Atlantis' import demand curve for shirts and Beltran's export supply curve for shirts. This result occurs at a price of $12 per shirt.

b Atlantis will import 6 million shirts per year.

9 a The effect of the $9 per shirt tariff is to shift the export supply curve (*S*) leftward. This outcome is shown as a shift from *S* to *S'* in Fig. 35.2 Solution. The price is now determined by the intersection of the *D* curve, which is unaffected by the tariff, and the *S'* curve. The new price of a shirt is $18.

FIGURE **35.2** SOLUTION

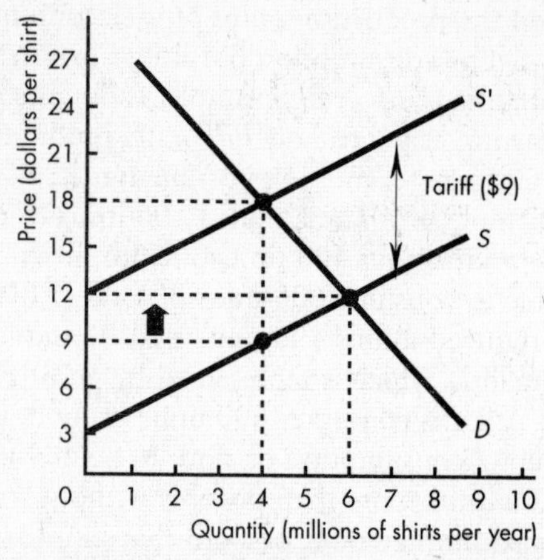

FIGURE **35.4**

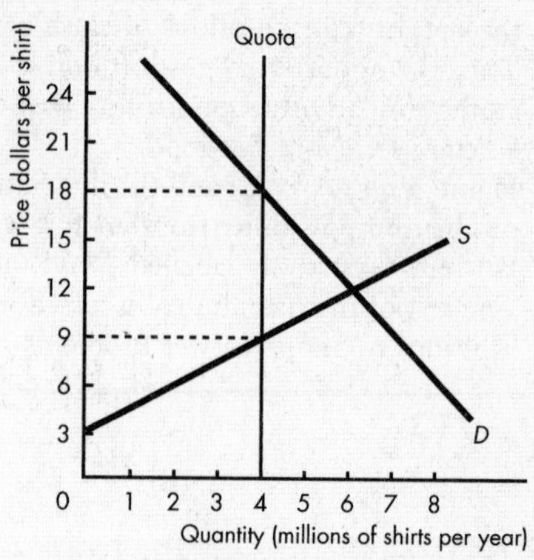

b Of this $18, $9 is the tariff, so the exporter only receives the remaining $9.

c Atlantis will now import only 4 million shirts per year.

d The tariff revenue is $9 (the tariff per shirt) × 4 million (the number of shirts imported), which is $36 million. This money is received by the government of Atlantis.

10 a The quota restricts the quantity that can be imported to 4 million shirts per year regardless of the price and is represented by a vertical line in Fig. 35.4 (which corresponds to Fig. 35.2). The market for shirts will thus clear at a price of $18 per shirt.

b This $18 price is received by the people who are given the right to import shirts under the quota. The amount received by the exporter is $9, given by the height of the *S* curve at a quantity of 4 million shirts per year.

c Atlantis will import 4 million shirts per year, the quota limit.

d The "excess profit" is $9 per shirt (the $18 received by the importer minus the $9 received by the exporter) × 4 million shirts, which is $36 million. This profit is captured by the importers who have been rewarded by the government of Atlantis because they have been given the right to import under the quota. This licence is essentially a right to make an "excess profit."

Chapter 36

The Balance of Payments and the Dollar

KEY CONCEPTS

Financing International Trade

The **balance of payments** accounts measure Canada's international transactions.

- **Current account**—net exports + net interest payments + net transfers.
- **Capital account**—foreign investment in Canada – Canadian investment abroad.
- **Official settlements account**—net changes in Canada's **official international reserves** (government's holdings of foreign currency)—if official reserves increase, official settlement balance is negative.

  Current account balance + Capital account balance + Official settlements balance = 0

- To pay a current account deficit we must borrow from abroad or decrease official reserves.
- Starting in early 1980s, a large current account deficit (and capital account surplus) emerged, but both had shrunk by 1996.

A country that in current year is borrowing more from rest of world than it is lending is a **net borrower**.

- **Net lender** lends more to rest of world than it borrows.
- **Debtor nation** has borrowed more than lent to rest of world over its history.
- **Creditor nation** has lent more over its history to rest of world than it has borrowed.
- Being a net borrower is not a problem if it is to finance investment that generates higher income to pay debts, as has been recent case in Canada.

Current account balance (*CAB*) is primarily determined by net exports ($NX = X - M$).

- Circular flow (Chapter 22) showed injections = withdrawals:
  - $I + G + X = S + NT + M$, or
  - Net exports = **private sector surplus** ($S - I$) + **government sector surplus** ($NT - G$).
- Since domestic and international sectors' deficits/surpluses are related, government deficit and current account deficit move together (**twin deficits**).

The Exchange Rate

Foreigners and Canadians exchange dollars for foreign currency in the **foreign exchange market**.

- **Foreign exchange rate** = price at which one currency exchanges for another (number of U.S. cents per Canadian dollar).
- **Currency depreciation** is decrease in value of dollar in terms of another currency, **currency appreciation** is increase.
- The Canadian dollar has fluctuated lots versus U.S. dollar since 1975, due to fluctuations in demand and supply for Canadian dollar.

The quantity of Canadian dollars demanded in the foreign exchange market = amount traders plan to buy at a given price—a *derived demand* based on demand for Canadian exports and Canadian assets.

- Decrease in exchange rate increases quantity demanded of Canadian dollars (movement down to the right along demand curve), because
  - exports become cheaper for foreigners, which increases demand for exports and therefore demand for dollars.

- expected profits increase from buying Canadian dollars and holding them until they appreciate, which increases demand.

◆ The demand curve shifts *rightward* if

- **Canadian interest rate differential** (Canadian interest rate – foreign interest rate) increases, increasing demand for Canadian assets.
- expected future exchange rate increases, which increases expected profits from buying Canadian dollars and holding them until they appreciate, which increases demand.

Quantity of Canadian dollars supplied in foreign exchange market = amount traders plan to sell at a given price in order to buy other currencies to buy imports and foreign assets.

◆ Increase in exchange rate increases quantity supplied of Canadian dollars (movement up to the right along supply curve), because

- imports become cheaper for Canadians, which increases demand for imports and therefore demand for foreign currency = increase in supply Canadian dollars.
- expected profits increase from buying foreign currency and holding it until it appreciates, which increases demand for foreign currency = increase in supply Canadian dollars.

◆ The supply curve shifts *leftward* if

- Canadian interest rate differential increases, decreasing demand for foreign assets, which decreases demand for foreign currency = decrease in supply of Canadian dollar.
- expected future exchange rate increases, which decreases expected profits from selling Canadian dollars and buying foreign currency and holding it until Canadian dollar depreciates, which decreases supply of Canadian dollar.

Market equilibrium determined by demand and supply, with exchange rate adjusting as required.

◆ Exchange rate is often volatile, because supply and demand often move together, creating big swings in value of exchange rate.

- Between 1986 and 1991, the Canadian dollar rose dramatically in value, mostly because people expected it to increase, increasing demand for Canadian dollar, decreasing supply of Canadian dollar.
- Between 1991 and 1998, opposite effect occurred.

Expectations of Δ exchange rate are due to the forces of **purchasing power parity** (two currencies have the same value or purchasing power) and **interest rate parity** (two currencies earn the same interest rate, adjusted for expected depreciation).

◆ If purchasing power parity does not hold, and Canadian dollar is more valuable than the U.S. dollar for purchases, then people expect it to appreciate, which increases demand for Canadian dollar, decreases supply—it does appreciate.

◆ Interest rate parity always holds (adjusted for risk), but if returns are higher in Canada, increased demand for Canadian dollar instantly increases exchange rate.

Bank of Canada can affect exchange rate in two ways:

◆ Use monetary policy to Δ interest rates, which leads to Δ exchange rate.

◆ Buy or sell Canadian dollars directly. Buying dollars increases demand, which increases exchange rate.

◆ Such interventions Δ official international reserves:

- Buying Canadian dollars requires selling foreign currency = decrease in official reserves.
- This requirement limits amount of intervention.

HELPFUL HINTS

1 There is an important difference between trade within a single country and trade between countries—currency. Individuals trading in the same country use the same currency, and trade is straightforward. International trade is complicated by the fact that individuals in different countries use different currencies. A Japanese vendor selling goods will want payment in Japanese yen, but a Canadian buyer will likely be holding only Canadian dollars. This chapter addresses this trade complication by looking at the balance of payments of a country, as well as the relation of the balance of payments to the foreign exchange rate.

2 It is important to understand foreign exchange rates as prices determined by supply and demand. They are prices of currency determined in markets for currency. The demand for Canadian dollars in the foreign exchange market arises from the desire on the part of foreigners to purchase Canadian goods and services (which requires dollars) and Canadian financial or real assets.

The supply of Canadian dollars is a special type of supply, because the offer to sell a

Canadian dollar is equivalent to an offer to buy foreign currency. Therefore it depends on the desire of Canadians to buy foreign goods and services (which requires foreign currency), and to buy foreign assets. Remembering that the supply of Canadian dollars equals the demand for foreign currency will help you to understand many of the shifts in the supply of Canadian dollars.

3 The exchange rate is often volatile because supply and demand often shift in a reinforcing manner, since they are both affected by the same changes in expectations. These changes in expectations are driven by two forces: purchasing power parity and interest rate parity. Each of these is a version of the law of one price, which states anytime there is a discrepancy in the price of the same good in two markets, natural economic forces (unless restricted) will eliminate that discrepancy and establish a single price. Suppose that the price in market 1 increases relative to the price in market 2. Individuals will now buy in the market with the lower price and not in the market with the higher price. This increase in the demand in market 2 and decrease in demand in market 1 will cause the two prices to come together. This principle applies to international markets as well: natural market forces will result in a single world price for the same good.

Suppose that purchasing power parity does not hold. For example, suppose that the price of good *A* in Canada is $6, and in Japan 600 yen, and that the exchange rate is currently 120 yen per dollar. The dollar price of *A* in Japan is $5 (600 yen/120 yen per dollar). People expect the demand for *A* in Canada to decrease (= a decrease in the demand for Canadian dollars), and the demand for *A* in Japan to increase (= supply of dollars rising), which would lead to the exchange rate depreciating towards 100 yen per dollar (the purchasing power parity level). Their expectations will lead to a decrease in the demand for the Canadian dollar and an increase in the supply of the Canadian dollar, so that the exchange rate will depreciate even before the demand for *A* adjusts!

The law of one price also holds for the price of assets such as bonds. If we recall that bond prices are inversely related to interest rates, we can see that interest rate parity is a version of the law of one price. For example, consider a situation where, taking into account the expected depreciation of the Canadian dollar, the Canadian interest rate was higher than the U.S. rate (which implies the price of bonds is lower in Canada). Buyers would demand Canadian bonds, raising their price and lowering Canadian interest rates. In addition, they would be selling U.S. bonds, lowering their price and raising U.S. interest rates. These actions occur until the interest differential between the two countries has shrunk to a level where it just reflects the expected depreciation of the Canadian dollar—interest parity holds.

4 In Chapter 28, we saw how monetary policy influenced the economy via changes in the interest rate, and changes in the exchange rate. This chapter fills in the details of the latter channel. A change in the money supply leads to a change in the interest rate, which changes the demand and supply of the Canadian dollar, and therefore the exchange rate, and therefore net exports and aggregate demand, and therefore inflation, real GDP, and unemployment.

There is also another international effect that the Bank of Canada often worries about. Imported goods play an important role in the production process, so that a depreciation of the Canadian dollar will increase the cost of production (Canadian dollar price of imports = foreign price/exchange rate). This depreciation in turn can create cost-push inflation. The Bank of Canada often works to offset temporary fluctuations in the exchange rate, or to smooth permanent changes in the exchange rate, in order to reduce fluctuations in the price level.

SELF-TEST

True/False/Uncertain and Explain

1 There can be no such thing as a balance of payments surplus/deficit, because by definition a *balance* of payments must always *balance.*

2 A larger government sector deficit leads to a higher current account deficit.

3 If a nation is a net borrower from the rest of the world, it will be a debtor nation.

4 If a country has a large government budget deficit and the private sector deficit is small, the balance of trade deficit will be large.

5 An increase in Canadian interest rates will lead to an increase in the demand for the Canadian dollar.

6 The demand and supply of Canadian dollars tend to move independently of each other.

7 Countries with currencies that are expected to appreciate will have higher interest rates than countries with currencies that are expected to depreciate.

8 If the yen price of the dollar is 100 yen per dollar and the price of a traded good is $10 in Canada, purchasing power parity implies that the price in Japan will be 1,000 yen.

9 If the exchange rate between the Canadian dollar and the Japanese yen changes from 130 yen per dollar to 140 yen per dollar, the Canadian dollar has appreciated.

10 If the foreign exchange value of the dollar is expected to increase, the demand for dollars increases.

Multiple-Choice

Financing International Trade

1 Which of the following statements is *true*? A high and persistent current account deficit implies Canada is

a a net borrower only.
b a net lender only.
c a debtor nation only.
d a creditor nation only.
e both a net borrower and a debtor nation.

2 $NX =$

a $C + I + G$
b $(S + I) - (NT + G)$
c $(G - NT) + (I - S)$
d $(S - I) + (G - NT)$
e none of the above.

3 Which of the following is one of the balance of payments accounts?

a current account
b borrowing account
c official lending account
d net interest account
e public account

4 Suppose Canada initially has all balance of payments accounts in balance (no surplus or deficit). Then Canadian firms increase their imports from Japan, financing that increase by borrowing from Japan. There will now be a current account

a surplus and a capital account surplus.
b surplus and a capital account deficit.
c deficit and a capital account surplus.
d deficit and a capital account deficit.
e deficit and a capital account balance.

5 The country of Mengia came into existence at the beginning of year 1. Given the information in Table 36.1, in year 4 Mengia is a

a net lender and a creditor nation.
b net lender and a debtor nation.
c net borrower and a creditor nation.
d net borrower and a debtor nation.
e net lender and neither a creditor nor a debtor nation.

TABLE **36.1**

Year	Borrowed from Rest of World (billions of dollars)	Lent to Rest of World (billions of dollars)
1	60	20
2	60	40
3	60	60
4	60	80

6 Assuming that Mengia's official settlement account is always in balance, in which year or years in Table 36.1 did Mengia have a current account surplus?

a year 1
b year 2
c years 1, 2, and 3
d years 1 and 2
e year 4 only

7 If Mengia's official settlement balance was in deficit every year, for which year or years in Table 36.1 can you say *for sure* there was a current account surplus?

a year 1
b year 2
c years 2 and 3
d years 1 and 2
e years 3 and 4

8 Suppose that a country's government expenditures are $400 billion, net taxes are $300 billion, saving is $300 billion, and investment is $250 billion. This country has a government budget

a surplus and a private sector surplus.
b surplus and a private sector deficit.
c deficit and a private sector surplus.
d deficit and a private sector deficit.
e surplus and a private sector balance.

9 Suppose that a country's government expenditures are $400 billion, net taxes are $300 billion, saving is $300 billion, and investment is $250 billion. Net exports are in a

a surplus of $150 billion.
b surplus of $50 billion.
c deficit of $150 billion.
d deficit of $50 billion.
e deficit of $250 billion.

10 The distinction between a debtor or creditor nation and a net borrower or net lender nation depends on

a the distinction between the level of saving in the economy and the saving rate.
b the distinction between the level of saving in the economy and the rate of borrowing.
c the distinction between the stock of net borrowing and the flow of net borrowing.
d the distinction between exports and imports.
e nothing really; they are the same.

11 If the current account is in deficit, and the capital account is also in deficit, then the change in official reserves is

a negative.
b positive.
c probably close to zero, but could be either negative or positive.
d zero.
e not affected.

The Exchange Rate

12 Suppose that the dollar-yen foreign exchange rate changes from 140 yen per dollar to 130 yen per dollar. Then the yen has

a depreciated against the dollar, and the dollar has appreciated against the yen.
b depreciated against the dollar, and the dollar has depreciated against the yen.
c appreciated against the dollar, and the dollar has appreciated against the yen.
d appreciated against the dollar, and the dollar has depreciated against the yen.
e neither appreciated nor depreciated, but the dollar has depreciated against the yen.

13 Suppose the exchange rate between the Canadian dollar and the British pound is 0.5 pounds per dollar. If a radio sells for 38 pounds in Britain, what is the dollar price of the radio?

a $19
b $26
c $38
d $57
e $76

14 The market in which the currency of one country is exchanged for the currency of another is called the

a money market.
b capital market.
c foreign exchange market.
d forward exchange market.
e international trading market.

15 If the Bank of Canada wishes to increase the exchange rate, it should

a lower interest rates.
b increase the money supply.
c buy foreign exchange.
d sell Canadian dollars.
e buy Canadian dollars.

16 Which of the following quotations best describes the purchasing power parity effect in action?

- **a** "The recent high Canadian interest rate has increased the demand for the Canadian dollar."
- **b** "The market feeling is that the Canadian dollar is overvalued and will likely depreciate."
- **c** "The price of bananas is the same in Canada and the United States, adjusting for the exchange rate."
- **d** "The expected depreciation of the Canadian dollar is currently lowering demand for it."
- **e** None of the above.

17 If you think that the exchange rate will depreciate over the next month, you can expect to make money by

- **a** only buying Canadian dollars.
- **b** only buying U.S. dollars.
- **c** only selling Canadian dollars.
- **d** only selling U.S. dollars.
- **e** both buying U.S. dollars and selling Canadian dollars.

18 Consider Table 36.2. Between 1994 and 1995, the Canadian dollar has __________ versus the mark and __________ versus the yen.

- **a** appreciated; depreciated
- **b** appreciated; appreciated
- **c** depreciated; depreciated
- **d** depreciated; appreciated
- **e** not changed; not changed

TABLE **36.2**

Currency	1994 Exchange Rate	1995 Exchange Rate
German Mark	2 marks/dollar	3 marks/dollar
Japanese Yen	120 yen/dollar	90 yen/dollar

19 Consider Table 36.2. Between 1994 and 1995, the yen

- **a** must have depreciated in value versus the mark.
- **b** must have appreciated in value versus the mark.
- **c** may or may not have appreciated in value versus the mark.
- **d** will have appreciated in value versus the mark if the mark has a higher weight in the Canadian trade index.
- **e** will have appreciated in value versus the mark if the mark has a lower weight in the Canadian trade index.

20 The Bank of Canada cannot just set the exchange rate at any level it desires because

- **a** such intervention violates international law.
- **b** the foreign exchange market is unregulated.
- **c** doing so would make Canada a debtor nation.
- **d** doing so would require constant changes in international reserves.
- **e** interest rate parity forbids it.

21 When would the exchange rate decrease in value the most?

- **a** When the supply and demand of dollars both increase.
- **b** When the supply of dollars increases, and the demand decreases.
- **c** When the supply of dollars decreases, and the demand increases.
- **d** When the supply and demand of dollars both decrease.
- **e** When there is intervention by the Bank of Canada.

22 Which of the following will shift the supply curve of dollars rightward?

- **a** An increase occurs in the demand for foreign goods by Canadian citizens.
- **b** A decrease occurs in the demand for Canadian goods by foreigners.
- **c** The dollar is expected to appreciate next year.
- **d** U.S. interest rates decrease.
- **e** None of the above.

23 Which of the following will shift the demand curve for dollars rightward?

- **a** An increase occurs in the demand for foreign goods by Canadian citizens.
- **b** A decrease occurs in the demand for Canadian goods by foreigners.
- **c** The dollar is expected to appreciate.
- **d** The dollar is expected to depreciate.
- **e** U.S. interest rates increase.

24 If the interest rate in Canada is greater than the interest rate in Japan, interest rate parity implies that

- **a** the inflation rate is higher in Japan.
- **b** Japanese financial assets are poor investments.
- **c** the yen is expected to depreciate against the dollar.
- **d** the yen is expected to appreciate against the dollar.
- **e** Canadian financial assets are poor investments.

25 The exchange rate is volatile because

a government intervention always make things worse.
b the demand curve is very flat.
c the demand curve is very steep.
d shifts in demand and supply are independent of each other.
e shifts in demand and supply are not independent of each other.

Short Answer Problems

1 What is the relationship between a country's trade deficit, its government budget deficit, and its private sector deficit?

2 What determines the value of the exchange rate?

3 What is purchasing power parity?

ⓒⓣ **4** Consider the following headline from the Friday, December 12, 1997 *Globe and Mail*: "Dollar hits new 11½-year low: Interest rate hike expected after recurrence of Asian flu forces Bank of Canada to intervene." Clearly the Canadian dollar's exchange rate was decreasing in value during December 1997. Explain briefly but carefully why an increase in interest rates by the Bank of Canada would help to reverse this decrease.

ⓒⓣ **5** Over its lifetime as a country, Canada has tended to be a net borrower more than a net lender. Is this outcome good or bad?

6 The international transactions of a country for a given year are reported in Table 36.3.

TABLE **36.3**

Transaction	Amount (billions of dollars)
Exports of goods and services	100
Imports of goods and services	130
Transfers to the rest of the world	20
Loans to the rest of the world	60
Loans from the rest of the world	?
Increases in official reserves	10
Net interest pyaments	0

a What is the amount of loans from the rest of the world?
b What is the current account balance?
c What is the capital account balance?
d What is the official settlements balance?

7 The information in Table 36.4 is for a country during a given year.

TABLE **36.4**

Variable	Amount (billions of dollars)
GDP	800
Net taxes	200
Government budget deficit	50
Consumption	500
Investment	150
Imports	150

a What is the level of government expenditure on goods and services?
b What is the private sector surplus or deficit?
c What is the value of exports?
d What is the balance of trade surplus or deficit?

8 Suppose that the exchange rate between the Canadian dollar and the German mark is 2 marks per dollar.

a What is the exchange rate in terms of dollars per mark?
b What is the price in dollars of a camera selling for 250 marks?
c What is the price in marks of a computer selling for 1,000 dollars?

9 Suppose that a personal computer sells for US$2,000 in the United States and C$3,000 in Canada.

a Where would you buy the personal computer if the exchange rate between the Canadian dollar and the U.S. dollar was US$0.80 per C$? Where would you resell it if you wanted to make a profit? (Ignore any taxes, tariffs, transportation costs, and differences in quality.)
b Does purchasing power parity hold?
ⓒⓣ **c** If many businesses acted like you, and if the exchange rate was flexible, what would happen to the value of the exchange rate? What would be the new equilibrium exchange rate that would make purchasing power parity hold for personal computers, if the U.S. dollar price and the Canadian dollar price stayed constant?

10 Go to the Government Documents Section of your library, or to the Bank of Canada Review, or to the Statistics Canada Web site (**http://www.statcan.ca**). Find data for the years 1985–95 on the value of the exchange rate in terms of U.S. cents, and data on Canadian and U.S. interest rates (use the prime interest rate banks charge to their best businesses). Construct a table of the Canadian interest rate differential versus the exchange rate, and discuss what kind of relationship you find.

ANSWERS

True/False/Uncertain and Explain

ⓒⓣ **1 F** Overall flow of money in/out of country = sum of the three balances of payment must balance. Individual balances may be in deficit/surplus/balance. (826–827)

ⓒⓣ **2 U** Depends on reaction of private sector surplus/deficit. (829–830)

3 U May or may not be true. Net borrower implies *current* net borrowing > 0. Debtor nation implies sum of *all* net borrowing > 0. (828)

4 T Balance of trade (negative) = government balance (large negative) + private balance (small negative). (829–830)

5 T Other things remaining the same, this increase will increase interest rate differential. (832–833)

6 F They are both affected by expected future exchange rate and interest rates, and so move together. (836–837)

ⓒⓣ **7 F** If expected to appreciate, this expected appreciation implies increased earnings in foreign currency terms, which increases demand for their bonds, which decreases interest rates until interest rate parity holds. (838)

8 T Under purchasing power parity, yen price identical in each country. $10 × 100 yen/$ = 1,000 yen. (838)

9 T Dollar is more valuable—takes more yen to buy one dollar. (831)

10 T Increase in foreign exchange value of dollar implies a profit opportunity, which increases demand for dollars. (833)

Multiple-Choice

1 a High current account deficit implies likely capital account surplus. It is unclear about debtor versus lender. (826–828)

2 e $(S - I) + (NT - G)$ by definition. (829–830)

3 a Definition. (826)

ⓒⓣ **4 c** Imports > exports implies current account deficit. Borrowing > lending implies capital account surplus. (Think about which direction money is flowing.) (826–827)

5 b Current lending > borrowing implies net lender. Sum of past borrowing > sum of lending implies debtor nation. (826–828)

6 e Official settlements balance = 0 implies current account surplus = capital account deficit, which occurs only when lending > borrowing. (826)

ⓒⓣ **7 e** Since current account + capital account + official settlements account = 0, when official settlements is a deficit, to be sure current is a surplus, it must be the case that capital is 0 or a deficit. (826–827)

8 c Government sector deficit = $NT - G = 300 - 400 = -100$. Private sector surplus = $S - I = 300 - 250 = +50$. (829–830)

9 d Net exports = $(NT - G) + (S - I) = 300 - 400 + 300 - 250 = -50$. (829–830)

10 c Net lender implies stock of investments rising. Debtor nation implies negative flow of interest payments on investments. (828)

11 a Official settlements balance = –(capital account + current account) = surplus, which implies change in official reserves < 0. (826–827)

12 d It takes less yen to buy dollar, which implies the dollar depreciated. Via inverse relationship, yen has appreciated. (831)

13 e $76 = £38 × ($2 per £). (831)

14 c Definition. (831)

15 e This increases demand for Canadian dollars. **a** decreases demand, **b–d** increase supply. (838–839)

16 c Two currencies have same purchasing power. (838)

17 e You will wish to buy foreign currency, since it will increase in value, which also requires you to sell Canadian dollars. (832–836)

18 a It takes more marks to buy $1 (increase in value), and less yen (decrease in value). (831)

ⓒⓣ **19 b** 1994:
1/60 mark/yen = (2 marks/$)/(120yen/$).
1995:
1/30 mark/yen = (3marks/$)/(90 yen/$).
Takes more marks in 1995 to buy 1 yen, so yen has appreciated. (831)

20 d Such intervention requires buying/selling Canadian dollars, which changes official reserves, which cannot occur forever. (838–839)

21 b Draw a graph. (836–837)

22 a Increased demand for foreign currency increases supply of Canadian dollars. (835)

23 c **a** has no impact on demand, **b**, **d**, and **e** shift it leftward. (832–833)

24 d Therefore Canadian dollar expected to depreciate, offsetting the interest rate differential. (836–838)

25 e They are both affected by the same expectations. (836–837)

Short Answer Problems

1 The national income accounting identities allow us to show that a country's balance of trade deficit is equal to the sum of its government budget deficit and its private sector deficit.

2 The value of the exchange rate is determined by supply and demand. The supply of the Canadian dollar is affected by two things—changes in the Canadian interest rate differential and changes in the expected future exchange rate. The demand for the Canadian dollar is also affected by the same two things.

3 Purchasing power parity follows from arbitrage and the law of one price. It means that the value of money is the same in all countries. For example, if the exchange rate between the dollar and the yen is 120 yen per dollar, purchasing power parity says that a good that sells for 120 yen in Japan will sell for 1 dollar in Canada. Thus the exchange rate is such that money (dollars or yen) has the same purchasing power in both countries.

ⓒⓣ **4** An increase in Canadian interest rates increases the Canadian interest rate differential, which increases the desirability of Canadian assets relative to foreign assets. This increase in turn increases the demand for Canadian dollars by foreigners, and decreases the demand for foreign exchange by Canadians, which decreases the supply of the Canadian dollar. These shifts in supply and demand will increase the value of the exchange rate.

ⓒⓣ **5** Being a net borrower is fine if the country is borrowing for investment purposes, and creating earnings to pay off what it owes. This situation has mostly been the case for Canada; so being a net borrower is good—it has allowed a resource-rich but capital-poor country like Canada to develop its resources.

6 **a** Current account balance + capital account balance + official settlements balance = 0, or (100 – 130 – 20) + (loans from rest of world – 60) + (–10) = 0, so loans from the rest of the world = 120.

b The current account balance is a $50 billion deficit: exports minus imports minus transfers to the rest of the world plus net interest payments to the rest of the world.

c The capital account balance is a surplus of $60 billion: loans from the rest of the world minus loans to the rest of the world.

d Because official reserves increased, the official settlements balance is –10.

7 **a** Since we know that the government budget deficit is $50 billion and net taxes are $200 billion, we can infer that government expenditure on goods and services is $250 billion.

b The private sector surplus or deficit is given by saving minus investment. Investment is given as $150 billion, but we must compute saving. Saving is equal to GDP minus net taxes minus consumption: $100 billion. Thus there is a private sector deficit of $50 billion.

c We know that GDP is consumption plus investment plus government expenditure on goods and services plus net exports (exports minus imports). Since we know all these values except exports, we can obtain that value by solving for exports. The value of exports equals GDP plus imports minus consumption minus investment minus government expenditure on goods and services; the value of exports equals $50 billion.

d There is a balance of trade deficit of $100 billion. This result can be obtained in two ways. First we can recognize that the balance of trade surplus or deficit is given by the value of exports ($50 billion) minus the value of imports ($150 billion). The alternative method is to recognize that the balance of trade deficit is equal to the sum of the government budget deficit ($50 billion) and the private sector deficit ($50 billion).

8 **a** If 1 dollar can be purchased for 2 marks, the price of a mark is 1/2 dollar per mark.

b At an exchange rate of 2 marks per dollar, it takes 125 dollars to obtain the 250 marks needed to buy the camera.

c At an exchange rate of 2 marks per dollar, it takes 2,000 marks to obtain the 1,000 dollars needed to buy the computer.

9 **a** The Canadian computer costs US$2,400 = C$3,000 × US$0.80 per C$. Therefore it is profitable to buy it in the United States for US$2,000 and sell it in Canada for US$2,400.

b No, the two currencies do not have the same purchasing power—U.S. dollars buy more.

ⓒⓣ **c** The extra demand for U.S. computers would tend to push up the demand for U.S. dollars, leading to an appreciation of the U.S. dollar (and a depreciation of the Canadian dollar). The value of the exchange rate that makes purchasing power parity hold would be the value *A* that solves US$2,000 = C$3,000 × US$*A* per C$, which is a value of 0.667.

10 The data is listed in Table 36.5. Your data may be slightly different, due to rounding errors, etc. in your data source.

TABLE **36.5**

Year	Differential	U.S. $/C$
1985	0.7	0.732
1986	2.27	0.72
1987	1.31	0.754
1988	1.43	0.813
1989	2.45	0.845
1990	4.06	0.856
1991	1.55	0.873
1992	1.23	0.827
1993	–0.07	0.775
1994	–0.38	0.732
1995	–0.17	0.729

Source: Bank of Canada *Review,* various issues.

We can see that there is a rough positive relationship between the differential and the value of the exchange rate. As the differential rose through the middle of the time period, so did the value of the exchange rate, driven by an increase in the demand for Canadian dollars and a decrease in the supply of Canadian dollars. As the differential fell towards the end, so did the exchange rate. The relationship is not exact, but it does meet the rough predictions of our theories.

Chapters

Part 10 Overview

35–36

Understanding the Global Economy

PROBLEM

You are an advisor to the prime minister, specializing in exchange rate considerations. The Canadian dollar is suffering from a crisis of nonconfidence on world markets, sparked by an economic crisis in Asia. Foreign investors are afraid that Canada's economy will be hurt by the Asian economic crisis, since Asia buys many commodities from Canada. The investors are afraid that profits and returns at Canadian companies will decrease dramatically. Foreigners start a selloff of Canadian assets.

a Explain to the prime minister (with the aid of a graph showing the demand and supply of dollars) what this will imply for the value of the Canadian dollar, as well as for interest rates, the value of the monetary base and the money supply, and the three balance of payments accounts. (The Bank of Canada is operating under a rule of trying to stabilize the exchange rate.)

b Another advisor to the prime minister has told her that the Bank of Canada should be ordered to increase the money supply to try and lower interest rates. What will this do to the value of the exchange rate and to foreign holdings of Canadian assets? Can the Bank of Canada do this and still maintain a managed exchange rate?

c The prime minister has received a phone call from the owner of Big Importer Company, complaining that the change in the value of the Canadian dollar has hurt his ability to sell imported whatzits in Canada. With the aid of a graph of the market for whatzits in Canada (with the vertical axis measuring the price of whatzits in Canadian dollars), explain to the prime minister what has happened to the price and quantity imported in this market. What has happened to exports? to the balance of trade?

ⓒⓣ **d** The prime minister asks you whether she should ask the Bank of Canada to defend the dollar even more strongly, or not. What do you think?

MIDTERM EXAMINATION

You should allocate 20 minutes for this examination (10 questions, 2 minutes per question). For each question, choose the one *best* answer.

1 The short-run adjustment costs in Canada associated with reducing the level of tariffs under a North American Free Trade Agreement will be borne principally by

a taxpayers, whose higher taxes provide the generous retraining programs.
b employers and workers in those sectors in which Canada has a comparative advantage.
c employers and workers in those sectors in which Canada has a comparative disadvantage.
d Canadian consumers of imported goods.
e Canadian producers of exported goods.

2 Which of the following quotations best describes the interest rate parity effect?

a "The recent high Canadian interest rate has increased the demand for the Canadian dollar."
b "The market feeling is that the Canadian dollar is overvalued and will likely appreciate."
c "The price of bananas is the same in Canada and the United States, adjusting for the exchange rate."
d "The expected appreciation of the Canadian dollar is currently lowering demand for it."
e None of the above.

3 Atlantis imports watches from Beltran and exports widgets to Beltran. Why would Atlantis prefer arranging a voluntary export restraint rather than a quota on watches?

a to not hurt Beltran's imports
b to prevent Beltran from retaliating by restricting Atlantis' exports
c to keep the domestic price of watches low
d to increase government revenue
e to help domestic producers

4 Which of the following would cause the dollar to depreciate against the yen?

a an increase in the Canadian monetary supply
b an increase in interest rates in Canada
c a decrease in interest rates in Japan
d an increase in the expected future exchange rate
e a decrease in the current exchange rate

5 If Fullofland is currently a net lender and a debtor nation,

a it has loaned more capital than it borrowed abroad this year, but borrowed more than it loaned during its history.
b it has borrowed more capital than it loaned abroad this year and also borrowed more than it loaned during its history.
c it has loaned more capital than it borrowed abroad this year and has loaned more than it borrowed during its history.
d its accounting system must be in error if it shows this nation to be a net lender and a debtor nation at the same time.
e its debts must be currently growing.

6 Suppose Musicland and Videoland produce two goods—CDs and videos. Musicland has a comparative advantage in the production of CDs if

a fewer CDs must be given up to produce one unit of videos than in Videoland.
b less labour is required to produce one unit of CDs than in Videoland.
c less capital is required to produce one unit of CDs than in Videoland.
d less labour and capital are required to produce one unit of CDs than in Videoland.
e fewer videos must be given up to produce one unit of CDs than in Videoland.

7 Suppose Musicland and Videoland produce two goods—CDs and videos—and Musicland has a comparative advantage in the production of CDs. If the countries trade, the price of CDs in terms of videos will be

a less than the opportunity cost of CDs in Musicland and greater than the opportunity cost of CDs in Videoland.
b greater than the opportunity cost of CDs in Musicland and less than the opportunity cost of CDs in Videoland.
c greater than the opportunity cost of CDs in both countries.
d less than the opportunity cost of CDs in both countries.
e dependent only on the relative size of each economy.

8 Which of the following quotations best describes the expected profit effect in action?

a "The recent high Canadian interest rate has increased the demand for the Canadian dollar."
b "The market feeling is that the Canadian dollar is overvalued and will likely depreciate."
c "The price of bananas is the same in Canada and the United States, adjusting for the exchange rate."
d "The expected depreciation of the Canadian dollar is currently lowering demand for it."
e None of the above.

9 Acadia and Breton are currently engaged in free trade. Acadia imports cheese from Breton and exports sheep to Breton. If Acadia imposes a tariff on cheese, Acadia's cheese-producing industry will

a expand, and its sheep-producing industry will contract.
b expand, and its sheep-producing industry will expand.
c contract, and its sheep-producing industry will contract.
d contract, and its sheep-producing industry will expand.
e expand, and its sheep-producing industry will be unchanged.

10 Canada has a trade deficit when the
- **a** value of Canadian exports of goods and services exceeds the value of Canadian imports of goods and services.
- **b** value of Canadian exports of goods and services is exceeded by the value of Canadian imports of goods and services.
- **c** value of Canadian exports of goods exceeds the value of Canadian imports of goods.
- **d** value of Canadian exports of goods is exceeded by the value of Canadian imports of goods.
- **e** current account balance is less than zero.

ANSWERS

Problem

a The fear of lower future returns leads to a decrease in the demand for Canadian dollar assets, leading to a decrease in the demand for Canadian dollars. In Fig. P10.1, this decrease, in turn, leads to a decrease in the value of the exchange rate from F_a to F_b. To keep it from decreasing even further, the Bank of Canada intervenes and buys Canadian dollars, supplying foreign exchange from official reserves. They also might shrink the money supply, which will tend to increase Canadian interest rates. (There are also potential supply effects not shown here.)

Foreigners are lending us less, so the capital account will move towards a smaller surplus or a deficit. The decrease in the foreign exchange value of the Canadian dollar will lead to a increase in exports and a decrease in imports (see part **c** below), so that the current account will move towards a surplus. Since the Bank of Canada is supplying foreign exchange, this is a decrease in reserves, or a movement towards a surplus.

FIGURE **P10.1**

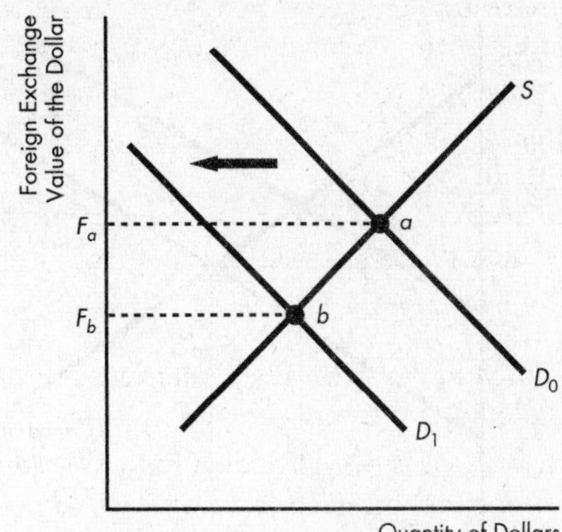

b A lower interest rate would spark a further decrease in the demand for the Canadian dollar, as foreigners buy fewer Canadian assets, given the lower Canadian interest rate differential. This would tend to push down the Canadian dollar's value, which would conflict with the Bank of Canada's attempts to stabilize the exchange rate.

c The market for whatzits is shown in Fig. P10.2. The new, lower exchange rate of fewer U.S. dollars per Canadian dollar means more Canadian dollars per U.S. dollar, and acts like a tariff—it increases the Canadian dollar price of the imported whatzits, shown as the shift leftward in the supply curve. This change leads to a new equilibrium, with a higher price, and a lower quantity imported and sold.

The market for Canadian exports would be acting in an opposite manner, with lower prices and more exports. The higher exports and lower imports will mean the balance of trade (and hence the current account) is moving towards a surplus.

ⓒⓣ **d** The answer is a value judgement, and depends on the value you place on defending the Canadian dollar (for example, helping the importer) versus the damage the defence might do to the Canadian economy. Defending the Canadian dollar will entail buying Canadian dollars (which will shrink the domestic money supply), and raising Canadian interest rates. Both of these actions will depress aggregate demand and put downward pressure on real GDP and jobs. It is your call.

FIGURE **P9.2**

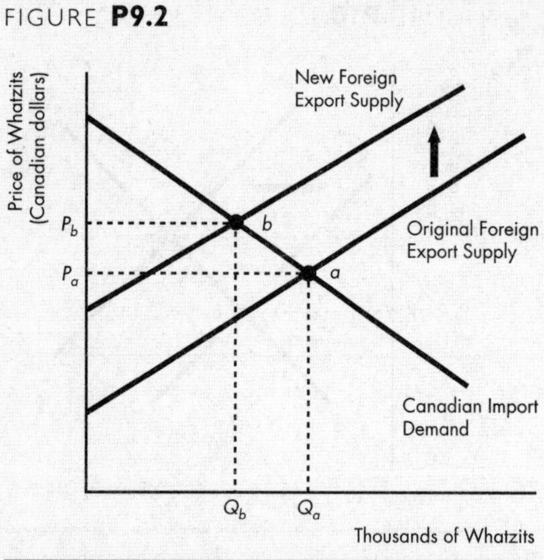

Midterm Examination

1 c Because decrease in U.S. or Mexican prices implies decrease in Canadian production. (816–817)

2 a If two currencies do not have the same interest rate, market conditions will change the demand for assets and the dollar. (838)

3 b Under a VER, exporting country gains excess revenue, which means it is less likely to retaliate, since hurt less. (809–812)

4 a **a** decreases interest rates, which decrease demand for Canadian dollars. **b–d** are increase in demand, **e** move along, not a shift. (832–833)

5 a Definitions of net lender and debtor nation. Debts are shrinking. (828)

6 e Definition. (803–804)

7 b Trade will only occur between these two prices, otherwise one or both countries are worse off from trade and will not trade. (804–807)

8 d Profit from holding Canadian $ is lower, so demand decreases. (832)

9 a Tariff increases domestic price of cheese, which decreases imports, which increases domestic production. Decreased imports = decreased exports in Breton, which decreases its income, which decreases its imports = decrease in Acadia's exports, decreasing Acadia's sheep production. (809–812)

10 b Definition of balance of trade. (826)